Building Better Beings

Building Better Beings

A Theory of Moral Responsibility

Manuel Vargas

OXFORD
UNIVERSITY PRESS

Great Clarendon Street, Oxford, OX2 6DP,
United Kingdom

Oxford University Press is a department of the University of Oxford.
It furthers the University's objective of excellence in research, scholarship,
and education by publishing worldwide. Oxford is a registered trade mark of
Oxford University Press in the UK and in certain other countries

Published in the United States of America by Oxford University Press
198 Madison Avenue, New York, NY 10016, United States of America

British Library Cataloguing in Publication Data
Data available

ISBN 978-0-19-969754-0

For my grandparents, Warren and Peggy DeCuir

Contents

Acknowledgments

As in many endeavors, the present visible product rests on a substrate of invisible efforts by many. So, first and last, thanks to my spouse Stephanie for putting up with and supporting all the special burdens involved in my writing this book. There were several moves, a good deal of work travel, and plenty of late nights. Such things are rarely easy, and this is all the more so when three young children are along for the ride. So thanks to Steph—and Athena, Satya, and Nike—for putting up with it all.

Internal to the world of philosophy, I have learned a good deal—but not enough!—from many friends and colleagues. Among them are Michael Bratman, Randy Clarke, Richard Holton, Michael McKenna, Al Mele, Eddy Nahmias, Derk Pereboom, John Perry, Tamler Sommers, Daniel Speak, Ken Taylor, Kevin Timpe, Jay Wallace, and Gary Watson. For all that and more, I'm especially grateful to John Doris, John Fischer, Heather Fox, Robert Kane, Jason Miller, Ben Mitchell-Yellin, Dominic Murphy, Dana Nelkin, Shaun Nichols, and Grant Rozeboom. They each read versions of this book that were much longer and considerably more foolish than the present version. Their superb feedback helped improve the book in a multitude of ways.

Ancestors of various chapters have also benefited from discussions with and the sometimes devastating criticism of many thoughtful people. Those folks include: Richard Arneson, Ruben Berrios, Gunnar Björnsson, David Brink, Andrei Buckareff, Eamonn Callan, Joe Campbell, Jonathan Cohen, Meir Dan-Cohen, Kristin Drake, Chris Franklin, Christopher Grau, Pete Graham, Alan "H-Bomb" Hájek, Caspar Hare, Elizabeth Harman, Chris Hitchcock, Nicole Hassoun, Brad Hooker, Nadeem Hussain, Aaron James, Agnieszka Jaworska, Matt King, Niko Kolodny, Josh Knobe, Janet Levin, Neil Levy, S. Matthew Liao, Simon May, Allegra McLeod, Christian Miller, Sarah Mrsny, Kieran Oberman, Katie Richardson, Debra Satz, Sam Scheffler, Tim Schroeder, Yonatan Shemmer, Saul Smilansky, Ken Stalzer, Jackie Taylor, Neal Tognazzini, Michael Torre, David Stump, David Velleman, Till Vierkant, Rico Vitz, Henrik Walter, David Widerker, Jim Woodward, Gideon Yaffe, and many audience members at conferences, symposia, colloquia, and reading groups over the past decade. Thanks to one and all, and my apologies to those whose feedback I've failed to acknowledge.

I have had the good fortune to spend several research leaves thinking and writing about these issues. For funding my research, hosting me, or otherwise providing support, my thanks to the Radcliffe Institute for Advanced Study at Harvard, the National Endowment for the Humanities, the McCoy Family Center for Ethics at Stanford University, the California Institute of Technology, the Mortimer Fleishhacker Family Endowment for Philosophy at the University of San Francisco, the Marion and Rogelio Vargas Foundation for Completion of Manuscripts, and Provost Jennifer Turpin of the University of San Francisco. I am especially grateful for the support of my colleagues at the University of San Francisco, who have tolerated my many comings and goings with considerable grace.

And Steph—again, thanks.

Sources

Parts of this book draw from material published elsewhere. In such cases, the present book tends to contain significant departures from those earlier publications.

Chapters 1–4 intermittently borrow material from all of the following:

Fischer, John Martin, Robert Kane, Derk Pereboom, and Manuel Vargas. *Four Views on Free Will*. Malden, MA: Blackwell, 2007.

Vargas, Manuel. "Responsibility in a World of Causes." *Philosophic Exchange*, 40 (2010): 56–78.

Vargas, Manuel. "Revisionism About Free Will: A Statement & Defense." *Philosophical Studies* 144, no. 1 (2009): 45–62.

Vargas, Manuel. "Revisionist Accounts of Free Will: Origins, Varieties, and Challenges." In *Oxford Handbook on Free Will* (2nd edn.), edited by Robert Kane. New York: Oxford University Press, 2011.

Vargas, Manuel. "Libertarianism and Skepticism About Free Will: Some Arguments Against Both." *Philosophical Topics* 32, nos 1 & 2 (2004): 403–26.

Chapter 5 is based on Vargas, Manuel. "Reasons and Real Selves." *Ideas y Valores: Revista colombiana de filosofía* 58, no. 141 (2009): 67–84.

Chapter 6 is based on Vargas, Manuel. "Moral Influence, Moral Responsibility." In *Essays on Free Will and Moral Responsibility*, edited by Nick Trakakis and Daniel Cohen, 90–122. Newcastle, UK: Cambridge Scholars Press, 2008.

Chapter 7 draws from Vargas, Manuel. "Situationism and Moral Responsibility: Free Will in Fragments." In *Decomposing the Will*, edited by Till Vierkant, Julian Kiverstein, and Andy Clark. New York: Oxford University Press, forthcoming.

Chapter 9 builds on material from Vargas, Manuel. "On the Importance of History for Responsible Agency." *Philosophical Studies* 127, no. 3 (2006): 351–82.

Thanks to the publishers of the above works for kind permission to reprint the relevant bits.

Introduction

1. What this book is about

Suppose that humans are a part of the ordinary causal fabric of the world, subject to the same physical, causal forces as everything else. If so, can normal adults be morally responsible for what they do? Other things that are subject to causal, physical laws don't seem to be. We don't suppose that quarks, agave plants, tornados, and newborn infants can be responsible. So what makes normal adult people responsible? What makes them deserve moral praise and blame? Or, perhaps, this all supposes too much. Perhaps moral responsibility is simply an illusion, an inherited prejudice of disputable value.

There is no easy path to answering these questions. One philosophically venerable point of departure is some or another aspect of common sense: by analyzing our standing practices, distilling implicit principles, and arguing from convictions that are widely shared, we can begin to fashion a satisfactory theory of moral responsibility.

Notice that such an approach makes a potentially dubious bet. The bet is that common sense is mostly reliable, or at any rate, reliable enough that our theories can help themselves to claims about the nature of responsibility, at least partly in light of coherence with ordinary responsibility-characteristic practices and convictions. However, if those convictions are incoherent, or aren't uniform across contexts, or are somehow disconnected from what truths there are about responsibility, then common sense is an unstable mortar for theory-building.

So, how might we anchor a theory of responsibility in aspects of common sense while acknowledging the possibility that our practices as we find them might be suspect? My answer comes in three parts. The first idea is a response to the immediate problem at hand. An adequate philosophical theory must be prepared to be *revisionist*, separating the theoretical wheat from the intuitional chaff that we find in common sense. What I will argue is that careful consideration of ordinary convictions about moral responsibility reveals that some aspects are problematic. Those aspects should be identified and rejected in a principled way. So, our theory must embrace revisionism. That is, as a matter of generating an accurate theory, we must abandon particular widespread intuitions (in particular: intuitions we have about alternative possibilities) and commit ourselves to a picture of responsibility at odds with aspects of common sense.

Pruning our conceptual commitments is just the beginning. Indeed, it may appear to leave us with more problems than before. Without recourse to the intuitive and powerful picture of ourselves as agents with metaphysically robust alternative possibilities, it isn't clear what, if anything, justifies our holding one another responsible. If so, then responsibility might indeed be an illusion.

In response to this concern, a second idea comes into play: *the agency cultivation model*. When we hold one another responsible, we participate in a system of practices, attitudes, and judgments that support a special kind of self-governance, one whereby we recognize and suitably respond to moral considerations. So, roughly, moralized praise and blame are justified by their effects, that is, how they develop and sustain a valuable form of agency, one we ordinarily have reason to care about. It is the tenability of this view that provides the basis for constructing a revisionist account. We thereby avoid, or at least forestall, the view that responsibility is a mere illusion.

When we turn to consider the viability of this account in light of scientific views about the nature of human agency, it may be tempting to think that we have indeed only forestalled the illusion conclusion. Whatever the appeal of the agency cultivation model might be, its presumptions about us appear to be at odds with the going scientific picture of human beings. In particular, contemporary psychology maintains that the causal sources of our actions have less to do with features of ourselves than they do with deliberatively irrelevant features of the situations in which we act. Moreover, much of human psychological activity amounts to automatic processes, often invisible and at odds with our awareness. If the going psychological picture of agents is right, then it isn't clear how we could be any good at recognizing and responding to moral considerations, as is required by the picture of agency postulated by the theory.

Here, though, a third idea comes into play—*circumstantialism* about powers. The operative idea in circumstantialism is this: the powers that matter for whether an agent is responsible are best characterized non-intrinsically, as functions of agents in circumstances. Circumstantialism, in this sense, contrasts with *atomism*, or the view that it is best to think of the relevant agent powers as intrinsic features of agents.[1] On the version of circumstantialism that I favor, the salient features of circumstances include abstract normative truths that arise from a complex of social and normative considerations. It is a view on which what we might think of as "moral ecology" matters, for the normatively relevant powers of agents are partly functions of circumstances. Those circumstances can be structured in ways that are more and less conducive to responsible agency.

These three ideas—revisionism, the agency cultivation model, and circumstantialism—do the heavy lifting. They are complemented by a suite of more familiar ideas, each recast in light of the larger features of the account. For example, responsible agency is properly understood as involving a kind of reasons-responsive agency, but one on which the involved capacities vary across contexts, structured by a complex of social and normative considerations. On the matter of desert, the notion of desert that is properly at stake in responsibility ascriptions rests on both teleological and non-teleological justifications. So, people deserve blame partly because it is good for both the blamer and the blamed. As for the norms governing the praise and blame of deserving agents, they have a neo-Strawsonian hue. Quality of will matters, but not merely as a brute psychological feature of creatures like us. Quality of will matters because of various normative considerations external to the mechanics of interpersonal expectations.

Together, these ideas constitute a systematic answer to questions about how we can be both part of the natural, causal order and at the same time deserving of moral praise and blame. We need not be agents radically separated from the causal order, nor need we be ultimate originators of our morally significant actions. Rather, we are beings for whom moralized praise and blame make sense, partly because of the effects of praise and

---

[1] I resist characterizing this view as *contextualist*, for contextualism is usually understood as a semantic thesis whereas the thesis I embrace concerns the metaphysics of the relevant normatively significant notion of capacities. Stretching the familiar term to cover my interests invites too much confusion.

blame. In their absence, we are less extraordinary agents. In their presence, we can become genuinely responsible agents.

The revisionist strand of my account is tempered by conservatism about the mechanics of our ordinary practices, our emotional responses, and the bulk of our characteristic inferences about what follows from them. The revisionism has some bite, however: complacency about our practices is not an option. Given that our powers are partly functions of circumstances, we have reason to be concerned about building better circumstances than the ones we find.

Revisionists cannot simply duck any purported counterexample by declaring that they are not beholden to commonsense intuitions. The revisionist about moral responsibility (and, as we'll see, free will) has no license to invoke revisionism about any inconvenient aspect of the theory. What license there is for revisionism is much narrower, focused on specific normative and conceptual aspects of responsibility assessments. Moreover, as with any proposal, a revisionist account will be constrained by considerations of consistency and coherence. Contradictory claims or implications are out of bounds for the revisionist as much as anyone else.

In contrast to scientific and philosophical skepticism about moral responsibility, my account maintains that we really can be responsible. The account conflicts with libertarian views, for it turns out that despite the grip libertarian pictures genuinely have on many of us, the justification of moralized praise and blame do not, in the end, require libertarian agency. In many ways, my account is closest to compatibilism. But standard compatibilists will object that I concede too much to incompatibilists, for on their accounts we never were incompatibilists. As they see it, incompatibilism was always just an error of the philosophers, and never an apt characterization of ordinary convictions.

A distinctive feature of my account is the extensive and explicit interpenetration of methodology and substantive commitments. Most accounts of free will and moral responsibility have comparatively little to say about methodology and how and why these things affect substantive philosophical positions. In contrast, this account holds that the seeming intractability of debates about free will and moral responsibility is at least partly a function of inattention to philosophical methodology.

Relatedly, the account holds that puzzles about free will and moral responsibility are not as insulated from larger philosophical issues as we might like them to be. It turns out that positions on the nature of language, metaphysics, and the relationship of these things to normative ethical concerns cannot be easily bracketed. What free will is turns out to be partly a matter of which practices we can justify and whether there is good reason to have responsibility practices at all.

These brief remarks about where all of this is headed are too compressed, of course. For better or worse, the decompression of the account is coming. The requisite scaffolding, definitions, and arguments will make up the rest of the book.

Let's get started.

2. Responsibility, praiseworthiness, blameworthiness

Consider the role of praise and blame in our social lives. In most contexts, we are alive to the possibility of being praised and blamed for anything we say or do.[2] Blame, especially, carries a distinctive set of costs that structure how we think about what options are available to us. When we are the subjects of blame we become stained, the subjects of practices and attitudes that we ordinarily seek to avoid. If I am viewed as blameworthy for some transgression, I potentially face expressions of disapproval, stigmatization, and avoidance—as well as outright rebuke. Blame and its costs are multifarious.

Something analogous arises in the case of praise. When praised, we become subject to a distinct web of practices and attitudes that reflect an altogether different way of being regarded by others. Those practices characteristic of praising have some variation, too. Among other things, praising practices can involve outright exclamations of one's excellence, expressions of enthusiasm, and the impulse to be affiliated with those marked out as praiseworthy.

Notice that our moralized praising and blaming present themselves as having what we might think of as standards of correctness. We can get praise and blame wrong, praising someone who doesn't deserve it or mistakenly blaming someone. We can also over- and under- praise and blame. We can praise and blame for the wrong reasons.

---

[2] Which "we"? Which "our"? The group I have in mind is at least the "we" of, roughly, the Anglophone members of NATO countries and their allies.

A crude (and not entirely innocent) way to characterize one aspect of the standard of correctness embedded in praise and blame is the following: we are right to praise when someone is responsible for having done the right thing and right to blame when someone is responsible for having done the wrong thing. This characterization requires a good deal of refinement, but it expresses a basic idea that will serve as our entry point: our suitability or worthiness for praise and blame depends on our *being responsible*.[3]

There are famously a number of senses in which one can be responsible. One can be *causally* responsible for something, in the way in which a cracked radiator can be responsible for the car overheating. One can be *legally* responsible, and open to various legal and economic consequences in light of that status.

This book is concerned with specifically *moral* responsibility. When we condemn someone for verbally abusing a subordinate, betraying a spouse, calling for genocide, or selling out one's friends for easy profit, we do not typically treat these violations in the same way as we would a bad move in a board game or a poor choice in home decorating. The typical social significance and emotional color are altogether different.

The aim of this book is to offer a theory of moral responsibility, or our being morally praiseworthy or blameworthy. In particular, I will focus on what I will call *the responsibility system*, or those judgments, practices, and attitudes that reflect assessments of the worthiness of moralized praise and blame.

The account will proceed in two main parts: first, an analysis of an important strand of how we think about responsibility (including its attendant drawbacks); second, a proposal for how we *ought* to understand responsibility in light of the diverse empirical, conceptual, and normative burdens on an adequate theory of responsibility.

3. The familiar chain of argument

For all the familiarity and importance of moral responsibility, it takes remarkably little work to motivate the thought that the whole business is

---

[3] I will revisit this presumption in chapters 6–7, so this should be understood as merely provisional and not a substantive conclusion sustained throughout the book.

rotten at its core. One does not have to look far to find *responsibility nihilists*, or those who maintain that no one is morally responsible.

There are several paths to nihilism about responsibility. Here is one, which I call *the familiar chain of argument*: if everything is caused, no one is genuinely free, and thus, no one can be genuinely morally responsible for anything. The force of the argument can be glossed in different ways. On one version, the idea is this: given that the rest of the world isn't subject to it, what makes us special enough to deserve moral praise and blame? On another version, the motivating idea is that if we think about things that get us off the hook with respect to blame, we'll see that the same basic structure exists everywhere we act.[4]

Outside of philosophy, perhaps the most common contemporary incarnation of the familiar chain of argument frames the threat in terms of the deliverances of contemporary science on the matter of free will. You don't have to look very hard to find people who will say, for example, that neuroscience or biology or scientific psychology has shown that we are not beings that act independent of the causal, physical order.[5] Sometimes explicitly, and often implicitly, we are told that modern science has sufficiently mapped out the underlying psychological, biological, or chemical roots of our behavior so that we can say with confidence that free will does not exist. Consequently, all those notions that depend on free will—ideas of praiseworthiness, blameworthiness, and merit—are in trouble as well.

It is easy to overestimate the conclusion of the familiar chain of reasoning. The argument does not claim that we make no difference to what happens. One can embrace the chain of reasoning while acknowledging that what happens to us sometimes happens precisely because of our participation in the causal sequence. One's sordid extramarital affair does not happen

---

[4] I am not convinced that these different glosses don't come to the same thing. Perhaps it is more accurate to say that there are numerous interrelated but distinct familiar chains of argument. Whatever the case may be, the Western intellectual tradition has been plagued by variants of the familiar chain of argument for literally millennia. Helpful discussions of the early roots of this chain of reasoning can be found in Susanne Bobzien, "The Inadvertent Conception and Late Birth of the Free-Will Problem," *Phronesis* 43 (1988): 132–75;— Richard Sorabji, "The Concept of the Will From Plato to Maximus the Confessor," in *The Will*, ed. Thomas Pink and Martin Stone (London: Routledge, 2003).

[5] John A. Bargh, "Free Will is Un-Natural," in *Are We Free? Psychology and Free Will*, ed. John Baer et al. (New York: Oxford University Press, 2008); P. Read Montague, "Free Will," *Current Biology* 18, no. 14 (2008): R584–R585; Susan Pockett, "The Concept of Free Will: Philosophy Neuroscience, and the Law," *Behavioral Sciences and the Law* 25 (2007): 281–93; Daniel M. Wegner, *The Illusion of Conscious Will* (Cambridge, MA: MIT Press, 2002).

without the causal chain working through one's body parts. The point of the argument is just that one should not be blamed for what one does, because it is part of an inexorable causal chain extending back in time prior to the existence of any humans.[6]

There are various difficulties with the chain of argument as I've construed it. One can spend a good deal of time making the argument more precise and responding with even more precise objections. This is important work, and I will do my part to keep the hamster wheel spinning in various parts of the book. However, my aspiration is to meet the spirit of the challenge in its own terms.

As I see it, the spirit of the challenge is to explain why some causes and not others are the sorts on which we might hang our assessments of moral responsibility. Matters of philosophical presumption come to the fore almost immediately. We could, for example, reject out of hand the idea that we are causally embedded, a part of the larger causal order of the universe. However, I'll proceed on the supposition that the familiar argument, for all of its coarseness, frames things correctly: there is a global threat to moral responsibility that derives from the very constituent elements of the idea that we are agents embedded in the ordinary causal order.

One motivation for accepting this way of framing things goes something like this: whatever one thinks about the possibility of our possessing non-physical elements, the physical stuff—our bodies, our nervous systems, and so on—seems to be of a piece with the larger causal order of the universe. When we focus on this thought, our agency and its distinctiveness dissolves into so many interlocking cogs of the universal causal machine. On this view, there is nothing obviously ontologically exceptional about us. So, if we are to be singled out for praise and blame then we need to say what it is that makes such assessments legitimate. On this picture, though, it is not obvious what that could be.

It goes almost without saying that there are other ways to approach questions of moral responsibility. Historically, concerns about divine fore-knowledge were an important path to theorizing about free will and moral responsibility. And, one could have concerns about free will that are not

---

[6] This chain of reasoning also does not claim that we must let all the criminals go. We would still have practical reasons to separate incorrigible cases from the rest of us. However, our treatment of criminals might seem closer to quarantine and rehabilitation than punishment in any conventional sense See Derk Pereboom, *Living Without Free Will* (Cambridge: Cambridge University Press, 2001).

necessarily connected with a conception of agents understood as part of the larger causal fabric of the world. For the present project, however, the challenge provided by the familiar chain of argument will serve as an organizing concern in what follows. That is, our question is whether the apparent fact of our being causally embedded in the physical order is compatible with moral responsibility, and if so, whether we have reason to think we are responsible. That's what the book is about.

4. Some aspects of the challenge

On the present approach, the apparent fact of causal embeddedness is the salient root-level challenge to responsibility. Conceiving of the challenge in this way leaves us with a broader challenge than the traditional threat to responsibility via determinism. (It is also distinct from theological concerns about how a divine being's omniscience or foreknowledge can be squared with freedom and responsibility.) Importantly, the details of how our little bit of the universe is causally ordered might generate distinct threats to responsibility. In light of this, a divide-and-conquer strategy is promising.

On the divide-and-conquer approach, we can ask whether the thesis of determinism would be a problem for moral responsibility. (Let *determinism* stand for the following thesis: the state of the universe at any prior time and the actual laws of nature are logically sufficient for the state of the universe at any later time.) We then ask a different question, whether responsibility is compatible with *in*determinism—roughly, the existence of multiple possible futures given the actual past and the actual laws of nature.

Notice that our interest in these matters need not be restricted to universalizing versions of these stories, i.e., stories on which every event is deterministic or, perhaps, every human decision is indeterministic. Determinism might exist in pockets around us, without holding everywhere in the universe at all times. Conversely, the universe might be fundamentally indeterministic, with large swaths of it operating in ways that are mostly indistinguishable from determinism (perhaps the indeterminism is ordinarily "drowned out" or only very infrequently relevant to the operations of super-atomic systems).

I will pursue a version of the divide-and-conquer approach, with an important wrinkle: in answering the deterministic threat, it will emerge that an adequate answer to this threat will give us some degree of insulation against global worries about indeterminism undermining responsibility. Once you see what properly matters for responsibility (which, again, is not precisely what we tend to think matters for responsibility), it emerges that indeterminism is threatening only to the extent it can disrupt what matters. However, nothing about indeterminism per se constitutes a global threat.

One consequence of framing what follows in terms of answering the challenge of the familiar chain of argument, is that it threatens to suppress other legitimate worries one can have about responsibility. For example, one could be worried about the consequences of reductionism of the mental (including whether our minds do anything, or whether they are epiphenomenal byproducts of more basic causal processes). Alternately, one might be worried that specific results in some or another science (usually, neuroscience but sometimes psychology) show that we lack some crucial power necessary for moral responsibility.

Although these are not my primary concerns, parts of what follow speak to these worries in different ways. A theme emerges, however: once we see what responsibility really requires, many of our diverse concerns about it can be allayed.

5. Free will and its terminology

My talk of causation, determinism, and threats from the sciences of the mind may give rise to the impression that what is really at stake is *free will*. Although this is partly right, we must be careful. The term "free will" has meant different things in different contexts.

As I'll be using the term, "free will" is a term of art that picks out some distinctive power or capacity characteristic of morally responsible agency.[7]

---

[7] As it will turn out, free will is neither sufficient nor necessary for moral responsibility. There are cases where one might have free will, but lack the relevant knowledge to be morally responsible. And, there may be cases where one is morally responsible for some outcome but lacking free will at the time of its undertaking, partly because one has knowingly arranged things such that it would rob oneself of free will at the time of decision.

In this, I follow perhaps the dominant strand of the recent philosophical literature, one on which free will is characterized in terms of a role that is explicitly connected to moral responsibility.[8]

It would be a mistake to claim authority over the term or unanimity about its usage. Philosophers have characterized free will as, among other things, the ability to do otherwise; a kind of control required for moral responsibility; decision-making in accord with reason; and a capacity to act with those powers ordinarily supposed when deliberating about what to do. A comparatively diverse range of characterizations crop up in the scientific literature as well, where free will has been equated to the feeling of conscious control,[9] "undetermined choices of action,"[10] and the idea that we make choices "independent of anything remotely resembling a physical process."[11]

(One can see how some of these notions seem, from the get-go, to settle the question of whether we have free will, given a broadly scientific picture of the world. This strikes me as a mistake. But never mind that right now.)

I am happy to allow that this diversity of meanings attached to free will may sometimes pick out genuinely distinct phenomena. I have no quarrel with someone interested in characterizing those other phenomena, and in attempting to discuss them in their own terms. Nor do I have a quarrel with someone wanting to call some other phenomenon "free will" if there is some plausible usage (or extension of recognizable usage, perhaps connected to the philosophical tradition) on which that phenomenon is plausibly the kind of thing people have sometimes pointed to when they talked about free will.

What I do have a quarrel with is any insistence that there is a single thing that is properly "the free will problem."[12] I grant that we could discover that there is only one thing at stake here. It is possible that all the phenomena

---

[8] For some examples (among many) of explicit appeals to a conception of free will picked out by its role in responsibility or responsible agency: John Martin Fischer et al., *Four Views on Free Will* (Malden, MA: Blackwell, 2007); Alfred Mele, *Free Will and Luck* (New York: Oxford University Press, 2006); Derk Pereboom, "Defending Hard Incompatibilism," *Midwest Studies in Philosophy* 29, no. 1 (2005): 228–47.

[9] Wegner, *The Illusion of Conscious Will.*

[10] Bargh, "Free Will is Un-Natural."

[11] Montague, "Free Will."

[12] I have discussed the issue at more length in Manuel Vargas, "The Revisionist Turn: Reflection on the Recent History of Work on Free Will," in *New Waves in the Philosophy of Action*, ed. Jesus Aguilar et al. (New York: Palgrave Macmillan, 2011).

I have mentioned reduce to some single, favored notion, and that the characterizations driving alternative conceptions are mistaken. However, this would be a *discovery*, and not something we should simply presuppose from the get-go. Moreover, given the diversity of things people have explicitly appealed to and the variety of ways people have characterized free will, the most reasonable thing to do is explicitly forgo the assumption that there is only one thing that is plausibly at stake when people discuss free will.

A recurring theme in this book is that the philosophical tradition sometimes exerts a form of conceptual tyranny on us. The issue of determinism has driven how we've conceived of the possibilities available as solutions to "the" free will problem. Although the main problem with which I am concerned derives from our causal embeddedness, most of the literature has approached these matters motivated by a concern with the relationship of free will to determinism. I will borrow some of that terminology, but that terminology's determinism-focused origins are worth bearing in mind.

Consider the term *incompatibilism*. Although I will introduce an important refinement in the coming chapter, for the moment we can say that incompatibilism about free will is the view that free will is incompatible with (the thesis of) determinism.[13] *Compatibilism* about free will is what you would expect: it is the view that free will is compatible with determinism. Importantly, a commitment to compatibilism or incompatibilism does not, by itself, commit you to whether the world is actually deterministic. "Compatibilism" and "incompatibilism," as I will use them, are simply labels for whether or not one thinks free will could exist in a deterministic world: the incompatibilist says "no" and the compatibilist, "yes." It is a further matter whether determinism is true, and for that matter, whether free will actually exists.[14]

---

[13] After this paragraph, I will usually drop the parenthetical bit of precisification. Strictly speaking, however, most appeals to the compatibility or incompatibility of things will be to those things and the thesis of determinism or indeterminism.

[14] Compatibilism is typically regarded as a success term. That is, the presumption is that if one holds a compatibilist theory, one thinks that we at least sometimes satisfy the requirements specified by the theory. Neil Levy has argued that this is too quick. There is room for a view on which one holds that free will and moral responsibility are both compatible with determinism, while also holding that for other reasons we do not have free will and/or moral responsibility. See Neil Levy, *Hard Luck: How Luck Undermines Freedom* (New York: Oxford University Press, 2011).

In embracing compatibilism about both determinism and indeterminism, the mainstream of contemporary compatibilism differs from its historical forerunners. Many historical forms of compatibilism included a requirement of determinism. It is for this reason that William James' terminology of "soft determinist" has rightly fallen out of favor in the current parlance: it misleadingly embeds a requirement of determinism into compatibilism that most contemporary compatibilists would reject. Instead, contemporary compatibilists usually embrace a kind of "supercompatibilism," holding that freedom and responsibility are compatible with both determinism and indeterminism.[15]

In recent years the terms "compatibilism" and "incompatibilism" have sometimes been used to refer to the relationship of moral responsibility and determinism. This usage can (but does not necessarily) overlap with compatibilism and incompatibilism about free will. Recall that, as I will be using the term, "free will" just is a distinctive power or capacity characteristic of morally responsible agents. So, (in)compatibilism about free will, thus construed, will ordinarily entail the same for moral responsibility. However, if one does not treat free will as the freedom or control condition on moral responsibility, then one cannot move so easily between (in)compatibilism about moral responsibility to the same about free will, and vice versa. I will have more to say about such views later, but given the conception of free will at work in this book, compatibilism simpliciter is a comparatively innocent bit of ambiguity.

So: free will is a power or capacity characteristic of morally responsible agents, and "compatibilism" and "incompatibilism" are terms about the relationship of either (or both) free will and determinism or moral responsibility and determinism. A further set of common terminology refers to species of incompatibilism. *Libertarianism*, in its original and still best sense, refers to the view that we have free will, and that it is incompatible with determinism. The incompatibilist denial of libertarianism has no commonly

---

[15] Outsiders to this literature are sometimes surprised to hear this, but the reasoning is relatively straightforward. Consider a broadly "identificationist" approach to responsibility: to act freely is, roughly, to identify with the relevant desires to lead to action. This condition can obtain under determinism or indeterminism. Now suppose one has a "reasons responsiveness" account of free will. On such an account, one maintains that one acts freely when one is responsive to reasons, this condition can be satisfied under determinism or not. Similar remarks hold for most contemporary compatibilist proposals. In what follows, subsequent usage of "compatibilism" should be read as referring to contemporary compatibilists, of the "super" variety.

accepted name, but I will call such a view *incompatibilist nihilism*. Incompatibilist nihilism is a species of responsibility nihilism, for it denies the possibility of responsibility, albeit on specifically incompatibilist grounds. However, since one could, at least in principle, be a responsibility nihilist on other grounds, it is useful to have the genus and species varieties of nihilism at our disposal.

Historically, the most influential strand of incompatibilist nihilism has been *hard determinism*, or the view that free will is incompatible with determinism and that determinism is true, and thus, that no one has free will.[16] This is a view that few philosophers hold any longer, mostly because philosophers have been inclined to accommodate the standard picture of quantum mechanics as irreducibly non-deterministic. These days, a more influential but still nihilist view is what Derk Pereboom has labeled *hard incompatibilism*. This is a "no free will either way" view, i.e., the view that we lack free will, and that free will is incompatible with both determinism and indeterminism.[17]

A final remark is in order about one of the central terms in this book. As we have seen, revisionism is the idea that our best theory of free will and moral responsibility will be one that conflicts with some aspect or aspects of commonsense thinking about free will and moral responsibility. A consequence of thinking about revisionism in this way is that an account can be more and less revisionist to the extent to which it conflicts with common sense. On the present regimentation of terms, revisionist accounts contrast with *conventional* accounts, accounts on which philosophical theorizing does not conflict with our pre- or loosely theorized convictions in some domain. So, revisionist compatibilism contrasts with conventional compatibilism in that its prescriptive theory—how we ought to think about responsibility after philosophical theorizing—conflicts with

---

[16] Notice that there is room here for a view on which free will is incompatible with determinism, but we lack free will apart from determinism, for there is some overdetermining factor such that even though determinism is true (and thus precludes free will), we would also lack free will because of this other free will-precluding thing.

[17] There is some complexity to how, exactly, we should characterize things. For example, we might distinguish between views that hold that we actually lack free will, and views on which we are merely *unlikely* to have free will. Similarly, we could distinguish between views that hold that free will is incompatible with determinism and indeterminism, and views on which free will is incompatible with all forms of determinism and indeterminism *that we are likely to have*. I believe Pereboom holds the latter view in each pair of disjuncts.

ordinary convictions about responsibility. In contrast, a conventional compatibilist account holds that there is no conflict. An account is a conventional compatibilist account if it maintains that how we think about free will is fine, and philosophy just explains how it is tenable, perhaps adding a few bells and whistles.

6. Putting the jargon to use

With some terminology in place, I can now sharpen up the characterization of what follows. The theory I offer in this book is one that, unlike conventional compatibilism, acknowledges the grip of incompatibilist intuitions. Like incompatibilist nihilist views, it rejects the tenability of libertarianism. However, it departs from responsibility nihilism on grounds that there are good reasons to think we are responsible, even though the basis and nature of that responsibility is at odds with important strands of how we ordinarily think about responsibility.

The account is revisionist; it insists that what we ought to think about responsibility conflicts with important threads of how we do think about responsibility, and so much the worse for ordinary ways of thinking about responsibility. So: it might be nice if we were libertarian agents, but we likely aren't. That's okay, because we can get genuine moral responsibility with less demanding forms of agency. Just don't think the picture agency that suffices for responsibility is the one we were initially looking for, because it isn't.

Revisionism offers something new to the debates about free will and moral responsibility: it provides us with a way to acknowledge the attractions of our concepts as we find them, while at the same time permitting us to bracket some problematic intuitions. Our task is to grapple directly with the matter of what forms of agency are required to justify attributions of praise and blame, given a causal, scientifically plausible picture of the world. In doing so, a revisionist approach provides a place for traditional metaphysical concerns without forgoing the normative questions that are obviously important for responsibility.

My rejection of responsibility nihilism in favor of responsibility revisionism partly stems from a conviction that for some time now philosophers have been circling around correct accounts of various aspects of moral responsibility, without quite seeing all the way through to how these things best hang together. I attribute the elusiveness of a more generally accepted solution to three things: (1) lack of clarity concerning methodological presumptions; (2) a failure to make explicit the success conditions of our accounts; and (3) a disposition to accept explanatory burdens that are familiar but neither necessary nor helpful. My aim is to assemble what I take to be the best partial truths of our state-of-the-art in these matters, improving them as I can, and displaying them in a way that allows each of them a role, if not quite the dominant role that they were conceived of playing.

With respect to the purported threat from contemporary science, I am concerned but undaunted. Contemporary science can illuminate particular cases, telling us important details about the presence or absence of things that matter for free will and moral responsibility. And, I think that one of the things that we learn from thinking about these issues in light of the existing scientific data is that our being free and responsible are considerably more fragmentary (less frequent, less unified) than we tend to suppose.

Importantly, however, transformation does not always entail elimination. Science can change our convictions, but these matters are only partly empirical. Much of what is at stake is normative. Science may give us reasons to accept that we make errors and that our convictions require deflation. What I conclude, however, is that there is enough secure foundation left upon which to build a credible account of moral responsibility.

7. Coming attractions

The book is divided into two main parts. Part I ("Building Blocks," spanning chapters 1 through 4) presents, refines, and reformulates the revisionist position. Part II presents a novel theory of moral responsibility.

Part I is primarily focused on three things: (1) characterizing a strand of ordinary convictions about free will and moral responsibility; (2) using that characterization to illuminate the puzzle of why debates about free will and moral responsibility have seemed so intractable; and (3) articulating what options are available to us in light of the empirical and normative difficulties facing the familiar theoretical options. Roughly, chapter 1 is about folk beliefs, chapter 2 is about libertarianism, chapter 3 is about nihilism and revisionism, and chapter 4 presents a framework for constructing revisionist accounts.

Part II ("A Theory of Moral Responsibility," or chapters 5 through 10) assumes the plausibility of revisionism and proceeds to build an original theory of responsibility. It is the heart of the book. Indeed, it might well have been the book, except that it seemed unreasonable to suppose that readers would have been sufficiently familiar with the latest version of my revisionist machinery, which animates the project throughout. Part II presents an account of responsibility understood largely in terms of the agency cultivation model, elaborating an account of the teleology of the responsibility system, and the role of praise and blame in fostering a particular form of agency. It explains how desert-entailing responsibility judgments can be preserved, even given what we know about our agency, and it emphasizes the fundamentally social dimensions of responsibility and our reasons-responsive powers.

Chapters 5 through 7 hang together. They are about, respectively, the centrality of reasons, the teleological structure of the responsibility system, and what it is to be a responsible agent. Chapters 8 and 9 extend and develop the account to address questions about exculpation, desert, and manipulation arguments. The tenth and briefest chapter ties up loose ends. Finally, the Appendix shows some ways to fruitfully connect this account of responsible agency with theories of action not centrally concerned with moral responsibility.

PART I
Building Blocks

1

Folk Convictions

... the idea of Free Will seems involved in a particular
way in the moral ideas of Common Sense.

Henry Sidgwick[1]

1. Fitting intuitions to theories

The ongoing philosophical grip that responsibility and free will have had on
us partly arises from conflicting intuitions that many of us have in a wide
range of contexts. By intuitions, I mean the beliefs and reactions initially
evoked in consideration of examples and principles. This chapter tries to
show some of how and why those intuitions have given us the familiar free
will debate.

The chapter aims at motivating three particular ideas: (1) we have diverse
intuitions, and some of those intuitions are plausibly understood as compatibilist, and others as incompatibilist; and (2) this result suggests that no
theory will accommodate all intuitions; but (3) the problem of intuitional fit
is more challenging for those constructing compatibilist theories.

The third claim may seem strange. If both compatibilist and incompatibilist theories imperfectly fit the intuitions, what is the basis on which incompatibilists theories have a comparatively better fit? Here's an idea that might
help. Imagine a tailor who discovers he has two batches of very large shirts.
He can be assured that neither batch will fit most of his clients—after all, both
sets of shirts are very large. However, one batch of these large shirts also lacks a
neck hole. In light of this fact, the tailor can be confident that the batch
without the neck hole will fit almost none of his clients. In contrast, the other
batch will fit a considerably greater number of clients.

---

[1] Henry Sidgwick, *The Methods of Ethics* (7th edn.) (Indianapolis, IN: Hackett, 1981), p. 284.

Here, intuitions are the clients, and theories are the shirts. Incompatibilist accounts provide the neck hole for incompatibilist intuitions. Compatibilist accounts don't. Even if no theory provides a perfect fit for widespread intuitions, and everyone is left with extra fabric, compatibilist theories are missing a place to put some widespread intuitions. Accounting for all the intuitions is hard on any theory, but it is especially difficult for compatibilist theories.

A further distinction between kinds of theorizing may help clarify the present approach and its commitments. One approach to theorizing can take as its aim the description of our intuitions, judgments, or concepts. Call this a *diagnostic* project. Diagnostic theorizing is akin to conceptual anthropology, revealing the contours of our present thinking about some matter. A different project is something we can call *prescriptive*. A prescriptive theory offers an account of how we *ought* to think about some subject matter, all things considered.[2]

In this chapter I'm concerned with diagnosis. Subsequently, I will be principally concerned with prescription. My goal in this chapter, though, is to offer an account of some aspects of common sense that have been significant for much of the traditional philosophical literature on free will and moral responsibility. In doing so, we will get a better grasp of why the free will/moral responsibility problem has persisted for so long, and why any candidate solution is bound to strike many people as deeply unsatisfying.

2. Incompatibilist inspirations

I have already suggested that a full accounting of our ordinary talk and reflection on free will and moral responsibility will find incompatibilist strands lurking more and less prominently in our thinking. That is, part of our shared conceptual framework for thinking about moral responsibility

---

[2] Because the "descriptive/prescriptive" distinction is significant in metaethics, I prefer to use the label "diagnostic." That said, I have no objection to using "descriptive" rather than "diagnostic," so long as we are careful to distinguish between accounts that endeavor to characterize our (perhaps latent) commonsense views and proposals for how, all things considered, we should characterize the matter. I've also avoided Sellars' terminology, for it may suggest that any prescriptive account will necessarily be "scientific," whatever that comes to. For an alternative (but, I think, compatible), tripartite division of theoretical aims see Shaun Nichols, "Folk Intuitions on Free Will," *Journal of Cognition and Culture* 6, nos 1 & 2 (2006): 57–86.

and free will has elements in it that entail that we cannot have these things if the world is deterministic.

Although I think that many of us have both incompatibilist and compatibilist intuitions in distinct contexts, I focus on incompatibilist intuitions. I've already said why: the theoretical commitments required to make good on incompatibilist commitments turn out to be especially problematic. Without them, we could get along just fine with shirts lacking neck holes.

In claiming that there are widespread incompatibilist intuitions, I do not mean to suggest that everyone necessarily has incompatibilist intuitions. Nor do I mean that those incompatibilist intuitions are pervasive in each and every judgment of freedom and responsibility. There might well be judgments of responsibility that do not contain incompatibilist presuppositions, even among people who regularly feel the pull of incompatibilism. What I do claim is that for a great many of us, there are contexts in which incompatibilist convictions are really, truly, genuinely part of the conceptual furniture with which we find ourselves. I will call this view *folk conceptual incompatibilism*, as distinct from the philosophical thesis of incompatibilism as such.[3]

The view I aim to motivate holds that folk conceptual incompatibilist commitments are *not* ersatz convictions. They are not merely theories projected on to us by ourselves or other philosophers. They are not simple misreadings of our existing commitments. Instead, they are really, truly, part of how a good many of us, much of the time, tend to think about the conditions of being morally responsible in as "deep" or "genuine" a sense as you like.

In what follows, I focus on five families of considerations that suggest that incompatibilist convictions play an important role in swaths of our thinking about the conditions on moral responsibility. I'll reject the first, but go on to accept a package of four considerations that individually and jointly motivate the conclusion that many of us (at least sometimes) have incompatibilist

---

[3] The label "folk" isn't supposed to be derogatory—it just refers to what we might think of as "ordinary folks"—i.e., not (just?) professional philosophers. Whether folk conceptual incompatibilism supports or even amounts to the philosophical thesis of incompatibilism is something I will take up later. In this chapter, the main interest is folk conceptual incompatibilism, and not the philosophical thesis of incompatibilism.

intuitions that invite accommodation in our philosophical theorizing. The considerations I largely accept as pointing in that direction include traditional philosophical arguments for incompatibilism, experimental data, the idea that there are culturally significant ideas that make sense of some of the other considerations, and the presence of a story about how those elements seem especially supported by how we understand our own decision-making.

None of these considerations are decisive. Nonetheless, the overall case for folk conceptual incompatibilism is strong.

3. Making and having choices

One place we might look for evidence of an incompatibilist conviction is natural language. For example, students will sometimes tell me that if determinism is true, no one ever *really* had a choice.

I find that "really," "genuinely," and "truly" often mark places where naked conviction hides an absence of good argument. However, in this instance it *is* plausible that there is a real distinction lurking here. It is just that it is insufficient to get us to folk conceptual incompatibilism.

Consider: Annie might choose to save Clio's life from, say, a rabid mongoose. In doing so, she might also insist that she had no choice but to do so. Such usage seems to reflect a distinction between *making* a choice and *having* a choice.[4] Making a choice is the forming of a decision or intention. Having a choice has something to do with the context in which decisions or intentions are formed, or perhaps their nature as they are formed. So: if determinism is true, we might have made plenty of choices, but nevertheless lacked a choice about which choices we made.

Does this distinction, plausibly embedded in natural language, reflect an implicit commitment to a metaphysics of incompatibilism? It would if by "have a choice" we mean something like "the agent makes a decision under conditions such that given the actual past and the actual laws, it is physically possible up until the moment of decision that the agent has available to him

---

[4] Van Inwagen, among others, has invoked this distinction. See Peter van Inwagen, *Metaphysics* (3rd edn.) (Boulder, CO: Westview Press, 2008).

or her that he/she *A* and that he/she not *A*, where *A* is some particular action."[5]

It is not obvious that appeals to having a choice necessarily mark a belief in metaphysically robust possibilities. Such language may reflect only a commitment to tracking when a bit of behavior's causal pedigree does not involve the customary forms of volitional control.

Consider reflexive actions. Suppose Jeff is frying potatoes and burns his hand, jerking it away from the stove. Later, Jeff might say that he had no choice but to pull his hand away from the stove. Perhaps Annie's saving of Clio is something like that. Even if it is not reflexive, something that bypassed deliberation about what to do, it might nevertheless have had an unusual or atypical causal history that does not involve the usual ways in which we recognizably control our selves.

All of this is compatible with non-deterministic pictures of action. Even if we tend to think of reflexive action as precluding metaphysically robust alternative possibilities, it might be that our reflexive actions are highly probabilistic in their ontological structure. That is, it might be the case that the particular reflexive action we undertake nearly always is arrived at indeterministically. So, perhaps Annie might have saved Clio by shouting, by throwing herself in the way of the mongoose, or by stomping on its head. Appeals to reflexive actions and the invocation of the "no choice" locution seem altogether neutral on this matter.

Moreover, some of our "no choice" talk seems to reflect assessments of undesirable or bad choice options. When I say "I had no choice but to pay my taxes" I do not mean that my paying taxes was reflexive or something that bypassed conscious, deliberative control. Instead, I am averring to, roughly, the absence of alternatives I regard as sufficiently appealing, or alternatives that would be rational for me to will.

When we have accounted for non-standard causal paths of choice and implicit assessments of the quality of choices, it is unclear whether there is much ground for invoking claims of an implicit incompatibilism in our distinction between the having and making of choices. We do plausibly have a distinction between the making of a decision (making a choice) and cases where that decision-making is sub-optimal or non-standard (reflexive action or poor choice options, wherein we are more inclined to say the

---

[5] Thanks to Jason Miller for suggestions on the wording.

agent lacks a choice, even if he or she made a choice). However, nothing in those distinctions seems to require that our analysis of folk convictions includes interestingly incompatibilist elements. So, I conclude that natural language does not, in this case, provide us with a compelling path to folk conceptual incompatibilism.

4. Traditional philosophical arguments for incompatibilism

Even if the bit of natural language considered above doesn't provide a path to folk conceptual incompatibilism, a more plausible path arises when we consider the *reception* of important philosophical arguments. In particular, I will focus on a family of arguments that include Peter van Inwagen's much-discussed Consequence Argument.[6] It is an argument for the conclusion that free will is incompatible with determinism.

Here is a very simple version of the argument, one that begins with only two important assumptions. First, let us suppose that free will requires the ability to do otherwise. Second, let us define determinism in the following way: determinism is the thesis that the state of the universe at any prior time and the actual laws of nature are logically sufficient for the state of the universe at any later time.[7] Here then is the heart of the argument: If determinism is true, then it seems to be a necessary fact that given the past and the laws, the world will turn out as it does. For someone to do otherwise in a deterministic universe, the agent would have to do something that results either in a change of the laws of physics or requires some

---

[6] Peter van Inwagen, *An Essay on Free Will* (New York: Oxford University Press, 1983). For an important antecedent, see Carl Ginet, "Might We Have No Choice?," in *Freedom and Determinism*, ed. Keith Lehrer (New York: Random House, 1966). A variety of incompatibilists have subsequently presented variations of the argument, designed to resist objections to earlier formulations. There is a voluminous literature on the particulars. For an overview, see Daniel Speak, "The Consequence Argument Revisited," in *The Oxford Handbook of Free Will* (2nd edn.), ed. Robert Kane (New York: Oxford University Press, 2011).

[7] Going forward, I will speak only of the past, as shorthand for "the state of the universe at any prior time." Notice, though, that "prior time" can be read as the present so long as it is prior to the future time whose present (plus the laws) are logically sufficient for that prior time. I should also note that characterizing determinism as it is used in the sciences is a difficult task, and there are distinct theses that can be rightly called determinism. My own sense is that these differences will not be crucial for what follows, so long as they entail the characterization on the table, or something similar in ramifications.

difference in the past. Since changing the laws and changing the past appear impossible, then in a deterministic world no one would have the ability to do otherwise. Thus, if determinism is true then we lack the ability to do otherwise. Since free will requires the ability to do otherwise, then if determinism obtains, no one has free will.

If we further suppose that free will is a requirement on moral responsibility, or that moral responsibility independently requires the ability to do otherwise, then the Consequence Argument drives us to a thoroughgoing incompatibilism. That is, determinism would be incompatible with free will and moral responsibility, precisely because it is incompatible with a requirement for both—i.e., the ability to do otherwise.

There are a number of ways to resist this argument. One is to challenge the idea that free will requires the ability to do otherwise. Another is to contend that the ability to do otherwise required by free will is not the sense of the ability to do otherwise that is ruled out by the argument. Another is to dispute one or another of the principles of reasoning in the argument. Yet another way is to grant the conclusion, but to argue that, whatever is the case for free will, *moral responsibility* does not require alternative possibilities of the sort that are incompatible with determinism.[8]

There is an impressively large and sophisticated literature on all of these possibilities, and simply canvassing that literature is a no trivial matter.[9] Moreover, there is some appeal to regarding the matter as reflecting an insurmountable standoff (the sort of thing John Fischer has helpfully labeled a "dialectical stalemate"). Convinced compatibilists usually find the arguments wanting, whereas self-identified incompatibilists frequently suspect resistance to these arguments is less a matter of any shortcomings of the argument and more a matter of disliking the conclusions that follow.

For my own part, I think the dialectical situation is a bit like fighting the hydra of mythology: for every difficulty found with these arguments, two new arguments emerge. (Well perhaps not *two*, but certainly another.) What I will focus on, though, is not the contents of the argument directly, but rather a different kind of argument, one that relies on the contents of traditional arguments only indirectly. To see what I have in mind, it helps to

[8] This approach has been famously developed by John Martin Fischer, sometimes in concert with Mark Ravizza. See John Martin Fischer and Mark Ravizza, *Responsibility and Control: A Theory of Moral Responsibility* (New York: Cambridge University Press, 1998).
[9] Speak, "The Consequence Argument Revisited."

think about *why* arguments such as the Consequence Argument for incompatibilism have been influential. What makes these arguments powerful is not so much that they rule out the possibility of compatibilism—they don't—but rather that they show how easily incompatibilism seems to capture ordinary ways of thinking about our own agency.

To see why this relatively innocuous point matters, consider perhaps the most influential line of criticism against the Consequence Argument and its successors (henceforth, Consequence-style arguments). Several critics have focused on how an antecedently compatibilist reading of the relevant ability term (for example, the ability to break the laws of nature) makes the argument unpersuasive against antecedently committed compatibilists.

Suppose these critics are right. If so, it would mean that Consequence-style arguments couldn't rule out the possibility of compatibilism. From this, we might think things look like a standoff, at best, and at worst a real problem for incompatibilism. Here, though, the innocuous point has some role to play: the "naturalness" or ease of the incompatibilist reading of the argument is itself evidence that the argument captures an important part of the contents and logic of commonsense thinking about these issues. Even if the contents of the argument cannot rule out a compatibilist reading, the ease with which we read the premises in consistently incompatibilist-supporting ways suggests that we can and do understand these issues in incompatibilist ways, at least sometimes.

Try it—present the Consequence Argument or its successors to a group of people and see how many people read it the first time (or even the fifth time!) in a way that exploits a compatibilist-friendly interpretation of "can" for any of the main premises. You won't find many people who read it in compatibilist-friendly ways. This provides one (defeasible) consideration for thinking that a natural, even default way of thinking about these issues leans incompatibilist.

If a compatibilist construal of our theoretical commitments on the freedom-relevant notion of ability were front and center in our thinking about free will and moral responsibility, it is difficult to see how Consequence-style arguments for incompatibilism would have been as persuasive as they have been to so many people. Indeed, the existence of incompatibilist intuitions seems the most straightforward explanation of how the argument could have ever seemed compelling.

So, even if the argument doesn't directly prove that common sense is incompatibilist (for we might discover that any such argument can be read in a way that favors the compatibilist), it provides indirect evidence for incompatibilism by being so naturally and widely read in incompatibilist terms.

Building the case for folk conceptual incompatibilism on the basis of the reception of arguments for *philosophical* incompatibilism obviously has its limitations. However, whatever else is true about such arguments, the Consequence Argument and its progeny have done an excellent job of making manifest an important and natural understanding of the sense of ability relevant to questions of free will. From the standpoint of diagnosing the state of intuitions, it puts the burden on compatibilists to show that a similar or better mustering of our intuitions and principles can be done on behalf of compatibilism.

5. An aside on Frankfurt cases

One way to respond to my construal of the power of Consequence-style arguments is to insist that folk conceptual compatibilists have better, or at least equally good tools to show that our ordinary thinking is thoroughly compatibilist in its commitments. Recall that the path to incompatibilism we have been considering works through a multi-step argument. First, we get the part of the argument that shows that determinism rules out the ability to do otherwise. Then we get the invocation of a principle that the ability to do otherwise is required for moral responsibility, what has become known as the Principle of Alternative Possibilities (or PAP).

An important family of thought experiments, drawing from the work of Harry Frankfurt, have been taken to impugn the plausibility of PAP.[10] Such cases—*Frankfurt cases*—are often regarded as demonstrating the failure of a crucial step in the argument, that alternative possibilities are required for

---

[10] These cases figured prominently in reconfiguring the recent history of the free will debate. For an overview of important elements of these cases, see John Martin Fischer, "Recent Work on Moral Responsibility," *Ethics* 110, no. 1 (1999): 93–139; David Widerker and Michael McKenna, eds, *Moral Responsibility and Alternative Possibilities: Essays on the Importance of Alternative Possibilities* (Burlington, VT: Ashgate, 2003). For my view of their more general importance to the literature, see Vargas, "The Revisionist Turn: Reflection on the Recent History of Work on Free Will."

moral responsibility. If so, one might conclude that it is a mistake to think that folk thinking is in any robust way committed to an alternative possibilities requirement for moral responsibility.

Here is an example of a Frankfurt case:

There is an agent facing a choice, where unbeknownst to that agent an intervener is prepared to induce some condition that brings it about that the agent make a particular choice (call it the Bad Choice), should the agent fail to make the choice on his or her own. Nevertheless, the agent makes the Bad Choice on his or her own, and the intervener never acts.

There are two crucial ideas at work here. First, there is the idea that the agent has a choice, but that unbeknownst to the agent there is really only one possibility about what will actually occur. This is because of the second important idea in the case: there is an intervener who is ready to act in a way that blocks access to any alternative outcome. Crucially, as things actually unfold, *the intervener never acts*. What blocks the presence of alternative possibilities is the preparedness of the intervener to intervene.

In Frankfurt cases, we are supposed to have the intuition that despite the absence of alternative possibilities, the involved agent is indeed morally responsible. If this is the intuition one has, then the conclusion that seems to follow is that PAP is false. That is, contrary to PAP, one can be morally responsible for a choice when there are no alternative possibilities. If all that is so, then the incompatibilist conclusion about responsibility is blocked: even if determinism rules out alternative possibilities, it does not rule out moral responsibility, for moral responsibility does not require alternative possibilities. Put differently, Frankfurt cases seem to show that our intuition about the responsibility-relevant sense of ability does not require alternative possibilities.

Again, the complexity of these issues makes a brief summary difficult, but I believe there are some reasonable conclusions that can be extracted from what has become one of philosophy's most refinement-laden literatures.

One thing to note is that it is now clear that the original cases, as Frankfurt first described them, simply do not work. The power of Frankfurt's original cases turned on under-description about the causal structure of the case. That is, the case only works if we obscure the matter of whether the scenario is deterministic or not.

If we stipulate from the start that the scenario *is* deterministic, and we attend to that fact, it isn't obvious that we conclude that the case is one of moral responsibility. On the contrary, if we stipulate that the scenario is *in*deterministic, then it looks like there are alternative possibilities in the case. The full realization of those possibilities in action is precluded by the presence of the intervener, but imperfect realization looks like it is enough for the having of alternative possibilities. That is, if the case is indeterministic, it looks like the agent has the ability to make a different choice, or at least to start to make a different choice—to start choosing otherwise—forcing the intervener to intervene. Call this *the dilemma strategy*.[11]

Something like the dilemma strategy defuses a good number of Frankfurt cases, beyond Frankfurt's original example. There are versions of Frankfurt cases where the dilemma strategy seems less compelling, though. In some examples, the alternatives can seem so feeble or disconnected from the context of choice that it seems strange to think that this is the sort of thing required for moral responsibility. Suppose the only alternative to the choice is something really bizarre (use your imagination). Would the bare presence of this alternative—irrespective of how strange it might be—be sufficient for responsibility?

Suppose you are trying to decide whom to vote for and there is only one possibility open to you. On the dilemma strategy, we would ordinarily hold that you are not responsible. But suppose that you suddenly gain an additional possibility—to, say, roast a chicken, as Michael McKenna has suggested.[12] Why would the addition of this possibility suddenly turn you into a responsible agent? If lack of alternative possibilities is what makes someone not responsible in a Frankfurt case, why would the addition of strange or trivial possibility suddenly make an agent responsible? How could roasting a chicken (or whatever bizarre alternative you imagined) be at all relevant to whether or not there is moral responsibility in the scenario? Call this response to the dilemma strategy *the normative relevance objection*. The idea is this: any possibilities that are radically disconnected from the

[11] This approach has been developed by, among others, Robert Kane, *Free Will and Values* (Albany: SUNY Press, 1985); David Widerker, "Libertarianism and Frankfurt's Attack on the Principle of Alternative Possibilities," *Philosophical Review* 104 (1995): 247–61; Carl Ginet, "In Defense of the Principle of Alternative Possibilities," *Philosophical Perspectives* 10 (1996): 403–17.

[12] Michael McKenna, "Robustness, Control, and the Demand for Morally Significant Alternatives," in *Moral Responsibility and Alternative Possibilities*, ed. Widerker and McKenna.

agent's concerns, deliberations, or values are, on this approach, obviously insufficient to ground the normative practices at stake in assessments of moral responsibility.

While there are a number of things that critics of Frankfurt cases might say at this point, I want to pause to consider something puzzling about the normative relevance objection, as a response to the dilemma strategy in the present context. Recall that what we have set out to do is to characterize commonsense thinking about free will and moral responsibility. Given this aim, it is not clear why the analyst of folk intuitions needs to suppose that normative relevance is a constraint on folk intuitions.

It is surely possible that our ordinary concepts have normatively irrelevant conditions built into them. Indeed, supposing anything else seems unduly optimistic. Given the varied quality of sources of our beliefs about ourselves and the world, some argument seems required if we are to suppose that our beliefs about moral responsibility reflect an antecedent commitment to conditions that earn their keep, given contemporary philosophical concerns. Instead, at least as theorists of the folk, we do better to accept the possibility that our moral framework has requirements that are gratuitous, or suppositions that are erroneous or unnecessary.

Allowing for this possibility permits us to make discoveries that we might not otherwise see, and it might permit us to explain puzzling aspects of philosophical disputes that take as their fuel the stuff of our ordinary moral framework. For example, one thing we might discover is that we really do have an alternative possibilities requirement in our thinking about responsibility, but that it does not do any justifiable work. Perhaps recent Frankfurt-style cases show this much. If so, this should be a discovery, and not something we rule out before undertaking the inquiry.

At the level of characterizing the architecture of our ordinary moral thought, the normative relevance demand is inappropriate. It may be a plausible requirement to invoke downstream in our theorizing. So, at least in the context of folk conceptual analysis, the dilemma defense can repel worries about normative relevance.

Consider a different concern about Frankfurt cases. Perhaps the most prominent latter-day Frankfurt-style strategy has been to build more elaborate cases that duck the various objections that have been lodged against earlier versions of the case. The growing number of epicycles on these cases (e.g., involving parallel brain processes, one indeterministic, the other deterministic) can do important work answering objections to less complex Frankfurt cases. However, the escalating complexity of these cases comes at a cost: it also makes it harder to get a clear-headed assessment of these cases as evidence that we do not ordinarily require alternative possibilities in our assessments of responsibility.

Inasmuch as we are plumbing the depths of our folk concepts of freedom and responsibility sufficiently complex cases run the risk of testing only the intuitions of philosophers with well-cultivated and deeply entrenched commitments about the matter. Moreover, the more a particular case relies upon mechanisms remote from our ordinary and perhaps naïve understanding of human agency the more likely it is that our commonsense understandings of these things will get distorted by the mechanisms imagined in the case. Although these issues remain unresolved, I am skeptical (perhaps more so than most) that we will be able to show that alternative possibilities aren't a persistent element of ordinary thinking about freedom and responsibility.[13]

6. Two points of clarification

Thus far, I have argued that there is good reason to think that folk convictions about moral responsibility tend to frequently involve an incompatibilist alternative possibilities commitment. Here, I wish to make two points of clarification about this picture of folk conceptual incompatibilism.

First: this account does not rule out the possibility of other, distinct incompatibilist threads in common sense. The folk conceptual incompatibilist picture I have been sketching has focused on the importance of alternative possibilities. Sometimes this is called *leeway* or *alternative*

---

[13] One might still wonder why I am comparatively sympathetic to the Consequence Argument and unsympathetic to Frankfurt cases. After all, both are contested arguments that depend on intricate details about which there is reasonable disagreement. Here is one reason why they appear to me to have different standing: Frankfurt cases were intended to overturn a principle that had, by and large, not been seriously contested, whereas the Consequence Argument is a regimentation of considerations that have long been a part of the literature. Although I am more persuaded by the Consequence Argument, even if I found it equally uncertain as Frankfurt cases, the background context of the argument seems to me to weigh more heavily in favor of a presumption for the Consequence Argument and against Frankfurt case. Consider: suppose you had two equally uncertain but powerful arguments, one in favor of high academic standards and another against representative government. In our present context, we should more readily accept the former and be reluctant to accept the latter, even if we are equally uncertain about both.

possibilities incompatibilism.[14] However, some incompatibilists—*source in-compatibilists*—argue that there is an important basis for incompatibilism that does not appeal to alternative possibilities. Instead, this form of incompatibilism appeals to a special form of causal origination, sourcehood, or ultimacy. On such accounts, if determinism were true, no agent could be responsible, quite apart from whether or not the agent has alternative possibilities.[15]

I am uncertain about whether and to what extent ordinary people are aptly characterized as specifically (folk conceptual) source incompatibilists. I am open to the possibility that the commonsense concept of moral responsibility does invoke a source requirement. I suspect that it is there in different degrees in different people, but somewhat less widespread than alternative possibilities intuitions.[16]

A second point of clarification: it is open to leeway incompatibilists to hold that alternative possibilities do not always matter.

One way that might be so emerges in so-called "tracing" cases. The standard tracing example involves knowing, intentional impairment of one's agency. So, for example, imagine a scenario in which Freddy goes to a Den of Iniquity, knowingly and voluntarily gets sufficiently iniquitous (say, drunk, high, or subject to other agency-corroding factors) that he fails to satisfy the conditions on responsible agency. Suppose that Freddy elects to leave that Den of Iniquity, and proceeds to drive home, destroying lives and property along the way. This looks like a case in which Freddy lacks some necessary condition on moral responsibility, but for which many of us will insist that he is genuinely responsible.

The standard way of addressing this lacuna, to which the leeway incompatibilist can appeal, is to stipulate that the agent's responsibility is derivative

---

[14] I believe the phrase "leeway incompatibilism" originates in Michael McKenna, "Source Incompatibilism, Ultimacy, and the Transfer of Non-Responsibility," *American Philosophical Quarterly* 38, no. 1 (2001): 37–51.

[15] There is some disagreement about the extent to which the alternative possibilities requirement is independent of sourcehood. For a sample of influential work on sourcehood and its relationship to alternative possibilities, see Robert Kane, *The Significance of Free Will* (Oxford: Oxford University Press, 1996); Pereboom, *Living Without Free Will*; McKenna, "Source Incompatibilism, Ultimacy, and the Transfer of Non-Responsibility"; Kevin Timpe, *Free Will: Sourcehood and Its Alternatives* (New York: Continuum, 2008).

[16] I believe that what intuitions we have about sourcehood are varied in origin. Some of it likely derives from the sensible thought that if the category of agents is treated as different than non-agents, this distinction is to be rendered in terms of agents being sources of actions. A less obviously respectable origin for sourcehood intuitions might be a tendency towards homuncularist interpretations of our agency, but this too cries out for a further explanation.

on some prior decision, when he or she knowingly and voluntarily undertook a course of iniquitous action.[17] Here, it may help to regiment some vocabulary. Call cases of non-derivative responsibility instances of *original responsibility*. When responsibility in some later case is parasitic on an earlier instance of original responsibility, call that later instance a case of *derivative responsibility*.[18]

These then are two thoughts worth keeping in mind: first, although the present account emphasizes leeway incompatibilism, we might be folk conceptual incompatibilists on other grounds; and second, even leeway incompatibilists need not hold that there will be alternative possibilities in every instance of original responsibility. Plausibly we are, as a matter of actual practice, variantists about alternative possibilities, invoking distinct conditions in different cases. Of course, if only very few or marginal cases are sensitive to alternative possibilities, then alternative possibilities will look less central to our conceptual framework of moral responsibility. Still, the upshot is that folk conceptual incompatibilist commitments cannot be easily disposed of by appeal to the odd thought experiment in which alternative possibilities do no work.

7. Experimental data

Traditional philosophical arguments provide some evidence of strands of persistent, broadly incompatibilist intuitions about free will and moral

---

[17] For critical discussion about such approaches and disputes about their limits, see Manuel Vargas, "The Trouble With Tracing," *Midwest Studies in Philosophy* 29, no. 1 (2005): 269–91; John Martin Fischer and Neal Tognazinni, "The Truth About Tracing," *Nous* 43, no. 3 (2009): 531–56.

[18] Might there be cases where, intuitively, we have original responsibility, but no alternative possibilities? Frankfurt cases were intended to be cases of just that sort. Even if we grant the existence of instances of original responsibility without alternative possibilities, the existence of such cases would not show that our judgments *never* reflect a commitment to a condition of alternative possibilities in cases of original responsibility. Such cases might simply show that our ascriptions of responsibility appeal to variable conditions: in some cases we invoke a requirement of alternative possibilities and in others we do not. This would be a version of variantism about alternative possibilities. Of course, as Jason Miller has rightly pointed out to me, this would be an important shift away from conventional "categorical" understandings of PAP. At the very least, it would plausibly shift the burden of proof to defender of some PAP-like principle, for we would need a characterization of *when* alternative possibilities matter for moral responsibility. For discussion about variantism about responsibility, see John Doris et al., "Variantism About Moral Responsibility," *Philosophical Perspectives* 21, no. 1 (2007): 183–21. For a critique of variantism and a defense of "unificationism" or invariantism about responsibility, see Dana Nelkin, "Do We Have a Coherent Set of Intuitions About Moral Responsibility?," *Midwest Studies in Philosophy* 31 (2007): 243–59.

responsibility. A different, potentially more powerful way to show that folk thinking has incompatibilist elements employs experimental data. I see no reason to think that philosophers are uniquely or even especially well equipped to determine the contents of commonsense beliefs. Indeed, the power of philosophical arguments about free will seems to rest on their intuitive force, on their ability to capture folk thinking about abilities, the meaning of *can*, and so on. If experimental data can tell us something about these things, then we should pay attention.

A number of psychologists and empirically oriented philosophers have studied these issues. One intriguing set of results come from the work of Shaun Nichols and his collaborators. In one experiment, they give subjects descriptions of two different universes, one in which everything is completely caused by whatever happened before it, and the other a universe in which almost everything is determined by whatever happened before it, *except* human decision-making. Then, they ask their subjects to identify which universe is more like ours. Strikingly high numbers of respondents (between 86 and 95 percent, depending on which particular study) describe the second universe—the one in which human decision-making was indeterministic—as the one most like ours.[19]

It is tempting to read these data as showing that our ordinary self-conception of human agency is incompatibilist, and specifically, libertarian. The reason: it is not obvious why we would suppose human decision-making is exempt from determinism unless we supposed ourselves to be agents of the sort libertarian theories endeavor to describe. However, it may be that our tendency to self-describe as indeterministic is not a reflection of libertarian commitments but rather an artifact of, for example, ordinarily interpreting our phenomenology as showing that our choice-making is indeterministic. One could think we are indeterministic in our choice-making without also thinking such indeterminism is required.

As a point about the logical space, that is surely correct. As a point about our self-conception, it is less persuasive. Or, at least, it seems to me more plausible to suppose that if we do take our phenomenology to be indicative of indeterminism, we are also prone to (for whatever reason) supposing that

[19] Nichols, "Folk Intuitions on Free Will"; Shaun Nichols and Joshua Knobe, "Moral Responsibility and Determinism: The Cognitive Science of Folk Intuitions," *Nous* 41, no. 4 (2007): 663–85; Hagop Sarkissian et al., "Is Belief in Free Will a Cultural Universal?," *Mind and Language* 25, no. 3 (2010): 346–58.

such indeterminism is required for responsibility. After all, it is presumably in light of our distinctive mental powers that free will and moral responsibility can arise, if they do.

Whatever the case about the source of our indeterministic convictions, it is also a striking fact that Eddy Nahmias and others have shown that *com*patibilist intuitions emerge in strikingly high numbers in a variety of contexts.[20] To my mind, the evidence for the general conclusion that high levels of ordinary persons make straightforwardly compatibilist judgments in a range of circumstances is quite good.

What explains these results? It is not entirely clear how to sort out what is going on, and research is ongoing. One promising hypothesis is that subjects tend to give compatibilist responses at higher rates in cases when the prompts are concrete, and where the examples trigger emotional reactions. To be sure, incompatibilist reactions never disappear entirely—they survive at rates roughly between a fifth to a third of respondents under virtually any prompt. The point, however, is that in many contexts our judgments seem to reflect compatibilist convictions.

Matters here are delicate, for it is not always obvious if there are reasons to take one or another alternative interpretation of the results. For example, one could read the data as indicating that we have distinct concepts of moral responsibility (and, correspondingly, of freedom). Alternately, we could interpret the same data as showing a performance error in one or another direction. There have been a number of attempts by thoughtful philosophers and experimentalists to tease out the details, and this is a literature very much in progress.[21]

Here, I will mention two promising possibilities. The first is that we will find that there is interaction between our conception of the metaphysics of

---

[20] Nichols, "Folk Intuitions on Free Will"; Robert L. Woolfolk et al., "Identification, Situational Constraint, and Social Cognition: Studies in the Attribution of Moral Responsibility," *Cognition* 100 (2006): 283–401; Eddy Nahmias, "Folk Fears About Freedom and Responsibility: Determinism and Reductionism," *Journal of Culture and Cognition* 6, nos 1–2 (2006): 215–38; Eddy Nahmias et al., "Is Incompatibilism Intuitive?," *Philosophy and Phenomenological Research* 73, no. 1 (2006): 28–53; Eddy Nahmias et al., "Free Will, Moral Responsibility, and Mechanism: Experiments on Folk Intuitions," *Midwest Studies in Philosophy* XXXI (2007): 214–41.

[21] For recent discussions of the state of the experimental literature, see Adam Feltz et al., "Natural Compatibilism Versus Natural Incompatibilism: Back to the Drawing Board," *Mind and Language* 24, no. 1 (2009): 1–23; Shaun Nichols and Joshua Knobe, "Free Will and the Bounds of the Self," in *The Oxford Handbook of Free Will* (2nd edn.), ed. Kane; Eddy Nahmias, "Intuitions About Free Will, Determinism, and Bypassing," in *The Oxford Handbook of Free Will* (2nd edn.), ed. Kane.

responsibility and somewhat looser, heuristics-driven practical considerations about holding one another responsible. The second is one I hinted
at in the preceding section: conceptual fragmentation, one version of which
might be variation in the conditions we invoke for responsibility.

Consider the first possibility. We might hold that what the experiments
are illustrating is the difference between, on the one hand, our genuine
theoretical beliefs about free will and moral responsibility, and on the
other hand, heuristics or "shortcuts" for assessing responsibility that reflect
a commitment to holding people responsible despite imperfect knowledge
of cases. When the assignment of praise, blame, and punishment to a
particular individual is not at stake, our reactions manifest a conception of
things that leans strongly incompatibilist. However, when the assignment of
praise and blame for a particular individual (fictional or real) becomes a live
possibility, this triggers our various heuristics for sorting out our best
estimation of a matter whose metaphysics is only indirectly available to us.

On this picture, pressures connected to the importance of holding people
responsible, and the thought that we should presume that norm violations
by adults ordinarily entail responsibility, may swamp whatever more nuanced requirements we have for free will and moral responsibility. This is
view on which, as a matter of ordinary cognitive and social practice, we take
it that there are good reasons to assume that people are responsible agents
unless we have reason to think otherwise. In particular, we need a pretty
good reason to *not* assign responsibility to people unfamiliar to us when they
violate some norm we value. Systems of sanctioning (punishment, both
formal and informal) are simply too important or too deeply ingrained to be
ignored. Determinism-resilient (i.e., compatibilist) judgments reflect the
pragmatic dimensions of a socially embedded practice whose efficacy
turns, in part, on swift responses to harm.

A different and not necessarily inconsistent explanation of the divergent
intuitions is this: our ordinary concepts of free will and moral responsibility
are not unified. On this view, we either inconsistently deploy different
concepts of freedom and responsibility, or there is a single concept with
different criteria under different circumstances, i.e., a form of variantism. In
the present context, disentangling the differences and similarities of these
latter two possibilities is not necessary. In either case, there remain good
grounds for concluding in favor of what I have been characterizing as a form
of folk conceptual incompatibilism.

Here is why. What incompatibilists about the folk concept must hold is that our ascriptions of free will and moral responsibility are at least sometimes committed to determinism being incompatible with people being responsible. Folk conceptual incompatibilists need not deny that there are conditions under which we utilize compatibilist notions of freedom. In contrast, folk conceptual *compatibilism* requires that there is *no* important sense or widespread context in which our ascriptions of free will and moral responsibility are incompatible with the thesis of determinism. Otherwise, the folk conceptual compatibilist will simply be conceding the point that incompatibilists insist upon: in a significant class of cases our responsibility depends on the thesis of determinism being false.[22]

The way I'm characterizing the terrain here (i.e., only some incompatibilism equals incompatibilism, full stop) may be a departure from how incompatibilism is used as a label of substantive prescriptive philosophical views. Philosophical (as opposed to folk conceptual) characterizations of compatibilism and incompatibilism have often treated these positions as all-or-nothing views on which all actions must satisfy, respectively, compatibilist conditions or incompatibilist conditions.[23] But I am not making any claim (yet) about what sort of view we should have about the philosophical matters. And, these are matters on which diverse combinations of folk and prescriptive theories are possible. Indeed, we might allow that a theorist might accept folk conceptual incompatibilism without being prescriptively incompatibilist. Since my focus in this chapter is restricted to the former and not the latter, this divergence in labeling conventions is philosophically innocent.[24]

[22] Notice that all of this is consistent with the aforementioned suggestion that our metaphysics and our practice of responsibility come into conflict.

[23] It is for this reason that, for example, Honderich claims that incompatibilism and compatibilism are both false and Smilansky claims that both are "partly true" but they agree that we have distinct conceptions of freedom and responsibility that fund compatibilism and incompatibilism, respectively. See Ted Honderich, *A Theory of Determinism* (New York: Oxford University Press, 1988); Saul Smilansky, *Free Will and Illusion* (New York: Clarendon Press, 2000). Among those who are plausibly interpreted as holding that there are recognizably forms of freedom and/or responsibility that admit of discrete (i.e., compatibilist and incompatibilist) conditions are: J. J. C. Smart, "Free Will, Praise, and Blame," *Mind* 70 (1961): 291–306; Honderich, *A Theory of Determinism*; Galen Strawson, "The Impossibility of Moral Responsibility," *Philosophical Studies* 75 (1994): 5–24; Kane, *The Significance of Free Will*; Smilansky, *Free Will and Illusion*; Pereboom, *Living Without Free Will*.

[24] It is not even clear that the purported divergence is a divergence from actual labeling practices. Oft-described incompatibilists—such as Kane—have rejected the claim that every instance of responsibility requires satisfaction of libertarian conditions. In contrast, I can think of no self-identified compatibilist

The main conclusion of this section is just that the experimental data do not support a unitary view on folk conceptual commitments about the compatibility question. Notably, the results show that many of us, even in the most compatibilist-friendly scenarios, seem to accept incompatibilist requirements on moral responsibility. Moreover, in moments of cool, abstract consideration, we tend to favor an incompatibilist conception of an alternative possibilities requirement on moral responsibility.

None of this entails that there are no non-philosophers with consistently compatibilist intuitions. Even so, such persons likely constitute a minority. Individual consistency on such matters appears to be the exception, not the rule. So, we should think that the typical mind—untempered in the forge of philosophy—will have mixed convictions about which powers are required for free will and moral responsibility.[25] If this is right, then some amount of incompatibilist convictions among the folk seems a pervasive feature of ordinary thought on moral responsibility.

8. Theological and psychological support

In the previous section I mentioned some empirical considerations for thinking that we have strands of incompatibilist commitments in our body of folk thinking about moral responsibility. Whatever the source of those elements, I suspect that these convictions, such as they are, have been buttressed by some elements of our contingent cultural history.

Here is one example of how that might have worked. If you accept that the mind or soul is fundamentally different than the physical world, it will be natural to have a conception of agency that is not governed by physical laws. There is, of course, a long tradition of just this sort of conviction in the Western world. Dualism is at least as old as Plato. Given the phenomen-

---

who thinks that there is an important class of cases where genuine, 100 percent Real Moral Responsibility requires alternative possibilities. So the parallel with philosophical in/compatibilisms seems fairly tight.

[25] This is a point that has been made by Honderich and Smilansky. See Ted Honderich, "After Compatibilism and Incompatibilism," in *Freedom and Determinism*, ed. Joseph Keim Campbell et al. (Cambridge MA: MIT Press, 2004); Smilansky, *Free Will and Illusion*.

ology of decision-making, and given a conception of agency ungoverned by physical laws, a libertarian conception of agency might seem a reasonable corollary to a dualistic metaphysics.

(This is not to suggest that *we* ought to suppose that dualism removes any and all puzzles about a libertarian conception of free will. Dualism does not obviously solve any of the main puzzles about free will, absent some account of the principles on which the mental stuff operates, and how it interacts with the physical stuff. If, for example, the non-physical stuff obeys deterministic laws, the positing of ectoplasm or a non-material thinking substance will have done nothing for the libertarian.)

Christianity and its theological tradition may have had some role to play in how these matters played out. Acceptance of dualism in the history of Christianity is notable. More importantly, perhaps, is the idea that libertarianism was (and continues to be) important to many (but not all) of the most influential figures in this history of Christian thought. For such theologians and philosophers, libertarianism is the best hope to explain how a loving, omniscient, and omnipotent God could permit so many harms in the world.[26] If there is some great value in libertarian freedom, and if we do have libertarian freedom, it allows us to make sense of at least some harms that God might have otherwise prevented.

The history of theology is a long and complicated thing, so caution is in order whenever one is tempted to make sweeping pronouncements about it. On the account I am offering, the persistence of libertarian impulses does not derive from the truth of some or another theological tradition. Nor am I claiming that the theological tradition in our current climate strongly supports or reinforces libertarian strands of conceptual commitments. What this picture requires is that at some point in time, in some culturally effective way, theological pressures that favored libertarian convictions came to attain comparatively wide cultural penetration, and that these convictions were then disseminated and taken in up in whatever way such things spread. It is a picture akin to one insisted on by Nietzsche: the power of a religion's metaphysical and moral picture persists long after

---

[26] Sociologist Randall Collins argues that the problem of free will arises in philosophical traditions around the world whenever there is a version of the problem of evil in the offing. See Randall Collins, *Sociology of Philosophies* (Cambridge, MA: Belknap, 1998).

religiosity is perceived as embarrassing, antiquated, or irrelevant to secular life.[27]

There are, of course, threads of the Christian intellectual tradition that cut against dualism and in favor of compatibilism. It is a variegated tradition. However, this fact leads to an obvious question: why, on this account, is it that a specifically incompatibilist conception of these things has taken root in ways that the specifically compatibilist strands of the tradition have not?

First, for all that I have said, it is possible that compatibilist strands of the Christian theological tradition *have* taken root in the larger culture, and that these convictions have generated a framework that takes on a life of its own, apart from the theological convictions. The point I am making does not preclude the possibility of multiple strands of influence, even inconsistent ones. My point is just that there is some plausibility to the idea that the familiar set of theological convictions that give rise to a kind of pressure for a libertarian conception of agency would have found its way into more popular conceptions of agency.

On the picture I am suggesting, even if compatibilist convictions took root, so too did incompatibilist convictions. In the latter case, they were presumably buttressed by several phenomena. So, for example, it might have been the case that aspects of our phenomenology of decision-making made a libertarian conception of agency seem especially appealing.[28] Or, it might have been that our naïve models of explanation provided fertile ground for the seeds of libertarianism.

Consider the following picture of how explanation works. When we know all the variables of a closed system and can accurately predict the outcome we will tend to suppose that the system is deterministic. Now consider what such a model would mean when directed at the human mind, given a once-plausible assumption that we were fully aware of our own mental states and motives. On such a picture of how explanation works, deterministic conceptions of agency would seem implausible. The

[27] See §9 of Friedrich Wilhelm Nietzsche, *On the Genealogy of Morality*, trans. Maudemarie Clark and Alan Swenson (Indianapolis, IN: Hackett Publishing, 1996). I find that professional philosophers (an overwhelmingly non-religious bunch) often forget the grip religious convictions have on many people.

[28] The point is not that our phenomenology *requires* a libertarian conception of agency. Rather the point is that a tendency towards libertarian extrapolation might derive from aspects of our phenomenology. For illuminating but contrasting discussions of this matter, see Richard Holton, "Determinism, Self-Efficacy, and the Phenomenology of Free Will," *Inquiry* 52 (2009): 412–28; Shaun Nichols, "Why Do We Believe in Free Will?," Unpublished manuscript (forthcoming).

first-personal unpredictability of even our own behavior in light of purportedly full knowledge of the causes of our action would have made non-
deterministic interpretations of human agency especially plausible. After
all, that I know both (a) what I want and (b) how I can get it does not
close off (c) the possibility that I will do something else. This I know from
my own experience of my mental states, so when I go to explain how my
mental life works, it seems apparent that I am an indeterministic system.[29]

So, here's what I suspect is going on. Both our phenomenology and the
structure of our explanations when turned towards our own psychology
provided a fertile soil for those libertarian conceptions of agency that arose
partly in light of pressure from various theological considerations. Minimally, religion lowered the cost of taking on board a libertarian conception of
agency, and given its potential of absolving the Judeo-Christian God
of responsibility for the world's evils, the attractions would have been
(and for many, continue to be) considerable. When such pressures com-
bined enthusiasm for an individualistic conception of the self and an impulse
to human exceptionalism, the result was a web of cultural reinforcement for
this metaphysically remarkable conception of ourselves. None of this precludes the possibility that compatibilist theological pressures played some
role, too, but it suggests that such pressures were unlikely to altogether
block the reception of incompatibilist pictures of agency.

A suitably informed critic might allow that this all sounds plausible
enough, but then insist that it runs afoul of some intriguing data that suggest
that what impulses there are towards incompatibilism are altogether detached from specifically Western cultural and theological convictions. In a
sample of four countries (including subjects in the U.S., India, Hong Kong,
and Colombia), researchers found majority incompatibilist replies to
prompts about whether human decision-making is indeterministic and
whether it is possible to be morally responsible in a deterministic universe.[30]
Since some half of these countries are not in the West, it shows that it
cannot be the particular cultural heritage of the West that does the work,

---

[29] This paragraph borrows extensively, if imperfectly, from Nichols, "Why Do We Believe in Free
Will?"

[30] See Sarkissian et al., "Is Belief in Free Will a Cultural Universal?" On the matter of whether
libertarianism is a cultural universal, this evidence strikes me as suggestive but unclear. Three of the
sample populations come from former English colonies. More compelling would be similar results from
Africa, central China, and other parts of the world less Westernized than the countries thus far studied.

and since the majority of these countries are not Christian, it cannot be the theological tradition of Christianity that is the culprit.

This evidence is interesting but it does not affect the account I have been motivating. I have not argued that our particular contingent cultural heritage is a unique path to libertarian convictions. Rather, my claim is only that the existence of such cultural elements has plausibly buttressed what impetus there is to incompatibilist thinking in the contingent cultural history of the West. So, this does not mean that in other places the local cultural and conceptual pressures to incompatibilism might arise and flourish without appeal to dualism, the problem of evil, or characteristically Western conceptions of the self. Perhaps incompatibilist intuitions have arisen without such things. Or, perhaps in such cases there are local analogs that do work in generating and supporting such intuitions.

I am presupposing that local cultural convictions can have real effects in what people believe. On the present picture, what we find intuitive is partly a function of what our local cultural forces provide us with as suppositions, as frameworks for thinking, and as guides to what is acceptable or not. And, I imagine that philosophical and theological reflection are not merely epiphenomenal, but that they sometimes go on to structure downstream cultural convictions. If one thinks all of these things, then the peculiar grip that libertarian convictions have on us becomes less an isolated ripple than the confluence of a diverse range of forces.

9. Ramifications

Reflection on the available evidence suggests that folk conceptual incompatibilism—the view that ordinary commitments have at least some strands of incompatibilist elements—is well-supported.

A natural question to ask about all of this is why it should matter. One might protest that for all that has been said in this chapter, precious little of it has do with the nature of free will itself, or the actual nature of moral responsibility. What we have learned, if anything, is only what the untutored mind thinks about these things. One might object that this is no more enlightening about responsibility than studying our naïve convictions about physics is enlightening about the nature of actual motion. As philosophers, we should aspire to more than armchair anthropology of concepts. What we properly want is an account of the Nature of Things, and not just our ideas about the nature of things.

It is time for the other shoe to drop.

Nothing in the argument for folk conceptual incompatibilism by itself entails philosophical incompatibilism. Nevertheless, folk conceptual incompatibilism does seem to favor at least attempting to develop an incompatibilist philosophical theory. Here's why: to the extent to which intuitions properly fund or constrain philosophical theories, folk conceptual incompatibilism looks like a kind of argument for incompatibilism. (It turns out we needed that neck hole after all.)

How much it counts in favor of philosophical incompatibilism depends on how strong folk conceptual intuitions are, and how pervasive those intuitions are across the variety of contexts in which we are called to make judgments of responsibility, and just what the relationship is between our diagnosis and our best prescription. Nonetheless, if ordinary convictions have strongly incompatibilist elements to them, it seems to put a thumb on the incompatibilist half of the scale at least to the extent to which we take our theories to be yoked to intuitions.

It is hard to do philosophical theory-building without intuitions in any form. We have no *responsibility-meter*, or some widely accepted independent way to adjudicate truths about moral responsibility. What we do have are our reactions and judgments to cases and arguments, our ability to examine the logical structure of arguments, and our creativity in constructing pictures that make better sense of what we have reason to think. The contours of ordinary thinking provide a parameter—one among several—that might be invoked in trying to understand the world and our talk about it.

Independent of some story that explains what bit of the world we are latching on to when we think and talk about moral responsibility, we are left doing metaphysics in the pejorative sense—conjuring up bundles of ideas with no connection to the things we care about, even if such bundles exist, subsist, or maintain some other ghostly but irrelevant existence. So, I think we must grant that our ordinary convictions about free will (along with reflections about concept use and social practices and so on) provide us with a sensible enough starting point. If they cut in incompatibilist ways, then this gives us reason to look for an incompatibilist theory first.

A conventional philosophical compatibilist might be tempted to reply that it is not the compatibilist's burden to defeat every conception of freedom and responsibility found in our ordinary thinking about responsibility. That is, what matters to the philosophical compatibilist is that there is an important way in which our ordinary way of thinking about responsibility is compatible with determinism.[31] The philosophical compatibilist, inasmuch as he or she is yoked to ordinary beliefs, concepts, or judgments, can get all he or she needs so long as there is at least one compatibilist construal of our convictions. Since I haven't denied that there are compatibilist strands to folk thinking, then philosophical compatibilism is fine.

Here, though, the relationship between intuitions and philosophical theorizing is thrown into sharp relief. The incompatibilist about both folk thinking and philosophical theorizing will object that it is not enough to note that there are concepts of freedom, and perhaps notions of responsibility that intelligibly deserve those labels. What is at stake, in both the present context and in the mainstream of wider philosophical work on free will, is the variety (or varieties) of freedom that are at stake in attributions of responsible agency and attendant judgments that people can deserve moralized praise and blame. If our best account of folk convictions reveals incompatibilist strands, the responsible responsibility theorist cannot just dismiss those intuitions simply because they are inconvenient or unwieldy. We need a T-shirt with the right openings.[32]

On the typical philosophical incompatibilist picture, we illuminate the nature of free will by looking at our concepts, and we do that by examining our intuitions. We do *not* have a good account of our shared concepts if we just start excising those elements that we do not like, even the ones that strike us as baroque or peculiarly demanding.

The frequency with which some commitment appears in our examinations can matter. If a commitment only is evident in rare circumstances and it has only the support of a small minority of our community of

---

[31] See Michael McKenna, "Compatibilism and Desert: Critical Comments on Four Views on Free Will," *Philosophical Studies* 144 (2009): 3–13.

[32] The philosophical compatibilist could object that the discovery of compatibilist strands in ordinary thinking reveals something, namely, that at least some aspect of our thinking about free will or moral responsibility is logically compatible with determinism. But I take it that the philosophical debate was never about whether there is *some* notion logically compatible with determinism, but rather, whether it is the notion we want, whether the powers it picks out can support the practices we associate with it, and so on.

concept-users, this is less of a problem. However, incompatibilist intuitions aren't like that. They are more widespread and more tenaciously held than that. Indeed, the prevalence of these attitudes in abstract conditions is especially important. After all, abstract conditions can exercise considerable influence in our formulation of policy and publicly stated principles. Thus, it will not do to pretend such convictions have no grip on us collectively, even if sometimes they have little grip on us individually or in particular instances.

Again, if some or another commitment is just an element of one person's thinking and no one else's, that commitment is poorly suited to making a claim as being part of our shared concept. But if you can easily get lots of people (or, at least university undergraduates!) to vigorously agree with you under suitable conditions, then it looks like you've got a candidate for a real part of one's conceptual commitments.[33] So, even if there are conditions under which we really are compatibilists, compatibilists will have hardly secured what they endeavor to secure if there are also a substantial number of conditions under which we are manifestly not compatibilists.

The compatibilist might, with some justification, reject any number of elements in this picture. Perhaps there is an error in folk attributions of responsibility, in just those cases when incompatibilist judgments are manifest. Or, perhaps it is an error to suppose that such judgments reveal anything about a shared concept of free will or moral responsibility.

Crucially, however, the compatibilist will need to offer *an argument* for why, when doing something like conceptual analysis, broadly speaking, we get to disregard some elements widespread in ordinary convictions, convictions that consistently show up in identifiable conditions in large numbers of people.[34] Without an argument—one that has not been made at least in this literature—it will surely look like the compatibilist is engaged in, well, "petty word-jugglery." That is, the compatibilist is cherry-picking strands

---

[33] Notice that what the incompatibilist maintains is that we are talking about the concepts of free will and moral responsibility, and not merely someone's idiosyncratic version or conception of these things. That is, depending on your favorite view of concepts, we are talking about the broad overlap of semantic, representational, causal, or inferential structures, structures which themselves permit an array of tokenings whose precise content is more and less elaborated.

[34] Suppose you reply with some remark about Quinean paraphrasing. I will then insist that paraphrasing is hardly basic conceptual analysis and, anyway, that it occludes too many issues in the present context. For explanation, see Vargas, "The Revisionist Turn: Reflection on the Recent History of Work on Free Will."

favorable to the compatibilist view and neglecting those elements of our thinking that disfavor it.

(In contrast: recall that many incompatibilists are prepared to allow that there are compatibilist strands to our convictions, but that they don't capture the "deepest" or "ultimate" forms of responsibility. Such incompatibilists might be mischaracterizing folk views, but if so, they can't be accused of failing to acknowledge the existence of compatibilist strands of thought.)

At least on the matter of characterizing folk thinking, the compatibilist cannot simply retreat to a defense internal to antecedent acceptance of a compatibilist viewpoint. In the face of existing data, there is simply too much that points to ubiquitous and pervasive strands of incompatibilist intuitions in our shared thinking about responsibility and free will. So, I think, the experimental data support the conclusion that a significant portion of ordinary thinking about free will has incompatibilist commitments.

Notice that the foregoing arguments hold even if our concept is somewhat fragmented, or we have multiple concepts of free will and moral responsibility, respectively. However, it is easy enough to see why philosophical incompatibilists have not been attracted to this sort of account, at least with respect to prescriptive theorizing. If one allows that there are cases of responsibility where the satisfaction of compatibilist conditions is sufficient for responsibility, it may seem that there is some pressure to explain why we should *ever* invoke more demanding incompatibilist conditions.[35]

On a wide range of approaches to constructing theories about moral responsibility, folk commitments do matter. If they matter, then it looks like

---

[35] Rightly or wrongly, I suspect that some are inclined to raise this sort of objection to Robert Kane's distinguished libertarian account of how one comes to be morally responsible in the earliest cases of formation of the self. On one interpretation of his account, it looks like some of the earliest moments of self-formation only satisfy compatibilist conditions. However, notice that in the context of diagnostic theorizing the "why then should we ever invoke incompatibilist conditions?" objection is not an especially trenchant one. A libertarian *could* reply: this just is the way we think about our agency. That is, it might be a brute fact about our self-conception that we are libertarians about some instances of action and not others, and in early life only compatibilist conditions are required. Now turn to the matter of our prescriptive theorizing. Suppose one thinks our prescriptive account of moral responsibility should reflect those convictions illuminated in our diagnostic theorizing. On such a view, then this brutely incompatibilist requirement will carry over into prescriptive theorizing. I do not know whether this sort of picture coheres to any significant degree with Kane's actual convictions, but it seems to me a possible libertarian view.

an incompatibilist diagnosis of folk commitments will give us reason to try to build an incompatibilist theory first. If such theorizing does not work, we may have reason to revisit the possibility of philosophical compatibilism. However, such compatibilism would not get to claim the mantle of being intuitive in the way in which compatibilists would ordinarily like it to be.

10. Original sins in philosophy

At the outset of this chapter I claimed that I would show how diagnostic work might help us understand why the debate about moral responsibility has been so intractable. It is time to make good on that promise.

At first blush, the diagnostic project helps flesh out one familiar idea. Philosophical compatibilism has little hope of providing a fully intuitively satisfying account moral responsibility precisely because folk conceptual incompatibilism is true. It might turn out that our best prescriptive theory is compatibilist, but such a theory will come at a clear cost. To the extent to which we have incompatibilist intuitions, even if only at the margins or in cases where we are judging matters in the abstract, such accounts will seem to many merely a dodge that is simply not responsive to their everyday convictions.[36]

A perhaps deeper payoff for starting with the diagnostic project is that it helps us see the seeming intractability of philosophical debates about responsibility as also plausibly rooted in pressures to "train up" our recalcitrant intuitions, rending them into a coherent package.

Consider the manner in which philosophers are cultivated. If the present account of our folk commitments is right, students come to the subject matter with mixed intuitions. That is, they have diverse pre-theoretical commitments that dispose them to make compatibilist judgments in some cases and incompatibilist judgments in other cases. However, the nature of philosophy being what it is, there is a pressure (from the professor, from the teaching assistant, from Theoretical Reason itself, and so on) to consistency. Students feel pressure to embrace some philosophical position that

---

[36] The view I will ultimately defend is that the best prescriptive accounts will not be fully intuitively satisfying. Instead, their virtue is that they are theoretically or "on balance" satisfying. Defending such an account is the work of later chapters; here my focus is only on diagnostic matters.

denies the presuppositions of the alternative. So, some commitments have to go.

Which commitments stay on and which are rejected is presumably part of a subtle process of belief adjustment in light of a variety of rational and non-rational pressures. Perhaps it involves an especially compelling presentation of a view by a charismatic or intimidating professor. Or perhaps it involves the contrary—an *under*whelming presentation of a view can just as easily lead one to regard the view dismissively. Or perhaps the student misunderstands a crucial argument, or stumbles on a novel consideration that tips the balance of considerations available to him or her at the time.

The net effect, however, is that over time the dedicated student of the literature on free will and moral responsibility has convictions that are pressured into a more consistent shape, whether compatibilist or incompatibilist.

By the time that undergraduate becomes a Ph.D.-holding professional philosopher invested in the free will debate, the years of rational and disciplinary pressure in favor of consistency will have led that person to reify those intuitions in one direction or the other. Correspondingly, he or she will dismiss, suppress, and often (even honestly) deny the presence of any intuitions to the contrary. In short, we unknowingly manufacture in our professoriate thoroughgoingly compatibilist convictions in some, and thoroughgoingly incompatibilist convictions in others. The result is that any contrary view appears counterintuitive, question-begging, evasive, confused, absurd, a cheat, panicky, or just downright puzzling. And so it goes.

I suspect the basic elements of this account generalize to a wide range of philosophical disputes. For all the skepticism about philosophical training that this account implies, it is comparatively optimistic when one compares it to the "insuperable cognitive limits" picture defended by Colin McGinn and others.[37] On those more radical accounts, the persistence of the free will problem is owed to our mental equipment being ill-suited to addressing problems of this sort. This is a view on which we are in the grips of a problem whose very nature is a result of the limits of human reason.

In the history of philosophy, something like this was suggested in Kant's antinomies: the nature of ordinary human reason inescapably leads to a

---

[37] Colin McGinn, *Problems in Philosophy: The Limits of Inquiry* (Cambridge, MA: Blackwell, 1993);Peter van Inwagen, "Review of Problems in Philosophy," *Philosophical Review* 105, no. 2 (1996): 253–6.

problem that is insoluble by the ordinary exercise of human reason.[38] On the insuperable cognitive limits picture, debates of free will can be understood as attempts to shift around a bump in the rug; the bump cannot be eliminated so long as we have only our ordinary rational powers at our disposal. Since we cannot escape our rational framework, what results is a series of predictable maneuvers that amount to re-characterizations of what must ultimately remain mysterious to us.

If one is convinced that we have free will but that the explanation of how is fundamentally beyond our rational grasp, free will and moral responsibility will seem mysteries without solutions.[39] Whatever the virtues of the cognitive limits view may be for explaining the general persistence of philosophical problems, it seems to me unwarranted in the case of free will. We do not need to posit that the persistence of the problem is some artifact of our cognitive limitations. We do not need to think that the best explanation of persistent failure to reach convergence on this issue is a result of an inevitable rational breakdown. All we need to explain the persistence of the debate are some naïve, divergent intuitions coupled with disciplinary and rational pressures to reify intuitions in a consistent way, and—*voilà!*— you have the tools to explain the origins and persistence of the problem.

So that's how we got here. Now let's get out of here.

---

[38] Of course, on standard interpretations, Kant also thought that he could provide a resolution to this puzzle, and that it involved his special transcendental philosophy.

[39] For pro and con regarding van Inwagen's prominent version of mysterianism, see Peter van Inwagen, "Free Will Remains a Mystery," in *Philosophical Perspectives (14: Action and Freedom, 2000)*, ed. James Tomberlin (Boston: Blackwell, 2000); Laura Ekstrom, "Free Will, Chance, and Mystery," *Philosophical Studies* 113, no. 2 (2003): 153–80.

2

Doubts About Libertarianism

The object of these commonplaces is to try to keep before our minds
something it is easy to forget when we are engaged in philosophy,
especially in our cool, contemporary style

P. F. Strawson[1]

1. Overview and caveats

In the last chapter, I contended that when we undertake a diagnostic
account of free will, we learn that there is good reason to think that threads
of ordinary thinking about free will and moral responsibility are incompatibilist. In particular, the idea of alternative possibilities (understood in an
incompatibilist way) plays an important role. I also noted that a special
conception of causal origin might fuel some incompatibilist intuitions. The
lesson I drew from those thoughts was this: folk thinking about moral
responsibility is at least sometimes recognizably incompatibilist, and therefore, any compatibilist philosophical account will fall short when it purports
to capture what we mean, and all we mean, by "free will" and "moral
responsibility."

In the present chapter I shift to the business of exploring our options for a
prescriptive theory of moral responsibility. That is, I am concerned to
develop an answer to the question of what theory we *ought* to hold about
the conditions on moral responsibility. In light of last chapter's incompatibilist diagnosis, there is pressure to develop a libertarian account. Partly,
the pressure arises from a widespread methodological presumption that
prescriptive accounts must respect the contours of ordinary thinking.

---

[1] P. F. Strawson, "Freedom and Resentment," *Proceedings of the British Academy* XLVIII (1962), p. 6.
Emphasis in original.

Given that ordinary thinking has incompatibilist (especially libertarian) strands to it, we must look to the prospects of an account that invokes libertarian requirements of agency. That is the task of this chapter.

In the present chapter, I argue that there are good reasons to doubt the prospects of libertarianism as a theory about what we ought to think about moral responsibility, all things considered. I begin with an overview of some libertarian options, and consider the significance of what I will call *the spookiness objection*. I find the spookiness objection wanting, but I go on to endorse two not-unrelated concerns about libertarianism's plausibility and its consequences for our moral practices.

The main upshot of this chapter can be put succinctly: there is no evidence in favor of libertarianism, and in light of this, it is unacceptable to treat people as blameworthy in light of a conviction that moral responsibility requires libertarian agency. I end with some reflections on other complaints about libertarianism and what they might mean for a theory of moral responsibility.

2. Libertarian options and the problem of spookiness

Outside of specialists working on free will and moral responsibility, there is sometimes the impulse to dismiss out of hand any form of libertarianism. Certainly in informal discussions among philosophers, the unsavory reputation of contemporary libertarian metaphysics is a familiar trope. Libertarianism's reputation is colored by the perception that it inevitably depends on an illicit Cartesian dualism, appeals to Kantian noumena, or other forms of "panicky metaphysics."

This is a real shame. Much of the high quality work on libertarianism by philosophers over the past two decades invokes little in the way of obviously objectionable metaphysical commitments. Unfortunately, this work has gone unrecognized outside of its subfield. Scholars unfamiliar with developments in the free will literature over the past twenty years are invariably unaware of the existence of libertarian theories that are designed to be compatible with a broadly scientific worldview.[2]

---

[2] See, for example, Bargh, "Free Will is Un-Natural"; Montague, "Free Will."

Nevertheless, building a libertarian account is no straightforward task. Consider an issue discussed last chapter: even though incompatibilist intuitions appear widespread, it is unlikely that everyone has them in all circumstances. There are at least two ways a prescriptive account might accommodate the fact of variably present incompatibilist intuitions. One approach would be to hold that the full flower of libertarian agency is properly required in each and every instance of original responsibility for some action.[3] This would be to stipulate a unity in the prescriptive account that does not obviously appear present in folk thinking. A different approach would accept the fragmentation of folk thinking and build it into the prescriptive theory.

For ease of exposition I will generally treat libertarianism as a unified, invariant view on which all instances of original responsibility require the exercise of indeterministic agency. This simplification should be regarded as just that. It is not a substantive claim about the options available to libertarians. To the extent to which libertarian requirements are treated as rare or exceptional in an account that variably requires it, it will obviously have consequences for the degree to which any problems particular to libertarianism ramify.

Even given this simplifying assumption, there are diverse ways to make good on the basic libertarian idea. Recall that libertarians are unified in the conviction that we are sometimes morally responsible, and that as a consequence, we must at least sometimes act in ways that are not determined by the conjunction of the prior state of the world and laws of nature. How this requirement (of non-determination by the laws and prior states of the world) is satisfied varies according to the theory.

We have already seen one way of carving the possibilities available to libertarians: we can distinguish between *leeway* and *source* versions of the view. The former emphasize alternative possibilities (holding fixed the laws and the actual past), whereas the latter emphasize the idea that agents must be appropriate origins of action. So, we can distinguish the options available to libertarians in terms of whether the accounts accept a leeway requirement, a source requirement, or both.

---

[3] This approach includes most tracing approaches; ordinarily, instances of tracing are derivative instances of responsibility, with the anchor for the trace being an instance of original responsibility.

A different way to sort the alternatives emerges when we focus on the *mechanism* or *manner* in which requirements of leeway or sourcehood are met on a given account. That is, we might ask about the where and the how of the non-deterministic element in the account.

On this way of approaching things, there is a conventional taxonomy of three main options: *uncaused event, event-causal,* and *agent-causal* libertarianisms. They differ in the non-deterministic condition to be met by agents, and each can (at least in principle) be matched with either or both leeway and source requirements.

The core idea of *uncaused event libertarianism* is that libertarian agency involves a mental event with no antecedent cause. Notice that on such a view, what one does freely is not a product of probabilistic prior causes, for the view is defined precisely by the thought that at the root of initiating a free action there is no cause at all.

Event-causal libertarianism generally accepts a broadly causal picture of agency where events are effects of prior causes, and themselves causes of later events. On this picture, indeterministic events are part of the general fabric of the ordinary causal order, and free agency is partly a function of the presence of such indeterministic events. So, free and responsible agency is caused, but not deterministically caused.

Agent-causal libertarianism is the view that agents are irreducibly non-deterministic causes of some events, and that they are non-deterministic causes of those events. On the most familiar way of understanding such views, agents are substances and causation by an agent is distinctive in that it is causation by a substance, as opposed to an event. There is variation in the kind of substance appealed to—sometimes it is immaterial (Thomas Reid), sometimes material (Tim O'Connor), but the core idea is that the causing is not a sole product of some prior event.

There are varied costs and benefits to each approach, even internal to the interests of libertarians. For example, libertarians disagree about whether worries about sourcehood or ultimacy can be captured by something short of agent causation, with agent causalists sometimes accusing interlocutors of going in for a "somewhat deflationary" picture of free will.[4] Other concerns generalize. For example, in relationship to all of these theories, critics have

---

[4] Timothy O'Connor, *Persons and Causes* (New York: Oxford University Press, 2000): 41–2.

raised worries about the involved notion of control and the role of action explanations in light of a need to appeal to reasons for action.[5]

I will have more to say about event- and agent-causal varieties in a bit. What I wish to emphasize here is a point of relative agreement between all these views, including uncaused event views: virtually all current instances of these approaches are designed to be compatible with a broadly scientific view of the world that does not require that everything be deterministic.[6] That is, the going instances of these accounts do not appeal to properties that are obviously incompatible with or somehow altogether separate from the ordinary causal order—even contemporary agent-causal accounts treat agents as part of the larger causal order. On typical accounts of this sort, the unique causal properties of agents are properties that emerge at high levels of thoroughly physical organization.

One way to characterize these things is to say that contemporary libertarian theories accept a *standard of naturalistic compatibility*. As I use the phrase, naturalistic compatibility refers to coherence with the known facts, along with compatibility with two further things: (1) the principle of the causal closure of the physical; and (2) acceptance of a principle of methodological minimalism.[7]

Methodological minimalism is the idea that additions to our ontology of entities and powers have to be earned in terms of familiar theoretical virtues like explanatory power, prediction, and so on. In concrete terms, what this means for contemporary libertarianism is that it does not (ordinarily) appeal

[5] See Randolph Clarke, "Incompatibilist (Nondeterministic) Theories of Free Will" <http://plato.stanford.edu/entries/incompatibilism-theories>, accessed July 19, 2010.

[6] So, for example, I take it that all of the following present libertarian accounts that are intended to be compatible with a broadly scientific conception of the world: Randolph Clarke, "Toward a Credible Agent-Causal Account of Free Will," *Nous* 27 (1993): 191–203; Laura Waddell Ekstrom, *Free Will: A Philosophical Study* (Boulder, CO: Westview Press, 2000); Carl Ginet, *On Action* (Cambridge: Cambridge University Press, 1990); Kane, *The Significance of Free Will*; Mele, *Free Will and Luck*; Alfred Mele, *Autonomous Agents: From Self-Control to Autonomy* (New York: Oxford University Press, 1995); Robert Nozick, *Philosophical Explanations* (Oxford: Clarendon Press, 1981); O'Connor, *Persons and Causes*.

[7] For some doubts about whether such cocktails of epistemic/methodological constraints and metaphysical commitments are stable, see Barbara Montero, "Post-Physicalism," *Journal of Consciousness Studies* 8, no. 2 (2001): 61–80.

to anything like the spooky powers of old: substance dualism, noumenal selves, or a "god-like" power to be a "mover unmoved."[8]

Importantly, contemporary libertarians can claim that acceptance of a standard of naturalistic compatibility does not signal a commitment to the view that one can offer a reduction of all action down to its event-causal components. Philosophers of varied predilections have thought that irreducible agential powers might emerge at sufficiently complex levels of organization, and openness to this possibility does not thereby amount to an abandonment of a broadly naturalistic picture. There are self-described naturalists who disagree, but there is room for diversity here. So, here's a first ruling on libertarianism: we should grant the libertarian that there are recognizable forms of naturalism compatible with strands of emergentism about causes and agents, of the sort that might be appealing to a libertarian.

Nothing in this ruling, and nothing in methodological minimalism, precludes the possibility that emergent powers might be earned or properly postulated. Such powers could be warranted in light of their explanatory payoff, coherence with other commitments, predictive utility, and so on.[9] Presumably, this is what libertarians of all stripes will insist is the case for their preferred accounts. Whether this is true in any given case is another matter. The point here, though, is that libertarians can and do accept a standard of naturalistic consistency; they do not *obviously* run afoul of some norm of theory construction that presumes a minimal ontology where "special" powers are added only if they pull some weight of explanation, coherence, or prediction.

Even when one rejects naturalism more generally, there can be good reason to be attracted to a theory that does not run afoul of compatibility with naturalism. A commitment to a standard of naturalistic compatibility loosely constrains metaphysics partly in light of an epistemological warrant: a philosophical theory that is in tension with our best science is a philosophical theory that is in tension with the overlapping consensus about one

[8] More formally, let "spooky" refer to those powers or entities we now regard as either methodologically mysterious or metaphysically extravagant for the purpose of action explanation. Ectoplasm is spooky. Neurotransmitters are not. Ghosts are spooky. Desires are not.

[9] I take it that the present standard is distinct from a standard requiring us to earn the right to "mock" Chisholm-style agent-causal theories, as suggested in David Velleman, "What Happens When Someone Acts?," in *The Possibility of Practical Reason* (Oxford: Clarendon Press, 2000).

of our best forms of knowledge. Running afoul of that consensus is a kind of cost to holding the theory.

Of course, that it is a *cost* does not mean it is an insurmountable cost. Still, as I read the literature, most libertarians in the past two decades have thought it best to respect at least a weak form of some naturalistic constraint.[10] So, a second ruling on libertarianism: contemporary versions of it do not run afoul of a standard of naturalistic compatibility.

If the foregoing is correct, it collectively suggests that there is nothing inherent to the *idea* of libertarianism that puts it necessarily at odds with a broadly scientific picture of the world. So, the spookiness objection should be put to rest.

3. The standard of naturalistic plausibility

Even if not spooky, there are reasons to be dissatisfied with libertarianism. The chief argument of this section is that libertarian accounts do not satisfy a reasonable standard of naturalistic *plausibility*. Failure to satisfy this standard gives us reason to reject this approach.

Unlike the aforementioned and widely accepted standard of naturalistic *compatibility*, on a standard of naturalistic *plausibility* the account requires something that speaks in its favor beyond mere coherence with the known facts and compatibility with minimal naturalistic doctrines. We seek a theory that has something to be said for it, in light of what we know about the natural world. Posits from the armchair are less compelling if not considered in light of what we have found in the world.

The motivation for accepting this more demanding standard is largely parasitic on the reasons for accepting the standard of naturalistic compatibility. That is, considerations grounded in rational norms of theory acceptance and the overlapping consensus about epistemic warrant are salient. If we

---

[10] Robert Kane has been especially clear about this matter, most recently in Robert Kane, *A Contemporary Introduction to Free Will* (New York: Oxford University Press, 2005), ch. 12. An important exception to the libertarian consensus *may* be Peter van Inwagen, who has repudiated naturalism in print, and has linked this repudiation to acceptance of a thesis that understanding free will may be beyond our ken. See, for example, van Inwagen, "Review of Problems in Philosophy." Also, compare van Inwagen, "Free Will Remains a Mystery."

accept that naturalistic compatibility is a virtue, a still greater virtue is naturalistic plausibility.

Regarding the precise characterization of the standard, matters are tricky. I don't want to pretend to give the idea of naturalistic plausibility more precision than it has. The general idea is just this: it is one thing for an account to be consistent with the facts and it is another for it to be a plausible theory, given what we know. More carefully, *the standard of naturalistic plausibility is satisfied if the account satisfies the standard of naturalistic compatibility and there are truth-relevant considerations that speak in its favor when it postulates requirements that exceed the known facts or the widely accepted ontologies of our current scientific understanding.*

Some clarifications about this idea are in order.

First, the "truth-relevant" stipulation precludes considerations that might speak in favor of accepting the theory, even if they have little direct connection with whether the theory is correct. A particular theory might score low for veridicality but high in whimsy, emotional appeal, or coherence with one's preferred self-image. These virtues seem irrelevant to the matter of truth, even if they might conceivably serve as tie-breakers in cases of theory underdetermination.

The truth-relevant constraint makes particular sense against the background presumption of the philosophical endeavor being oriented to veridicality. On this picture, philosophical theorizing is something like an attempt to generate probable truths in domains in which we lack reliable, widely accepted methods for determining the truth. Supposing that one has broadly naturalistic sympathies, a truth-relevant constraint on plausibility seems like the right way to think about these matters.

Where the first point of clarification about the standard concerns the sort of considerations that shape our theorizing, the second concerns the relationship of those commitments to our current understanding of science's commitments. Here, the philosophical details are, again, difficult to nail down. But again, the basic idea is simple enough. The greater the departure from what science now countenances, the worse something fares in terms of plausibility.

This issue of plausibility, even in these very general terms, can be cast in at least two ways. Naturalistic plausibility admits of either a *threshold* conception or a *scalar* conception. When characterized in threshold terms, the standard of naturalistic plausibility enjoins us to measure whether some proposed account has passed a particular threshold of plausibility. On a scalar conception, truth-relevant considerations land an account on a spectrum of plausibility.

Going forward, I am interested in questions that map on to both notions. First, there is a weak threshold notion that I am interested in: is there any reason to think the special commitments of libertarianism have evidence in their favor? Second, there is scalar element to my inquiry: how do a libertarian's commitments compare in plausibility to alternative accounts?

In invoking a standard of naturalistic plausibility, I am supposing an ontological monism that does not rely on the supernatural, and that methodologically takes current science as the paradigm of our epistemically best practices. The position does not close off whether there are truths ultimately intractable in terms of the diverse methods of the sciences. However, the most salient upshot of the standard is that all things being equal, a theory with substantive commitments that are less distant from our current scientific understanding of the matter ought to be treated as more plausible than a theory whose commitments require radical revisions or additions to existing ontology.

4. Event-causal libertarianism and the threshold demand

The foregoing leaves us with the idea that the standard of naturalistic plausibility challenges prescriptive theories with naturalistic sympathies in two ways: first, it asks us to consider whether there is any positive truth-relevant evidence for the account, and second, it asks us to consider the comparative plausibility of available accounts. Libertarianism fails to deliver on either measure.

Let's start with the question of whether libertarianism satisfies the threshold demand of the standard of naturalistic plausibility. On this interpretation of the standard, the question is whether there is any positive evidence in favor of the theory. I do not think any going libertarian account can answer this question in the affirmative, but to illustrate the idea I will focus on Robert Kane's influential account of event-causal libertarianism.

On Kane's account, paradigmatic instances of free will, what he calls SFAs, or "self-forming actions," are results of a particular kind of indeterministic brain process. The idea is that torn decisions—moments of conflict or uncertainty, where there are multiple but mutually exclusive aims we would like to attain—stir up a chaotic system in the brain that becomes sensitive to lower-level indeterminacies in the brain. As Kane himself notes, chaotic systems are usually understood to be deterministic, so it is crucial that the account invoke amplification of lower-level indeterminacies. These low-level indeterminacies (presumably at the quantum level) influence an agent's decision by affecting the sensitive chaotic system generated by the agent's desiring mutually exclusive aims. The result is an SFA, or an instance of free will.

Notice just how demanding the theory's commitments are: not only do agent mental processes have to turn out to be indeterministic, but they must also be indeterministic in a very particular way. If multiple mutually exclusive aims did not cause the brain to go into a chaotic state the theory would be disproved. If it turned out that neurological systems weren't sensitive to quantum indeterminacies the theory would be disproved. If it turned out that neurological systems were sensitive to quantum indeterminacies, but not sufficiently sensitive to amplify quantum indeterminacies in a way that affects the outcome of choice, this too would disprove the theory. These are not marginal or insubstantial bets about what brain science will reveal to us. So, we can see how the comparative worry generated by the scalar dimension of the standard arises in this case.

Important to answering the threshold question is whether there is any positive evidence in favor of our being agents of the relevant sort. In Kane's case, what we ask is whether there is any evidence to think that our neurological structures are as he has described. Although the account might be consistent with brain science, I am not aware of any independent reason for thinking that the brain is organized as he has described. Or to put the matter differently, if suitably sophisticated Martians came and looked at the available neuroscience data, they would not infer Kanian agency from it. I see no evidence for it, and I do not think Kane takes himself to have provided positive evidence for the view.

(At various points in time Kane has noted that aspects of his picture cohere with various ideas in neuroscience, but as far as I know he has never argued that there is neuroscientific evidence for quantum amplification in each and only in each case of torn decisions.)

I am not arguing that the trajectory of neuroscience is deterministic. In earlier work I maintained that Kane's account was inconsistent with the trajectory of neuroscientific understandings of the brain, which seemed to operate with largely deterministic presumptions. Kane has rightly argued otherwise, and I am now persuaded that going neuroscientific theories are not explicitly deterministic.[11] To be sure, brain scientists will often treat determinism as an aspiration for their accounts, but this is more presupposition than principled conclusion.[12] So, I agree with Kane that in general, the scientific issues surrounding the causal powers of the brain are not settled. Indeed, I can imagine that I could be talked (back, autobiographically speaking) into libertarianism if scientists found solid empirical data that showed that indeterminism is present in exactly all the right spots and few, if any, of the wrong ones.

Even though Kane and I mostly agree about the state of the brain sciences we disagree about what conclusion to draw from it. In my view, it is striking that nothing in the brain sciences would lead an independent observer to conclude that we must be libertarian agents. In a recent survey of the state of the neuroscience literature, Adina Roskies concludes that the epistemic limits of neuroscience preclude any warranted conclusions about whether the brain operates indeterministically or not. As she puts it "in order to make judgments about determinism from the neuroscientific data, we would need to know far more about the microphysical makeup of neurons than our neurophysiological techniques tell us, as well as to have complete information about the global state of the system impinging upon the neurons from which we are recording" (112).[13]

So, if one is optimistic about the existence of libertarian agents, the optimism must come from somewhere else. Perhaps some libertarians will be inclined to appeal to religious commitments. However, I take it that the permissibility of this appeal in the context of philosophical theorizing is

---

[11] Fischer et al., *Four Views on Free Will*, ch. 5.

[12] See Adina Roskies, "Neuroscientific Challenges to Free Will and Responsibility," *Trends in Cognitive Science* 10, no. 9 (2006): 419–23.

[13] Adina Roskies, "How Does Neuroscience Affect Our Conception of Volition?," *Annual Review of Neuroscience* 33 (2010): 109–30.

suspect, unless such appeals can be shown to satisfy a demand of publicly accessible truth-conduciveness. However, if religious commitments can do that, then it only seems likely to do some in some way that renders it detachable. That is, whatever those publicly accessible considerations are will be doing the work of sustaining libertarianism's plausibility, independent of the particular religious concerns. So, we are left with puzzlement about what evidence there is that supports libertarianism, given that the most frequently invoked sciences purportedly relevant to the matter are (at best) devoid of any real evidence for libertarianism.

Compare a belief in ESP (extra-sensory perception). Perhaps ESP is *compatible* with the state of brain science. However, compatibility does not mean plausibility, and I do not see why the fact that ESP is not ruled out by brain science means that we should find it plausible. If we are to find ESP plausible, we would need some independent piece of evidence for its plausibility, and this is what we have yet to hear from proponents of ESP. Similarly, what the libertarian needs is an account of *why* we should be optimistic that libertarianism will be vindicated by science.

To this, one might reply that this analogy is inapt, for unlike ESP, there are a variety of elements in at least Kane's account that have more substantial connections with contemporary science. Unlike ESP, Kane's libertarianism invokes phenomena that, even if speculative, are not completely disconnected with contemporary scientific theory.

I don't disagree that Kane's account is, with respect to its global scientific credentials, in better shape than ESP. And, indeed, there are aspects of Kane's account, which he emphasizes, that dovetail with going accounts of neurological activity. However, the intended force of the ESP analogy is not about global scientific credentials of Kane's account but about the specifically libertarian requirements in it.

A contrasting case may sharpen the point. Compare an account of ESP to a controversial (but conventionally scientific) account of paralimbic dysfunction as one of several elements that are at the neurological root of psychopathy. In the case of the paralimbic-hypothesis, the motivation for adopting the hypothesis includes behavioral evidence, brain-scanning data, and a body of established research on the paralimbic system and its operations.[14] In contrast, there is no comparable evidence, no background body of data that makes plausible the ESP hypothesis in the same way.

Now let's reconsider Kane's libertarianism. In contrast to the paralimbic system hypothesis, both ESP and the specifically libertarian structures of Kane's account seem to be in the same boat: neither has anything like the evidential basis that would lead a disinterested observer to conclude from the evidence that we have ESP or that we have said the Kane-specified neurological structures. So, again, the sense in which Kane's libertarianism is more like the ESP hypothesis than the paralimbic-hypothesis is that it is hard to see what in the evidence specifically fuels the specific commitments that constitute the particular libertarian structure of the account.

In light of these considerations, I am inclined to think that the most reasonable thing for us to believe is that it is unlikely that our agency is of a sort described by Kane, but that it remains an open question what follows from our not having this agency. (This latter issue is the subject of the next chapter.)

Kane, or a like-minded libertarian, does have available a further reply. The reply might be this: since our self-image is libertarian, and since it is an open question whether science will bear out of self-image, we should proceed cautiously. The default assumption should be that our self-image is basically correct, and that assumption should only be abandoned in the face of compelling evidence to the contrary. Because we lack such evidence, there is no compelling reason to yet abandon libertarianism.

To adopt this position, one must reject the application of the threshold conception of the standard of naturalistic plausibility, which rejects libertarianism on the grounds of there being no truth-relevant consideration in favor of the conclusion that our agency is of that sort. One must also reject the scalar conception of the standard, or at least, reject the conclusion that there are comparatively more plausible alternatives available to us. However, rejecting the standard of naturalistic plausibility comes at a steep price, and so it seems best to accept the standard and to therefore conclude that libertarianism fails to meet the standard.

---

[14] For an overview of current neurological hypotheses about psychopathy, see Kent A. Kiehl and Joshua W. Buckholtz, "Inside the Mind of a Psychopath," *Scientific American Mind* (Sept./Oct. 2010): 22–9.

The significance of having implausible beliefs—even beliefs whose implausibility one acknowledges—is a complicated business. Some libertarians may argue that considerations not relevant to the truth can play a role in the appropriateness of belief, adherence to a belief, and pursuit of an apology for the belief.[15]

Still, non-veridical considerations, even if subjectively warranted, strike me as orthogonal to the matter at hand. Return to the idea that libertarians are in a position similar to researchers hoping to demonstrate the existence of ESP. There may be reasons for particular individuals to believe in the truth of ESP. Perhaps there is some personal experience that generates a warrant for the belief, or perhaps the belief is especially important to that person's well-being or conception of the world. More generally, there might be benefits derived from doing research on ESP (e.g., personal satisfaction, interest, and the various unanticipated but beneficial side-effects of doing research). Indeed, for all we know, ESP may yet turn out to be vindicated. However, from where the rest of us stand, such considerations give us no reason to think ESP—or libertarianism—is true.

5. Comparative plausibility

In the last section I primarily focused mainly the plausibility of libertarianism given a threshold conception of the standard of naturalistic plausibility. Here, my focus is on the implications of the scalar interpretation of the standard. Libertarianism comes at a high cost: it requires that indeterminism be present in our agency in a very particular way, at very particular times, in the process leading up to or in the decision about what to do. Just how the indeterminism operates varies by the particular theory, but all libertarian theories are committed to non-deterministic phenomena showing up in the world at *particular* times and places. It is not enough that there be non-deterministic events in the larger causal order. According to libertarians, the non-deterministic phenomena must be located in some places and not others. So, in contrast to any theories that make no claim about

---

[15] This is a strategy that Daniel Speak has advocated. Daniel Speak, "Towards an Axiological Defense of Libertarianism," *Philosophical Topics* 32, nos 1 & 2 (2004): 353–69.

indeterminism showing up in particular places and times libertarianism will also come out to be comparatively implausible.

One might think that we face a tradeoff between preserving our self-image (as libertarianism does) and comparative plausibility. For example, one could hold that the absence of positive evidence is sufficiently damning as to make us think that nihilism about moral responsibility is in order. Such a view would not run afoul of the standard of naturalistic plausibility, even if it forces us to give up our supposition that we ordinarily are morally responsible. Alternately, one could think that the right resolution to the tradeoff is to abandon the conviction that a prescriptive account of free will must reflect the full set of our pre-philosophical suppositions about free will.

I consider these options in greater detail in the next chapter. Here, though, it is enough that there are such options. To see why, consider the relationship of libertarian views to prescriptively compatibilist views. What marks out the difference between libertarians and compatibilists is not (typically) a dispute about whether there are compatibilist conditions on free will and moral responsibility. Rather, the dispute is over whether a further, indeterministic condition must be satisfied. Libertarians need not and typically do not deny that there is a range of conditions on free will and responsibility that are accurately rendered by compatibilists (for example: being responsive to reasons, or perhaps identifying with the action, and so on).[16] However, for virtually any libertarian theory, there is an additional requirement it is bound to have, above and beyond the non-skeptical competitors.

Note that the point is not that we lack some special reason to think the world is indeterministic. Most parties could agree that there is good reason to think that at least some parts of the universe are indeterministic. The special burden of libertarianism is that it must hold that the indeterminism shows up at particular times and places. Libertarianism is in this sense more demanding than non-skeptical alternatives. We do not know where science will lead us and it takes a puzzling sort of confidence to simply assume that

---

[16] Some libertarians have been very explicit about this. See Chris Franklin, "The Problem of Enhanced Control," *Australasian Journal of Philosophy* 89, no. 4 (2011): 687–706. Elsewhere, I've argued that one important advantage of "incorporationist" or "piggybacking" approaches is that it provides resources for deflecting traditional concerns about the Luck Problem for libertarianism. See Manuel Vargas, "Why the Luck Problem Isn't, then," *Philosophical Issues: A Supplement to Nous* 22 (forthcoming).

future discoveries will vindicate the more demanding theory. They might—or they might not.

For us, the issue is what we have reason to think will be more likely. The growth of human knowledge has frequently been unkind to the products of the philosophical imagination. All things being equal, it seems a bad idea to bet on the truth of the more demanding theory.

The upshot of these remarks is that libertarianism faces a general worry about its plausibility: compared to any alternative, and in the absence of any evidence for the theory, these accounts will be less likely to be vindicated by future discoveries about the nature of human beings, all other things equal. The libertarian might argue that all other things are not equal. The libertarian could argue that there is some special reason why we should be committed to a picture of human agency with indeterminism nested in particular places and times along the pathway to human decisions, even if this makes the theory less plausible than alternatives. I will consider this possibility later. However, for the moment let us allow that the general plausibility worry only has force—to the extent that it does have force—if all other considerations are equal.

6. What about agent causation?

At this point, a critic could allow that the problems I have identified for libertarianism are unique to Kane's account, or perhaps to event-causal accounts more generally, but the critic might yet insist that this does not mean that libertarianism is incapable of satisfying the standard of naturalistic plausibility.

This would be a striking position to adopt, precisely because there are independent arguments that a special version of empirical implausibility arises in the agent-causal case. In this section I consider this objection, a possibly reply, and conclude that agent causation does not obviously fare any better than event-causal libertarianism on these matters.

Consider an agent-causal account on which agents are at least partly physically constituted. If so, then those parts must be consistent with the local causal structure of such constituent parts. However, if libertarian agency is supposed to be a feature of creatures embedded in the physical, then it looks like the libertarian faces a dilemma: either such agents violate the causal organization of the natural order or they run afoul of what Pereboom has called "the problem of wild coincidences."[17]

Here's the problem: it is difficult to see how the action of libertarian agents can cohere with the underlying causal structure of things while at the same time figuring in any explanation of what happens. Suppose the underlying causal regularities have some event happening 69 percent of the time. If the intervention of libertarian agency makes a difference to that probability, then we have a violation of the statistical frequency of the event. This looks like exactly the sort of implausibility libertarians have been hoping to avoid—i.e., positing powers of agency that require us to suppose that we regularly violate the existing causal, physical organization of the natural order. So, instead suppose that when libertarian agency is exercised, it does not make a difference to the probability of the event and it remains at 69 percent. What then is the role of libertarian agency? What does it explain?

Pereboom makes the point in this way:

That the agent-cause is a causal factor distinct from the factors that incline her is underscored by her capacity to act in opposition to them. For instance, even if her reasons incline her very strongly toward performing an action at each opportunity for performing it, she can choose to refrain every time. But what mechanism could then explain the agent-cause's conforming, in the long run, to the same frequency of choices that would be extremely likely to obtain on the basis of the inclining factors alone? On the agent-causal view, if the agent-cause is truly free, there is no mechanism that could provide this explanation. We would therefore have a match in frequencies without an explanation—a wild coincidence. (84–5)

I think this is an intriguing objection. Indeed, sometimes I am even persuaded by it. However, I do think one can motivate legitimate concerns about the objection as formulated. For example, it seems to me that the dedicated libertarian might justifiably wonder how we are to understand the idea of antecedent probabilities, independent of the agent's actual choices. For my part, I do not find especially problematic the idea that the physical constituents of agents possess objective probabilities concerning their operations. The trickier part comes with wondering if those probabilities turn out differently if we accept the idea of emergent causal powers.

---

[17] Pereboom, *Living Without Free Will*, p. 84.

Here's an idea: it might be the case that the causal probabilities of, let's say, particular neurological systems have a fixed distribution if there are no causal powers above and beyond the constituent elements of the system. However, once we countenance emergent causal powers the situation may change. In this case, let us suppose that sufficiently complex neurological systems give rise to powers not reducible to their parts—agent-causal powers. Upon the emergence of these powers, the objective probabilities of the constituents might change so as to not coincide with the prior objective probabilities. Why? Well, you might think that if the underlying causal properties don't change, you can't have any properly non-reducible, *emergent* causal powers.

If this is right—and I'm not saying that it is—then it looks like the wild coincidences problem does not arise. Even if we know the antecedent causal powers of pre-emergent constituent parts of the agent-cause of some action, these facts become irrelevant when agent-causal powers emerge, just because the underlying causal structure would be *re*-structured by the emergence of agent-causal powers. So: constituent-level probabilities might not coincide with the probabilities in the world that you would expect to find.

Notice that one need not hold that such powers are always online, as it were. One could be an *Occasional Agent Causalist*. On this view agent-causal powers emerge only intermittently: perhaps in moments of torn decisions or the like. That is, only under particular conditions will new causal powers emerge, restructuring the arrangement of lower-level probabilities of the relevant constituent parts of the agent.

I am uncertain what conclusion ought to be drawn about these difficult matters. Perhaps there is a viable web of philosophical commitments about agent causation, emergent causal powers, and the restructuring of prior causal probabilities of constituent parts of the agent that might avoid the problem of wild coincidences. However, even in the absence of a firm verdict about these matters, I think there is enough reason to think that agent-causal views of libertarianism will run afoul of the broader application of the standard of naturalistic plausibility. That is, if event-causal libertarianism fares badly on the standard, agent-causal libertarianism can hardly do better.

On the scalar conception of the standard, agent causalism ordinarily looks worse than event-causal libertarianism, given that it asks us to add to our ontology a unique set of causal powers, beyond the powers asked for by any other account of agency. So if we find event-causal libertarianism troubling on that account, then we should find agent-causal libertarianism even worse. On the threshold conception, agent causalism certainly fares no better than event-causal libertarianism. Agent-causal accounts equally lack any positive evidence in favor of the special powers they postulate. Indeed, I am unaware of any agent causalist ever having tried to make a serious case for the idea that there is evidence in favor of our being agent causes. One might be able to find bad arguments—appeals to phenomenology, for example. However, the main appeal of agent-causal views seems to have rested largely on their capturing aspects of our folk thinking,[18] and the tantalizing promise that such accounts can resolve theological worries. So, I think, agent-causal views are no exception to basic worries about naturalistic plausibility.

7. The moral argument

Until this point, the argument of the chapter has been about the failure of libertarianism to meet a standard of naturalistic plausibility. Here, I wish to raise a further argument, one that derives from the failure to satisfy the threshold demand of the standard of naturalistic plausibility. The argument is a moral one, and to my mind it is a damning one for libertarianism. Moreover, it is one that would persist even if libertarians find a way to satisfactorily meet the comparative plausibility gloss on the standard.

The conclusion of the argument is this: in the absence of any positive evidence in favor of libertarianism, adoption of a prescriptive libertarian theory would entail that we either abandon holding people responsible or that our continuing to hold people responsible is an injustice. Here's the argument.

---

[18] There is obviously more to folk notions of responsible agency than just alternative possibilities, and perhaps, a sourcehood commitment. So, for example, I take it that part of our self-conception on these matters includes the idea that we are active with respect to action, and that we are not just passively implementing the actions given to us by our antecedent desires. (Although I am dubious that this is universally regarded as entailing that we are something above and beyond our familiar psychological states.) At any rate, nothing I say here is meant to preclude the possibility that some of these other elements may provide some of the motivation for seeking a libertarian theory, even if capturing such ideas does not provide direct evidence of the truth of the theory.

Some (though not all) of our blame and punishment practices, in conception or in practice, presuppose libertarian free will. Most libertarians will concede this point. However, given the truth of the argument in the prior section, there is no evidence in favor of our being libertarian agents. This creates a problem. For any amount of blame and punishment based on the supposition that the agent has free will we face a problem of justification. (Note, again, that we need not suppose that all blame or punishment presumes libertarianism. I am merely considering the aspects of those things that do make such a supposition.)

Consider what we can say to someone I'll call "Barrows." Barrows is a skeptical subject of such blame and punishment. Perhaps she faces the death penalty, if that is permissible, and if not, then some very significant censure, where that variety or some large quantum of that censure (whether blame or punishment) depends on the presumption of libertarian agency. In light of her skepticism, Barrows demands to know *why* such treatment is justified. At this point the libertarian must acknowledge that such treatment is justified if libertarianism is true, and that we hope—although we have no evidence to support such a hope—that Barrows is, indeed, a libertarian agent.[19]

At this point, Barrows may grant the possibility that she is, indeed a libertarian agent. After all, she might say, such a possibility is not incompatible with anything she knows about science. Nevertheless, she is likely to protest that the mere *possibility* that she deserves some extra quantum of blame or punishment does not, by itself, make such treatment justified. After all, there is also a chance that she—and everyone else—might not be a libertarian agent. Indeed, this strikes her (especially now!) as far more plausible. If she is not a libertarian agent, according to the libertarian theory it would be grossly unjust to hold her accountable to any degree beyond those things justified by non-libertarian considerations. On the presumption that one should avoid gross injustice when one can do so, and that it is wrong to blame when there is no evidence that the target is responsible, the only defensible course of action is to abandon holding Barrows (and everyone else) responsible in whatever degree the presumption of libertarian agency entails.

---

[19] Pereboom has also noted that the epistemic requirement on punishment puts pressure on libertarian punishment practices. See Pereboom, *Living Without Free Will*, pp. 161, 198–9; Derk Pereboom, "Kant on Transcendental Freedom," *Philosophy and Phenomenological Research* 73, no. 3 (2006): 562–4.

Notice that the force of this objection diminishes if one thinks that the quantum of blame or censure accorded to agents on a libertarian basis is small. Notice too that the importance of libertarian agency for moral responsibility diminishes the smaller that portion of blame becomes. So, the moral problem that libertarianism's epistemic position gives rise to only goes away on pain of undercutting the impetus to libertarianism.

As I see it, libertarianism is left with a simple but deep problem. To the extent to which we sometimes blame and punish on putatively libertarian grounds (which, again, libertarians think we ought to), we had better have a justification that runs deeper than the wish or hope that we are libertarian agents.

8. Conclusion

Prescriptive libertarianism requires us to accept a comparatively implausible view without evidence, and which entails that in praising and blaming on libertarian grounds we do wrong. To be sure, virtually all philosophy is somewhat speculative, and in the context of a constructive, theory-building account of something, we will be almost inevitably invited to take on commitments that outstrip our evidential basis. Still, failing to meet the standard of naturalistic plausibility comes at a high price, high enough that, for now, I will close the matter of whether we can generate an intuitively satisfactory prescriptive account of moral responsibility, without violating the standard.

I harbor no illusion that my anti-libertarian musings will convince a dedicated libertarian. Proponents of libertarianism will object that their preferred form of libertarianism has the resources to address the objections I raise. Although critics of libertarianism will have less to quarrel with, they will likely insist that the objections I make are mostly familiar.

Fair enough. These are complex issues, the resolution of which is more likely to be a product of re-thinking our options than yet again returning to already well-plowed fields. Hence, this chapter's primary goals have been to explain why libertarianism is problematic, and to provide some important reasons for taking seriously the impulse to look elsewhere. The next chapter begins to develop a map to that elsewhere, arguing that the considerations animating the present chapter do not entail responsibility skepticism.

3

Nihilism and Revisionism

1. Elimination or...?

In the last chapter, I argued that the libertarian strands of commonsense thinking about responsibility are unlikely to be vindicated. The present chapter considers what options remain for us, once we conclude that the costs of a prescriptively libertarian account are high, both from the standpoint of what we can claim is plausibly true about us, as well as from the standpoint of our moral practices. I argue that we should regard responsibility nihilism as a position of last resort, and further, that there is one position left that must be considered before we accept nihilism. I call the position *revisionism*. Arguing for the existence of this alternative, and for its general plausibility, is the task of this chapter.

Recall that nihilism (or eliminativism) about responsibility appears to many as the only viable option if we accept the following conjunction: (1) libertarianism is wanting; and (2) an adequate prescriptive theory must accept incompatibilism.[1]

I reject the second conjunct, and the nihilist conclusion. My rejection of nihilism is grounded in considerations about the conditions under which nihilism is a serious option. Although the basic idea admits of many formulations, a reasonable principle here is that we ought to abandon our standing commitments only as a last resort. Call this the *principle of philosophical conservation*. When we do abandon our commitments, there is pressure to minimize the consequences, limiting the scope of revision or elimination.

---

[1] Here, I use "nihilism" and "eliminativism" interchangeably to refer to the view on which no one is ever morally responsible. I generally prefer to speak of "responsibility nihilism." However, in those contexts where I am calling attention to parallels with other domains where the idea of eliminativism plays a similar role to that of responsibility nihilism, I tend to refer to "eliminativism about responsibility." This difference in terminology is only one of presentation. It is not intended to mark a difference in substantive commitments.

The presumption of local or limited revision derives from at least two considerations. First, there is a general tendency that the larger the revision, the more general doxastic stability is threatened and the larger the tear will be in the fabric of interlocking justification and explanation that ordinarily develops among our beliefs. There can, of course, be cases where the presumption is overturned. Large swaths of beliefs might be in error, and the evidence might be compelling. Alternately, a set of beliefs might be sufficiently isolated from an agent's other beliefs so that there is little cost to excising them, at least in terms of the impact on the interconnectedness of belief and the attendant patterns of justification.

The second factor in the presumption of limited revision derives from the fact of our being finite agents. For creatures like us—that is, cognitively finite systems with limited resources—there is a kind of cost to belief revision, and the larger and more sweeping the revision, the larger the cost will ordinarily prove to be. Again, there will be cases where this is just not true. However, in cases where the relevant beliefs are intimately connected with practical matters, where those beliefs structure our practices and interactions with one another, the costs of belief revision are particularly high because revision disrupts entrenched dispositions of action and patterns of concern.

The point is just this: sometimes, we can just change our minds about the nature of something or what it involves, rather than abandon the concept and its associated practices. When there is some reason to revise, rather than eliminate, elimination looks like a hasty and unmotivated option.[2]

Revision of our beliefs can be more and less momentous. If I think it is not going to rain today, and it starts raining as I leave my house, I'll simply update my beliefs to reflect my conviction that it is indeed a rainy day. Other changes, however, can demand more subtle readjustments in our network of beliefs.

Consider a theist who thinks that the content of morality is and must be determined by the decrees of God. Now suppose that this person—call him

---

[2] Put slightly differently, the rational authority of the principle of philosophical conservation plausibly derives from those principles that govern our ordinary mechanisms of belief formation and management in the real world. It wouldn't do to constantly inquire into the status of every belief we have. If beliefs are to be useful to us, if they are to help us get around, they must have some degree of de facto stability. So, unless there is some special pressure to revise them, they rightly have a kind of doxastic inertia, continuing as they were. And, when we have cause to revisit and revise beliefs, there is a presumption that such revisions will be local.

Friedrich—starts to doubt whether or not God exists. He eventually becomes an atheist. Consider what Friedrich might now say about morality, given his newfound atheism.

Friedrich could reject morality. Given his conviction that morality re-quires God, he might conclude that morality is a sham. Having rejected morality, Friedrich might go on to think that we have good reason to act as though morality were not a sham. Or, he might not. Perhaps he would think it is a good thing if we all realized the illusory nature of morality. Practical considerations aside, however, if Friedrich followed this line of thought to its conclusion, he would hold that morality ought to be elimin-ated from the catalog of what truly exists in our world. Call this view *eliminativism* about morality.

It should be apparent that eliminativism is not Friedrich's only option. Instead of thinking that morality should be rejected, he could think that what needs rejection is his conviction that morality requires God's existence. This might be an especially tempting option if he came to believe that morality's distinctive judgments and practices could be grounded in practical reason (or sentiment, or human functioning, or ideal social ar-rangements with which no one could reasonably disagree, or...). Of course, Friedrich would have to acknowledge that atheism changed things for him. He would not regard morality in quite the same way as he had before. Nevertheless, if he reasoned in this way he would likely insist that morality should be included in the catalog of what truly exists in our world. Notice, though, that if Friedrich's former theistic conception of the foundations of morality were widespread, his newfound convictions about morality would put him at some distance from conventional ways of thinking about it. To mark this fact, we can call this view *revisionism* about morality.

Eliminativism and revisionism are not positions limited to morality. When the biological notion of race came under widespread criticism, there were some who thought that the defects of the biological notion showed that there were no races. Others thought that the right view was to hold that although races exist, the nature of race was not biological. The former reaction was eliminativist and the latter revisionist. When cognitive science and neuroscience put pressure on standard taxonomies of mental terms, there were those who took this to show that eliminativism about folk psychology was the correct view. Others thought that, at best, the threats from the sciences of the mind showed that we needed to revise some of our folk psychological categories. So, eliminativism and revisionism constitute options in a variety of theoretical domains.

The argument of the rest of this chapter—and the rest of the book, really—is that revisionism is the best philosophical position available to us. The motivating thought is that our prescriptive theory of responsibility need not be constrained by our folk conceptual incompatibilist commitments. If our prescriptive theorizing can be decoupled from any libertarian folk elements (which is not to say from *all* folk commitments), we can avoid nihilism. Even better, we can do it without denying the existence of those intuitions that tend to lead to skepticism about responsibility.

In itself, weakening the connection between folk and prescriptive theories about moral responsibility should not seem like an especially radical idea. If we have learned anything from the sciences, it is that the nature of things seldom neatly reflects our naïve conception of it. In the present case, it is hard to make out why this should be an exception. That is, there does not seem to be any special reason to suppose that free will and moral responsibility will provide us with a fortuitous alignment between conception and reality.

Nearly *any* significant concept—physical, moral, or otherwise—that has a long enough history is unlikely to survive unrevised in the face of growing knowledge about the world. Given that the notion of simultaneity proper to physics, our conception of water's essence, our moral notions of what constitute virtues, and our conception of marriage all have been subject to revisions in various ways, it is not obvious why we must suppose that our concept of responsibility is immune to revision. Indeed, given the particular sociocultural history of the idea of responsibility, and in particular, the role it played in Christian theology and pre-scientific conceptions of the self, it seems unduly optimistic to suppose that this particular culturally inherited concept will have come down to us in a form that is smoothly compatible with a contemporary scientific view of the world.

It is striking that responsibility nihilists have given us startlingly little reason to suppose that the incompatibilist element of our ordinary convictions is really a(n immutable) part of moral responsibility, as opposed to a contingent feature of how we currently, and perhaps erroneously, think

about it.[3] Without some principled reason to suppose that moral responsibility cannot be other than as we conceive of it, or some explanation of why
it is different from so many other concepts that have undergone change as
we learned more about the world, it threatens to be sheer prejudice to insist
on a tight connection between our current historical conception of free will
and the world.

Perhaps the ready acceptance of nihilism derives from the implicit recognition that if we accept that moral responsibility may be more or less than
we ordinarily suppose, the status of many important arguments in the
literature becomes considerably less clear. Standard arguments are ordinarily
taken to show something about the nature of free will and moral responsibility. If we accept the possibility of revision in our commitments, however,
it threatens to obviate the utility of many of the standard philosophical
arguments, including The Consequence Argument, Frankfurt cases, the
Four Case Argument, the Basic Argument, and so on. Such arguments do
not have any obvious warrant for teaching us about more than the manifest
image of these things. If we want our philosophical theories to be about
moral responsibility, and not just our thoughts about moral responsibility, it
is not clear how we do this once we accept that the contours of our thought
are not reliable guides.[4]

At least in conversation, some philosophers are tempted to respond
to these thoughts with a philosophical throwing up of the hands: They
say that because we do not have any other way to get at the nature of moral

---

[3] Susan Hurley has argued that it is problematic on nearly any plausible view about language to think
that responsibility should be *essentially* impossible. See her "Is Responsibility Essentially Impossible?,"
Philosophical Studies 99 (2000): 229–68. Her position is compatible with the one I offer here, but one
advantage of the position I develop in this chapter is that it also applies to nihilist views that do not insist
that responsibility is impossible, just not had for contingent reasons. What we *think* is essential might not
be; what we associate with the idea might prove to be gratuitous or unnecessary. And anyways, as John
Perry once remarked, whenever a philosopher invokes the idea of something being essential, it's a pretty
good sign that the argument is a bad one.

[4] Dana Nelkin has suggested to me that it is more charitable to interpret incompatibilist concerns
about, say, fairness as a kind of argument in favor of the revision-resistant nature of incompatibilist
commitments. If that's right, then it is not accurate to say that such arguments never take us beyond
received views about moral responsibility. That's reasonable, but as a substantive matter it strikes me as
pushing around the bump in the rug, for it is hard to see what incompatibilists will have then illuminated
beyond our received view on responsibility *in light of fairness* (or what have you). The core issue to be
settled is whether responsibility is revision-resistant, once we get all the concerns on the table, and not
just those that motivate incompatibilists. The revisionist position is one that is afforded, if it is, by
showing that a package of normative and naturalistic considerations favor revision.

responsibility other than conceptual analysis, the requirements on moral responsibility must be as conceptual analysis reveals them to be.

Even bracketing the specific question of responsibility, this is a puzzling reaction. It is a familiar complaint about simple forms of conceptual analysis that they presuppose that the nature of the world is to be read off of our current epistemic limitations. Perhaps there is no way to ever understand the nature of free will and moral responsibility, independent of conceptual or semantic analysis. Nonetheless, this truth would not entail that the nature of moral responsibility is settled once we have done conceptual analysis. Conceptual analysis may guide our attempts to understand free will by giving us an account of what to look for in the world, but it remains possible that the world will teach us things that require us to revise our conception of free will.

2. Against libertarian–style alternative possibilities

I have thus far objected to what seems to be a widely accepted but nearly always undefended premise: that the requirements of responsibility must be as we imagine them to be (and as a consequence, that the failure of libertarianism entails a collapse to nihilism). In this section, I offer some considerations that count against the apparent necessity of libertarian-style alternative possibilities in particular. In discussing these matters, I'll be canvassing a set of substantive philosophical issues that have been the subject of considerable discussion in the literature. I won't pretend to break a lot of ground in this discussion. Instead, my aim is to motivate and stake out a position, with an eye towards showing the place of these familiar thoughts in the larger dialectic of skepticism about responsibility nihilism.

Consider how we go from being unfree and non-responsible to free and responsible. This is something that will need to be explicable on any account of moral responsibility, but there is something especially challenging about this matter when we think about it in prescriptively libertarian terms. As children, we either had the indeterministic structures favored by your favorite version of prescriptive libertarianism or we lacked them. If we lacked them as children, we might wonder how we came to get those structures. We might also wonder what the evidence is for thinking that we do develop said structures.

Suppose the libertarian offers us an answer to these questions, and the quasi-empirical challenges I have raised in this chapter. We would still face another puzzle, one expressed by compatibilists at least since Hume: what does the indeterminism add, exactly? Here, the concern is less metaphysical than it is a normative. It is a concern about what work the indeterminism does in libertarianism, apart from providing a way to preserve our default self-image as deliberators with genuine, metaphysically robust alternative possibilities.

Consider the relationship between control and moral responsibility. On one plausible view, an act of free will is partly constituted by the agent having some control over what he or she does. (You could hold that you act freely when you lack control, but this is an unattractive picture for free will when it is understood as the freedom condition on moral responsibility. An absence of control hardly seems like the way to become a responsible agent.) So, responsible agency is going to presume some notion of control. Here, then, is the nub of the matter: what, precisely, is the work of the indeterminism? Is indeterminism required for control or is it required to elevate an agent who already has control into a free agent?

Suppose that the work of the indeterminism is to bestow control. Consider, however, the nature of an agent's first moment of free will. Inevitably, that moment will not derive from prior free aspects of character, inclination, standing policies, and so on. It is, after all, the *first* free act. What then makes it count as free, as the kind of thing that could underwrite attributions of responsibility? Presumably, the causal forces that lead to that first willing will be constituted by a web of events, inclinations, character traits, decisions, and so on, for which the agent was not responsible and lacked the requisite form of control. Out of these things a first free act is generated.

Suppose the libertarian accepts that we can have responsibility-supporting control generated out of mental elements, the possession and nature of each of which was beyond our control. This strikes me as the kind of thing that one ought to say. There is disagreement about this, however. Responsibility nihilists like Galen Strawson insist that one must have control over all the elements that led to a free choice, and that this is impossible.[5]

Even if you thought that it was intuitively plausible that we must have control over all the elements that led to a free choice, this doesn't show we

---

[5] Strawson, "The Impossibility of Moral Responsibility."

didn't have responsibility-supporting control. The availability of the revisionist option would remain: the requisite control might be different than we imagined, or it might be that we can otherwise reform our understanding of the necessary form of control.

If we do acknowledge that control can be attained out of elements that are not themselves controlled in their acquisition or content (something that some libertarians—at least Kane—seem prepared to allow), it begins to sap some of the motivation for prescriptive libertarianism. Here's why: it is hard to see what indeterminism adds to control, *given that the options indeterministically available to the agent were all products of things beyond the control of the agent.*[6]

In the case considered above, the first instance of free will, and in every instance that follows, what control the agent has is a function of what options the world bestowed on that agent (through experience, heredity, socialization, circumstantial luck, and so on). Any control the agent has must be built up out of those constraints. Given that even the indeterministic options are thusly constrained, and the elements that gave rise to those options (experience, heredity, socialization, the circumstances one finds oneself in) were not in control of the agent, what does the indeterminism give the agent in the way of control? Why doesn't the indeterminism simply open up multiple paths to an agent, where the constitution and sources of those paths were not something over which the agent had control?[7]

Consider an agent who had all of the requisite capacities for control but lacked the indeterminism. Call him Max. The libertarian would insist that Max would not satisfy the freedom condition on moral responsibility. But what exactly would the freedom given by indeterminism provide for Max? Like anyone reading this book, Max already deliberates about what to do,

---

[6] Such thoughts sometimes give rise to the conviction that alternative possibilities need to be supplemented with a suitably robust sourcehood requirement. Whatever one's sourcehood requirement comes to, it had better be the kind of thing that we could have, at least in principle. (Again: essentially impossible powers have no place here; their invocation suggests the diagnosis went wrong at least in part because it is hard to square such demands with plausible pictures of language use.) So, the prescriptive agent causalist can agree to this demand, if he or she thinks that agent-causal powers suffice to provide some special further degree of control. The issue would then be whether such extra control is *required* for moral responsibility.

[7] Such thoughts have often fueled compatibilist objections that incompatibilist accounts are committed to a picture of agency vulnerable to responsibility-undermining luck. I'm not going to pursue that particular issue here, beyond noting that I'm unsold on it being an insurmountable problem. For discussion, see Vargas, "Why the Luck Problem Isn't."

decides some things are better and worse, responds to reasons or doesn't, and decides to do some things rather than others. The only thing he is lacking is indeterminism.

Were Max to suddenly be bestowed with indeterminism (in whatever way the libertarian likes), this wouldn't change the way his deliberations appear to him. He would still be deciding between options. And, the mental elements out of which his control was constituted and out of which the indeterministic possibilities would be shaped would not suddenly become under his control if they were not already. So, whatever indeterminism bestows on Max is nothing that changes the way his deliberations will appear to him, or the control he rightly has access to thinking he has when he acts.

The libertarian might protest that Max would gain *this* further power: the power to do X rather than Y, given the laws and the past.[8] I'm not convinced that it would, but even if it did, I don't see why this matters *for responsibility*.

To begin with, there is the familiar challenge of explaining how the addition of alternative possibilities gives the agent power over what happens, as opposed to introducing new possibilities over which the agent has no special power. Rolling a 20-sided dice does not give an agent more power over outcomes than rolling a 6-sided dice. There is certainly not greater control here and it is not obvious that the sense in which there is greater freedom here rightly counts as something belonging to the agent.[9] Even if we grant that there is sense to be made of the idea that there is a further power here, and a difference in the probabilities concerning what happens, it does not follow from the fact of a further power that there is more agent-level *control*. I plausibly have the power to make inadvertently specious arguments. The addition of that power to my dialectical arsenal does not give me more control.

But let us suppose that indeterminism does give us further control. Why is that control required for *responsibility*? On standard accounts, the addition of the indeterminism-specific power would make *no difference* to what options Max takes to be available to him, to whether he succeeds in doing

---

[8] Robert Kane makes this point in Robert Kane, "Review of *Libertarian Accounts of Free Will*," *Mind* 115 (2006): 136–42. See also Franklin, "The Problem of Enhanced Control."

[9] Van Inwagen has emphasized this concern in a number of places. For a recent exposition, see his *Metaphysics*.

what he endeavors to do, and whether in general he can do such thing in deliberatively similar circumstances. Why would an indeterminism-dependent power be *uniquely* necessary for responsibility, such that no other combination of powers could suffice to generate responsibility? What would an argument for that conclusion even look like?

I see no easy reply here. There is an alternative story available to the libertarian, though. On the alternative story, indeterminism doesn't bestow control but rather adds freedom to an agent already possessing control. What would the picture of control be, however? Presumably, an agent could be said to have control by possessing some complex arrangement of agency, given a particular environment or range of environments. For example, control in an environment presumably relies on capacities to be sensitive or responsive to stimuli in the environment, the capacity to make decisions, the ability to reliably predict what effects one's actions will have on the environment and vice versa. And, plausibly, none of these things requires indeterminism. (Indeed, this would seem plausible even if we weren't assuming that control does not require indeterminism.) Indeterminism, on this picture, would be something superadded to control. Indeterminism would transform an already controlled agent into an agent with free will.

One appealing thing about this picture—where indeterminism adds freedom but not control—is that it seems to preserve an important theoretical burden for indeterminism: it is the difference-maker between free and unfree action. However, again, it is not clear what such freedoms add by way of making sense of praiseworthiness or blameworthiness. Again, were Max to be granted the requisite indeterminism, this wouldn't change the way his deliberations appear to him. He would still be deciding between options, the mental elements out of which his control was constituted and out of which the indeterministic possibilities would be shaped would already be under control (or not). So, whatever freedom indeterminism bestows on Max is nothing that changes the way his deliberations will appear to him, or the control he, by hypothesis, has access to thinking he has when he acts. So, on this version of the role of the indeterminism, it brings freedom of a sort, but it is not clear why such freedom does any work in making him responsible.

The prescriptive libertarian might be tempted to reply that the work left over for indeterminism—whether construed as important for freedom or for control—is crucial in at least the following respect: without it, Max would fail to be an intuitively free and responsible agent. Fine. At this stage, however, we are beyond mere intuition description. We can grant that common sense has these commitments. What we are presently attempting to determine is whether there is anything besides our self-image that hinges on the success or failure or our turning out to be indeterministic in some libertarian fashion. What we need is an explanation of what *normative* work indeterminism does in generating responsibility. It is difficult to see what explanation the libertarian might offer.

These issues dovetail with yet another sort of reply that incompatibilists can offer. On this further approach, the presence of alternative possibilities means that *the agent* can make a difference to the causal order. Making that sort of difference is crucial to understanding the normative work of indeterminism, according to this account.

It is difficult to put the above thought precisely. How we should understand the idea of agents "making a difference" partly depends on questions about the level of explanation that is being claimed for the difference-making, and how we think of agents in the ontology of the world. For example, agent causalists will insist that non-reducible powers of agency are the key to making sense of this idea, but event-causal or uncaused event libertarians might reject this supposition. I think we can side-step this issue. That is, let us grant that there is a kind of difference that we could only make if we were not determined (and, let us suppose, if we were agent causes). Even so, it does not suffice to show that such a power is necessary for moral responsibility.

An explanatory gap persists, even for the difference-making approach. What is missing is an explanation of why this particular version of difference-making is *necessary* for moral responsibility. Importantly, there are alternatives available, suggesting that such work is not necessary. For example, one could hold that the proper necessary condition in this area is something like our being *indispensable* to the causal chain.[10] After all, if the motivation for thinking that difference-making matters is the thought that without that force, the universe would continue as it was without the contribution of the agent, then it looks like that difference-making can be discharged without requiring leeway incompatibilism. On this view, the

---

[10] This important idea has been developed John Fischer in various places. See John Martin Fischer, *My Way: Essays on Moral Responsibility* (New York: Oxford University Press, 2006).

agent (or the agent's intentional action, or the agent's mental states, or the agent's deliberations) makes a difference by being a crucial part of the causal order, without which the outcome would not have the character it has.

These are difficult matters, and arguably the core of the debate between compatibilists and incompatibilists. There is, without a doubt, considerably more than can be said pro and con. However, these thoughts leave us with two basic challenges for the prescriptive leeway incompatibilist. First, we need an explanation why difference-making has some privileged normative link to moral responsibility. Why does difference-making in this sense generate responsibility? Second, we need an argument for why, in the absence of difference-making understood in the leeway incompatibilist fashion, we *cannot* have moral responsibility. It is this last bit—the exclusion of alternatives—that is crucial. In its absence, the prescriptive incompatibilist will have only shown that difference-making is, presuming satisfaction of other background agential requirements, sufficient for responsibility. However, this would not show that there are no other ways sufficient for generating responsibility.

Of course, we could still grant that it might be attractive to offer an account of responsibility that has the resources to explain how we might make a difference to the causal order and how we can do so in some way that is not arbitrary. Even better, it would be desirable to show how the agent is not a passive conduit for the causal order. However, the foregoing shows that we should not suppose that indeterminism *uniquely* provides this, and anyway, even if it did, that responsibility cannot be obtained in its absence.

Apart from the inertia of present habits of mind, it is unclear why we should think that libertarian-style alternative possibilities are *required* for moral responsibility. By itself, this does guarantee that there is a viable revisionist alternative. It may yet turn out that there is no plausible revisionist account of moral responsibility, an account sufficient to justify the forms of life in which responsibility matters. If so, then responsibility nihilism awaits. Until such time, we have good reason to explore revisionist options.

3. What revisionism is

If we are going to explore revisionist options, it is helpful to introduce some terminology. That is what I aim to do in this section.

As a first pass, whether an account is revisionist with respect to something depends in part on our ordinary commitments about that thing. If, for example, no one was ever really committed to a divine command theory of morality, then a proposal for the non-divine foundations of morality would not automatically count as revisionist. Similarly, for a theory of free will to be revisionist, it must propose an account that departs from our ordinary commitments about free will.

These thoughts permit us to fix some terminology. *Conventional* accounts entail a kind of consistency between prescription and diagnosis.[11] So, an account that concludes with compatibilism about diagnosis (folk conceptual compatibilism) and about prescription (philosophical compatibilism) is a conventional compatibilist account. Conventional libertarianism is the view that, as a matter of both our folk concept and our best prescriptive theory, responsibility is incompatible with the thesis of determinism and we have free will. *Revisionist* views are those on which the proposed prescriptive account conflicts with the diagnostic account.

Notice that prescriptive accounts may be compatibilist or incompatibilist: there can be revisionist compatibilists and revisionist incompatibilists. So, whatever else is true, revisionism is not co-extensive with conventional approaches to compatibilism. Revisionism may be wretched, but it is no subterfuge. What sets revisionist accounts apart from their conventional counterparts is the contention that we should abandon some commitments that constitute our ordinary way of thinking about moral responsibility. The greater the departure, the greater the degree of revisionism.

A revisionist account is one where the commitments of the prescription conflict with the commitments of the diagnosis. The requirement of a conflict in commitments is important. If revisionism were characterized as a view on which there is merely some—*any*—difference between diagnosis and prescription, then revisionism would threaten to collapse into an uninteresting category. After all, many conventional accounts of X invoke commitments that are not a part of ordinary beliefs about X, but are consistent with those beliefs.[12]

---

[11] I recognize that there is some infelicity here, as "conventional" can also describe things whose truth conditions appeal to conventions. I mean conventional in the "customary" or "ordinary" sense of the word.

[12] This is an objection that Michael McKenna rightly made against my earlier characterizations of revisionism. See McKenna, "Compatibilism and Desert: Critical Comments on Four Views on Free Will." The present account, which follows, is intended to supersede my previous response in Manuel

For example, a particular deontological account of morality might stipulate the requirement that moral truths about some considered course of action are to be determined by testing the potential maxims under which one acts against the demand to treat people as more than mere means to some end. Even if it turned out that ordinary beliefs about morality did not involve a commitment to maxims, beliefs about treating others as mere means, and so on, it would be strange to insist that such commitments constitute a revisionist account of morality—*unless such elements were in conflict with ordinary moral commitments*. On this characterization of revisionism, an account of free will that, for example, invoked the idea of neurological magnification of quantum indeterminacies would not be revisionist unless the idea of such magnification was inconsistent with commonsense commitments about moral responsibility.

So, revisionist accounts recommend a positive account of free will that not only departs from, but also conflicts with, aspects of commonsense thinking about responsibility. It is why revisionist accounts are at odds with conventional accounts of responsibility.

Characterizing revisionist accounts in this way may suggest that revisionism and eliminativism are kin, from the standpoint of types of theories. Although this was once my view, I now think that is a misleading way to characterize the relationship of these positions.[13] Revisionism and conventionalism are views about the relationship of our prescriptive theories of the nature of free will with our pre-philosophical views about these things. Eliminativism is a position that denies the existence of free will, regardless of whether our best theory of it is revisionist or conventional. Of course, most revisionist and conventional accounts of free will are intended as success-theories, that is, committed to the existence of the thing in question (free will). Still, revisionist and conventional accounts need not reject eliminativism, even if they ordinarily do.[14]

Vargas, "Revisionism About Free Will: A Statement & Defense," *Philosophical Studies* 144, no. 1 (2009): 45–62.

[13] Manuel Vargas, "The Revisionist's Guide to Responsibility," *Philosophical Studies* 125, no. 3 (2005): 399–429.

[14] On this way of fixing terminology, one could be a nihilist about free will and either a conventionalist or a revisionist. Improbable though it may be, nihilist revisionism would be a view on which one the prescriptive theory on offer conflicts with the commitments of common sense, but that we nevertheless lack moral responsibility. Notice, too, someone who thinks that moral responsibility is compatible with

4. Varieties of revisionism

So, revisionism is distinct from conventional compatibilist and incompatibilist accounts. Although broadly revisionist approaches have some currency in other fields, internal to the literature on free will and moral responsibility (at least self-described) revisionism is something of a newcomer. So, some remarks are in order about how to understand the options in this domain.[15]

Recall Friedrich and his reconsideration of the divine command theory of morality. Let us suppose that Friedrich comes to regard eliminativism with suspicion and begins to weigh up his non-eliminativist possibilities. He might conclude that his initial diagnosis of his convictions was in error. He could think he misdiagnosed his actual beliefs about morality. Perhaps he concludes that even though he might have explicitly avowed a divine command theory of morality, he was not actually committed to it, and it was his acceptance of atheism that helped him see that his avowals were not reflective of his genuine commitments. Whatever the plausibility of this maneuver, it is not a revisionist one. At best, it is a convoluted path to a conventional account. On this story, Friedrich does not hold that there is a conflict between the proper diagnosis and the proper prescription, as revisionists do. He simply holds that the initial diagnosis was in error. Call this possibility *diagnostic correction*.

The properly revisionist route begins not from amending the diagnostic account. Instead, it proceeds from accepting the diagnosis that one's actual commitments contain an important error. In Friedrich's case, this would require that Friedrich, in his now purportedly enlightened state, regards his prior commitment to divine command theory as an error, something to be abandoned. It is hard to say what sort of thing it is that he now thinks he

---

determinism but that we lack it for other reasons, could be a conventional compatibilist and an eliminativist/nihilist.

[15] I'm open to the thought that any number of figures might properly count as revisionist, but I take it that the particular concerns and framework for thinking about the problem space is a matter on which most authors have been silent or limited to remarks that might be read in conflicting ways. I don't have an axe to grind here about whether a given figure could or should be regarded as a revisionist in my sense. Elsewhere, I have explored whether and to what extent other authors are profitably thought of as revisionists. See, for example, Vargas, "The Revisionist's Guide to Responsibility"; Manuel Vargas, "Compatibilism Evolves? On Some Varieties of Dennett Worth Wanting," *Metaphilosophy* 36, no. 4 (2005): 460–75; Manuel Vargas, "Revisionist Accounts of Free Will: Origins, Varieties, and Challenges," in *Oxford Handbook on Free Will* (2nd edn.), ed. Kane.

must abandon (a belief? the concept? a conception?), but for present purposes whatever it is that he abandons will be significant in one of two ways.

First, he could be giving up mental content that plays no role in fixing the referent of the term, something we can label *connotational content*. That is, Friedrich's beliefs about divine command theory could be irrelevant to reference. They would be, roughly, beliefs he associates with morality, but the corresponding semantic content would do no substantive work in designating some property in the world. Indeed, Friedrich might take the fact of some alternative proposal for understanding morality (e.g., Kantian, contractualist, consequentialist, virtue theoretic) to count as evidence that his divine command theory beliefs were only connotational, despite his prior belief that they were essential to reference-determination.[16] If so, then Friedrich is a *connotational* revisionist.

A second possibility: Friedrich could be giving up some reference-fixing content. If so, one might think, Friedrich is really committed to nihilism. After all, he is advocating giving up commitments that do work in referring to morality.

Matters are delicate on this point. While it does seem that Friedrich is a nihilist, there is a kind of revisionism lurking in the neighborhood. Suppose that Friedrich thought that there is some nearby property, very much like morality, which exists and to which we could refer. Moreover, suppose that the property obtains in all the places where we customarily attempt to refer to morality, and its presence or absence licenses the practices and attitudes characteristic of morality. For example, suppose the not-really-morality-but-pretty-close-to-it account of contractualism explained the truth of various not-really-morality-but-pretty-close-to-it claims, claims that license morality-characteristic reactions, attitudes, and practices. Friedrich might couple his nihilism about morality (in the original sense) with a bit of referential re-anchoring, precisely because he thinks that the lurking-but-thus-far-not-usually-referred-to target property gets all the important things right. By hypothesis, the new target preserves the primary inferential roles we take to organize our beliefs about morality and it regiments our practices and characteristic attitudes in familiar ways. Moreover, the

---

[16] Notice that those beliefs about his theoretical commitments count among connotational content; his prior beliefs about whether those other beliefs were reference-fixing do no work in fixing reference.

new thing weighs in our deliberation in just the same way that morality-in-the-strict-and-unrevised sense does, and in general, it preserves morality's characteristic normative import.

If all this were true, Friedrich might think that a revision of reference, *denotational revision*, is warranted. In doing so, he would be advocating that we change the topic, in some sense. Importantly, though, it would be a principled change, one that respects what I call "the work of the concept." I will say more about this idea in the next chapter, but by "work of the concept" I mean the primary inferential roles figuring in those forms of life connected to uses of the term. Indeed, if all this were true, Friedrich-the-denotational-revisionist would think the onus is on traditional nihilists about morality to explain why we should care about the loss of morality in the old, non-actual, maybe impossible sense. After all, Friedrich-the-denotational-revisionist would say, we have a plethora of non–divine command accounts that preserve the import of morality and adequately explain the practices, attitudes, and inferences that we take to make up our moral lives and discourse.[17]

Another possibility: in opting for revisionism about morality, Friedrich may be unsure about whether he is committed to connotational revision or denotational revision. As I noted above, ordinarily available evidence may be insufficient to settle matters. Consequently, Friedrich might accept a kind of *semantic agnosticism*, if he were unsure about how to parse questions of whether his old, problematic beliefs about divine command theory were connotational or denotational. For him, the important thing is that, either way, he accepts a revisionist account.

The main three possibilities I have just canvassed—diagnostic correction, connotational revision, and denotational revision—are instantiated in the free will debate in relatively straightforward ways.

The best-known instance of theorists who championed a diagnostic correction may be classical "conditional analysis" compatibilists. Such compatibilists were sometimes prepared to grant that people might have *said* that they believed in a "categorical" or non-conditional conception of "can." However, on this view, what the folk failed to see was that any such notions

---

[17] Should we call this replacement, rather than revision? I suspect that we will have no luck in finding hard and fast rules here. I favor "revision" when the main inferential roles are preserved, and "replacement" when they are not; there will surely be cases that fall in the middle of that spectrum or that are otherwise mixed in ways that do not admit of any easy call.

in fact refer to a conditionalized ability. Similarly, contemporary compatibilists and their near relatives will sometimes grant that people have incompatibilist intuitions about free will. However, careful philosophical
reflection shows that such characterizations are at root failures to appreciate
one's more modest actual commitments. So, on a diagnostic correction,
what needs correction is not our commitments, but our appraisal of them.[18]

Connotational revisionists hold that we need to expunge aspects of folk
thinking about free will, but that in doing so we do not disrupt reference.
According to this view, we have been talking (successfully, let us presume)
about free will all along, even if we had erroneous beliefs about it.

Denotational revisionists hold that we need to expunge aspects of folk
thinking about free will, and that in doing so we will re-anchor the referent
for "free will." What makes a denotational revision possible is that we can
re-anchor our talk of free will on some property whose existence is in most
or even all of the places we used to refer to free will (in the pre-revised way),
and the fact that its presence or absence warrants the typical inferences,
reactions, and social practices that are characteristic of free will.

Notice that revisionism (whether denotational or connotational) can be
mostly neutral about how we should think about concepts in general.[19] The
salient issue is whether the element to be revised is connotational
or denotational in its significance. Depending on one's theory of concepts,
and how one sees the relationship between concepts, beliefs, and reference,
one will say different things about the significance of revisionism for
concepts. So long as we can render the distinction between connotational
and denotational revisionism, though, we have all that we need to capture
the main contours of what is significant about revisionist accounts.[20]

---

[18] Fischer has suggested that he is non-revisionist about the concept of responsibility, but revisionist about "the conditions of application." See Fischer et al., *Four Views on Free Will*, ch. 8. I remain puzzled about how to reconcile Fischer's ongoing concern for, say, the outcome of Frankfurt cases and the obviousness of responsibility, if he is willing to decouple his prescriptive theorizing from ordinary intuitions. As I understand Fischer's general approach, he starts by identifying intuitions and then argues that the theory should respect the identified intuitions. Such an approach is methodologically at odds revisionist theory building, so it seems best to understand his account as closer to a diagnostic correction. Fischer may disagree. My suspicion is that a neat taxonomical fit with the present characterization of revisionism is unlikely for any theory constructed antecedent to and independent of the methodological issues that have been my concern.

[19] For dissent, see Derk Pereboom, "Hard Incompatibilism and Its Rivals," *Philosophical Studies* 144 (2009): 21–33.

[20] In prior work, I have distinguished between weak, moderate, and strong revisionism. Weak revisionism is what I am here calling diagnostic correction. Strong revisionism is eliminativism.

In the next two sections, I will unpack some of the general motivations that favor adopting either of the two main strands of revisionism, with a special eye towards how these accounts fit with standard accounts of language. The general upshot is that while revisionism is not compatible with any possible view about language, it is compatible with a wide range of plausible views—i.e., if you want to reject revisionism as a possible kind of view, you are going to have to saddle yourself with a really peculiar view about language.

5. Reference, meaning, and revision

Although I am officially agnostic about how reference works out for responsibility, I find connotational revisionism to be the most appealing revisionist position. My present aspiration is to present an account that is compatible with many (although presumably not all) plausible theories about how the term "responsibility" refers to the world, and to the main views about the relationship between referent and meaning. The terminological differences, the distinction between connotational and denotational revisionism, serve to keep straight what the ramifications are if things turn out one way rather than another.

Here's the crucial thought that motivates my agnosticism about the referential picture and its contribution to meaning: if we can satisfactorily organize our practices and statuses without appealing to incompatibilist convictions, then the rest is bookkeeping. I'm inclined to think that if we can justify the bulk of our practices and the familiar pattern of judgments and practices, this is enough to earn the right to calling it a theory of responsibility. What licenses calling it a revisionist account is that we can

---

Moderate revisionism was ambiguous between connotational and denotational revision. I am now unhappy about the weak/moderate/strong distinction for several reasons. First, moderate revisionism's ambiguity between connotational and denotational revisionisms invited confusion. Second, weak and strong revisionism are not ordinarily revisionism at all. Weak revisionism (diagnostic correction) is a conventionalist's admission that he or she mischaracterized our commonsense views about free will. Strong revisionism (eliminativism/nihilism) is a view that holds that we should reject the existence of free will, irrespective of whether our best account of free will's nature is at odds with our folk conception of it. So, I now propose that we regiment terminology in the way I have suggested here, reserving "revisionist" for those theories that are committed to either denotational or connotational revision.

show that the proposed account conflicts with widespread features of how we ordinarily think about it.

Declarations of indifference are well and good, but it is worthwhile to earn indifference about the particulars of how reference and meaning work out. So, what I'll do in the remainder of this section is sketch some reasons for thinking that we can flesh out the requisite details in a revisionist-friendly way on any of the main approaches to these matters.

Consider the possibility of revisionism under broadly internalist theories of reference, where what settles reference is meaning, and where meaning just is whatever we think about some thing. On this view of responsibility, responsibility is whatever we think it is. Here, it is natural to think that since, for example, we think responsibility requires incompatibilist alternative possibilities, then the having of such possibilities is what we mean when we say someone is responsible. The claim that "X is responsible for action A" refers to, among other things, X's having of alternative possibilities.

There are at least two paths to revision on this picture of responsibility. First, we could conclude that the above picture is compatible with revisionism by a form of fiat. Consider the nature of a touchdown. A touchdown is whatever it is that we (or some relevant subset of our community, anyway) say a touchdown is. Right now, a touchdown is 6 points in the context of a game of American football. We (or, again, the relevant subset of us) could change that. If the rules committee of the NFL decided to make a touchdown worth 7 points or 5 points, then a touchdown would effectively become worth that new amount.[21] On this view, we could accept that there is some tight connection between how we think about free will and moral responsibility and the nature of these things in the same way we accept that there is such a relationship of touchdowns to how we think about such things. If responsibility is like that, then the fact that we think about responsibility in one way (as involving alternative possibilities, say, or unmoved mover-hood, or what have you), would not be a barrier to our revising what such notions include or entail.

At this point, it will be natural to insist that there are important disanalogies between touchdowns and free will. However, if one were a

---

[21] Notice that there are constraints even here. If the rules committee proposed changing the rule to minus 5 points, or a forfeiture of the game, this presumably would entail destruction of the practice, not revision. So, even constructivist accounts can find comparatively fixed points that are revision-resistant.

conventionalist about moral terms, holding that the nature of moral terms is constituted or rests on complicated facts about human conventions, such differences might not be telling. That is, if one is a conventionalist of some or another sort about morality, then it would not be unthinkable to hold that free will and responsibility are sufficiently stipulative so as to permit revision away from its incompatibilist elements. And that's the key to this path to revisionism, given an internalist picture: if we can change what we mean by fiat, through convention, or by some other coordinated change in our practices or understanding of the term, then revisionism just is a proposal to change what we mean in that way.

Internalists about reference have a second path available to them, one that does not appeal to perhaps troublesome changes by fiat, or fiat-like transformations of meaning. Internalist revisionists can appeal to the satisfaction of some privileged requirement of the usage, conceptual significance, or social practice of responsibility. The idea here is to isolate some referentially privileged feature of our thinking about responsibility, hold that this is preserved, and argue that anything else is connotational and thus severable from our understanding of the term.

One reason for thinking there is a referentially privileged element of our thinking about responsibility comes from the fact that our concepts of free will and moral responsibility are important for helping us to organize, track, and justify different ways of treating each other. On this approach, if we can show that there is something sufficient to justify such activities, or that otherwise provides a warrant for some flexibility between what we think and what is the case, then revisionism is a live option.

To see how this works, consider a view modeled on Lewis's approach to defining theoretical terms, one where we match our maximally consistent platitudes about moral responsibility with those properties that best correlate with those usages.[22]

Right away, it should be apparent that responsibility nihilism is an unpromising view on this approach. Why? Rather than an absence of realizers, there is an embarrassment of realizer riches. In particular, the compatibilist literature on free will and moral responsibility is rife with

[22] See David Lewis, "How to Define Theoretical Terms," in *Philosophical Papers* (New York: Oxford University Press, 1983). For a related proposal that focuses specifically on moral terms (something "free will" conceivably is), see Frank Jackson and Philip Pettit, "Moral Functionalism and Moral Motivation," *The Philosophical Quarterly* 45, no. 178 (1995): 20–40.

proposals about which properties can do the requisite work of grounding the bulk of platitudinous ascriptions (e.g., intentional action with morally significant outcomes plus either identification, reasons responsiveness, conditional abilities, or...). What a Lewis-style picture suggests is not that there is no plausible reference to free will, but rather, that there are a variety of candidates in the world that would render true the platitudes, without invoking incompatibilist metaphysics. Revisionism goes along with this picture of language like ice cream with apple pie. While it might turn out that there are some elements of ordinary thinking (say, libertarian-style alternative possibilities) that do not survive the correlating of platitudes with property, the bulk of the familiar convictions, inferences, and practices look to be in good shape.

The nihilist might still argue that the abundance of candidate properties points to there being no single best property that corresponds to responsibility's conceptual role.[23] From this claim, the nihilist might insist that, at best, ascriptions of responsibility would be referentially indeterminate.

If this is what is left of the nihilist option to revisionism, it is a pyrrhic victory, at best. If there are a number of properties in the world that correspond to the conceptual role played by free will, then there are a number of ways in which we can rightly, plausibly, truly be said to have free will. What we don't get to say is that there is no free will. If we are concerned about ridding ourselves of potential semantic indeterminacy we can make something of a semantic decision, where we specify which property we aim to track, thus anchoring free will ascriptions in a unique property. So, revisionism would be a solution to semantic indeterminacy, and not precluded by it.

Although the viability of revisionism under internalist theories of language depends on the particulars of the theory, I take it that the foregoing considerations provide reason for thinking that adoption of an internalist theory of reference does not, by itself, rule out the possibility of revisionism. A brief consideration shows that something similar is true of externalist theories, too.

---

[23] This is a rather different state of affairs than one in which there are *no* candidate properties that cover a significant range of ordinary ascriptions, and we are left with a motley that can only be expressed as a grotesque disjunction (to borrow a phrase from Hurley). The bountiful variety of compatibilist accounts that are recognizably accounts of moral responsibility constitute counterexamples to the plausibility of us encountering a grotesque disjunction when we search for realizer properties.

By an externalist theory of responsibility, I have in mind any account on which the property of responsibility is picked out by more than just what thoughts we happen to have about it. This would be an account on which reference is fixed by, for example, ostension or alternately by some causal link to a kind (whether social, artifactual, natural, or other).

On such accounts, it is relatively easy to see how connotational revisionism might be true. Responsibility is like, say, the concept of race was in the nineteenth century: understood to be one thing but really something else. For race, it was perhaps understood to require biological kinds; for responsibility, it has been understood to require an incompatibilist conception of alternative possibilities. For race, revision was, say, in the direction of requiring social categories with a particular history; for responsibility, revision may be in the direction of, say, pedestrian powers to recognize and respond to moral concerns

Whether moral and other normatively laden parts of language function in externalist or "referentialist" ways is a matter of ongoing dispute. However, if one accepted a view on which moral terms in general (or even just responsibility in particular) operate on an externalist picture of meaning and reference, then connotational revisionism will be especially appealing. What such a revisionist would purport to offer is the correct account of responsibility, and what the folk conceptual diagnosis would illuminate is the connotational (but not reference-fixing) elements of our thinking about responsibility.[24]

In both internalist and externalist cases, it seems possible that reference might shift to a legitimate inheritor or successor property if some privileged aspect of the term were better satisfied by the successor property. Re-anchoring seems especially warranted when something does a better job of supporting the beliefs, practices, and inferences that were our concern in the first place. We now think water is H_2O, not one of the four basic indivisible substances; we now think marriage is a privileged living arrangement between two people, and not a property exchange between two men

---

[24] One interesting consequence of adopting this picture of the meaning of responsibility is that it makes it puzzling how responsibility could be "essentially impossible," as some responsibility nihilists have thought. If meaning is fixed by elements outside the head, it is unclear how an impossible (and thus, non-existing) target can become part of the essential meaning of the term. For elaboration, see Hurley, "Is Responsibility Essentially Impossible?"

involving the exchange of a daughter for some goods.[25] It might be surprising, but not entirely scandalous, if we concluded that these transformations were re-anchorings of old notions on to new successor references that did a better job with roles that (at some suitable point) mattered more. The same may yet be true of responsibility.

6. Against the obviousness of responsibility

Some philosophers have maintained that it is obvious that we are responsible, and thus, any view that is skeptical of the kind of free will that is required for moral responsibility must be false.[26] On the face of it, this conclusion seems unwarranted. Surely we could be wrong about whether or not we are morally responsible creatures in the same way in which some people were wrong about water being basic and indivisible, in the way people have been wrong to think of women as property, and in the way in which it was a mistake to deny people the right to vote because of their skin color.

However, it may be that the range of attitudes and practices characteristic of our holding one another responsible are impossible to get rid of, as P. F. Strawson has suggested.[27] Although Strawson didn't seem to think so, it is plausible that our judgments that someone is responsible, and the various reactive attitudes we take towards others as a consequence are not purely affective, devoid of any cognitive content.[28] If that is right, then the beliefs or cognitive content that lurk behind our judgments and reactions may well be in error. However, once we allow for this possibility, that the cognitive content implicated in our reactive attitudes may be mistaken,

---

[25] The possibility of revisionism does not depend on responsibility being a natural kind term, as Daw and Alter suppose in their reply to Heller on the possibility of externalism about free will. See Russell Daw and Torin Alter, "Free Acts and Robot Cats," *Philosophical Studies* 102, no. 3 (2001): 345–57; Mark Heller, "The Mad Scientist Meets the Robot Cats: Compatibilism, Kinds, and Counterexamples," *Philosophy and Phenomenological Research* 56 (1996): 333–7. There are obviously attractions to a view on which responsibility is not an entirely gerrymandered thing, but I take it that there are a variety of ways of thinking about kinds and categories that give us something that is neither a natural kind nor entirely gerrymandered.

[26] Van Inwagen, *An Essay on Free Will*, 162, 188. In a compatibilist vein, see Strawson, "Freedom and Resentment." The idea that it is compelling to think we are morally responsible (and relatedly, that we do well to embrace a theory that makes this fact resilient to future discoveries) has also played a prominent role in the work of John Fischer. See the introduction to Fischer, *My Way*.

[27] Strawson, "Freedom and Resentment."

[28] Susan Wolf, "The Importance of Free Will," *Mind* 90 (1981): 386–405.

there is enough space to insert the thin edge of the nihilistic wedge into this sort of "obviousness of responsibility" argument.

One virtue of a revisionist-style reply to nihilism is that it does not run afoul of supposing that nihilism is simply off the table. Even better, most revisionist accounts will be able to appeal to the idea that we can be in massive connotational error (e.g., pervasively supposing that free will requires some form of libertarian agency) without this error necessarily affecting reference or our prescriptive theorizing.

As we have seen, any divergences from our prescriptively favored notion of responsibility will: (1) tell us little or nothing about the property in the world that is the best candidate for a truth maker; and (2) tell us little or nothing about the kind of thing that defines the conceptual role that free will plays in our lives. That a theoretically defined term could turn out to be modestly revisionist does not speak against its ontological and conceptual importance any more than changes in the post-Einsteinian conception of simultaneity that is proper to physics speaks against the importance, both ontological and conceptual, of the revised notion of simultaneity.

If revisionism carries the day, our pre-theoretical notion might persist in various parts of our linguistic community long after we have settled on a particular account of the best theoretical specification of free will. However, once we have a successful theoretical definition on our hands, the persistence of these other notions is at best a curiosity and at worst an impediment to the spread of knowledge.

On the present approach, we are looking for a property that can do the relevant conceptual work: in this case, organizing responsibility-characteristic practices, licensing judgments of praise and blame, distinguishing between free and unfree cases, warranting the reactive attitudes, and so on. However, this project may raise the worry that the revisionist is helping him- or herself to a too-easy defeat of eliminativism about responsibility. The critic might worry that on this approach, responsibility nihilism is simply off the table. If that is so, then we have theoretical theft over honest toil.

There is plenty of toil here. Nothing about the framework of revisionism as such entails that responsibility nihilism is necessarily unavailable. To see this, it helps to consider cases where the mismatch between concept and world is especially large. In these cases, elimination is appealing. Consider phlogiston. Phlogiston was thought to be an element that facilitated combustion, where it was released. The now conventional view about these things is that phlogiston does not exist. In the ostensions of early scientists attempting to dub something phlogiston, we now tend to think that there was no suitable property they were picking out. So: eliminativism about phlogiston at least retrospectively looks like the right conclusion.

Perhaps scientists could have re-worked the relationship between terminology, beliefs, and the world, so the match between the idea and the world was better. There were serious difficulties for any attempt to go the revisionist way, however. The standard theory of phlogiston was that it escapes from an object when the object is burned to ash. Unfortunately, experiments showed that some purportedly phlogisticated metals (e.g., magnesium) actually *gained* weight when burned. Attempts to rescue the theory persisted (phlogiston has negative weight!). Eventually, however, scientists came to accept that it was better to jettison the phlogiston theory and work with a different notion that picked out a different property. Scientists could have spoken of dephlogisticated air. But this would have made it look like that stuff—dephlogisticated air—was doing some work, in spite of the fact that the notion of phlogiston didn't seem to find purchase in the growing body of scientific results, and could not do the things for which the term was originally introduced. So, oxygen displaced phlogiston in our explanations of combustion.

Of course, we can imagine that things might have worked out differently. If scientific practice, beliefs, and attendant conceptual commitments had adjusted to the world in a different way, perhaps scientists would have concluded that phlogiston was different than it had initially been conceived. If so, though, presumably the grounds for it would have been that enough of what mattered to scientists about phlogiston was preserved across old and new understandings of it to warrant the change.

This much seems right: in the case of preserving a term's usage, beyond preservation of principal inferential roles and some inchoate sense of similarity, it is difficult to formulate hard and fast rules about revision as opposed to elimination. This will be especially true in cases where there is non-trivial but partial consistency of usage, inferential roles, and similarity. Nevertheless, what the phlogiston case shows is that revision is never guaranteed, even when there is conceivably a path to it. In the present case, the only way to ensure that the mismatch between our ordinary convictions about responsibility and the world do not entail nihilism is if we earn the survival of the term "responsibility." What it takes to do *that* is the subject of the next chapter.

4

Building a Better Theory

[I]t goes without saying that I do not deny, presupposing I am no fool, that many actions called immoral ought to be avoided and resisted, or that many actions called moral ought to be done and encouraged—but *for different reasons than formerly.*

F. Nietzsche, *Daybreak* §103

Suppose we want to construct a revisionist account of moral responsibility, one that eschews those strands of incompatibilist thought lurking in ordinary convictions about free will and moral responsibility. That is, suppose we want to construct a prescriptively compatibilist account. How do we go about doing that? What are the proper constraints on the construction of that account? These are the main questions I aim to answer in this chapter.

1. Revisionisms: systematic and repurposing

There are two ways we might go about developing a revisionist theory. One route I will call *repurposing revisionism*. The other route I will call *systematic revisionism*.

Repurposing revisionism is accomplished by taking your favorite compatibilist proposal of free will and declaring that it is not beholden to commonsense intuitions about responsible agency and free will. Instead, the positive compatibilist proposal is a purely prescriptive account of how we ought to think of free will and moral responsibility. The virtue of this approach is twofold: it is both methodologically simple and endowed with the not insubstantial resources of already existing compatibilist theories.

The alternative to repurposing revisionism is systematic revisionism. What makes systematic revisionist distinctive is that it proceeds from the ground up on the basis of attempting to provide an intentionally and explicitly revisionist proposal of free will. On this approach, we attempt to construct an account of responsibility out of independently plausible resources, resources that may or may not generate an account similar to familiar compatibilist accounts. Whereas repurposing revisionism endeavors to simply repurpose familiar compatibilist accounts, systematic revisionism accepts the burden of constructing a theory anew, where the various commitments of the theory are constructed with an eye towards the particular demands of revisionist theory construction.

The present account aspires to systematic revisionism.

Although it is more labor-intensive (for both the writer and the reader!), I think there is good reason to adopt the systematic approach over the repurposing approach. Here's why: conventional compatibilist theories of the sort repurposing revisionists are apt to appeal to are usually generated under non-revisionist constraints. That is, conventional compatibilist accounts are constructed under the presumption that strong intuitions are firm limits on the theorizing. As a consequence, conventional compatibilist accounts are more likely to contain elements in them that are responsive to ordinary (incompatibilist) elements, elements that in the present context we seek to avoid.[1]

None of this should be taken to suggest that we can't get convergence between the present project and potential proposals that pursue repurposing revisionism. I believe that many accounts are in the neighborhood of The Truth, even if methodological confusions and the absence of some crucial distinctions obscure matters. Moreover, I won't pretend that the account I generate has no connection to existing compatibilist accounts. I intend to enthusiastically poach where such poaching is valuable, avoiding the more problematic global commitments of conventional compatibilist approaches. That said, it remains to be seen whether this initial foray

---

[1] By way of preview, in chapter 9, I will argue that there is a historical condition on moral responsibility that is accepted by many compatibilist accounts, but that (as far as I can make out) has roots in incompatibilist convictions that have no obvious normative foundation. If that is right, this is one example in which conventional compatibilist accounts attempt to take on board convictions ultimately rooted in incompatibilist demands that we do well to reject.

into revisionist theorizing is best served by endeavoring to provide a systematically revisionist account.

In rest of this chapter, I outline what I take to be the best path to developing a prescriptive, systematic revisionist account of moral responsibility. I begin by invoking two standards governing subsequent theory construction. Then, I focus on ways to delimit the subject matter, or the subset of our practices, attitudes, judgments, and statuses that are characteristic of moral responsibility (*the responsibility system,* as I called it in the Introduction). I proceed by outlining aspects of the internal logic and structure of the responsibility system that I take to be especially salient for the revisionist approach I recommend. I conclude by reflecting on the relationship of this revisionist approach to theorizing in metaethics and normative ethics.

2. Two standards

Although I aim to elaborate the methodological features salient to my particular revisionist approach, there is surely room for variation that produces distinct revisionist accounts. This raises the following puzzle: were we to have multiple revisionist accounts, on what basis would we properly decide which to accept? Here's an answer: competing revisionist accounts would have to be weighed against each other in all the usual ways, i.e., weighing their explanatory power with the number and nature of ontological commitments, and looking to the coherence of it all with any favored methodological precepts.

More concretely, recall the idea, introduced in chapter 2, that an adequate prescriptive account must satisfy a *standard of naturalistic plausibility.* A proposal is more plausible if it doesn't make a bet that science is going to turn out substantially differently than we now understand it. It also gains plausibility by having evidence in its favor, or if the picture of agency it requires relies on things that are independently part of our ontology of agents and actions. So, competing revisionist accounts can be measured on this standard, too.

The fundamentally normative nature of prescriptive theorizing about moral responsibility merits some special attention. It should be clear that on the current approach, any adequate prescriptive account of responsibility (but *especially* one that embraces revisionist conclusions) must cohere with various familiar normative concerns. One way to express this idea is in the form of *a standard of normative adequacy*.[2]

The governing idea of a standard of normative adequacy is this: any prescriptive account of responsibility must be well integrated with our network of mutually supporting moral norms, practices, and theories thereof. This standard can be divided into five distinct sub-requirements. First, the *integration* requirement: the account should explain the relationship between a theory of responsibility and broader philosophical accounts of morality. Second, the *distinctiveness* requirement: the account should say something about the distinctive normative structure of responsibility. What the distinctiveness requirement demands is an explanation of those normative features that animate justified concern for the praiseworthiness and blameworthiness of agents (see §5 of this chapter for more on this idea). Third, there is the *justification* requirement: an adequate account should explain how responsibility attitudes, practices, and judgments can, at least in general, be justified. What the justification requirement demands is some account of why we are rightly concerned with responsibility, to the extent to which we are, and when we are justified in praising and blaming. Fourth, there is the *relevance* requirement: an adequate account should be able to explain how the features of agency and/or the aspects of the practice of responsibility invoked in the account have some relevant connection to what is at stake in attributions of moral responsibility. Appeals to powers that bear no discernible or credible relationship to being responsible, or being held responsible, should be viewed as a cost to the theory. Fifth and finally, there is the presumption of *conservatism*, which carries over from antecedent commitment to a standard of philosophical conservation. Other things being equal, we should favor accounts that do a minimum of violence to other independently plausible normative notions, such as "don't punish the innocent." A prescriptive account of responsibility that made responsibility-characteristic practices immune to considerations of proportionality in praise and blame, or that failed to make distinction between agents that

---

[2] I believe this standard should be accepted by *any* prescriptive account of moral responsibility, revisionist or not. Indeed, I think it is in fact (implicitly) accepted by most theorists of moral responsibility. However, it is another matter entirely whether this standard is accepted by those principally interested in the metaphysics of free will.

are capable of moral responsibility and those that are not, would likewise come at a significant cost.

One reason to accept this standard derives from the fundamentally normative nature of moral responsibility, and the task of giving a normative prescriptive account of responsibility. Unless a proposal engages with the normative dimensions of moral responsibility, the account threatens to collapse into mere fictionalizing or speculative anthropology for a non-actual world. However, a different reason for accepting the standard derives from commitment to a principle of philosophical conservation. That is, even though we are entertaining a revisionist proposal, there is still reason to limit the scope of revisions. Consequently, any account that entails radical departures from independently plausible normative principles will give us reason to regard the account with skepticism if the revisions are unmotivated or there are alternatives that are comparably justifiable without entailing similar revisions.

In the context of revisionist theorizing, invoking a standard of normative adequacy can sometimes give rise to the following worry: how are we to justify responsibility-characteristic practices independent of an antecedent account of moral responsibility and those concepts that depend upon it? This worry can have special pressure if one holds that libertarian free will is foundational to *all* other moral notions.[3] However, the same basic worry arises even if one thinks that only a good many moral notions depend on free will and moral responsibility. The fundamental worry is that we are left with too depleted a stock of moral notions on which to build any account of the justification of our moral responsibility practices if we look to things external to (or normatively independent of) moral responsibility.

There are several things to be said by way of reply. First, the scope of moral notions that are conceptually dependent on an antecedent notion of moral responsibility is not as large as this objection suggests. For example, it is plausible to think that many aretaic or characterological notions are altogether independent of responsibility assessments.[4] Whether or not

---

[3] Although the exegesis is hardly straightforward, this is plausibly the view expressed in §§ 1744–9 of the *Catechism of the Catholic Church* (2nd edn.) (New York: Doubleday, 1997).

[4] This is a point that Michael Slote has emphasized, and that has also been suggested by J. J. C. Smart. See Michael Slote, "Ethics Without Free Will," *Social Theory and Practice* 16, no. 3 (1990): 369–83; Smart, "Free Will, Praise, and Blame." The matter is complex, however. Gary Watson has argued that there is a "face" of responsibility under which aretaic judgments are subsumed. See Gary Watson, "Two Faces of

I am couth, charming, or irritating are matters that can be settled without any appeal to whether I am also morally responsible. This is not to say that moral responsibility could not interact with these assessments. You might regard my being unkind differently in cases where you think I am responsible for that fact of my character than you would in those cases where you regard me as not responsible for that fact. However, *whether* I am unkind is fundamentally independent of questions about free will and moral responsibility.

Second, beyond characterological notions, there seem to be a wide range of normative notions to which we can appeal that are plausibly antecedent to, or at least independent from, moral responsibility. Although there is some dispute about it, many conceptions of distributive justice and fairness can be advanced independent of some antecedent account of moral responsibility or free will. Moreover, considerations of fairness, net utility, and instrumental rationality (given some specification of independently desired ends) are all normative notions that plausibly persist independent of facts about whether agents are morally responsible or possess free will in some libertarian sense.

To see why, it may be helpful to compare two universes, one in which agents possess libertarian free will (Universe A) and another in which they lack it (Universe B). When we look to Universe B, we can say that some arrangements in that universe are fair and others are not, some practices and actions are utility-producing and other utility-diminishing, and that various actions turn out to be rational relative to various values, aims, and desires that agents have. Of course, it is missing something that Universe A possesses, but that difference does not seem to affect assessments of fairness, utility, and rationality in any robust way.

Perhaps you have different intuitions about such cases. Still, I am unaware of any *argument* why we should dismiss the judgment that these normative notions could survive in a world without libertarian free will. As I see it, the work these various notions do, the concerns to which they are responsive and the reasons for which these notions have come to have a place in our conceptual economy, seem not to depend on assessments of freedom and

Responsibility," *Philosophical Topics* 24 (1996): 227–48. For discussion of the various commitments of different conceptions of responsibility, see John Martin Fischer and Neal Tognazinni, "The Physiognomy of Responsibility," *Philosophy and Phenomenological Research* 82, no. 2 (2011): 381–417.

moral responsibility. So, in the absence of some argument otherwise, we have good prima facie reason to permit appeals to widely accepted normative notions not directly at stake in ascriptions of responsibility.

Note too that the discovery that some normative notion appears to have a conceptual link to a prior notion of freedom or responsibility would not suffice to show that it does. As we saw last chapter, it may be that what we will discover is that the connection is only connotational. If so, then it is not telling about the essence or reference-fixing features of the property. Anyway, the proof will be in the pudding. If we find that the ensuing account appeals to notions that can themselves be shown to rely on a notion of libertarian free will, then I grant that this would constitute a serious difficulty.

3. The work of the concept

Responsibility-characteristic phenomena are obviously diverse in their occurrence and complex in their particulars. So, if we are to offer a revisionist account of responsibility, it will require some picking and choosing among what is more and less central to the proposed account of responsibility. This is especially so if one maintains (as the revisionist does) that responsibility is somehow other than we tend to think of it.

It is therefore especially helpful to have in hand some proposal about the general conceptual role of responsibility. A revisionist with an account of *that* has some place to stand with respect to claims about why the account constitutes an account of responsibility, and not some other thing. Central to my own approach to these questions is the idea of *the work of the concept*, or roughly, the characteristic roles played by the collection of beliefs, commitments, and distinction-making characteristic of moral responsibility.[5]

As I understand them, concepts carve up and categorize parts of the world. Concepts do a kind of work for us: they demarcate one thing from

---

[5] This is a picture of concepts that is broadly psychological. Concept talk should be understood loosely. I don't have much invested in these thoughts turning out to fall under some or another privileged notion of what it is to be a concept. My main interest is in characterizing the kinds of things that responsibility thoughts do for us.

another. Relatedly, they identify a collection of (we suppose) interrelated inferences we can make about things.

So, for example, the concept of "car" does the work of capturing a subset of transportation-related thoughts we have: a car is likely to have a motor, it is likely to travel on wheels, it is likely to be used as transportation for small groups of people on paved streets, and so on. The work of the concept of "llama" is to specify a cluster of inferences regarding a particular kind of mammal in the world; the work of the concept of "felony" is to specify a set of inferences regarding a legal status; the work of "touchdown" is to specify a set of inferences regarding a scoring event internal to the game of American football. In short, *the work of a concept* is defined by its primary, general inferential role.

Nothing in this picture requires that all concepts necessarily do an identifiable piece of work for us. Perhaps there are concepts that do not have any practical or theoretical inferential role in our thinking or practices. This picture also does not presume that the work of a concept is always univocal. Indeed, some concepts are very highly contested, subject to substantially different individual conceptions of what counts as the principal work of the concept.

Consider the concept of marriage. It has done the work of keeping track of, for example: (1) a legally sanctioned and privileged relationship; (2) a religious sacramental relationship; (3) a property relationship; (4) a privileged emotional relationship; and/or (5) conditions of socially sanctioned sexual intercourse. If the conceptual work of "marriage" is different for you than it is for your neighbors, you are likely to disagree with them about the propriety of different ways of extending the concept.[6]

Importantly, the fact of a concept having a role does not guarantee that the concept as we have it or use it does a good job of fulfilling that role. In the fifteenth and sixteenth century, the Spanish Empire's notion of *limpieza de sangre*—"cleanliness of blood"—might have been like this. As a somewhat unstable amalgam of ancestral religious origin, social class, and something like race, *limpieza de sangre* did ineffective work at characterizing real human kinds and descent groups. At least two things account for its

---

[6] Much of the recent rhetoric concerning gay marriage in the U.S. appears to reflect a disagreement about the work of the concept of marriage. One's conception of the work of the concept plays a big part in the ways in which one is willing to think a novel proposed usage is an apt one. Disagreement about the work of a concept is obviously both possible and sometimes actual.

ineffectiveness. First, there was nothing in the world that neatly corresponded to blood cleanliness, as those concept-users conceived of it. Second, what work the concept did in practice fell considerably short of the role for which it was generally understood to have. Rather than tracking real, essential "cleanliness" of a blood line, it tracked various contingent social and class differences. The lesson here is that the work of a particular concept might not be well executed by the concepts we have. And anyway, the world might not cooperate.

Turning to the case of moral responsibility, I propose that we understand the work of the concept of moral responsibility as having to do with regulating inferences about differential moral praiseworthiness and blameworthiness, marking those who are praiseworthy or blameworthy and those who are not.[7] People who knowingly and intentionally do the wrong thing deserve condemnation. People who do the right thing deserve approval. Keeping track of when people deserve praise and blame is the work of the concept of moral responsibility. It is, in some sense, *why* we rightly have a concept of moral responsibility.

This is not a historical claim. It is a claim about why—whatever its history—we *now* have reason to deploy this concept. Of course, it could turn out that we are tracking something illusory, or that there is some independent reason to abandon that network of practices, judgments, and statuses that surround it. An account of a function does not entail that the function is instantiated or well fitted to the world.

If the work of the concept is tied to regulating moralized praising and blaming, anchoring a revisionist account of moral responsibility will presumably require an explanation of the justification of our responsibility-characteristic practices. Why? By showing such practices are justified independent of the considerations that drove us to revisionism, we show that it accounts for the core work of the concept, and thereby earns the right to count as a theory of responsibility.

---

[7] This characterization of the work of the concept is intended to be largely innocent, that is, the kind of thing that most theorists working on responsibility could accept. This is not to say that it is vacuous: if one rejected the Strawsonian thought that reactive attitudes have some connection to responsibility, this would presumably run afoul of how I have proposed to understand the work of the concept. One reason to resist this characterization might come from thinking about responsibility for "morally neutral" action. I say more about this in chapter 10.

4. Reflective equilibrium

One might be tempted to say that the analysis of the work of the concept provides comparatively fixed points in the process of establishing reflective equilibrium for a theory of responsibility. On such a view, systematic revisionism along the lines I propose constitutes a particular version of the method of reflective equilibrium. Non-revisionist and repurposing revisionist approaches would be their own forms of achieving reflective equilibrium, with the former giving especially heavy weight to folk intuitions.

Depending on what one means, it may well be true that the present approach counts as an instance of the method of reflective equilibrium.[8] However, characterizing an account as committed to the method of reflective equilibrium is familiar and obscure in equal measure. I believe we are better off abandoning such invocations altogether. That an account is committed to reflective equilibrium tells us almost nothing substantive or distinctive about the methodological details of the account. Few philosophers who invoke the idea bother to explain why some recalcitrant intuitions are to be tolerated and not others, on their version of the method. Whatever its utility in Rawls, it is simply unclear what commitments one means to take on board by invoking reflective equilibrium.[9]

Rather than perpetuating the ritual of invoking the method of reflective equilibrium, I prefer to be explicit about the various methodological aims and constraints of the present approach. I have said which intuitions are problematic and why, and I am here endeavoring to provide an explicit statement of what burdens I take the theory to have and why. In contrast, standard appeals to reflective equilibrium do not distinguish between diagnosis and prescription, do not purport to offer an account of the work of the

---

[8] Indeed, on some conceptions of it, the method of reflective equilibrium amounts to something like rational theory building, as such. See Michael R. DePaul, "Why Bother With Reflective Equilibrium?," in *Rethinking Intuition: The Psychology of Intuition and Its Role in Philosophical Inquiry*, ed. Michael R. DePaul and William Ramsey (Lanham, MD: Rowman & Littlefield, 1998). For some of the varied conceptions of reflective equilibrium, see many of the essays in DePaul and Ramsey, eds, *Rethinking Intuition: The Psychology of Intuition and Its Role in Philosophical Inquiry*.

[9] For an overview of Rawls' approach, and subsequent developments, see Norman Daniels, "Reflective Equilibrium" in *the Stanford Encyclopedia of Philosophy* (Spring 2011 Edition) <http://plato.stanford.edu/archives/spr2011/entries/reflective-equilibrium/>, accessed January 23, 2012. There, Daniels makes a remark that should give proponents of reflective equilibrium some pause: "a full defense of reflective equilibrium as a method would require a more developed response...than exists in the literature."

involved concept, and do not specify standards governing proposed revisions of conceptual and practical commitments.

If every bit of philosophy is an instance of reflective equilibrium, or if the mere act of rational reflection is implementation of reflective equilibrium, then revisionism is a kind of reflective equilibrium. Of course, if that is all reflective equilibrium in practice really is, it isn't clear what it rules out. (Again, Rawls' own picture was rather specific, and for that matter its relationship with Goodman's original work on this matter is complex.) If the invocation of the method of reflective equilibrium is intended to be a substantive methodological commitment, then philosophers need to say more about the theoretical aims of their accounts, the role that intuitions play in them, and the basis on which such intuitions are to be accepted or rejected. In the absence of such specifications, it is much harder for us to evaluate when two or more accounts are in genuine disagreement as opposed to, for example, differing in the subject matter or theoretical aim of the account. Getting a grip on these matters is what the account of revisionist theory construction in this chapter is supposed to provide. As such, it seems a rather different beast than the more familiar ritual invocation of reflective equilibrium.

5. Aspects of the responsibility system

In the previous section, I claimed that the work of the concept of moral responsibility is to regulate our assessments of praiseworthiness and blameworthiness. Here, I say a bit about these notions and related ideas that will be the subject of the ensuing account of moral responsibility. In doing so, I will necessarily invoke theory-laden characterizations of those phenomena. These are not intended to be immutable substantive commitments. They are provisional characterizations intended to provide an initial grip on the subject matter.

I will focus on several ideas—being responsible, holding responsible, responsible agency, exculpation, blameworthiness, blame, and desert—that constitute the core phenomena of the responsibility system. There are plausibly other aspects of the system sometimes salient for proper ascriptions of moral responsibility. Among them, I include epistemic conditions and some sense of the agent being active with respect to the action. I will have things to say about these issues in later chapters, but I take them to be less central to the propriety of moral responsibility.

A. *Holding responsible and being responsible*

Consider the act of holding someone responsible. On at least standard usage, it seems to require a judgment that someone has done something with a moral valence, and that reaction to it is permitted, prescribed, or proscribed by praising and blaming norms. However, holding someone responsible is not just a matter of behaving in praise- or blame-like ways. We can feign praise and blame. We can also judge that praise and blame are justified without feeling inclined to express praise or blame. Indeed, we can even judge that one is blameworthy without also thinking that it is fair to blame someone.[10] In short, there is considerable complexity to our judging and holding others and ourselves responsible.

Here is an initial thought, one first introduced at the outset of this book: judging that someone is responsible involves acceptance of a (at least implicit) judgment that the evaluated agent is a special kind of agent, what I will call *a responsible agent*.[11] Chinchillas, blue jays, and newborn humans are not ordinarily candidates for moral praise and blame; they are not responsible agents. So, we need a theory that recognizes a restriction on the kinds of agents that are properly subject to moral praise and blame.

Of course, it is not enough to conclude that someone is a responsible agent. To be praiseworthy or blameworthy, a considered agent has to have done something that merits praise or blame. As a first pass, our assessments of moral praiseworthiness and blameworthiness appear to be parasitic on our

---

[10] Suppose we had a practice of excusing some initial infraction for which someone is morally responsible, but that we arbitrarily decided not to excuse some transgression in a particular instance. In such a case, the targeted agent is plausibly responsible although it would be unfair to hold him or her responsible. I discuss this case and its significance for Wallace's fairness-focused account in Manuel Vargas, "Responsibility and the Aims of Theory: Strawson and Revisionism," *Pacific Philosophical Quarterly* 85, no. 2 (2004): 218–41.

[11] Other familiar locutions for this idea include that claim that the agent is *accountable* or "in the ballpark" for attributions of responsibility. See, among others, R. Jay Wallace, *Responsibility and the Moral Sentiments* (Cambridge, MA: Harvard University Press, 1994); Fischer and Ravizza, *Responsibility and Control: A Theory of Moral Responsibility*.

assessments of what morality requires of us. Moralized blame presumes that we have done wrong.[12] Moralized praise presumes that we have done right.

These thoughts help illuminate the idea that our responsibility assessments have an apparently cognitivist, or truth-functional surface structure. An ascription of responsibility presumes at least two things: (1) the judgment that the targeted agent is indeed a responsible agent; and (2) the agent has done (whether by act or omission) something that merits praise or blame. Errors can occur in both of these domains. We might be mistaken about whether a given agent is a responsible agent, and we might be in error about whether what is done merits praise and blame. So, an account of responsibility that elaborates the conditions for being a responsible agent and/or some account of right and wrong action will have the resources to explain the thought that there is an apparent fact of the matter about responsibility attributions, and that we can be in error about such facts.[13]

A further facet of the phenomenon of holding responsible is worth flagging. When we make judgments of responsibility, there is a collection of attitudes and dispositions that typically follow in its wake. We can characterize that collection of attitudes and dispositions as a kind of stance we take towards agents of the relevant sort. The stance is constituted by the disposition to regard some agents as appropriately subject to praise and blame, to see various actions as worthy of blame and praise, and to view agents as culpable at least partly in light of his or her actions and omissions.

To be sure, those dispositions of reaction can be masked or removed by various particulars of the case. I might be less prone to expressing blame at those I hold in high esteem. You might regard yourself as lacking the standing to criticize another for something, if you think you are subject to a similar criticism. Still, holding someone responsible ordinarily involves both a presupposition about the nature of the agent and engagement of those dispositions that constitute the characteristic stance of holding agents

---

[12] For a dissenting view, see Thomas Scanlon, *Moral Dimensions: Permissibility, Meaning, Blame* (Cambridge, MA: Belknap Press of Harvard University Press, 2008).

[13] The nature of these facts has been subject to dispute. For example, Wallace holds that it is implausible to think that there is an "independent" order of prior metaphysical facts to moral responsibility, antecedent to facts about the fairness of holding agents responsible. Although I am unpersuaded by some of the particulars of the fairness-focused account he gives, I am very sympathetic to the thought that what facts there are about moral responsibility are structured by normative features of our practice. For more on this matter, see Vargas, "Responsibility and the Aims of Theory: Strawson and Revisionism."

responsible. So, it seems that adoption of this stance seems to have an expressive function, or at any rate, in adopting it we thereby express a distinctive (if implicit) regard for the agency of those viewed through this lens. Its targets are not *mere* agents, but agents vulnerable to judgments of blame and the attendant reactions and attitudes that we take such judgments to license.

B. *Excuses and exemptions*

Any adequate account of moral responsibility will need to account for the conditions under which someone is responsible and not. Minimally, this involves some account of responsible agency and some account of what gives rise to proper moral praise and blame.

In the larger literature on these matters, this task is frequently framed in terms of providing an account of exculpation. The reason for this is simple: ordinarily, we assume agents are responsible so what needs special explanation are the conditions under which agents are not responsible. Here, the presumption is that we need an explanation of why responsible agents are responsible for outcomes when they are; in accounting for that, a theory of exculpation will follow. Still, it may be helpful to keep in mind that what we are looking for is an explanation of both matters, even if they prove to be different sides of the same coin.

As we have already seen, being responsible requires that one be an agent of the proper sort, and that one has done something that licenses moral praising and blaming. Adapting a distinction Gary Watson finds in the work of Peter Strawson, we can distinguish between two ways the license can be disrupted.[14] The first we can label *exemptions* and the second *excuses*.

Roughly, exemptions track the nature of the agent. An agent is exempt when he or she is the wrong sort of agent to be properly subject to norms of praise and blame. As we saw above, it is not as though any agent can count as a candidate for assessments of moral praise and blame. A theory of *responsible agency* provides an account of which features of agency constitute those required for responsibility. With it, we can draw the line between those

---

[14] Gary Watson, "Responsibility and the Limits of Evil," in *Responsibility, Character, and the Emotions,* ed. Ferdinand David Schoeman (New York: Cambridge University Press, 1987). A similar distinction can also be found in, among others, Wallace, *Responsibility and the Moral Sentiments*; Fischer, and Ravizza, *Responsibility and Control: A Theory of Moral Responsibility.*

agents exempt from responsibility and those that are candidates for evaluation in light of the norms of praise and blame.

Exemptions arise because of failures to be the right kind of agent. Excuses arise in cases where the action was not of the right sort. Even if an agent is a responsible agent in the to-be-given sense gestured at above, the agent might still fail to be praiseworthy or blameworthy because of the kind of action it was, or the manner in which the action was produced. Typical excuses invoke ignorance, unintentional action, or lack of freedom. What unifies these things, if anything does, is that something about them disrupts the ordinary pattern of responsibility assessment among responsible agents. Articulating an account of the proper structure of our excuses is a burden for a theory of excuses, and it is surely part of any plausible account of moral responsibility.

One notable implication of this way of thinking about exculpation is that it provides us with the tools for clarifying something that is often ambiguous in ordinary language. When we say that someone is responsible, we can refer to either or both (1) someone being an agent of the right sort to be evaluated in terms of norms of moral praise and blame; and (2) that the agent under consideration is both a responsible agent and in fact blameworthy or praiseworthy for some act.

Two more remarks about excuses are in order. First, the language of excuses is infelicitous when applied to praise, for we do not often talk about being excused from praise. Despite the violence to ordinary language, as a conceptual matter it is plausible to think that people can be properly excused from praise because the apparently praiseworthy action was a function of, for example, ignorance about the praiseworthy effect. Suppose Grant was unaware that his wrestling to the ground a random passerby in front of the police was in fact the successful collaring of a criminal mastermind that the police had been hunting for years. When this fact comes to light as he is getting booked at the local jail, this should not license adulation and praise for Grant's actions even if we think that, on balance, his successful takedown of said criminal was a good thing.

Second, there is a distinction in the law between excuses and justifications that may or may not map on to the present distinction between excuses and exemptions. There is some dispute in the law about how to draw the distinction between excuses and justification, and different ways of drawing that distinction are more and less friendly to the distinction I've drawn here. For example, in the law insanity is usually regarded as an excuse. Here, though, it is more plausibly an exemption for it points to some fundamental (if local) defect of agency, instead of an ordinary disruption in the production of action. In the law, self-defense is regarded as a justification. Here it a better candidate for excuse.

There are cases of legal excuse that focus on the apparent difficulty of the agent for compliance with the law, and such cases look like analogs for some excuses. So, there may be some overlap. Moreover, in chapter 8, I will argue that if we have a sufficiently nuanced grasp of how exemptions work, some of the pressure diminishes for treating many "difficulty with compliance" cases as instances of (moral) excuses. So, for the moment, we should be neutral on the extent to which the present distinction between excuses and exemptions corresponds with or perhaps underdescribes a related distinction in the legal theory.

C. Desert

Reflecting on the idea of being responsible and the ways in which we can fail to be responsible may give rise to the thought that when we judge that someone is morally responsible, what we are committed to is the idea that the targeted agent *deserves* praise or blame for the considered action. After all, when we blame someone, it suggests a kind of culpability in the agent, that the thing for which the agent is being blamed is not just a fault, but the *agent's* fault.[15]

Earlier, I noted that other forms of plausibly moralized assessment—such as the judgment that someone is greedy, charming, or irritating—can be neutral on the matter of whether the agent is at fault for possessing that quality. We can conclude that an agent is charming or irritating through no fault of her own.

However, in the ordinary course of things we typically do conceive of such defects and virtues as belonging to the agent in a way that can give rise to the imputation of desert for the virtue or vice. We might praise John for

---

[15] As J. J. C. Smart once noted, praise works differently than blame in this respect. We can praise something in a way that need not impute a special relation between the agent and grounds of the praise, only a "grading" of excellence on some measure. In conjunction with skepticism about libertarian agency, Smart thought that the proper counterpart to praise is not blame but "dispraise."

being generous with junior members in his professional field, thinking that he is to be credited for having developed that virtue. And, we might believe that Christina's haughtiness is not only a shortcoming, but that it is her own fault for not having suppressed or blunted it or its expression in interpersonal or professional situations.

Matters here are tricky along several dimensions. First, there is the question of whether it is right to think of responsibility as paradigmatically involving desert at all (as opposed to, say, appropriateness or fittingness). I am inclined to think that this is a sufficiently prominent feature of how we think and talk about responsibility to merit treating it as one of the phenomena that ought to have a recognizably important place in the account. It need not be a necessary feature of every responsibility judgment, however. More on that in a bit.

Second, even if we accept the desert-entailing picture, the details of how desert operates are obviously complex. For example, there is the question of whether an agent deserves blame for acquiring the trait, for retaining the trait once acquired, for acting on the trait, or for not attempting to suppress action on the trait to the extent to which he or she is capable. Responsibility for action and responsibility for character unfilosofo have a complex relationship. However, in each case of the sort I just mentioned, it is not unreasonable to think that the matter of moral responsibility is paradigmatically the matter of deserving moralized praising and blaming. We might thus express the desert-as-central thought as the idea that *a responsible agent can deserve praise or blame only if that agent has violated, met, or superseded some moral norm governing that action type.*

A few brief points of clarification are in order.

First, by invoking the idea of a moral norm, I simply mean to mark that normative element, however it is best understood, in virtue of which some actions are regarded as "to be done" or "not to be done" according to the correct account of morality. It would have been easier to say that "a responsible agent can deserve blame only if she has done something wrong." However, this way of putting it fails to reflect the possibility that agents may be praised for meeting or exceeding some requirements.

Second, it is plausible that in some cases the satisfaction, violation, or superachievement of these norms will admit of degrees. How we ought to respond to various degrees of satisfying, violating, or superseding a norm can be a scalar matter.[16]

Third, notice that although this formulation invokes a requirement of responsible agency, it is neutral on the matter of the conditions for responsible agency and whether such conditions can obtain if determinism is true.

On this construal of the central phenomena of moral responsibility, praise and blame get their pride of place because of they are things that are deserved.

There is some appeal to framing matters in this fashion, although it may run the risk of making desert both more important and more mysterious than it needs to be. I will have more to say about desert in a later chapter, but for the moment let us bracket worries about desert and instead focus on the blame element.

D. Blame 1: a judgment-like attitude

"Praise" and "blame" are ambiguous terms. Sometimes they refer to judgment-like attitudes, and other times to the characteristic attitudes and practices which the appropriateness of these judgment-like attitudes are taken to license. I'll remark on each phenomenon.

As an initial characterization, we can say that the first sense of blame (i.e., the notion of blame as a judgment) is this: blame is a judgment of *pro tanto* license to a class of characteristic interpersonal reactions.[17] In this sense of blame, it is not the exercise of that license that constitutes the blame, but rather the judgment. The language here invites confusion, for it permits us to say that we can blame without blam*ing*, which may sound odd. Nevertheless, it seems possible, and occasionally, actual. It might happen when you judge that a close friend, lover, or spouse has done something wrong to a third party but you cannot bring yourself to feel anger or indignation over the act, even while acknowledging that the act is worthy of blame. Or, it might happen when one regards someone's act as wrong but views oneself

---

[16] My focus is on blaming judgments and reactions. Inasmuch as blame-expressing practices extend to punishment, the present picture allows for scalar punishment that reflects scalar degree of response to the degree of violation of the responsibility norms.

[17] As noted before, I will largely bracket the matter of praise. One difference between praise and blame emerges in the following way: praise is paradigmatically triggered by, in some cases, meeting a norm, and in other cases (e.g., the supererogatory), for exceeding the demands of some norm. In contrast, blame is paradigmatically triggered only by failure to meet a norm.

as not having an interest in, or the standing to respond in the characteristic ways.[18] We can therefore call the judgment-like sense of blame *a judgment of blameworthiness*. And, as was suggested by the earlier distinction between responsible agency and blameworthiness, it is a judgment that the evaluated agent is both a particular sort of agent (a responsible agent) *and* that blame-characteristic attitudes are licensed.

The preceding characterization of this sense of blame—blame as judgment, or blameworthiness—raises a puzzle if we think assessments of responsibility embed the idea that persons deserve blame for wrongdoing. A *license* falls short of judgment that someone *deserves* something. If you are licensed to interrupt a speaker with a question of clarification, it does not follow that you *deserve* to interrupt that speaker. This suggests that either the analysis of judgments of blameworthiness-as-licensing is mistaken, or else imputations of desert are not, in fact, central to responsibility.

However, an alternative is to hold that blame judgments admit of two species and desert is central to only one. To see why, consider a case where one judges one's spouse blameworthy for some infidelity. On the present suggestion, one is committed to the idea that resentment or other characteristic interpersonal reactions are licensed. However, if *all* one believes is that, say, resentment is acceptable without being deserved, then one has formed a judgment of blameworthiness, but only in a somewhat attenuated sense. In these judgments, desert has no role to play. Let us call such attenuated judgments, devoid of desert attribution, *minimal judgments of blameworthiness*.

These thoughts bring us back to the phenomenon of holding responsible. Note that minimal judgments of blameworthiness are insufficient for what we might think of as full-blooded *holding* responsible. A minimal judgment of blameworthiness suggests a kind of detachment from the emotionally engaged and often messy business of holding someone responsible.[19] Here,

---

[18] We might not have an interest in blaming if doing so would detract from the pursuit of some other project we regard as trumping in urgency or importance. And, one might view oneself as lacking the customary license to praise and blame if, for example, it would be hypocritical to do so or if there is some overriding moral consideration that precludes expressions of praising and blaming judgments. In such a case, however, one is still committed to the view that in some sense the characteristic interpersonal reactions are licensed, even if the license does not hold, all things considered, in one's own case.

[19] Ordinary linguistic practices may sometimes mislead on this point, suggesting that it is possible to hold someone responsible simply in virtue of forming a minimal judgment of blameworthiness. Perhaps there is some semantic shift underway in our current practices. For example, in the theater of public

though, is where desert has some role to play. One thing that is needed to transform a minimal judgment of blameworthiness into something that constitutes an instance of holding someone responsible is for the evaluating agent to judge that someone *deserves* resentment, indignation, moralized anger, or the like. Such a judgment of blameworthiness signals a stance, a disposition of regard towards another agent that includes the commitment that said agent deserves a reaction for what he or she has done. Call these desert-imputing judgments *robust judgments of blameworthiness.*

It is plausible to say that forming a robust judgment of blameworthiness ordinarily counts as an instance of holding responsible, even when there is no opportunity to express or experience the characteristic reactions. In the normal case of forming a robust judgment of blameworthiness, both the experience and expression of the characteristic emotional responses follow quickly. However, there are situations where the disposition to experience those emotions persists without the experience, perhaps because of more pressing concerns or emotional exhaustion. For example, one can form a robust judgment of blameworthiness about a life-threatening injury caused by one child to another, but because of the immediate severity of the threat to the injured child and the need to attend to that threat, an adult caretaker may fail to experience the ordinary suite of emotional reactions that typically accompany robust judgments. Still, it seems proper to say that in such cases where the ordinary emotional reactions have not had time to engage, one is indeed holding the involved party or parties responsible.[20]

To sum up this picture of blaming judgments, we can say that there are two main varieties, minimal and robust. In the case of minimal judgments of blame, what we have is merely a judgment of license for engagement of the characteristic stance or framework of emotional reactions, without any

political denunciations it is distressingly common that people will declare that they "hold someone responsible" while giving no evidence that they are committed to the target of responsibility deserving resentment, indignation, moralized anger, and what follows. If such views of holding one responsible sufficiently infect larger patterns of usage, then minimal judgments of blameworthiness might indeed count as holding someone responsible.

[20] A different case might be one where someone forms a robust judgment of blameworthiness—that Neal deserves blame, for example—but where the person making the judgment has no inclination (because of concerns of standing, say, or perhaps just expedience) to express blaming reactions. Although I think there is room to disagree, I still find the present regimentation the most appealing. That is, in this case, the agent making the robust judgment of blameworthiness holds Neal responsible; he just does so in a way that does not involve expression of the typical blaming reactions. I say more about the blaming reactions in the next section.

further commitment on the part of the adjudicating agent. In the robust case, the adjudicating agent is committed to the deservingness of praise, blame, or other characteristic interpersonal reactions. Between these two ways of blaming, however, only the last counts as an instance of holding responsible.

E. Blame 2: blaming reactions

In the section prior to this one, I focused on blame as a kind of judgment, or as a set of broadly cognitive commitments. If we focus on just the cognitive aspect of blaming, we run the risk of presenting a pallid picture of responsibility, drained of its characteristic affect.[21] After all, it seems that we can hold someone responsible simply by experiencing a characteristic attitude of interpersonal reaction. Indeed, this might be the usual case. So, it seems that the experience or operation of this reaction constitutes a second sense of blame: blame not as a judgment-like attitude but as a kind of emotion-laden reaction we can identify with blam*ing*.

Blame in this second (blaming) sense typically encompasses two things: (1) what P. F. Strawson called "the reactive attitudes," that is, attitudes of gratitude, resentment, indignation, and the like; and (2) expressions of these attitudes in the form of characteristic behavior, such as verbal condemnation, calls for censure or shame, and more common forms of reaction such as avoidance, emotional distance, or retractions of interpersonal warmth. Both (1) and (2) are what I will call *blaming reactions*.

Judgments of blameworthiness and blaming reactions stand in a complicated relationship to one another. Sometimes, we draw the conclusion that

---

[21] This is an objection that Jay Wallace has made against Scanlon's recent account of blame, on which blaming is a change in the way an agent regards his or her relationship with another agent. See, respectively, R. Jay Wallace, "Dispassionate Opprobrium: On Blame and the Reactive Sentiments," in *Reasons and Recognition: Essays on the Philosophy of T. M. Scanlon*, ed. R. Jay Wallace et al. (New York: Oxford University Press, 2011); Scanlon, *Moral Dimensions: Permissibility, Meaning, Blame*. The force of this criticism turns on a complex issue about how best to understand Scanlon's intriguing account, apart from how Scanlon himself presents the account. For example, we could think of it as characterizing an underappreciated but distinct notion of blame, separate from the notion that Wallace (and, I think, most of the responsibility literature) is concerned. Alternately, we could regard it as a competitor account of the same notion of blame at stake in Wallace's work. I am inclined to think that it is plausible that there are various notions of blame that can be systematized in distinct ways, each of which may have imperfectly overlapping explanatory scope. So, I think, it is an open question which systematization best serves our interests and why. However, the notion of blame with which I am concerned and the systematization I provide does take the affect-laden (or at least, affect-disposed) aspect of blame as central to (1) how we (at least right now) engage in blaming, and (2) some forms of holding responsible.

someone is blameworthy because we experience blame reactions towards that person. Other times, the blame reactions follow (sometimes slowly, sometimes swiftly) from judgments of blameworthiness. Here though, we should not *under*intellectualize the facts. There is a direction of normative dependence here, with blaming reactions depending for their license on an assumption of a warrant for a blaming judgment. Unless one regards the target as accountable, or as a responsible agent, then the reactive attitudes are out of place. One can be in error about whether there is such a warrant. And, one can discover this after the fact, when one experiences the reactive emotions and follows them back to their initially presumed, but upon reflection, implausible assessment of the agent in question. My anger at being excluded from a mezcal tasting party hosted by a good friend evaporates when I learn that it was my spam filter that stymied the delivery of the invitation.

There is, then, an interconnectedness of cognition and affect. When one forms a robust judgment of blameworthiness, in the normal case this judgment is coupled with the experience of the reactive attitudes. And, when one experiences the reactive attitudes, the appropriateness of doing so depends on an assumption of responsible agency. In both cases holding responsible significantly depends on a conviction of the agent being responsible. In the absence of the blamer's conviction that the target is a responsible agent, the blamer cannot be said to genuinely hold the blamed to be responsible. So, the second sense of blame turns out to be connected to the first.

At this point, it may have occurred to the reader to wonder whether it is only in the case of blameworthiness, and not responsible agency, that questions of desert arise. Desert can arise in the context of considering responsible agency, on at least on one reading of desert. That is, we might ask whether there is anything an agent deserves in virtue of the bare fact of being a responsible agent. In asking this, though, I think we are asking about something different than the sense of desert discussed above. We are asking about something like the kind of characteristic regard or respect owed to responsible agents. Here, the notion of desert is distinct, decoupled from moral praise or blame (except, perhaps, indirectly). On the notion with which I am concerned, paradigmatically one has to have *done* something with a moral valence to deserve praise or blame. Normal agents engaged in activities with no moral valence are not obviously deserving of moral praise and blame for those morally neutral acts.

What this suggests is that there may be a notion of desert that can arise in the context of reflections about responsible agents as such, distinct from the sort that is central to praise, blame, and the business of holding one another morally responsible. However, it does so in a manner distinct in content and significance from the notion of desert that arises in the context of assessments of blameworthiness.

6. Realism, relativism, and quietism

One could think that any adequate theory of moral responsibility must somehow reflect the idea that there can be a fact of the matter about whether someone is morally responsible for some action or outcome.[22] One motivation for it seems to be this: it is very natural to speak of it being *true* that someone is morally responsible, and that there are *facts of the matter* about whether someone deserves blame. If any bit of moral language presents itself as truth-functional, responsibility talk does.[23] It was in anticipation of these thoughts that I noted above that there is a relatively straightforward way to account for the apparent truth-functional surface structure of responsibility talk.

Consideration of these facets of responsibility talk may fuel the thought that realism about responsibility is an important aspect of the structure and logic of the responsibility system. If so, then it ought to be a part of any revisionist account, or if not, it should explicitly be counted among the revisionist elements of the account.

I disagree.

---

[22] Richard Double was perhaps the first to note how widespread this assumption was, and the role it seems to play in structuring philosophical disputes about free will. See Richard Double, *The Non-Reality of Free Will* (New York: Oxford University Press, 1991); Richard Double, *Metaphilosophy and Free Will* (New York: Oxford University Press, 1996).

[23] Defenses of broadly non-cognitivist accounts of responsibility tend to elicit complaints precisely because they do not allow for a natural way to allow for the apparent truth-functionality of responsibility talk. Reactions to P. F. Strawson's work on this front are indicative. See Daniel Dennett, *Elbow Room* (Cambridge, MA: MIT Press, 1984); Wallace, *Responsibility and the Moral Sentiments*; Watson, "Responsibility and the Limits of Evil."; Wolf, "The Importance of Free Will." For discussion of it, see Vargas, "Responsibility and the Aims of Theory: Strawson and Revisionism."

These matters are obviously entwined with a wide range of complex metaethical issues. However, if a non-cognitivist account—one where moral language is not truth-functional—is going to carry the day, it will need to be able to explain the apparent cognitivist or truth-functional surface structure of moral language. That is, the non-cognitivist will need to be able to accommodate the fact that ordinary moral language presents *the appearance* of truth-functionality and the predication of moral properties.[24] The fact of a cognitivist surface structure for moral language simply clarifies one of the explanatory burdens for a non-cognitivist analysis of moral language. Whether non-cognitivism has the resources to adequately model this feature without running afoul of other problems remains a contested matter in metaethics.

For my own part, I find it natural to speak of moral responsibility in cognitivist terms. I believe that there are justified practices, attitudes, and statuses that play the characteristic roles we associate with moral responsibility. So, I am inclined to think that there is something that moral responsibility *is* and that this is precisely what we are endeavoring to describe and explain when we offer a theory of it. I take it that all of this constitutes my having roughly realist sympathies.

That said, it is not obvious that any revisionist account needs to reflect such sympathies. In acknowledging the cognitivist surface structure of discourse of responsibility a revisionist need not commit him- or herself to the truth of cognitivism, or the existence of moral properties in any particularly contentious sense. One can accept that a piece of language has a cognitive surface structure, but still insist that the proper analysis will reveal the apparent truth functionality of that bit of language to be merely apparent.

On the general matter of realism about responsibility, consideration of a particular version of denotational revisionism suggests that asking if one is a realist about responsibility is the wrong question. Recall that a denotational revisionist holds that we should re-anchor reference, so that responsibility talk and thought picks out a different thing than before. I've already noted

---

[24] The explanation for why has to do with the Frege/Geach problem of embedding: moral claims are easily embedded in chains of reasoning that are, upon inspection, straightforwardly valid but which cannot be so if the meaning of the same moral predicates is both emotive and stable across occurrences in the premises of the valid argument. For discussion, see Mark van Roojen, "Moral Cognitivism vs. Non-Cognitivism" <http://plato.stanford.edu/archives/fall2009/entries/moral-cognitivism/> accessed July 19, 2010.

that one way to end up with such a view is to think that nothing satisfies our pre-revised notion of responsibility, but that there is a better (and existent!) thing we can refer to that is sufficiently close in structure and what it justifies so as to merit the name.[25] One might think of this as a kind of eliminativism coupled with revisionism: eliminativism about the old referent, connotational revision to a new referent, with the claim of revision getting licensed by the preservation of the majority of old conceptual and linguistic roles across the revision.

Would the proponent of the picture I just sketched be a realist or not? The view holds that there is something that merits the name, but it does not pick out the property that we customarily picked out, even though it does the conceptual work characteristic of the old notion. What such a possibility suggests is that questions about realism or anti-realism about responsibility are typically too coarse-grained to give us any informative conclusion. Rather than trying to answer the "is it realism?" question, we are better off focusing on more fine-grained questions about successful reference, truth-functionality of a given bit of discourse, licensed inferences, and the status of imputed properties.

On the account I offer, it is plausible to think that talk of responsibility successfully refers, that the conditions I offer constitute at least a partial statement of the truth conditions, and the justification I offer properly counts as part of the story about what licenses inferences about responsibility. I see no reason to think such commitments will be a part of all revisionist accounts.

The present position might give rise to a distinct metaethical concern about how far the account travels. Even if responsibility talk refers in such a way that it makes sense to speak of responsibility's truth conditions and the like, these remarks hardly settle the question of whether responsibility is properly thought of as only locally true (like, say, claims about the side of the road on which one should drive) or more universally true (like, say, how we ordinarily talk about the impermissibility of murdering innocents).

Indeed, we might imagine two objections against any position pretending to offer truth conditions for the property of moral responsibility. The first is

---

[25] Another way to end up a denotational revisionist: think there is some thing that better does the work of the concept than the kind of thing we have been referring to, and to call for revision in that direction.

a global version of the argument from disagreement. On this objection, the motivating thought is that across the planet there are diverse intuitions about free will and moral responsibility. So, for example, it may turn out that close study of the anthropological record reveals that there are societies in which attributions of responsibility make no appeal to anything like a control or freedom condition. Assume we can agree that such diverse practices can count as responsibility practices. If so, then the global version of the argument from disagreement maintains that what explains this fact is not that there is some independent property of moral responsibility that we are tracking. Rather, it is simply local ways of organizing normative practices.[26]

A second, local version of the argument restricts itself to the data I have already employed: even amongst ourselves—again, roughly Anglophone populations in NATO countries and their allies—there is disagreement about whether, for example, moral responsibility requires incompatibilist alternative possibilities. In light of this, we should think there are simply different concepts at work masquerading under the same term "moral responsibility." If these different concepts reflect different forms of life, at best we should expect to get a relativistic account of moral responsibility, one indexed to subpopulations.

Although these strike me as concerns worth having, I do not think either gives us reason to abandon the project as I have thus far characterized it. Start with the local version of the argument from disagreement. Here, I am completely unpersuaded that the best we can hope for is a kind of relativistic standoff between subpopulations of compatibilists and incompatibilists (and between source theorists and leeway theorists, and between reductionists and anti-reductionists, and...). Some of the considerations that arose in thinking about the work of the concept and the justification of the practices can do work here. Notice that even if the configuration of intuitions differs internal to local subpopulations, the work of the concept (regulating

---

[26] I take it that this is the position taken in Tamler Sommers, *Relative Justice* (Princeton, NJ: Princeton University Press, 2011). There is a growing literature in psychology and experimental philosophy about the idiosyncratic nature of the intuitions of affluent, well-educated Westerners. For some examples, see Joseph Henrich et al., "The Weirdest People in the World?," *Behavioral and Brain Sciences* 32, nos 2–3 (2010): 1–23; Sarkissian et al., "Is Belief in Free Will a Cultural Universal?"; E. Machery et al., "Semantics, Cross-Cultural Style," *Cognition* 92 (2004): B1–B12; Jonathan M. Weinberg et al., "Normativity and Epistemic Intuition," *Philosophical Topics* 29 (2001): 429–60.

differential moralized praise and blame) is plausibly consistent across many populations. And, inasmuch as this concept helps us coordinate our shared normative practices, there is pressure to find a way to organize, unify, and render coherent the logic of those practices in a prescriptive account of responsibility. As long as large percentages of us have incompatibilist commitments, the fact of our local social interconnectedness gives us some reason for rejecting a relativist prescriptive account of responsibility— quite apart from whether there is some independently good reason to favor realism about moral responsibility.

Matters are more complicated when we consider the global version of the argument from disagreement, for the presumption of our lives being interconnected to a sufficiently high degree, in ways that are governed by shared cooperative norms, does not hold. Given conceptual fragmentation across different communities of "us," revisionists have a number of options.

First, we theorists of responsibility can accept relativism in this more global form. That is, we might simply accept there is a fundamental degree of conceptual fragmentation across societies or groups of people, and that what normative pressures there are for internally coherent and plausible accounts of responsibility will be indexed to those societies and the forms of life they give rise to.[27]

Second, we could accept a kind of quietism about moral responsibility. That is, we might insist that we have reason do our own normative housekeeping, repairing our own practices and judgments, but we can remain agnostic on whether some objectivist, agent-independent realism about responsibility is true, and whether our favored local systematization of the concept tracks that objective fact.

Third, we might argue—as many realists of other stripes have done—that the fact of global disagreement about moral responsibility is no evidence whatsoever that there is no fact of the matter. On this view, the various considerations brought to bear in favor of the proposed account of responsibility just are reasons for thinking that it is an account of the true nature of moral responsibility. There will, of course, be disagreement about this in much the same way that there is ongoing disagreement about a range of true

---

[27] I have already acknowledged that the present account makes no pretense to accommodating more than broadly Western features of our thinking about responsibility. So, I wouldn't be terribly surprised if there were societies that lacked convictions that freedom was required for moral responsibility, much less specifically libertarian freedom.

accounts. However, the truth is notoriously consistent with disagreement and this may be especially so in the case of moral notions.

Adopting any of these positions would bring varied benefits and costs. I take it that all are available to revisionists of different stripes. For my part, I am inclined to embrace quietism. I see no reason to pick among the global relativist and robust responsibility realist positions on these matters. We can get on with the business of improving our understanding of moral responsibility regardless of whether what is understood turns out to be indexed only to us or to the world at large. If push comes to shove, we can retreat to one of the other positions.

7. The limited ethics approach

In this section I address two issues connected to wider issues in normative philosophy: (1) the extent to which the account legitimately relies on other normative notions, notions not impugned by the rejection of the folk notion of responsibility; and (2) the degree of entanglement between those notions and larger commitments to a theory of normative ethics.

The position I take is one that employs a range of widely employed normative notions, but emphasizes near-neutrality about any particular theory of normative ethics. I'll start with the first issue, the reliance on normative notions.

Consider a view on which the construction of a theory of responsibility ought to proceed without appeal to robustly normative notions. The most obvious way to do this would be to adopt a reductive approach, on which the normative features of moral responsibility would be analyzed in terms of non-normative phenomena or properties. This would be a *no normative* approach—*no nomo*, as it were. Such an approach would leave us with the demanding task of accounting for the normative foundations of moral responsibility without recourse to any normative notions.

There are a variety of reasons we might wish to avoid undertaking construction of a theory of responsibility under this constraint. For example, one might suspect we cannot adequately account for the normative foundations of moral responsibility without appeal to any normative notions whatsoever (or, in less drastic form, without appeal to specifically moral notions). Nevertheless, a proponent might think that the no nomo approach makes theorizing about responsibility a task that neatly parallels—perhaps even constituting a proper part of—familiar metaethical projects that seek to provide an analysis or reduction of normative vocabulary to non-normative notions.

The success of such a project would have obvious virtues. However, the project is a notoriously difficult one to pull off. Even bracketing the matter of whether it is desirable to give such accounts, it strikes me as unnecessary to do so. What is a problem for any account is no special problem for a theory of moral responsibility. That is, in accounting for our various moral notions, we will presumably be pulled in the direction of employing concepts and vocabulary that—normative or not—will presume some or another foundation for that vocabulary.

Unless we have reason to suppose that a given account is positing some peculiar element of agency or some unusual normative property, there is no special explanatory burden that rightly attaches to the account. We have seen one place where this can happen: libertarian conceptions of agency. And, of course, it remains an open question whether there are further cases where there is some unusual property invoked by the proposed account. However, from the standpoint of assaying our methodological options, there does not seem to be any special reason to think that we cannot appeal to normative notions in our account of moral responsibility.

We could, of course, invoke global skepticism about normative notions, or perhaps skepticism about just moral notions. That would be a much bigger fish to fry. If we are going to fry it, the burden of doing so does not plausibly fall on the responsibility theorist. So, while it might be appealing to some were we to have a non-normative, reductionist account of moral responsibility, it does not appear *necessary* for a plausible (enough) account of moral responsibility.

Once we allow that moral notions can have a role to play in the construction of a theory of responsibility, there are a variety of configurations that role might take on. Consider an account on which a theory of responsibility is permitted to invoke the full complement of normative notions afforded to us by one's favorite account of normative ethics, or one's theory of those volitional, characterological, or actional features in virtue of which things (states, events, actions, agents) are ethically right or wrong. This possibility might give rise to a very specific view about the

128 BUILDING BLOCKS

methodological relationship of responsibility to normative ethics. On the view I have in mind, we are not only permitted to, but we *ought* to take as prior some specific normative ethical theory, extending that theory to account for moral responsibility. Call such an approach an *ethics partisan* approach to the theory of moral responsibility. What makes an ethics partisan approach distinctive is that it insists on the methodological priority of normative ethics to the theory of moral responsibility.

Accounts of responsibility like Moritz Schlick's or J. J. C. Smart's, i.e., classical consequentialist accounts of responsibility, constitute examples of this approach.[28] These are accounts on which one begins with an antecedent commitment to some or another consequentialist theory of normative ethics, and then proceeds to construct a theory of responsibility informed by that antecedent commitment.

Here's a worry about ethics partisan approaches. In starting from antecedent commitments to a particular theory of normative ethics, one too easily runs the risk of deforming the distinctive normative and conceptual structure of moral responsibility, in a rush to apply the particular resources of one's favored theory of ethics.[29] Perhaps ethics partisan approaches prove to be too ideological to adequately reflect the phenomena as we find them. If so, this would be an especially significant cost in the context of revisionist theorizing. After all, the revisionist is under special pressure to constrain departures from the familiar notion of responsibility, lest he or she be accused of avoiding what is at stake in these debates.

Although revisionist accounts might go any number of ways, I will adopt what I call a *limited ethics* approach. The operative idea here is that we account for the foundations of the responsibility system at least partly in terms of moral notions, but without appealing to a particular antecedent theory of normative ethics. On this approach, we are permitted to appeal to widely shared moral notions, patterns of reasoning, and approaches to

[28] Moritz Schlick, *The Problems of Ethics*, trans. D. Rynin (New York: Prentice Hall, 1939); Smart, "Free Will, Praise, and Blame."

[29] The extent to which contemporary accounts of responsibility proceed in an ethics partisan way is unclear. My sense is that the approach is not particularly prominent in the recent literature, and that when philosophers have worn their commitments to some or another normative ethical theory on their sleeve, there tends to be comparatively little uptake of that work internal to the subfield concerned with free will and moral responsibility.

justification that can be countenanced under a range of plausible theories of ethics.

It may be helpful to consider an example. Think about the notion of a moral consideration. On most theories of normative ethics, there is sense to be made of the idea that there are considerations with moral significance, considerations that ordinarily have some appropriate role to play in an agent's deliberations about what to do. What individual theories tend to disagree about is the nature of such considerations, and what it is that makes those considerations distinctively moral. On a limited ethics approach, employment of the notion of a moral consideration does not require taking a stand on these more global questions. It is enough that moral considerations are countenanced by a wide range of theories of ethics and practical reason.

The limited ethics approach suggests (but does not require) the possibility of a distinctive way of thinking about the relationship of responsibility to normative ethics. As I framed the presuppositions behind the ethics partisan approach, the idea was that a theory of moral responsibility is either a subset, or otherwise dependent on, the proper view of normative ethics. However, one might accept that moral responsibility, as a moral notion, is in the domain of normative ethics without accepting that the correct *theory* of moral responsibility is interestingly dependent on the true theory of normative ethics.

Here is the idea: it might turn out that moral responsibility has its own autonomous normative structure, a structure that will need to be integrated with a larger theory of normative ethics but that nevertheless remains distinctive and badly apprehended if we approach it in the top-down manner suggested by starting with normative ethics. Something like this was already suggested by the idea that on the present methodological approach we take the various distinctions internal to moral responsibility as a given, rejecting pictures that presume that wholesale replacement of those distinctions is the order of the day.

Although I am neutral on the matter, one could even turn on its head the ethics partisan suggestion that theories of normative ethics constrain our theories of moral responsibility. Rather than taking a "top-down" approach, one that treats moral responsibility as methodologically secondary to normative ethics, one might instead regard moral responsibility as methodologically prior to normative ethics, influencing which theories of normative ethics we judge as better and worse. Such a view would be compatible with the conclusion that at the end of theorizing, the theory of moral responsibility might be viewed as part of our larger theory of normative ethics.

There is a further reason for adopting a limited ethics approach over an ethics partisan approach. It is hardly news that there is widespread yet reasonable disagreement about substantive issues in philosophical ethics. In the absence of such consensus, a limited ethics account offers the possibility for ongoing improvement of our understanding of responsibility even if there is no consensus about the best approach to normative ethics. Moreover, it promises to do so in a way that is sensitive to this fact of disagreement, as it relies only on normative notions that have widespread currency among plausible approaches to normative ethics.

It goes almost without saying that revisionist accounts are not faced with a stark choice between limited ethics and ethics partisan approaches to moral responsibility. Plausibly, the convictions of individual theorists will appeal to will be a combination of those that are widely countenanced on any theory of ethics and those that reflect that theorist's more considered commitments on some specific normative matters. For my account, however, a limited ethics approach is operative.[30]

8. Two questions

I intend to provisionally accept the apparent general internal structure of the responsibility system as it stands, including the overall pattern of inferences from judgments of responsibility, the ordinary pattern of psychological reactions, and the familiar range of social practices. A failure to retain the bulk of these characteristic statuses and patterns of inference would make it less plausible to claim, as I do, that my proposed revisionist prescription constitutes an account of moral responsibility. Thus, the guiding interest

---

[30] Here's a bet: if we are cognizant of different possible presumptions of the relationship of normative ethics and the theory of moral responsibility this will help us to recognize when commitments to substantive normative ethical theories (implicitly) play a role in theorizing about moral responsibility. For example, we might learn that Dana offers an account of responsibility that proceeds from an antecedent commitment to Kantian ethics, that Shaun offers a no-nomo account, and Michael offers a limited ethics account. If so, one might worry that the chance of cross-talk in such contexts will be high, unless we identify these implicit views about normative ethics.

for any systematic revisionist account responsive to the concerns in chapters 1–3, is to establish whether or not the logic and structure of the responsibility system can be explained and suitably grounded, independent of a commitment to libertarianism.

It is conceivable that someone could pursue systematic revisionism in a less conservative mode. One could, for example, proceed on the supposition that the entire framework of the responsibility is to be overturned, not because of concerns about the involved picture of agency but because one independently regards as problematic the framework of responsibility statuses and judgments ("is responsible," "deserves blame").[31]

Radical replacement can be fine if you have powerful—really powerful—independent considerations fueling the theory. However, we shouldn't underestimate what is needed to justify our walking away from comparatively fundamental aspects of our shared normative discourse. I am inclined to think that there are no such considerations in play, at least pending the results of serious engagement with a more conservative approach to revisionism about responsibility.

So here, finally, are the questions that will shape Part II of this book. The first question is this: *Is there anything that would, in general, justify our participation in practices of moral praising and blaming?* If there is, we may be licensed in our ongoing participation in those practices. The second question is this: *Can we explain our patterns of responsibility assessment in ways that make it plausible that they are tracking normatively relevant features of agents and the world?*

In addressing the second question, we are looking for a connection between the normative status of the practice (i.e., whether there is justification sufficient for sustaining such practices), normatively significant features of agents, and our ordinary patterns of responsibility-characteristic inferences and judgments. That is, we want the bulk of our ordinary practices, attitudes, and judgments concerning moral responsibility to be

---

[31] Consider what a global consequentialist might say about the responsibility system. Global consequentialism is the view that *everything* is to be assessed in terms of its consequences for value. On such a view, the question of whether someone deserves blame would be severed from the question of whether the agent is the right sort of agent to be subject to praise and blame. Instead, all questions about responsibility-characteristic practices would be answered entirely in terms of whether their enactment has the correct consequences for whatever the target value(s) turns out to be. So, a global consequentialist's approach to the responsibility system would constitute a gross framework replacement, one that opts for a wholesale jettisoning of the conceptual or analytic relations distinctive of moral responsibility.

appropriately connected to both the general justification for engaging in such things and to particular facts about agents. Those facts need to help make sense of the idea that people can be praiseworthy and blameworthy, that it is possible that they *deserve* to be blamed, and that they can be held responsible. In the absence of the appropriate normative ties, the logic of the responsibility system would lack the normative force we ordinarily associate with it.

I've claimed that in constructing a prescriptive, revisionist account of moral responsibility we face a question external to the responsibility system (about the general justification of those practices) and a question about the internal structure of that system (about the grounding of particular statuses and judgments). Here is why I think it is important to try to answer both of these questions.

Imagine that we have an answer to the justification question, but no explanation of how assessments internal to those practices reflect the normative status of our ordinary practices, statuses, and judgments. If so, then we face the following worry: we might be able to justify holding one another responsible, but this might amount to little more than a reason to keep up an illusion. That is, a critic could object that all that has been shown is that we have a justification to *act as though* people are responsible. In contrast, if we can explain both the general justification of the practice and the normative structure of judgments internal to it, we thereby make it plausible to think the account is indeed describing the nature of moral responsibility—or, at any rate, something with comparable credentials.

One might still object that answering the first question—about the justification of the system as a whole—is superfluous once we have answered the second question by, for example, demonstrating that the ordinary statuses, judgments, and so on are individually well grounded. After all, we might be able to provide an account of how our assessments track some normatively relevant feature of agents and the world, without needing to say anything about the justification for praising and blaming practices as a whole.

I agree that the justification question is unlikely to be answered in complete independence of some or another provisional commitments about at least some aspects internal to the responsibility system. However, consideration of the general justification question gives us some insight into the internal logic of the responsibility system. This idea plays an important role in Part II, to which we now turn.

PART II
A Theory of Moral Responsibility

5

The Primacy of Reasons

1. The story thus far

The core argument from Part I can be summarized thusly:

(1) Libertarian accounts are not naturalistically plausible.
(2) Therefore, we should accept responsibility nihilism or revisionism.
(3) Considerations favoring philosophically conservative approaches favor revisionism.
(4) So, we should attempt to construct a revisionist theory.

Part II attempts to make good on the conclusion of that argument.

The present chapter is concerned with reasons for selecting what I call a Reasons account. Subsequent chapters go on to develop a Reasons account in the context of the ideas of moral influence, circumstantialism, and social self-governance as a way of delivering a systematic revisionist account of moral responsibility.

2. Old beginnings

Most compatibilist accounts of responsibility (and, arguably some incompatibilist accounts) begin from either of two prominent points of departure: the idea that an agent must have some characterological or expressive connection to the action, or alternately, the idea that an agent must be responsive to reasons in some suitable sense.[1] Indeed, we might even

---

[1] In what follows I will bracket what is arguably a third alternative in debates about responsibility—"attributionist" accounts of the sort given in T. M. Scanlon, *What We Owe to Each Other* (Cambridge, MA: Belknap Press of Harvard University Press, 1998); Angela Smith, "Responsibility for Attitudes: Activity and Passivity in Mental Life," *Ethics* 115 (2005): 236–71.

understand much of the past couple of decades of philosophical work on moral responsibility as concerned with investigating which of these two approaches offers a superior account of moral responsibility.

In this chapter, I will embrace a general conception of responsible agency as concerned with responsiveness to reasons, as opposed to the character-ological expressiveness approach. That said, at this point the argument is only concerned with motivating the general approach. In chapter 7, I will return to the matter of characterizing how the capacity to recognize and suitably respond to reasons (or moral considerations, on my account) constitutes responsible agency. In the present chapter, the aim is more modest: it is to motivate the general approach, saying something about the appeal of it and its advantages over the characterological approach.[2]

One theme that emerges in this chapter is that the relationship between the two familiar approaches to responsibility is much more complicated than is ordinarily assumed. I argue that there are reasons to think that what is attractive about the characterological approach turns out to be a manifest-ation of the features of the other view, and if not, that there is nevertheless reason to think at least some characterological approaches have misidenti-fied the features of agency relevant to moral responsibility. I label the resulting view *the primacy of reasons*.

To be sure, there are any number of places we can start the construction of a substantive theory of moral responsibility, and the present approach, which begins with a theory of responsible agency, is only one. However, I begin here for two reasons. First, the ideas developed in the present chapter provide some of the raw materials that will be crucial to the account of the justification of our practices of responsibility that I offer in the next chapter. Second, reflection on these matters provides a natural way to connect my account with familiar concerns that have governed conven-tional compatibilist accounts. Although I aspire to provide a systematically revisionist approach, this is one place where there are benefits from making use of familiar ideas developed in conventional compatibilist contexts. At the very least, it helps to situate my account with respect to some important ideas in this domain.

---

[2] One might wonder about mixed views, which emphasize both responding to reasons and char-acterological expression. I'm presuming that at this stage, parsimony favors adoption of one or the other. If, however, we could show that neither theory is by itself satisfactory, this would presumably favor a mixed approach.

3. Real Selves and Reasons: initial considerations

I began with the idea that there are two competing touchstones for a good deal of theorizing about moral responsibility: the idea that an agent must have some characterological or expressive connection to the action, or alternately, the idea that an agent must be responsive to reasons in some suitable sense. One inspiration for accounts of the former—accounts that emphasize a characterological or expressive connection between agent and action—is the idea that it can only make sense to hold someone responsible if the action in some way expresses a deep fact about the particular agent.

Contemporary versions have variously emphasized that the agent needs to "identify" with the motives that lead to the act, or the act has to be expressive of a "Real Self," or expressive of the agent's values, or the action has to be an expression of the regard in which the agent holds others.[3] Following the parlance given to us by Susan Wolf, I will call such accounts Real Self views, or RS views.[4] The label is imperfect, for it is not obvious that all accounts that appeal to a condition of identification or self-expression need be committed to the existence of a "real self" in any substantive way. In this context it is nevertheless a serviceable misnomer, because it emphasizes the idea of some special or privileged subset of psychological states in relation to which the agent's actions must stand for there to be responsibility.

If an RS account emphasizes that the mark of responsible agency is the presence of psychological structures that, roughly, express some privileged view of the agent, the mark of its alternative—*a Reasons account*—is the presence of a particular power to respond to the world. On this latter approach, the agential contribution to responsibility is a power to respond to the reasons that arise from the world or the agent's psychology's inter-

---

[3] Philosophers have given various treatments of what it means to identify with the motives with which one acts, e.g., to be satisfied with the motivating desires, to view those desires as expressing one's true self or true values, and so on. Variants of this picture, broadly construed, have been offered in David Hume, *A Treatise of Human Nature*, trans. L. A. Selby-Bigge, and P. H. Nidditch (2nd edn.) (New York: Oxford University Press, 1978); Harry Frankfurt, "Freedom of the Will and the Concept of a Person," *Journal of Philosophy* 68, no. 1 (1971): 5–20; Gary Watson, "Free Agency," *Journal of Philosophy* 72, no. 8 (1975): 205–20; Gerald Dworkin, *The Theory and Practice of Autonomy* (New York: Cambridge University Press, 1988); Michael E. Bratman, "Identification, Decision, and Treating as a Reason," *Philosophical Topics* 24, no. 2 (1996): 1–18.

[4] Susan Wolf, *Freedom Within Reason* (New York: Oxford University Press, 1990).

action with the world. On this approach, what makes responsible agency distinctive is that the agent's response to the world is structured by reasons in a particular way. It is not the projection of the agent's identity or convictions that makes action responsible but rather how the agent's actions express (or don't) due sensitivity to reasons.[5]

Characterized in this way, the purported difference between RS accounts and Reasons accounts may seem like a matter of labeling, rather than a substantive disagreement among distinct parties. If the manner in which one responds to reasons just is a way of expressing one's character, commitments, or values, then the difference evaporates. Similarly, if one's character, commitments, and values say something about what the agent regards as reasons-giving, these approaches may seem to come to the same thing. Even if RS views and Reasons accounts can claim to have different points of theoretical departure, those departure points are surely not far apart.

4. Motivating a Reasons account

Although it might seem that these accounts come to the same thing, there are some differences in apparent motivations and implications that emerge if we focus on the appeal of Reasons accounts.

Although it is doubtful that there is any single idea that has drawn philosophers to Reasons accounts, there are at least four ideas that might be thought to explain their appeal.

One reason for embracing a Reasons account derives from the thought that in calling one another to account, in (especially) blaming one another and in judging that someone is responsible, we are suggesting that the evaluated agent had a reason to do otherwise. One might think that the mere having of alternative possibilities, even on the most metaphysically demanding conception of these things, is of little use or interest in and of itself. It is a condition on the possibility of an alternative *being relevant to the agent* that there be a reason in favor of it. Moreover, this seems true for both

---

[5] I have in mind views of the sort expressed in, for example, Wolf, *Freedom Within Reason*; Wallace, *Responsibility and the Moral Sentiments*; Fischer and Ravizza, *Responsibility and Control: A Theory of Moral Responsibility*; Nomy Arpaly, *Unprincipled Virtue: An Inquiry into Moral Agency* (New York: Oxford University Press, 2003); Dana Nelkin, "Responsibility and Rational Abilities: Defending an Asymmetrical View," *Pacific Philosophical Quarterly* 89 (2008): 497–515.

the purposes of calling someone to account, and for an agent trying to decide what to do. In the absence of the ability to discern or act on a discerned reason in favor of that possibility, it seems to be something of an error or confusion to blame the agent for failing to have acted on that alternative (unless, perhaps, the agent knowingly undermined or destroyed his or her reasons–responsive capacity).

This first reason is connected to a second. A paradigmatic feature of holding one another responsible is the thought that the critic has a reason or justification for criticism, and that the only way to escape such criticism is for the target to have some suitable explanation of the bit of behavior that is criticized. The act of calling one another (and sometimes, ourselves) to account appears to presume a capacity to offer and exchange in reasons-giving. Where such reasoning capacities are occurrently absent, it does not seem possible to call an agent to account in a way characteristic of ordinary responsibility practices. Where those capacities *were* absent, it seems inappropriate to call the agent to account for those actions.

Third, Reasons accounts provide us with a comparatively straightforward account of our apparent uniqueness in having free will and being morally responsible. To the extent to which we are responsive to a sufficiently wide class of reasons in general, or perhaps more plausibly, to a special class of considerations, this form of agency stands out against the fabric of the universe. Our possession of this capacity constitutes a particularly notable and rare form of agency.[6]

Fourth and finally, Reasons accounts appear to cohere with the bulk of ordinary judgments about cases (e.g., why young children are treated differently than normal adults, why cognitive and affective defects seem to undermine responsibility, why manipulation that disrupts people's rational abilities seems troublesome, etc.). So, there is a "fit" with the data of ordinary practices and judgments.

On this latter point, the proponent of any Real Self account will surely insist that his or her account is at least as well suited to capture the range of phenomena at stake. RS theorists can plausibly argue that if their accounts

---

[6] I should note that, as far as I can make out, there is a currently uncontested consensus about the possibility of reasons sensitivity even under determinism. Such a view is held by, for example, Dennett, *Elbow Room*; Fischer and Ravizza, *Responsibility and Control: A Theory of Moral Responsibility*; Wolf, *Freedom Within Reason*; Wallace, *Responsibility and the Moral Sentiments*; Pereboom, *Living Without Free Will*; Kane, *The Significance of Free Will*.

did not cohere with a suitably large class of judgments about ordinary cases, these accounts would have no widespread appeal. Since such accounts do have wide appeal, this is reason to think that RS accounts can (and at least sometimes do) capture our intuitions sufficiently well.

Similarly, it seems that RS views can make good sense of the business of calling one another to account. The grounds for calling the agent to account is to be understood as tied to something like the agent's disclosure of his or her agency in action. Roughly, we are to morally evaluate what is disclosed. On this account, the importance of moral responsibility arises because particular forms of agency—complex agents like us, whatever that turns out to mean—have moral significance. The why and the how will vary across RS theories, but a natural way to understand this view is as an extension of the idea that moralized evaluation just is evaluation of an agent, and praiseworthiness and blameworthiness are, roughly, assessments of the moral significance of that person writ in action. Calling an agent to account invites the agent to defend his or her person as it was writ in action.

Matters are more complicated when we consider whether RS accounts have natural analogs to Reasons views for accommodating the idea that agents must be able to do otherwise. For starters, it is less obvious that the notion of being able to do otherwise has an especially natural home in an RS account. It is not that it cannot be paired with such an account. Surely, it can. Rather, the thought is just that there is no obvious need to appeal to such a notion on an RS account, even in an etiolated way, at least as compared to Reasons accounts.[7] Moreover, if one were suspicious about such demands, RS accounts will seem especially appealing precisely because they provide the form of an explanation for why such possibilities are irrelevant to moral responsibility.

According to the RS view, in assessing responsibility, we are tracking features of the Real Self, whatever that comes to. Now we *could* invoke some conception of alternative possibilities as partly constitutive of that Real Self. However, it is not obvious that we need to do so. After all, one of the main ideas behind an RS view is the thought that in assessments of moral responsibility we are evaluating the moral quality of the agent as expressed

---

[7] To be sure, a Reasons account need not appeal to alternative possibilities. In the present context, though, where we are attempting to construct a revisionist account that does minimal violence to ordinary convictions, allowing some room for alternative possibilities is a plus.

in action. If for some reason the agent's character or quality is not expressed in the action (for example, when the agent is coerced), it is the disruption of that expression that explains the absence of responsibility. The presence or absence of alternative possibilities has no necessary role in such explanations.

Guided by these thoughts, we might conclude that what the Real Self provides is a privileged stopping point for attributing the source and quality of the act to the agent, irrespective of considerations about whether there were unexercised possibilities available to the agent. Acts that are relevant to responsibility are those that express some privileged feature of the agent, and those that aren't are those that fail to express those features.

If this is right, these considerations suggest an intriguing hypothesis: Part of the appeal of RS accounts is rooted in the ease with which such accounts have resources for making sense of sourcehood intuitions. Correlatively, part of the appeal of Reasons accounts is rooted in the comparative ease with which such accounts have resources for making sense of intuitions about alternative possibilities.[8]

Depending on how one felt about the comparative importance of these notions for responsibility, this might provide some reason for initially favoring one over the other. For the moment, I want to bracket this possibility, for two reasons. First, I am at least in principle willing to countenance both sets of intuitions, but second, I worry that sourcehood commitments are really byproducts of libertarian intuitions that we should seek to avoid in the construction of a systematically revisionist prescriptive account of responsibility. I will return to these issues later, however.[9]

What remains is the question of whether either of these general approaches offers a better provisional starting point for a theory of moral responsibility. In the next section, I suggest some initial reasons for concern about RS accounts.

---

[8] If this is right, it is no accident that Frankfurt's work figures prominently both in the rejection of the Principle of Alternative Possibilities and in the development of RS views—embrace of either will recommend (but not require) the other. Also on this matter, see chapter 5 of Timpe, *Free Will: Sourcehood and Its Alternatives*. As Timpe sees it, at least one paradigmatic Reasons account—Fischer and Ravizza's—is centrally concerned to address sourcehood problems that arise in Frankfurt's account. I think that's right. So, whatever one's starting point, you might yet wish to accommodate the commitments that have their most natural home in accounts of the other sort.

[9] In the Appendix, I grant that there is a sense of origination and action that is plausibly not rooted in lingering libertarian impulses, but I go on to argue that it can be accounted for in a way consistent with the Reasons approach I pursue here.

5. Some worries about RS accounts

Consider a paradigmatic RS account—Harry Frankfurt's early account of moral responsibility.[10] On Frankfurt's account, an agent is responsible for some action if and only if at the time of action the agent had a particular second-order desire—i.e., a desire that the motivating first-order desire be effective in action. Notice that the higher-order desire need not be causally efficacious itself—it could be "along for the ride," so to speak. Its presence or absence might play no causal role in whether the agent acts on some particular first-order desire. So, on Frankfurt's account, a willing addict is morally responsible for a decision to take his drug of choice even if the higher-order desire that one act on the drug-taking desire plays no causal or explanatory role in the taking of the drug.

Frankfurt's account and its subsequent developments have been construed in different ways—as, for example, a picture of autonomy, of free will, of responsible agency, of "strong agency" and so on.[11] Construed as an account of the kind of agency required for moral responsibility, however, the picture in "Freedom of the Will" provides at least three reasons for consternation. First, on Frankfurt's account, all that matters for securing responsibility is the presence of the requisite psychological structure, regardless of its origin. This entails some startlingly counterintuitive possibilities. For example, an agent who has an alien set of values or higher-order desires transplanted by coercive indoctrination, brainwashing, or (currently science fictional) neurological implantation would, it seems, count as straightforwardly responsible for any action subsequent to the implantation. One could bite this bullet, but without some explanation it is obviously a cost to the theory.

Second, no matter how self-identified, a systematically delusional agent who is incapable of knowing any better is hardly a model of responsibility.[12]

---

[10] Frankfurt, "Freedom of the Will and the Concept of a Person." Henceforth: FWCP.

[11] See, for example, some of the varied uses to which Frankfurt's account has been put in James Stacey Taylor, ed., *Personal Autonomy: New Essays on Personal Autonomy and Its Role in Contemporary Moral Philosophy* (New York: Cambridge University Press, 2005). See also Michael E. Bratman, "Autonomy and Hierarchy," *Social Philosophy and Policy* 20, no. 2 (2003): 156–76.

[12] Compare Susan Wolf, "Sanity and the Metaphysics of Responsibility," in *Free Will*, ed. Gary Watson (New York: Oxford, 2003). Wolf uses the notion of "sanity" in an arguably idiosyncratic way, but the general thrust of her argument, as I understand it, is to emphasize how those psychological structures that constitute "real selves" require further supplementation by something akin to a reasons condition.

Yet, on Frankfurt's account it seems that we must say that such an agent is a responsible agent. A natural way to respond to such worries is to appeal to the rationality of the agent's beliefs, or to a connection between agents, norms, and the structure of the world. But if we supplement the account in this way, then it looks less distinctive as an alternative to Reasons accounts.

Thirdly, the account is silent on the matter of why, precisely, it is that second-order desires are the sorts of things that provide a basis for moral responsibility.[13] A second-order desire is still a desire, and the fact of it being of the second order does not seem to, by itself, constitute any reason to regard it as expressing where the agent stands. One way of understanding the criticism is that it is unclear why the fact of where some agent stands, were it tractable in terms of hierarchies of desire, should be the kind of thing in virtue of which moral praise and blame make sense.

In the present context, the force of these criticisms is less clear than they might ordinarily seem, for in the present context we are explicitly willing to entertain counterintuitive accounts. In particular, counterintuitiveness that derives from abandonment of some aspect of folk thinking that is problematic or gratuitous to an adequate prescriptive account of moral responsibility is not particularly problematic.[14] Nevertheless, ongoing commitment to a principle of philosophical conservation gives us some reason to regard counterintuitiveness as a prima facie cost, even if we might yet conclude that the cost is not very high or worth paying for some or another reason.

Nevertheless, it seems that we need some account of why those psychological elements identified by an RS account are sufficient for grounding the appropriateness of praise and blame. In the present context, part of the force of this concern arises out of the thought that any account of responsibility will need to be normatively adequate, which entails (among other things), that the entities postulated have some relevant connection to moral responsibility. One way to appreciate the force of the worry is to consider an appeal to psychological states that are manifestly irrelevant to grounding moral praise and blame. For example, if someone were to argue that it was hierarchies of jealousy, or hierarchies of beliefs, or hierarchies of hunger that

---

[13] This objection was first made in Watson, "Free Agency."

[14] Recall that the goal here is to abandon the incompatibilist elements of folk commitments, and anything that depends on such intuitions that cannot be given some independent license or justification. The hope is that we will discover that libertarian elements are relatively inferentially isolated, or that any connections to other things can be replicated in a different way.

determined the appropriateness of moral responsibility, we would surely demand an explanation of why such things are at all relevant to moral responsibility. In the case of desires, the idea that they have some connection to warranting praise and blame is an old one. Nevertheless, we can and should ask why hierarchies of desires should be the sorts of things that warrant praise and blame.

There are a number of things the Real Self theorist might say in the face of this challenge.[15] I've suggested one already: these features mark out what it is for the agent's "real" or privileged self to be expressed in action. We might worry, though, that this simply forestalls the basic question. After all, *why* should the expressions of those particular features of agency count as the ones that license praise and blame? We might agree that in assessing blameworthiness and praiseworthiness we are evaluating some fact about the agent, but the question is why those features of agency identified by the account, whatever they turn out to be, should be the ones that generate the morally loaded evaluation of the agent in terms of praise and blame. After all, why couldn't it be any of those other features of agency, not identified with the RS, which constitute the praise- and blame-engendering features of agency expressed in action?

Here is one form of a response available to the RS theorist. Perhaps the reason why higher-order capacities are significant for moral responsibility is because they reflect some *further* fact about the agent, and in virtue of that further fact, praise and blame come to make sense. Frankfurt suggests something very much like this in the context of considering whether creatures other than humans might count as having higher-order desires. He writes, "No animal other than man, however, appears to have the capacity for reflective self-evaluation that is manifested in the formation of second-order desires" (12).

If I understand Frankfurt rightly, his claim is that there is a comparatively unusual capacity required before one can have second-order desires, some-

---

[15] Indeed, there is more that Frankfurt went on to say. But in those papers that followed FWCP, the machinery of desiderative hierarchies was re-purposed to account for other agential phenomena (identification, whole-heartedness, and so on) and the matter of responsibility disappeared. In a conversation I had with Frankfurt in 1999, he said that his views about the requirements for moral responsibility had not changed since FWCP, which further suggests that those later hierarchical accounts, in which "moral responsibility" virtually never occurs, are not intended as replacements of the earlier account of moral responsibility. So, what follows here are thoughts on how an RS theorist might try to address worries about the account as an account of responsible agency, using the resources of FWCP.

thing he calls "the capacity for reflective self-evaluation." It is this capacity that sets humans apart from other animals, and it is in virtue of this capacity that we come to be able to have second-order desires. Higher-order desires are a kind of proof for this capacity's existence, for one could not have such desires without a capacity for reflective self-evaluation. So, perhaps, the thought is that those capacities are part of what makes the presence or absence of hierarchies of desire relevant for moral responsibility.

The existence of this enabling capacity raises some puzzles about Frankfurt's account. In particular: what is doing the explanatory or normative work in the account? If higher-order evaluations are really products of some more basic feature, why not look to that distinctive capacity as the locus of freedom, personhood, and moral responsibility? Indeed, what seems to give those higher-order desires any force or relevance at all for the matter of responsibility is that they are the products of reflective self-evaluation. For example, if they were simply brute desires, or products of unmediated instinct, it would be difficult to see how they could support the distinction Frankfurt is looking for, one where on one side we have unremarkable animals, and on the other side we have agents capable of personhood, freedom, and moral responsibility. What makes second-order desires special seems to be precisely that they are the products of reflective self-evaluation. So, perhaps what Frankfurt should have said is that it is not second-order desires, per se, that matter for distinguishing responsible agents from non-responsible agents. Responsible agents are, in some way, a byproduct of a more fundamentally important capacity, and it is something about this underlying capacity that makes sense of the appropriateness of praising and blaming.

One consequence of replying in this way is that Frankfurt's account threatens to collapse into a de facto Reasons account. It is difficult to see how the capacity for self-reflection is not just self-directed rational assessment. Frankfurt's "reflective self-evaluation" seems to be a self-aware, self-directed form of those capacities emphasized by Reasons accounts: i.e., reflective self-control, or the capacity to recognize and appropriately respond to reasons. To be sure, he seems to have in mind a particular subset, or perhaps a particular application of those abilities—namely, those tied to self-awareness. Still, ultimately we are left with an appeal to a species of rational power. If so, then we have come to the startling conclusion that Frankfurt's account is really committed to a species of the Reasons approach.

The foregoing suggests that the paradigmatic RS account is not itself a genuine, distinctive option in the way ordinarily regarded in the literature.[16] Call the present view about these matters *the primacy of reasons* thesis about responsible agency. On this view, our rational capacities are central to moral responsibility, and purportedly alternative accounts will, on closer inspection, either smuggle in a commitment to rational capacities or prove to be inadequate.

In the face of such a view, one could rightly object that even if one accepts that Frankfurt's account is vulnerable to concerns about its force deriving from the role of rational powers, this need not be true of any and every RS account.[17] It would require a good deal more discussion than I have offered to show that other or all RS accounts ultimately bottom out into a story of rational powers.

Still, the present reflections generate a standing challenge to extant RS accounts: is there any reason to think that the psychological features highlighted by one's preferred RS account have some special status, apart from their genesis in the rational faculties of agents? Put differently, what RS theorists need are two interconnected things: (1) an account of why the psychological structures they identify are the kinds of things in virtue of which agents can be responsible; and (2) an explanation of why the normative relevance of those structures is not ultimately parasitic on, or reducible to the exercise of the capacities that constitute the heart of Reasons accounts.

---

[16] For discussions that take RS views, under one or another name, to be an important alternative to what I have been calling Reasons approaches, see, for example: Wolf, *Freedom Within Reason*; Fischer and Ravizza, *Responsibility and Control: A Theory of Moral Responsibility*; Elinor Mason, "Recent Work on Moral Responsibility," *Philosophical Books* 46, no. 4 (2005): 343–53.

[17] There are other ways one might build an RS account. As previously noted, one could appeal to the role of an agent's values, or of the agent's valuings, as part of an account of what constitutes the agent's real self. For an attempt to explain how one might answer the challenge he put to Frankfurt without giving up on what I have been calling an RS picture, see Watson, "Free Agency." Alternately, one could appeal to an agent's self-governing policies and their role in securing cross-temporal identity of the agent. See Bratman, "Identification, Decision, and Treating as a Reason." Either approach has distinctive resources for addressing the concerns raised here. In the Appendix, I argue that some of those resources can *supplement* a Reasons account, but that the core features of responsibility turn out to be best understood in a Reasons framework. The payoff of the present discussion, then, is twofold: (1) appreciation of some complexities obscured by the familiar RS/Reasons distinction; (2) some motivation for starting with a Reasons view, even if it does not completely put to rest the viability of RS accounts.

6. A new argument for RS theories?

Going forward, I will assume that RS accounts face the two-pronged challenge mentioned above. In the present section, I consider one way in which the proponents of RS accounts might reply. In its basic elements, the reply is this: the reason those psychological structures appealed to on an RS view count as the features in virtue of which agents are responsible is that those structures are the focus of our existing judgments of responsibility, and moreover, that RS accounts are uniquely well suited for capturing such judgments.

In appealing to these ideas, the proponent of RS would need to also invoke something like the principle of philosophical conservation. That's fine, though. As we have seen, this is already a commitment that plays some role in the construction of the present prescriptive account. So, if RS accounts mesh uniquely well with the contours of our ordinary responsibility assessments, and can explicate what is important about such judgments, that is a virtue. Even if the RS–identified structures are parasitic on reasoning capacities in some fundamental way, the RS theorist could insist it is those higher-level psychological structures to which we are responding in our responsibility assessments, and it is the presence of these specific structures (and possibly, the absence of specific structures or properties) *even if the warrant for their normative significance derives from the lower-level capacity.* On this account, the gap between those psychological structures that give rise to the Real Self and the warrant for praise and blame is bridged by our basic epistemology of moral responsibility.

One virtue of this reply is that it permits the RS theorist to concede a kind of dependence on underlying rational capacities, without thereby surrendering the need for a distinctively RS account of moral responsibility. However, for this strategy to succeed it needs some warrant to motivate its central claim that RS views are uniquely good at capturing the phenomena of ordinary judgments of responsibility. And, the RS theorist might think, there is evidence of just this sort in the experimental data.

Consider a series of provocative experiments conducted by Woolfolk, Doris, and Darley.[18] What these experiments seem to show is that attributions of responsibility tend to track an agent's identification with the action;

[18] John Doris and Stephen Stich, "As a Matter of Fact: Empirical Perspectives on Ethics," in *The Oxford Handbook of Contemporary Philosophy*, ed. Frank Jackson and Michael Smith (Oxford: Oxford

identification or its absence is the most salient trigger of our assessments of responsibility. If that is correct, then this is exactly the sort of evidence the RS theorist might hope to find: evidence for a tight conceptual link between RS-favored psychological structures and the warrant for praise and blame.

Woolfolk et al. have subjects consider a scenario in which they are told about two couples that are friends, returning from a vacation together. One of the members of this group of four adults, Bill, has learned that his wife (Susan) and his best friend (Frank) have been involved in an illicit love affair with each other. The subjects are told that Bill has just discovered proof. The subjects are then given one of several different versions of the case. In the low-identification version of the case Bill decides that he is going to confront Susan and Frank, but that he has resolved not to stand in their way if they want to be together. In the high-identification version of the case, Bill decides that he will kill Frank. The philosophically interesting results emerge in the high-identification case. Subjects in the high-identification version of the case are told that before Bill does anything, hijackers take over the plane and things eventually get to a situation where Bill is ordered by the hijackers to shoot Frank, and he does so. What Woolfolk et al. discovered was that subjects are more willing to judge high-identification Bill as more responsible, more appropriately blamed, and more properly subject to guilt than low-identification Bill. Even more remarkably, this was so even in scenarios where the hijackers were described as having additionally administered to Bill a "compliance drug" that forced him to behave exactly as they ordered. That is, even in the presence of multiple overdetermining elements to Bill's action, subjects were more willing to hold high-identification Bill responsible, as compared to low-identification Bill. So, what Woolfolk et al. seemed to have found was that ascriptions of responsibility very tightly track identification.[19]

In light of results such as these, the RS proponent might have some reason to claim that RS theories are *uniquely* well suited to capturing distinctive phenomena of the sort manifested in the Woolfolk et al. results.

University Press, 2005); Woolfolk et al., "Identification, Situational Constraint, and Social Cognition: Studies in the Attribution of Moral Responsibility."

[19] This scenario was tested precisely because of concerns that in less coercive versions of the case, there remained alternative possibilities that might fuel an incompatibilist reading of the evidence.

(Indeed, one could even think that not only do these results favor a specifically identificationist RS account, they even suggest—as Frankfurt himself famously argued—that alternative possibilities are no requirement on moral responsibility.[20]) So, one might think we have an answer to the challenge facing RS views. The evidence for our tracking identification in responsibility ascriptions seems to support the idea that identification is central to our concept and practices of moral responsibility.

7. Against the new argument for RS theories

The Woolfolk et al. results are provocative, but less than the RS theorist needs. First, it is far from clear that empirical data alone will be sufficient to demonstrate that RS accounts can explain the special status of those psychological features they identify, apart from their relationship to rational capacities. That is, even if there are some phenomena that RS theories are particularly well suited to explain—let us suppose the Woolfolk et al. capture such phenomena—these considerations have to be balanced against the costs of accepting the theory, especially given the costs and benefits of alternative accounts. (Here, recall the aforementioned worries regarding manipulation and sanity.) So, the most we can expect from data of this sort is support for one premise in a more complicated argument for RS views.

There is a second, and more powerful reason to doubt the overall utility of these examples. Simply put, you don't need an RS theory to account for

---

[20] Doris and Stich explicitly appeal to these results to argue against the intuitiveness of incompatibilism, both of the leeway and source varieties. See Doris and Stich, "As a Matter of Fact: Empirical Perspectives on Ethics." It is not clear to me why. Even if one thought that the results cut against leeway accounts, it is less obvious that they raise concerns for source accounts. Recall that according to source incompatibilists, the removal of alternative possibilities does not, by itself, mean that the agent wasn't the ultimate source of the action. Conceivably, a source incompatibilist might argue that Bill was ultimately responsible (assuming he wasn't subject to causal determinism), and that his ultimate responsibility was not gotten rid of simply because he lacked alternative possibilities. Doris and Stitch could emphasize that under manipulation, the person isn't the ultimate source. However, it all depends on how sourcehood and ultimacy are understood. I do not see any obvious reason why the case of Bill prevents source incompatibilists from offering an account compatible with the case as it has been described. (Compare the case they rely on with one where the hijackers give Bill a pill that deterministically makes him identify with whatever action they give him. If Bill didn't previously identify with the action, this sort of coercion strikes me as undermining sourcehood. I wager it would also undermine the rate at which respondents attribute moral responsibility.) Moreover, there is no reason a source incompatibilist could not help him- or herself to a tracing approach (see next section), and thus dodge the consequences of the Woolfolk et al. evidence in this way.

these results. To see why, think about the question of how we become responsible for what flows from our habits and character. A very natural way to accommodate the idea that we are responsible for actions deriving from character and habit is to think that our choices shape us, and that in turn, we are shaped by those features of our character that are built up out of individual choices. On this picture, as we make choices they slowly come to form settled habits of character.[21] Sometimes this operates on the basis of habituation. In other cases, it might arise as a consequence of settling on an explicit, self-governing policy that filters the agent's downstream deliberative options.[22] If I have a policy of starting the coffee pot immediately after getting out of bed, it will typically filter out other potential deliberative options when I first get out of bed (e.g., reading the latest news, going for a run, firing up the waffle iron, etc.). Whether by habit or self-governing policy or both, guidance by prior choices permits us to extend the efforts of agency into the future in comparatively stable and reliable ways.

Such considerations have given support to a notion I first introduced in chapter I—tracing. On a tracing theory, one way we can be responsible for what we do is by being responsible for who we are. This capacity is important, as much of what we do is a product of habits, policies, and character traits. It is by being responsible for the formation of these habits, policies, and character traits that we come to be responsible for much of what we do. That is, we can trace our responsibility for actions that derive from habits, policies, and character traits back to our antecedent choices that led to those aspects of ourselves.[23]

Tracing is an important part of the repertoire of most theories of responsibility. Tracing helps to explain away many of the cases that might otherwise appear to be accommodated only by an RS account. Tracing does this by permitting us to say that for any putative instance of responsibility, responsibility need not be accounted for by appeal to the presence of (for example)

---

[21] Kane has proposed a picture along these lines. See Kane, *The Significance of Free Will.*

[22] This aspect of agency plays an important role in much of Michael Bratman's work. See, for example, many of the essays in Michael E. Bratman, *Structures of Agency: Essays* (New York: Oxford University Press, 2007).

[23] Most contemporary accounts of responsibility invoke some notion of tracing. For some comparatively explicit appeals to tracing, see Fischer and Ravizza, *Responsibility and Control: A Theory of Moral Responsibility*; Kane, *The Significance of Free Will*; Ekstrom, *Free Will: A Philosophical Study*; Peter van Inwagen, "When is the Will Free?," in *Philosophical Perspectives, 3, Philosophy of Mind and Action Theory, 1989*, ed. James E. Tomberlin (Atascadero, CA: Ridgeview, 1989).

rational capacities at the time of action. Instead, all that is needed is some prior decision, character trait, habit, or policy that itself constitutes responsible choice (where this includes possession of some suitable knowledge), under conditions where those things were arrived at through the operations of the requisite agential features.

An example illustrates the point. Suppose Kevin has the deplorable policy of insulting any student who comes to speak to him during office hours. And, suppose that Kevin is no longer reflective at all about this practice, and not sensitive to moral considerations that weigh against it. However, when Kevin formed this policy he was alive to those considerations and simply decided to dismiss them—perhaps even welcoming their deterrent effect on students visiting him during office hours. Now, though, when Kevin's students arrive during office hours, he habitually says (with a loud chuckle): "What stupid question are you too dumb to answer on your own?"

On a tracing theory, the most natural thing to say about Kevin is that he is responsible for insulting his student. After all, he was carrying out a policy that he formed freely and responsibly (e.g., on a Reasons account, under conditions of rational self-governance). That his later deployment of that policy was unreflective and automatic is immaterial given the presence of that prior anchor in suitable features of agency.[24] Similarly, a drunk driver does not get off the moral hook simply because at the time he hit someone with his car he was especially intoxicated, and thus not responsive to reasons. In such cases, we look back to earlier decisions to, for example, begin drinking when there was reason to think one might come to drive, or in adopting habits of excessive drinking, or in deciding against being cautious about the risks of drinking, and so on.

Once we recognize the possibility of tracing, it is difficult to see how examples of the sort generated by Woolfolk et al. require an RS view. Opponents of RS views can insist that Bill's responsibility for his killing Frank is grounded in his (free) decision to kill Frank, prior to the actions of the hijackers. While Bill might not have envisioned the particular details of how we was going to kill Frank, his deciding to do so is a sufficient anchor

---

[24] In contrast, without appealing to tracing, an RS account can hold that Kevin is responsible for insulting his students precisely because his doing it is something that expresses his RS (i.e., that he identifies with, that he endorses, that expresses his regard for students, etc., etc.). Notice that an RS view may appeal to tracing, but it is not obvious that it must. Or, at any rate, if it must, it need not do so very often.

for tracing responsibility. As long as there is no reason to suppose the prior decision violated one's (non-RS) conditions of responsible agency, then there is no reason to rule out this sort of tracing. That the hijackers coerced Bill might involve some diminution of responsibility—which is, anyway, consistent with the responses Woolfolk et al. received. However, such concern does not mean that Bill cannot be held morally responsible for pulling the trigger.[25]

So, a critic of RS theories is unlikely to be moved by the Woolfolk et al. evidence. However, the proponent of an RS theory will surely object that there is a crucial element of the results that have not yet been addressed: where there is more identification there is more willingness to ascribe responsibility. Indeed, one might think, this is the most important result arising from those experiments. So, the RS proponent might say, even if critics can explain why people might think Bill is responsible in cases where there is a compliance drug present, the data still support the idea that what is central to our ascriptions of responsibility is identification.

In reply: while it is true that the data provide something of an initial warrant for thinking that identification is central to how we ascribe and think about the requirements for moral responsibility, this is also consistent with thinking that identification matters to us only evidentially. That is, our tracking whether an agent identifies with some outcome or act is a piece of evidence for some more metaphysically or normatively salient property to which identification points. That is, the attempt to provide an epistemic bridge between identification and the rational reflective capacities required for identification leaves identification with no independent significance of its own.

Suppose, for example, that we had the view that responsibility depends on, roughly: (1) whether an agent is capable of rational self-governance in that particular context; and (2) whether the agent has done something morally wrong. On this view, we ordinarily have good reason to track whether an agent identifies with his or her action in a given context.

---

[25] To be sure, this does not end the possible dialectic. Doris and Stitch might reply that Frank's decision isn't causally implicated in killing *on the plane*. To which, one possible reply is to point out that most decisions are fairly open about how the end is achieved, and that we fill in the details as required. (So: there is a decision to kill, and that becomes a decision to kill here and now under various conditions.) In cases where the details are relatively specified at the outset, it does not seem to be irrational to allow opportunistic transformations of the operative plan. A plausible theory of responsibility should allow for this, I would think. So again, I don't see anything that obviously favors the RS theorist.

Whether an agent identifies with an act counts as a good piece of evidence for thinking the agent has the relevant rational capacities in that context. Why think that? Well, one might think it for exactly the sort of reason suggested by Frankfurt in "Freedom of the Will and the Concept of a Person": identification strongly suggests—even ultimately requires—the presence of rational self-governance. Where there is identification there is rational agency. Note, moreover, that this is a perfectly general point, one that does not necessarily require a Reasons view. For example, suppose you thought that the agential feature that is paradigmatic of moral responsibility is the presence or absence of ill will.[26] On such a view, identification will plausibly be important to our epistemology of responsibility. However, its importance is derivative. It is a byproduct of our inability to directly access what we are really interested in, whether it is ill will, rational capacities, or something else.

So, it seems, the Woolfolk et al. data do not settle the matter or even obviously favor the RS theorist. Consequently, RS theorists have not yet identified a special conceptual connection between, on the one hand, praise and blame and on the other hand, those psychological structures implicated by RS views.[27] Minimally, what is required is a different set of experimental results, results whose experimental model controls for the possibility that identification (or some other RS property) has only an evidential role to play. Until we see such an experiment and the attendant results, it seems that the RS theorist cannot appeal to experimental data for forging a link between the theory's preferred psychological structures and praise and blame.

---

[26] See Strawson, "Freedom and Resentment."

[27] A further reason for caution about the evidence invoked by Doris and Stich hinges on a complexity of responsibility attributions. In a different set of experiments, Nichols and Knobe discovered that responsibility attributions are sensitive to the way a case is framed. See Nichols and Knobe, "Moral Responsibility and Determinism: The Cognitive Science of Folk Intuitions"; Nichols, "Folk Intuitions on Free Will." In concrete, high affect contexts, the folk will ascribe responsibility even if they are told it happens in a deterministic scenario. However, when a case is discussed abstractly, in low affect terms, responsibility attributions become much more sensitive to disruption because of determinism (i.e., in high affect contexts, responsibility attributions are resilient in a way they do not tend to be in lower affect contexts.) And, in the Woolfolk et al. experiments, the cases are described in concrete, high affect ways. So, there seems to be a further variable here that needs to be disentangled from their results. For a further worry about the importance of whether examples are presented as pertaining to this or another world, see Adina Roskies and Shaun Nichols, "Bringing Responsibility Down to Earth," *Journal of Philosophy* 105, no. 7 (2008): 371–88.

8. Is the best defense a good offense?

Thus far, I have argued that the familiar distinction between RS and Reasons approaches to moral responsibility is less clear than one might think. In particular, RS views are under pressure to show that there is some reason to think that the psychological features highlighted by one's preferred RS account have a special status, apart from being evidence of the rational faculties of agents. If they cannot show this, then it suggests that RS theorists fail to have a distinctive approach to accounting for moral responsibility, and more importantly, that the focus on a Real Self constitutes a misidentification of the features of agency in virtue of which moral responsibility obtains.[28]

I then considered a line of reply that makes use of recent empirical data suggesting that ordinary attributions of responsibility tightly track identification. However, appeals to tracing and the evidential role of identification permit non-RS accounts to explain away the experimental evidence. The appeal to tracing, though, is important. Without tracing, Reasons accounts do not obviously have the resources to explain away the persistence of our responsibility attributions under conditions where agents do not seem to be actively exercising rational capacities.

It is on this issue where RS theorists might plausibly go on the offensive. Although tracing is common in the literature of responsible agency, I've elsewhere argued that these accounts are plagued by an under-appreciated difficulty. The difficulty is this: in many circumstances the anchoring traits, habits, or policies are adopted under conditions in which the agent has poor epistemic access to the consequences that flow from having adopted that trait, habit, or policy.[29]

It is perhaps a truism that I cannot be held responsible for some outcome unless it was reasonably foreseeable—except where my lack of foresight is

---

[28] Of course, we do not yet have an account of why a capacity for reflective rationality should underwrite praiseworthiness and blameworthiness, either. However, the task of this chapter is relatively modest, circumscribed by the question of which of the two considered approaches presents a better starting point. Concluding that Reasons accounts provide the better starting point does not obviate the need for an account of why the involved capacities are the ones that appropriately connect to responsibility assessments. This is an issue I return to in chapter 7.

[29] Vargas, "The Trouble With Tracing." I will have more to say about tracing in chapter 9, as well. For a reply to my earlier concern about tracing, however, see Fischer and Tognazzini, "The Truth About Tracing."

itself something for which I am responsible. In the context of tracing theories, the worry is this: in a wide range of cases, the aspects of our self, character, or policy which provide the basis for many of our actions were acquired in circumstances under which we could not foresee the implications for our future actions of our acquiring them. Or, to put it somewhat differently, the anchors for our responsibility traces cannot secure responsibility when the downstream effect was not reasonably foreseeable at the time of the anchoring decision. Indeed, the more remote—temporally or recognitionally—the context of action is from the context of the acquisition of the trait, habit, or policy, the more significant we should expect the epistemic defect to become. Many of the characteristics I inculcated in myself in junior high school were doubtlessly acquired under conditions when I would or could not know about their consequences in my more mature adult life.

How ubiquitous this problem is remains an open question. As a problem for theories of responsibility, it depends in part on the frequency with which the theory relies on tracing. Accounts that hold that we have free will somewhat infrequently will face a version of this problem to a greater extent than theories that require little or no tracing, or whose tracing does not typically involve significant temporal extendedness. It is on this point, however, that the thin edge of the RS wedge might be inserted. Earlier, I noted that RS theorists could make use of tracing, but need not. Indeed, the ability of RS accounts to make sense of the responsibility of cases like Kevin (the grumpy professor) and Bill (the homicidal cuckold) suggest that RS accounts might yet have some decisive advantage over Reasons accounts. That is, RS accounts might have a particularly effective way of accounting for responsibility attributions if it turns out that tracing is as problematic as the above argument suggests.

I think the problems I identified with tracing, if they are genuine problems, do not arise in relatively localized instances of tracing. Instead, they tend to rely on temporally extended traces of considerable magnitude. Since comparatively localized instances of tracing are plausibly operative in the cases now under consideration, I don't see an easy way for the RS theorist to recruit tracing concerns on behalf of the RS vs. Reasons dialectic.

If I am wrong about this—that is, if tracing worries extend even to relatively localized instances of tracing, or one were committed to temporally extended tracing being the main way of anchoring responsibility in, say, adulthood—then it would open some space for the possibility that RS theories have appropriately identified the correct locus of concern for moral responsibility. Even then, however, matters would not be settled so directly. If one were concerned about manipulation or implantation scenarios on RS accounts, or if one were moved by the thought that RS agents can be unacceptably detached from what reasons there are in the world, then a different possibility emerges. One might begin to take seriously the prospect of a distinctive form of moral responsibility skepticism. On that view, one might not think that responsibility is altogether impossible—only much less frequently present than our ordinary practices would suggest. On this more skeptical view, the problems with tracing and any reliance on comparatively few instances of original responsibility would be the right position, not necessarily an RS view.

Here, though, I think the Reasons theorist should resist capitulating too quickly to either the RS view or the attenuated skepticism just mentioned. One reason to think that tracing's troubles are not particularly dire in the present context is that, at least on the face of it, even habitual, personal policy-dictated actions can be sensitive to reasons. That I habitually empty my pockets on a bookshelf when I get home from work does not preclude the following: were there something I perceived as more important, I would respond to those considerations. I do not wish to deny that our habits, traits, or policies can make us less able to detect relevant considerations, moral or otherwise. At the same time, those same mechanisms can enhance our responsiveness to considerations. Were I to have no habit of asking my children how their day went, I would presumably fail to be aware of some considerations that should weigh in my deliberations at least some of the time. The operative thought here is that while habit, traits, and policies might sometimes diminish our appreciation for some reasons, they can also work to make us more aware of these things than we might otherwise be. All of which is to say that we should not so readily accept that our reasoning capacity is paralyzed whenever it is silent in action production.

It is time to draw some provisional conclusions. One aim of this chapter has largely been to show that the relationship between RS views and Reasons theories is considerably more complicated than ordinarily presumed. A second aim was to argue that this further complexity does not generally favor RS views. The upshot of these arguments was this: there are reasons to favor a Reasons account.

The reasons that favor the primacy of reason are not obviously decisive. Reasons accounts face difficulties of their own. They must explain how we can have adequate sensitivity to reasons in cases where reasons seem to play no active role in the production of action, but where we nevertheless find ourselves inclined to assign responsibility. I have gestured at some initial considerations why one might think that a Reasons account could meet this challenge, but more needs to be said.

If it turned out a Reasons account cannot sustain an adequate theory of moral responsibility, this would give us cause to restart the project of systematic revisionism from an RS basis. However, I think I can show that a Reasons account can, when sufficiently refined, do the work it needs to do.

In the next chapter, these issues will recede a bit as I focus on the justification of the responsibility system. In chapter 7, though, the nature of responsible agency will resume its place on center stage, and the matter of how to characterize my version of the Reasons approach will become the heart of the remaining program of the book.

6

Justifying the Practice

The task of this chapter is show that there is justification sufficient for holding one another responsible, irrespective of whether we are libertarian agents. I begin by exploring and rejecting several familiar approaches for justifying our responsibility-characteristic practices. I then go on to argue for an account that makes use of some of the ideas in these rejected approaches, in the form of a Reasons account of the sort gestured at in the preceding chapter. I call the resultant account *the agency cultivation model*.

Recall that there are two reasons for considering what, if anything, might justify our ongoing promulgation and participation in responsibility-characteristic practices, apart from belief in libertarian free will. First, if we can justify the practice of holding one another responsible, we undercut the appeal of responsibility nihilism. That is, if we have justification for holding one another responsible, even if we are not in fact responsible, the non-reality of moral responsibility is of diminished practical significance. Second, I have suggested that considerations rooted in *why* we are justified in holding one another responsible may illuminate something about the internal structure and logic of the responsibility system. What I hope to show is that the justification-generating features of our practices have an important connection to the normative structure governing the regulation of praise and blame.

1. The sense of justification

What we are looking for is some justification of holding one another responsible. Although broad, the notion of "justified" at work here should be recognizable. There are some activities we engage in that make good sense, that we have reason to be engaged in, or that are well supported by our various interests and cohere with our not-indefensible commitments. Those are justified. There are other activities that we engage in that seem to lack those features, or that have them in very limited degrees. Those are typically unjustified. So, slavery: not justified. Concern about whether one's pattern of activity is healthy for oneself: justified. Laws about what side of the road to drive on: arbitrary, but justified.

On the broad sense of justified that is at issue here, one could maintain that a way for some practices to be justified is that they reflect some important truth. If there are moral truths, we might think that such truths are central to why slavery is unjustified. In light of such considerations, we might think that what makes it justified that we hold one another responsible is the fact that we are, in fact, sometimes morally responsible. This thought pushes us back in the direction of a conception of moral responsibility as depending on some antecedent fact about us or the world. As we have already seen, however, the most familiar route to that sort of justification story is not open to us precisely because the matter of what responsibility facts consist in is in dispute.

What we require to pursue the present project of justification is a picture of the normative anchors for our responsibility-characteristic practices, a picture that (ideally) also provides resources for illuminating the internal structure of the responsibility system. So, rather than appealing to some prior account of the truths about moral responsibility, we instead endeavor to provide an account of what could justify our responsibility-characteristic practices. We judge that proposal on the basis of its fruitfulness in fulfilling the various burdens outlined last chapter (e.g., naturalistic plausibility, normative adequacy, and informativeness about the familiar logic and structure of the responsibility system).

To be sure, the *variety* of justification provided (pragmatic vs. moral) might matter. If the only justification available to us is a pragmatic one, we might worry that even if we undercut the significance of responsibility nihilism we won't have gotten what we want. A pragmatic solution might succeed in undercutting the significance of responsibility nihilism to the extent that we would still have reason to hold one another responsible. However, if all that is available to us is a prudential justification for responsibility, one might think we lose the distinctively moral normative force that the various judgments and statuses internal to the responsibility system present themselves as having.[1]

Bracketing some complexities about these issues, the idea is that we'd like a more-than-merely pragmatic justification, ideally something rooted in features with significant normative heft. In the next two sections I consider some promising but ultimately insufficient strategies for doing this. What I'll argue is that the right approach borrows aspects from each of the strategies that otherwise fail on their own.

2. Strawsonian psychologism

Given that we cannot appeal to some prior account of facts about moral responsibility, one place to look for the justification of our responsibility-characteristic attitudes and practices is in the psychology operative in holding one another responsible. This strategy is perhaps most commonly associated with P. F. Strawson's account in "Freedom and Resentment."

On this approach, what is central to the practice of holding one another morally responsible are our expectations about how we are to be treated, and our dispositions of reaction to violations of those expectations. That is, ordinary human adults are attuned to what Strawson called "the quality of will" evinced by others. When someone's action fails to demonstrate a kind of concern for us that we expect, we react with anger, resentment, indignation, and so on. On this picture, when one acts with a bad will, one is blameworthy and where one acts with a good will, one is praiseworthy. Blameworthiness and praiseworthiness are statuses that simply reflect our assessments (or perhaps norms of assessment) that grow out of concern for

---

[1] Here are some of the complications. First of all, if it turns out that the proper way to understand the normative force of morality is in broadly prudential terms, then the mere fact that a justification is "pragmatic" would not necessarily undercut the normative adequacy of the proposed account. Second, fictionalism might remain an option. On one way of characterizing this view, moral claims are systematically false, but there are good prudential reasons to perpetuate moral practices, and moreover, that adopting an attitude of pretense about them (pretending that they are true, or engaging in make-believe when it comes to morality) can yield the same benefits and range of reactions that follow from genuine belief in morality. If one accepted fictionalism as a description of our *actual* moral discourse, then a prudential justification that could secure the perpetuation of our ongoing pretense and its connections to motivation (and so on) would attain all the normative force we require.

quality of will. Judgments about responsibility express an underlying framework of attitudes built around inter- and intra-personal demands for concern.

I think this account of blameworthiness is mostly correct, as far as it goes. Construing judgments of blameworthiness as judgments about quality of will makes good sense of much of the internal logic of the responsibility system. On the account I favor, the norms of praise and blame are sensitive to the intentions of agents and what those intentions reveal about whether those agents were acting with the sort of concern due to agents in light of morality. I take it that the structure of standard excuses tracks this fact in just the way Strawson describes: ignorance is ordinarily an excuse because it shows there was no ill will on the part of the offending agent. Similarly, difficulty mitigates blameworthiness partly because the requisite quality of will can require effort that is difficult to sustain in some circumstances and not others. Of course, the notion of ill will can stand some unpacking. And, judgments of blameworthiness presume a picture of responsible agency concerning which agents are properly subject to the quality of will-sensitive norms of praise and blame. Nevertheless, in its general contours, the broadly Strawsonian account of blameworthiness is compelling.

Alas, the virtues of the Strawsonian account of blameworthiness do not extend to providing a satisfactory answer to questions of justification that are in some sense external to the practice. The Strawsonian picture comes up short in the face of skeptical concerns about the integrity of the practice. Strawson's thought was that we could answer the justification question by looking to the immutability (in most of us) of those attitudes on which the particular stance of holding one another responsible rests. I am doubtful this part of the Strawsonian approach works.

On the picture I'm characterizing as Strawsonian, the crucial bit is the idea that our native framework of attitudes—what he called "the participant stance"—is an inescapable feature of our natural psychological endowment. It is simply not open to us to give it up.[2] Moreover, even if we somehow could give it up, and came to contemplate doing so, the only basis on which we could decide the matter would be in light of the "the gains and losses to human life, its enrichment or impoverishment" (13).[3] So, the significance of

---

[2] Strawson need not deny that there are some agents that lack this framework. His point is that for those of us with it, it is a non-optional feature of how we see and react to our social world.

[3] Strawson, "Freedom and Resentment."

the fixed attitudes, and the constitutive roles they purportedly play in our lives is this: they deflect the demand for justification. Once we recognize the fact that our practices are an outgrowth of attitudes that are fixed and, anyway, could only be abandoned at cost of our entire way of ordinarily relating to one another, it simply does not make sense to continue to ask whether we are justified in holding one another morally responsible.

The plausibility of this line of argument, at least as I have been characterizing it, rests on the twin presumptions that the responsibility-characteristic attitudes cannot be abandoned, and that abandonment of them would require the abandonment of our entire framework of interpersonal attitudes. However, both of these presumptions have been called into question.[4] I won't rehearse the full details here, although I think it is implausible to hold that our attitudes are all "of a piece" with the larger participant framework (as Strawson insisted), and that they cannot be attenuated or reformed in various ways. Instead, I want to focus on whether the fixity of psychological reaction would suffice to end questions about justification.

To see why psychological inevitability does not deflect questions about the justification of practices, even practices that rest on implastic psychological elements, consider Jealous Dave:

Whenever Dave's spouse Michelle spends time with opposite-sex friends, Dave experiences strong pangs of jealousy. This doesn't strike him as bizarre or unusual. After all, he was raised in a context where after puberty (and frequently before then) opposite-sex relationships of more than the most distantly formal sort were looked down on. And really—what kind of married woman wants to have friends of the opposite sex, anyway?

In light of such convictions, when Dave has had pangs of jealousy connected to Michelle's interactions with other men, he has always been quick to express them. Over time, in a wide range of ways, he does what he can to restrict Michelle's time with members of the opposite sex.

However, not all is lost, for Dave is a sometimes reflective and frequently curious guy. He tends to pick up and read any old thing lying around. Sometimes it is a celebrity gossip magazine at the dentist. Other times it is a short wave radio repair manual at the hobby store. One day while waiting at the optometrist's, he stumbles across an article that makes him wonder about the larger significance of his attitudes

---

[4] See, for example, Lawrence Stern, "Freedom, Blame, and the Moral Community," *Journal of Philosophy* 71, no. 3 (1974): 72–84; Watson, "Responsibility and the Limits of Evil"; Pereboom, *Living Without Free Will*.

towards gender and relationships. Maybe it is a bit of Faludi or Valenti or hooks. Whatever it is, he starts to think that there is a larger significance to how he treats Michelle's relationships to other men. Nothing changes right away, of course. However, over time he starts to wonder. He persists in feeling that his underlying attitudes of jealousy are natural and unavoidable, but he starts to think that his behavior in this respect is unjustified, and that really, he ought to do his best to refrain from acting on his feelings of jealousy.

Is Dave making a mistake when he thinks that his behavior might be unjustified? I don't think he is, and I think it is reasonable for him to think this even if he is right that his feelings of jealousy are a fixed feature about himself. Now you might object that this is implausible. Perhaps it is. Perhaps feelings of jealousy are not so implastic as Dave thinks. Still, I'm not sure why this fact, a fact of which he is unaware, would change anything. Moreover, we can tinker with the example so as to have jealousy play a role that is comparably crucial for Dave's particular life as, say, feelings of resentment can be in a person prone to easily experiencing that emotion.

For example, we can imagine that throughout his transformation, Dave regards his feelings of jealousy as crucial to his identity, as partly constitutive of the kind of person he wants to be. Perhaps he regards it as a crucial contributor to his being able to make good on something else he values, such as his monogamy. When tempted to stray, he reflects on his feelings of jealousy, and he reasons that Michelle would surely feel similarly were he to break his vows, and that thought makes it easier to remain faithful. Or, perhaps he simply thinks that a life devoid of any sexual jealousy would be less vibrant and less worth having.

Even with such thoughts a part of Dave's convictions, it does not strike me as insensible for Dave to conclude as he does. That is, while he cannot and would not do away with his feelings of jealousy, his own behavior or practices—practices that depend on the existence of that jealousy—would be unjustified. Indeed, it seems to me that were he to come to accept this judgment, he might even go on to think Michelle should reproach him for acting on such feelings when he does. The inevitability of an emotion does not entail the justification of its expression or those practices that presuppose its expression.

Similar thoughts hold in the case of our responsibility-characteristic attitudes—those feelings of resentment, indignation, and the like that give rise to our praising and blaming practices. What reflection on Jealous Dave suggests is that neither the immutability of our emotional dispositions nor our being wedded to the experience of such emotions is sufficient to show that the attendant practices are justified. If that's right, then the immutability of our reactive attitudes would not block or satisfy the demand for justification.

(Notice that this idea is distinct from the idea, mentioned in chapter 4, that there is a difference between being unable to *hold* someone responsible and that person *being* responsible. This latter distinction was important for complaints that Strawson did not properly recognize the intelligibility of responsibility nihilism. Here, my interest has been whether the purportedly fixed and implastic nature of our attitudes would suffice to show that the resultant responsibility practices are *justified*.)

It is open to the Strawsonian to insist that in the case of praising and blaming, there is a special necessity that attaches to the responsibility-characteristic attitudes, such that (unlike feelings of jealousy) they *must* be expressed, and that they must be expressed in roughly the ways characteristic of our responsibility practices. Either of those two claims is much stronger than anything ordinarily attributed to Strawson, and anyway, it is very difficult to see how the argument for such claims would go. Even were we to have such an argument, I cannot see how it would change the dialectical situation. It would not show that we are justified in having those practices, only that we can't help having them.

If Dave can endeavor to swallow his jealousy and refrain from the relevant coercive behaviors, then there is no reason to think that the inevitability of his jealousy suffices to justify the attendant behavior. Similarly, if we can swallow our reactive attitudes, then there is no reason to think that the inevitability of our having such attitudes suffices to justify the perpetuation and promulgation of our practices of praising and blaming. So, if we wish to justify our holding one another responsible, we need to look elsewhere.

3. Responsibility as morality's enforcer

A different place to look for the justification of responsibility practices is in their ineradicably social character. Such a route was initially suggested by

Strawson's own approach, which began by considering what function various social practices might have. Here, the theorists faces a choice—pursue an answer to the justification challenge in the psychology of holding responsible (the Strawsonian path) or pursue an approach that tries to locate justification in some feature of the practices themselves. Strawson's account was constructed partly as a response to an approach that took this latter tack: the old consequentialist picture of moral responsibility. On perhaps its simplest version, the attitudes and practices characteristic of moral responsibility are justified because such practices influence or pressure agents to behave in morally desirable ways.[5]

Although such accounts are now much reviled, it is worth recalling why such accounts had at least some allure to a number of philosophers throughout the first two-thirds of the twentieth century. One virtue of the old consequentialist approach was that it seemed to contain a natural account of responsible agency. That is, it drew the distinction between responsible and non-responsible agents in approximately the right place. Even better, it did so without appealing to what P. F. Strawson later described as "panicky metaphysics." In cases where there is no point to influence or pressure—e.g., coercion, ignorance, or insanity—this sort of account maintained that the considered agent ought not to be held responsible. Where influence can be effective, we can and do hold people responsible.

Perhaps the deepest appeal of these accounts (for those not already committed to consequentialism) derived from the psychological thesis that praise gets us to do good things and blame gets us to avoid doing bad things. From this presupposition came two attractive ideas and one ugly one. The attractive ideas were these: (1) we have reason to *care* about moral responsibility inasmuch as we care about getting people to behave in the right ways and getting them to avoid behaving in the wrong ways; and (2) praising and blaming are *justified* (and their practices structured) by their role in encouraging pro-social or utility-enhancing behavior.[6] The former rooted our interest in responsibility in our interest in morality, and the second anchored

---

[5] The classic statement of a theory of this sort is Schlick, *The Problems of Ethics*, ch. 7. Elements of this account are also widely associated with Smart, "Free Will, Praise, and Blame." Richard Arneson has recently offered a rehabilitation of Smart's account that is congenial to some of what I will go on to argue for. See Richard J. Arneson, "The Smart Theory of Moral Responsibility and Desert," in *Desert and Justice*, ed. Serena Olsaretti (Oxford: Oxford University Press, 2003).

[6] Strawson, "Freedom and Resentment."

a justification for holding one another responsible in their effects. The ugly idea was that praise and blame are merely forward-looking attempts to influence the behavior of others.[7]

For ease of exposition, call any account committed to the idea that we can justify the practice of holding one another responsible in light of its consequences *a moral influence theory*.

As I suggested above, these views have gone the way of waxed handlebar mustaches. The consensus—and it is virtually unanimous among philosophers of free will and moral responsibility—is that moral influence theories are total failures. P. F. Strawson pointedly objected that "[moral influence] is not a sufficient basis, it is not even the right sort of basis, for these practices as we understand them," while Scanlon has concluded that "the difficulties with this theory are, I think, well known."[8]

It is perhaps no surprise, then, that what I aim to do is to defend the moral influence account. Perhaps "defend" is too strong. What I aspire to do is to identify and rehabilitate an important insight that rests at the core of traditional moral influence theories. I think this insight can be developed in a way that sidesteps the traditional objections directed against moral influence accounts. To avoid confusion, I will call the picture I favor *the agency cultivation model*. If carefully deployed, the agency cultivation model explains how our practice of holding one another responsible can be justified and how that picture of justification illuminates some aspects of the nature of logic of the responsibility system. I am less concerned with whether or not the resultant account is properly regarded as an instance of the moral influence approach. For present purposes, however, I will treat it as an instance of the general family of moral influence accounts.

The insight I aim to make use of from classical moral influence accounts is roughly this: the justification of our praising and blaming practices derives, at least in part, from their effects on creatures like us. Here, some of the Strawsonian work on the moral psychology of responsibility can actually

---

[7] There is a companion thesis one might have about the function of conscience, one given expression by a character in Lowry's *Under the Volcano*: "conscience had been given man to regret it only in so far as that might change the future." See Malcolm Lowry, *Under the Volcano* (New York: Harper Perennial, 2007), 113.

[8] Strawson, "Freedom and Resentment," 4; T. M. Scanlon, "The Significance of Choice," in *The Tanner Lectures on Human Values*, ed. Sterling M. McMurrin (Cambridge: Cambridge University Press, 1988), 159.

help. On my account, it provides a way of thinking about some of the constraints on a system of influence. Of course, whether the agency cultivation model works depends, in part, on whether the familiar traditional objections to moral influence theories can be addressed. So, I'll start by presenting the traditional objections to moral influence accounts. I'll then present the agency cultivation model, and argue that it has the resources to overcome traditional objections to moral influence accounts.[9]

4. Objections to moral influence

The following six objections are the ones I take to constitute the most significant criticisms directed against the classical moral influence account over the past 50 years or so.[10]

The first two are different versions of the idea that moral influence theories are too coarse-grained to make the distinctions required of a theory of moral responsibility. First: moral influence (MI) theories cannot make suitable distinctions among kinds of agents. Second: moral influence itself cannot be distinguished from other kinds of influence.

Take the matter of distinguishing between intuitively responsible and intuitively non-responsible agents. MI theories maintain that agents are responsible when they can be influenced in the ways characteristic of holding people responsible. On this account, the threat or promise of our anger, indignation, gratitude, praise, blame, punishment, or reward is the substance of moral responsibility. But, if it is mere susceptibility to influence that marks out responsible agents from non-responsible agents, then we do not have any principled way to distinguish intuitively responsible agents (normal adults, for example) from intuitively non-responsible agents

---

[9] I do not take a stand on whether standard criticisms of the traditional view *ought* to have felled traditional moral influence accounts. My concern here is simply whether we can re-purpose some ideas from the classical approach in a way that avoids the main complaints about the approach.

[10] Important objections to the approach have been offered in: Strawson, "Freedom and Resentment"; Jonathan Bennett, "Accountability," in *Philosophical Subjects: Essays Presented to P. F. Strawson*, ed. Zak Van Straaten (Oxford: Clarendon Press, 1980); Scanlon, "The Significance of Choice."; Wallace, *Responsibility and the Moral Sentiments*. Until very recently, to find a notable defense of it you had to go back more than twenty-five years to Dennett, *Elbow Room*. Significantly, reviewers with widely divergent estimations of that book generally agreed that Dennett's defense of moral influence was unsatisfactory. See Gary Watson, "Review of *Elbow Room*," *The Journal of Philosophy* 83, no. 9 (1986): 517–22. See also Gerald Dworkin, "Review of *Elbow Room*," *Ethics* 96, no. 2 (1986): 423–5.

(infants, most non-human animals). After all, members of both groups can be moved by a range of "influencing" behaviors (cajoling, threatening, enticing, and so on). So, even if an MI account can explain the pointlessness of blaming someone who acted out of ignorance, it cannot explain why we should, in the ordinary case of blaming, hold normal human adults to a kind of moral standard we do not intuitively think appropriate to hold of infants and most (or perhaps all) non-human animals. It thus fails to adequately account for the difference between responsible and non-responsible agents.

Now consider the second objection of coarseness. This complaint holds that MI accounts do badly in distinguishing between moral and non-moral forms of influence. If holding someone morally responsible just is to treat them in ways that would influence them to behave better, then we have no way to distinguish intuitively genuine blaming from feigned blaming. Indeed, we would have no way to distinguish moral influence from a range of manipulative behaviors that aim to shape others and their actions without any attendant moral judgment.

The natural place to look for a distinction between moral and non-moral influence is internal to the act of influence (say, an instance of moral blaming). But on the moral influence account it is difficult to see how there could be a relevant "internal" feature, given that MI accounts construe responsibility and its attendant judgments and practices in terms of some external relation (namely, whether the influence is efficacious). So, here too a moral influence theory is simply too ham-fisted. Its failure to distinguish between kinds of agents and its inability to distinguish between responsibility and manipulation shows it to be an inadequate theory of responsibility.[11]

Here's a third objection: the MI theory conflates being responsible with judgments about the appropriateness of holding responsible. On a standard moral influence theory, an agent's being responsible is fixed by facts about when and/or whether it is appropriate to hold the agent responsible—that is, whether we can influence an agent (or others) to behave in a suitable

---

[11] For objections in the spirit of what I have been discussing, see C. A. Campbell, "Is 'Free Will' a Pseudo-Problem?," *Mind* 60, no. 240 (1951): 447. See also Strawson, "Freedom and Resentment." I should also note that it is open to the moral influence theorist to insist that we are better off without these distinctions, but it is clear that in going this route we would be abandoning a substantial part of our given conceptual furniture associated with moral responsibility. Relatedly, concerns about scapegoating can arise in this context. I'll say more about this worry in §7.

way. However, at least in commonsense moral thinking, whether someone is responsible and whether it is appropriate to hold that person responsible come apart. Suppose that we have a policy of never holding people responsible for, say, the first impolitic remark they make. Now suppose that we make an arbitrary exception, and hold one and only one person responsible the first time he or she makes an impolitic remark. It looks as though we can say of this case that even though the agent is, in fact, morally responsible for the first impolitic remark, it would be inappropriate to hold him or her responsible. Thus, a theory that collapses the issue of when someone is morally responsible with the issue of when it is appropriate to hold someone morally responsible will be unsatisfactory.[12]

A fourth objection is that MI accounts fail to accurately describe how we hold people responsible. It is entirely compatible with a moral influence account that one never need experience what Strawson called the reactive attitudes—the responsibility-characteristic attitudes of resentment, indignation, gratitude, and so on—and could instead feign these things as part of an attempt to influence others. On the moral influence account, genuine resentment, indignation and so on, are never actually required. In fact, an MI theory might recommend (or perhaps even require) something like an emotionally disconnected, almost therapeutic approach to influencing others by the most expedient means. However, reflection on how we in fact hold people responsible shows that "blame-related responses all involve something like hostility towards the subject; whereas a [moral influence] therapist, though he may have to feign ill-feeling for therapeutic purposes, can in fact be in a perfectly sunlit frame of mind."[13] Even if the practice of holding people responsible sometimes amounts to an attempt to influence people, it is surely a mistake to claim that we are always attempting to influence others.

A fifth objection is that MI theories misdescribe what we are doing when we hold people responsible. In many cases where we assess responsibility, we are making judgments that look like they have no hope of influencing

---

[12] If I understand him properly, Scanlon seems to have something like this in mind when he claims that the theory appears to conflate the question of whether moral judgment is applicable and the question of whether it should be *expressed* (in particular, expressed to the agent). See Scanlon, "The Significance of Choice," p. 159. I say a bit more about gratitude in the fifth objection.

[13] See Bennett, "Accountability," p. 20. Strawson makes the same criticism in "Freedom and Resentment."

anyone, both as a matter of what I might believe and as a matter of what is actually possible, apart from my beliefs. If I admiringly praise a dead relative for her dedication to the fight against the now-extinct disease of kuru, I need not presume to be influencing that relative.[14] Influencing the dead is, I suspect, substantially beyond my limited powers of persuasion.[15] It is also implausible to suppose that my judgment is an attempt to influence, for example, myself, or my acquaintances to fight kuru. After all, kuru become extinct a few decades back.

I suppose we *could* imagine that I might be motivated to praise my dead relative for her fight against kuru as part of an elaborate attempt to get me or people I know to fight diseases in general, or even to just dedicate some part of our lives to a worthwhile cause. But this certainly doesn't seem necessary for me to make the judgment that my relative was praiseworthy for her endeavors. Yet, the classical influence story seems to require that my particular praising or blaming have these effects *in this particular case* for us to rightly care about praiseworthiness and blameworthiness. So, whatever it is that we are tracking with our concept of moral responsibility, it looks like the classical consequentialist story misses the mark.

A related way of putting the objection from misdescription of our practice focuses on the moment of moral concern. On the classical moral influence account, it seems to locate our concern in the present or the future, and never in the past. Sometimes, however, assignments of responsibility are backward-looking. That is, they are assessments of the way an agent was, and have little or nothing to do with the influence that the reactive attitudes or associated practices might have on this agent or others in the future. As I just noted, we surely can have responsibility-characteristic attitudes such as gratitude towards parents, grandparents, friends, and mentors even if they are dead or otherwise incapacitated. Even if it turned

---

[14] Kuru was a disease afflicting the brain that came to international attention in the 1950s because of an outbreak in Papua New Guinea; one acquired it by eating dead humans, especially their brain and nervous system. It appears to have gone extinct within a generation after Australia's 1957 ban of cannibalism.

[15] One might think it is a somewhat common and ordinary thing to influence the dead with, say, prayers of petition. But it does not seem plausible to think that the ordinary case of making a responsibility judgment about the dead *requires* that this possibility be "live," so to speak. In a different vein, one might think that one can influence the dead by changing relational properties that include the dead as one of the relata. My grandparents can be made more genetically successful by my procreative endeavors, and in this way, I might be said to exert some influence on them, even in death. But this sort of influence does not seem relevant or even required in the case of ordinary judgments of praise and blame.

out that such attitudes had some justification because of their effects on the living, this again seems to be the wrong kind of justification for gratitude. Our judgments of responsibility often express a legitimate concern for the past, and the traditional moral influence account has no way to accommodate this point.[16]

A sixth and final objection is a simple but not insignificant one. It is the objection that moral influence theories are unacceptably tied to consequentialism. If one finds consequentialism troubling on independent grounds, any theory of responsibility that presupposes some form of consequentialism will seem troubling for that reason. A somewhat more nuanced version of this worry arises from the "limited ethics" approach outlined in chapter 4. The idea is that given the contentious nature of normative ethics, a theorist of responsibility should treat it as a desideratum that any proposed account of moral responsibility be somewhat insulated from commitments to a specific theory of normative ethics. If we accept this methodological constraint, moral influence theories are problematic not because of consequentialism as such, but because they imply a commitment to a specific theory of normative ethics.

Individually, and sometimes jointly, these six objections have been widely taken to show the inadequacy of the MI account as a theory of moral responsibility.

5. Distilling the spirit of the influence theory

The most important flaw of traditional MI accounts is that they overreach, attempting to account for too many things with the comparatively limited idea of moral influence. It is a mistake to generate a comprehensive account of responsible agency, blameworthiness, praise and blame, and (perhaps) an

---

[16] Dworkin writes that "Any attempt to forge as close a link between responsibility and modifiability . . . ignores those ascriptions of responsibility which are not oriented toward the future but are, so to speak, for the record. And since they are for the record, justice requires that we pay attention only to the details of a person's circumstances, and not to what is true in general or true of individuals very similar to her." See Dworkin, "Review of *Elbow Room*," p. 424. Similar objections can be found in Wallace, *Responsibility and the Moral Sentiments*, pp. 56–7; Kane, *The Significance of Free Will*, p. 83; Campbell, "Is 'Free Will' a Pseudo-Problem?," p. 447.

account of the justification of the responsibility-characteristic practices, all from the same materials.

If the idea of moral influence has any plausibility, its plausibility is restricted to the justification of responsibility-characteristic practices. However, scaling back the scope of application for the idea of MI is not enough. The idea of moral influence itself requires refinement.

In section 3, I noted that traditional MI accounts were committed to three ideas: (1) we have reason to care about moral responsibility inasmuch as we care about getting people to behave in the right ways and getting them to avoid behaving in the wrong ways; (2) the justification for praise and blame comes from their effects; and (3) praise and blame are forward-looking attempts to influence behavior in socially desirable ways. It is the second claim that I think is roughly right, though perhaps not in the way moral influence theorists have traditionally argued. (I remain ambivalent about the first idea; I think the third is dead wrong.)

There is, I think, a temptation on the part of both moral influence theorists and their critics to think of the justification of moral influence in terms of the efficacy of particular tokenings of praising and blaming, of the practices of expressing those judgments and acting in characteristic ways upon them. So, when, say, Lori criticizes Dan for being overly self-conscious, proponents and critics of moral influence accounts have tended to think that the justificatory force derives from the efficacy of the particular instance of so criticizing or praising in that particular time and circumstance.

That's a view. A more plausible view, however, construes the justification for moral praise and blame as arising not at the level of particular interpersonal interactions, but instead, at the level of a general practice. On the model I propose, the justification arises from the group-level effects of justified norms that are ubiquitously internalized by members of the community and regularly put into practice.[17] This difference—both a scaling back of ambition and elevation of the source of justification from

---

[17] A note about the locution "justified norms": for present purposes, very little turns on whether you think norms are best understood as *justified* or *true* or *appropriate* or what not. What I need is some notion of privileged norms of the sort with suitable standing to guide our practical deliberations. As I think about it, norms are ubiquitous (perhaps they are abstract propositional-like entities, roughly imperatival in structure), but only some have any claim on us, and only some of those with any claim on us go on to have corresponding social currency and psychological uptake of the sort that counts as internalization. I use the notion of "justified" to pick out norms that have that normatively privileged status.

tokens to the in-practice effects of the system of norms of praise and blame as a whole—turns out to dissolve many of the familiar objections to the idea of moral influence.[18]

I'll have more to say about this idea in a moment, but let's assume it is on the table. We can now move another piece already on the table into position. Recall an idea from the previous chapter: we should understand responsible agency in terms that emphasize our distinctive reasoning capacity. There are a lot of ways we can develop the basic idea of the primacy of reasons, but let us suppose the way to do this is to emphasize *responsiveness to moral considerations*. This too will need unpacking, but let's assume we have some way of doing that. If you give me all of that (provisionally—and yes, I know my promissory notes are stacking up here), then we're in a position to see how the picture comes together.

Here's the crucial conjecture at the heart of what I've been calling "the agency cultivation model": *what would justify our responsibility characteristic practices, is if these practices fostered a distinctive form of agency in us, a kind of agency sensitive to and governed by moral considerations.*

A characteristic feature of responsible agents is the ability to entertain moral concerns and decide upon courses of action in light of these considerations. On this picture, the capacities tied to moral concerns are the hallmark of responsible agency, and *this* is why praise and blame that responds to and reacts to those capacities is properly a subject of such intense concern for us. Moreover, there is some reason to think that our moral considerations-sensitive agency is intrinsically valuable, or even just substantially important for other things we care about, including how we structure shared social space and our expectations concerning interpersonal possibilities.

Whether any of this works depends on what the pieces come to. So, a preliminary outline of those ideas is now in order.

A. Teleology

Start with the observation that this picture is modestly teleological. Justification for holding agents responsible, for perpetuating our practices of praise

---

[18] To be sure, framing matters in this way invites concerns of the sort that arise for two-tiered consequentialism, including worries about the theory being self-effacing. Although I will address some of those issues as they seem especially pertinent to the case of responsibility, I won't fend off every analog of every worry that arises in the case of two-tiered consequentialist accounts. I'm betting that the general strategy is viable. And, so far as we know, it is.

and blame, derives from those things contributing to the achievement of an outcome. Unlike the classical MI theory, on the agency cultivation model the relevant outcome is not utility or welfare. Instead, the relevant outcome is the development or achievement of a form of agency.

This modestly teleological picture of the responsibility-characteristic practices can suggest a larger picture of the responsibility system as a whole. If our practices can be justified by this kind of effect, we might be tempted to expand the scope of the idea. That is, we might conjecture that the responsibility system is justified because of its role in bringing about agents of this sort.[19]

On this picture, the internal logic of the system is properly shaped by those statuses, practices, and judgments that play some role in achieving the outcome. On an ambitious version of this conjecture, it is not merely the defensibility of our practices of holding responsible that are at stake. It is also the *truth* of various statuses, and the appropriateness of various connected attitudes, that turn out to be at stake.

Recall that even if we justify the practice of holding one another responsible, it might be that we conclude that the practice presumes something false. However, in chapter 4, I argued that if we can work out an adequate justification for our responsibility practices, this might provide us with an independent standpoint from which to anchor a revisionist account. That is, it might provide us with an account of what makes it the case that various paradigmatic responsibility statuses, such as *being responsible* are had, so that we could see how truths about such things might be sustained in the face of skeptical threats.

The ambitious, truth-determining version of this conjecture is compatible with the idea that there are other variables structuring the particulars of the responsibility system, apart from those elements that contribute to cultivation of the target form of agency. Minimally, there are facts about our psychologies and the circumstances in which we conduct our norm-shaped lives, and there are the larger conceptual demands about the role that responsibility plays in our lives with respect to regulating praise and blame and the connection of these things to concepts like right and wrong action.

I am tempted by the more ambitious conjecture. For the moment, though, all I hope to make plausible is the more modest thought that the

[19] I will thus sometimes speak of "the aim" of the responsibility system. This locution is not meant to imply that the responsibility system is somehow an agent, possessing desires, intentions, or similar mental states. Rather, it is simply shorthand for the idea that the responsibility system can be justified by its role in cultivating the relevant form of agency.

responsibility-characteristic practices of holding one another responsible could be justified if those practices foster a special kind of agency.

B. *Internalization of norms*

Return to idea that we would be justified deploying responsibility-characteristic practices where such practices, as a whole and over time, foster the development of moral considerations-responsive agency. Internalization of norms of praise and blame is key. Without internalization of such norms, it is hard to see how actual practices could be suitably stable and reliable enough to yield the relevant result.

A guiding presumption here is that effective responsibility practices will exploit our psychology, and are largely parasitic on it. On this picture *expressions* of praise and blame—and characteristic behavior that flows from blaming reactions[20]—initially work by providing external motivation for agents to track moral considerations and regulate their behavior in light of them. For creatures like us, at least when we are acquiring our habits of normatively structured dispositions, praising reactions typically encourage and blaming reactions usually discourage.

The important point is this: norms for which we start off having only external motivations to obey will, under many conditions, go on to become internalized. When that happens, the norms are experienced as intrinsically motivating, and such agents will typically go on to both perpetuate and enforce those norms.

How this happens, and the variety of conditions that facilitate or frustrate that process—at a time and across generations—remains a matter of some speculation. It seems clear that there are distinctive aspects of our affective endowments that play an important role in the acquisition of norms and how we regard them as reasons giving.[21] What appears indisputable is that norm internalization does happen, and there is good evidence that humans are especially receptive to norm internalization through early adolescence.[22]

---

[20] See chapter 4, §4d–e.

[21] See Shaun Nichols, *Sentimental Rules: On the Natural Foundations of Moral Judgment* (Oxford: Oxford University Press, 2004), ch. 7.

[22] For an overview of that literature, and a general proposal for the involved mechanisms, see Chandra Sripada and Stephen Stich, "A Framework for the Psychology of Norms," in *The Innate Mind: Volume 2: Culture and Cognition*, ed. Peter Carruthers et al. (New York: Oxford University Press, 2006).

The present proposal is that norms of moralized praise and blame work in this fashion. Initially, they operate by providing external incentives. However, in the ordinary case, those norms are internalized and come to motivate without the work of external sanctions. To be sure, in the case of norms of praise and blame, an advantage of internalization is that it can facilitate avoidance of sanction and pursuit of positive social recognition. However, once norms of moralized praise and blame are internalized, the external sanctioning element need not play any role at all in the considered agent's deliberations. Internalization ordinarily entails the norm is experienced as intrinsically motivating. Indeed, the benefits that flow from internalization of the norm can be entirely beside the point from the standpoint of the agent's deliberations.[23]

Internalization of norms of praise and blame does more than structure the conception of action possibilities. It also structures the agent's self-assessments of praiseworthiness, blameworthiness, and desert. So, internalized norms of moralized praise and blame come to shape both the agent's prospective and retrospective self-assessments. In turn, such assessments license a range of evaluative and emotional responses from blame and recrimination to positive self-regard and self-satisfaction.

Internalization does not ensure perfectly compliant behavior. Agents might be akratic with respect to internalized norms. Moreover, any given agent might decide that there is some reason that trumps the edicts of the praising and blaming norms. Some agents might even conclude that one's own internalized norms are not actually justified. What matters for the present account, though, is that norms of moral praise and blame can come to structure the deliberations of agents even when actual expressions of praise and blame are unlikely or absent.

If all this is right, then here another piece of the picture: norms of praise and blame ordinarily come to be internalized, and once they do, they motivate agents and structure their assessments independently of any external sanctions. To the extent to which such norms reflect concerns for moral considerations, internalization of those norms will be one avenue by which

---

[23] Elements of this basic picture obviously have a long history, stretching back at least to accounts of the internalization of norms found in Nietzsche and Freud. Nietzsche, *On the Genealogy of Morality*; Sigmund Freud, *Civilization and Its Discontents* (New York: Norton, 1989). Both accounts share the thought, crucial here, that moral norms come to shape the psychology of agents even under conditions where no external threat is present.

practices of praise and blame foster forms of agency that are suitably responsive to moral considerations.

C. Indirect effects and the limits of our psychology

The justifying effects of the practice need not be direct, for many of the
effects are mediated by aspects of our psychology that function on the basis
of other concerns and principles.

The agency cultivation model's teleological, norm-internalizing picture
of moral influence allows us to see why it is a mistake to think that moral
influence must be direct, expressed in each tokening of blame or praise.
First, there is no need for every instance of praise or blame to directly
contribute to the cultivation of the requisite form of agency. All that is
required is that the system as a whole produces agents that, over time and in
a wide range of contexts, are suitably responsive to moral considerations.
Thus, there can be a certain degree of slack between norms, their expressions, and their effects. Moreover, some apparently non- or even wrongly
influencing instances of blaming and praising may indirectly contribute to
the general efficacy of the practices over time.

To motivate the picture of how indirect effects might contribute to the
justification of our responsibility practices, first consider a non-moral case.
Suppose that the aim of the practice of football includes fun for the
competitors and entertainment for the spectators. The rules of football
may sometimes require games where a sequence of foul calls is neither fun
for the competitors nor conducive to the entertainment of the fans. However, having a regular, stable system of foul calls in place surely contributes
to the fun and entertainment of the sport over time. Analogously, there may
be instances where my gratitude or indignation may fail to influence anyone
in the proper fashion. Nonetheless, my gratitude (or indignation) can have
an appropriate role, internal to a system of moral influence, because the
prevalence of such attitudes and corresponding practices contributes to the
efficacy and stability of the responsibility system over time.[24]

---

[24] In broad outlines, this sort of idea has been developed and defended by Robert Merrihew Adams,
"Motive Utilitarianism," *Journal of Philosophy* 73 (1976): 467–81; Richard B. Brandt, *A Theory of the Good
and the Right* (Oxford: Clarendon Press, 1979); David Copp, *Morality, Normativity, and Society* (New
York: Oxford University Press, 1995); Brad Hooker, *Ideal Code, Real World: A Rule-Consequentialist
Theory of Morality* (New York: Oxford University Press, 2000).

A second point to recognize is that our psychology puts limits on the justified norms of praise and blame. As we have seen, the efficacy of the norms depends partly on their internalization. However, given that our psychologies are messy (that is, many of the mechanisms involved have functions and histories that do not neatly map onto existing social roles), it is likely that some of the psychological mechanisms on which internalized responsibility norms depend play diverse roles in our psychological economy. Anger, resentment, satisfaction, and so on can have both moral and non-moral roles in that economy.

The various roles these attitudes play and the psychological mechanisms they rely upon may impose limits or create psychological phenomena that—at least from a specifically moral perspective (or even a more limited perspective exclusively concerned with moral responsibility)—are undesirable or in tension with the distinctly moral roles for which those mechanisms have been appropriated. Our complete psychological economy is complex; the individual mechanisms of influence and motivation play various roles that are not likely to be optimized exclusively for the subtle and complicated mechanisms of moral appraisal. So, here too, we find reason for slack between mechanism and effect.

A third way in which our psychology is relevant to the content and operations of the responsibility norms has to do with the possibility that some of the responsibility-characteristic attitudes may be unavoidable and largely unchangeable. For example, we may discover that feeling resentment at being a target of apparently unjustified ill will is a largely implastic piece of our cognitive and affective architecture.[25] If so, a theory of responsibility will have to allow for resentment, even if resentment generally fails to contribute to a system that fosters moral consideration-sensitive agency. Even the most effective set of practices will contain concessions to our psychologies, and every (plausible, implementable) theory of responsibility will be constrained by the limitations of human psychology. The best we can hope for are practices that, as a whole, work reasonably well with and for creatures with psychologies like ours.[26]

---

[25] This is a much more limited hypothesis than the one entertained by Strawson: it does not presuppose that all reactive attitudes are implastic, or that they stand and fall together.

[26] Two notes about the foregoing: First, the potential discovery that the operations of gratitude and the other reactive attitudes are generally inescapable consequences of our psychology is compatible with those inescapable features having indirect benefits. Second, resentment could thus turn out to be

This last point is an important one, and it returns us to the point I opened with: the justification of holding responsible should be understood as the justification of a network of norm-structured practices and attendant attitudes, judgments, and statuses. Individual practices or attitudes may not serve to influence a particular agent in a suitable fashion. However, if those practices or attitudes are necessary upshots of a psychology-dependent system that enables us to promote the relevant justified ends, then norms that respect that fact are perfectly acceptable and, indeed, required.

What matters is the overall efficacy of the responsibility system in influencing us, and not a particular instance of holding someone responsible. The norms that are justified just are those norms whose currency in the psychology and practices of a community would, in fact, foster among us the kind of moral considerations-responsive agency that is the responsibility system's concern.[27] Plausibly, many of these norms will be expressed in practices that, in their exercise, conception, and application have no element of immediate concern with influence.

This point allows us to see something about what I'll call *practical spandrels*,[28] as distinct from indirect effects. What is distinctive about practical spandrels is that they are side-effects of an otherwise effective system. Whether something is an indirect effect or a practical spandrel depends on whether it contributes to the aim of the responsibility system or whether it is a byproduct of something else that is necessary for pursuit of the aim of the responsibility system, respectively.

Suppose we learn that moral revulsion can be jettisoned, psychologically and socially speaking. Further, suppose we learn that it does not directly contribute to the fostering of moral considerations-responsive agency. Before we recommend excision of it from our moral practices we would need to know two things. First, we would need to know if it indirectly contributes to the overall efficacy and stability of the responsibility system over time. If it does, then it may have a place in a justified system of practices in light of its indirect effects. If it does not, then we still need to ask whether

unjustified in some "normatively best" or otherwise ideal sense, but justified in the "best we can do, given our natures" non-ideal sense. I am only concerned to meet the second "best we can do, given our natures" sense.

[27] This account of the justification of the responsibility norms has some parallels with the account of the justification of norms given in Copp, *Morality, Normativity, and Society*.

[28] Thanks to John Fischer for suggesting the label.

it is a practical spandrel, a byproduct of something that does play an appropriate or necessary part of our responsibility practices.

If moral revulsion were a practical spandrel—a necessary or inescapable byproduct of an imperfectly efficient system—then it would be safe from complaint for just this reason. Like the various forms of gas produced by human digestion, it might be the sort of thing that we put up with, manage, or ignore but whose elimination would (presumably) require drastic measures we are unwilling to undertake.

My point is *not* that moral responsibility is like indigestion. Instead, my point is that one can allow that the justification of praise and blame might derive from the efficacy of those norms in influencing us, without thereby committing ourselves to the view that every instance, or even every type of characteristic emotional reaction, thereby contributes to influencing us in the appropriate way. Sometimes, counter-productivity is a necessary consequence of the most effective available system.

Consider a case in which a particular agent would be unmoved by praise, blame, or some display of responsibility attribution. On the traditional MI account, that agent could not be responsible for his or her actions. On the agency cultivation model, whether the agent is morally responsible for his or her actions is not a function of that particular agent's susceptibility to influence in that particular circumstance. Instead, it is a function of two facts: (1) whether the agent is suitably responsive to moral considerations (yes, I know—I still owe you an account of this); and (2) what the norms of praise and blame say about the actions of that type in that context. At a general level, the norms of praise and blame just are those that are most effective at collectively influencing agents in the appropriate way.

Again: the content of the responsibility norms need not have a consequentialist character. Indeed, it seems implausible that they would, given the kinds of psychologies that we find ourselves with, and given the virtues of comparatively coarse-grained and simple principles for structuring our actions and guiding our evaluations of ourselves and others. It is for this reason that I think the quality of will account I started with does plausible work here, although one can imagine various alternative characterizations of those norms. As I see it, the quality of will story provides a unifying characterization of what sorts of norms might plausibly be those that cultivate considerations-sensitive agency. The result is a package of views that can combine the centrality of "quality of will" blame norms with the justificatory power of the teleological account.

D. On the matter of individual cases

As I noted above, on the agency cultivation model the norms of praising and blaming are structured by a range of concerns tied to the aim and justification of the responsibility system, the facts of human psychology, and the contexts in which the norms are applied. And, as we have seen, the responsibility norms will plausibly be structured by larger theoretical demands, such as stability and psychological efficacy. Here, I will remark on how some familiar concerns about the relationship of systemic justifications to individual cases.

Consider the psychologies we plausibly have: multi-purposed, emotionally complex, norm-structured systems. It takes time for us to acquire the relevant sensitivities and responsibility-characteristic reactions. Given such psychologies, a frequently fluctuating network of norms and practices would be a disaster for our ability to govern ourselves and others in compliance with justified responsibility norms.

Now consider one familiar objection to rule-utilitarianism: it collapses into act-utilitarianism because the best system of rules would be the one that has rules about individual cases. In at least the case of moral responsibility, the second-order moral influence theory is buttressed against such a collapse by the realities of our psychologies, including the length of time it takes to develop and refine moral attitudes, the flexibility of our attitudes, the cognitive burden involved in assessing responsibility, and the overarching need to have a stable and efficacious system of influence. Collectively, these considerations will tend to weigh against something like act- or token-specific norms of responsibility.

One might grant all of this yet still ask how we move from the justification of the responsibility system as a whole to the more particular justification for individual instances of praising and blaming. That a norm of coming to a complete stop at a traffic stop sign might be generally justified does not answer the question of whether adherence to it is justified in this case. It might, from a practical standpoint, be justified enough if I think I am in the ordinary case. But, if I am asking whether I am in that case, knowing that the norm is generally justified does not seem to settle the question. If the question is unsettled, it is not clear whether praise or blame is in fact licensed.

In general, facts about whether a given responsible agent deserves praise or blame for something will be settled, at least internal to the norms of moral responsibility, by what the norms say about cases of that type. The justification in the individual case follows this relation of fact to type. Since the norms are given in part by their general efficacy, we can expect that most cases will fall unproblematically under their scope, as instances where praise and blame plausibly play the right sorts of roles, given facts about the agents and their circumstances. These will be cases where praise and blame are justified or at least permitted as a tokening of those practices or judgments that are, in fact, justified in the ways I have described.

In the individual case of an assignment of responsibility, the most we can reasonably demand is something like a pragmatically warranted judgment about what seems to be the case, normatively speaking, in the circumstances we find ourselves. Given that we accept that the norms of responsibility are justified as a whole, at least partly in light of how they contribute to our being moral considerations–responsive agents, it seems to me that we will ordinarily have adequate grounds for believing that, in any typical case, these norms will likely apply.

On this point, the possibility of indirect effects, practical spandrels, and our ordinary psychological messiness can do some work in helping us see how we ordinarily have at least a pragmatic warrant for thinking praise and blame are justified in the usual sorts of ways even if we might wonder about the status of some norm in a particular case. That is, there might well be cases where praising or blaming is not justified even if in general such acts are. Such cases would be relatively isolated from wider practices and principles. Otherwise, the practical and cognitive costs of adopting a different set of norms about this and related cases might well exceed the advantages of the alternative norm. (Indeed, one reason for avoiding thinking too much about the status of particular cases is that it might weaken the grip that the norm has on us!) So: exceptional, norm–divergent cases aren't ruled out on this approach, but there is no reason to think they will be the standard case.[29]

---

[29] One might wonder what happens if the marginal cases are frequent. But there is something incoherent about the worry. What justifies the whole of the system is precisely that it gets the right

There is one important class of cases where the usual pragmatic warrant might be defeated. These are cases with agents in new, unusual, or particularly challenging contexts of action. In such cases, though, it looks like the right place to look for settling whether praise and blame are justified is not so much the theory of responsibility norms but, perhaps somewhat surprisingly, the account of responsible agency.

Here is why: if the threat to a responsibility ascription operates via some threat to the normal capacity to respond to moral considerations (as seems more likely in cases of new, unusual, or particularly challenging contexts of action), then the issue is how these concerns are accommodated internal to some account of the capacities required for being subject to the responsibility norms. In other words, we look to our theory of responsible agency. Once the capacity issue is settled, there may be some features of that agent that become relevant to the assignment of praise and blame (for example, perhaps the difficulty of responding to moral considerations is not high enough to render that agent a non-responsible one in that circumstance, but perhaps it is high enough to fund a degree of mitigation). Nevertheless, the basic issue seems to be a challenge to the details of a theory of responsible agency more so than the details of a theory of the responsibility norms. So, at least internal to the norms of responsible agency it seems we can account for the justification of most concrete cases of praise and blame.

Since the blame norms and their attendant practices receive their justification from more general facts about their efficacy in a community, one might be worried that we can adopt a standpoint external to them and ask whether there is justification for the enforcement of those norms in a particular case, if we do not necessarily take ourselves to be bound by responsibility norms in general.

These issues are difficult, but it seems to me that there are two lines of reply.

First, I see no reason to suppose that a theory of responsibility must provide a decisive answer to the more basic normative question of what

results in the majority of cases. It might be conceivable that there is a world in which there is no system of internalized and practicable norms suffices to generate justification for holding agents responsible. Such a case would provide grounds for skepticism about the whole project of moral responsibility, funding a kind of skepticism about moral responsibility that would respect its conceptual and practical role in a way that most prominent forms of responsibility skepticism do not. But the circumstances of such a case seem very remote from our own.

one ought to do, all things considered, even in cases where what is at stake is some matter of moral responsibility. This is because a theory of responsibility must be silent on those considerations whose origin or normative force places them external to the norms of responsibility. This more fundamental normative or deliberative task—settling the all-things-considered practical matter—even in cases concerning responsibility, is more clearly a task for a theory of normative ethics or a theory of practical reason. So, if we adopt a standpoint external to the norms of responsibility or from a standpoint that is skeptical of moral force in general, and ask how to close the gap between the justification for the responsibility norms and the justification of some particular instance of praise and blame, the question becomes uninteresting for a theory of responsibility. If the edicts of the responsibility norms are only inputs into some greater normative, practical calculation, a piece of deliberation where responsibility norms can be trumped by other concerns, then when we ask this question external to the norms of moral responsibility we cease to be talking about a question that must be answered by a theory of moral responsibility. At best, the responsibility norms identify the salient normative facts relevant to concerns of responsibility, but the ultimate question of whether one is justified in blaming, all things considered, is to be decided by appeal to considerations beyond the scope of this account.

A second line of response focuses on the externality issue in a different way. Given that the justification for any particular instance of blaming hinges on normative issues outside of merely a theory of responsibility, what may be at stake in asking the question (whether some particular case of blaming is justified) is only whether we can re-establish the warrant for adopting a standpoint internal to the norms of responsibility. As this warrant is funded by some confidence in our moral assessments, the generally justified status of the norms, the ordinariness of our case and so on, all we can do is rehearse the reasons for caring about moral responsibility, working through the arguments for its importance. In re-establishing our confidence in those things, we re-establish confidence in our judgments of concrete particular cases of responsibility ascriptions.

To sum up: depending on what is asked, we can answer the questions about whether it is justifiable to blame in a number of ways. The basic picture here is that blame norms are justified as whole in light of their role in fostering a kind of agency. Or, in the particular form important to this account, quality of will norms and associated practices are justified by their role in cultivating a form of agency sensitive to moral considerations. Whether it is justifiable to blame in a particular case derives from the status of the agent and the action, given the justified norms. It is, as it were, a question internal to the practice of moral responsibility. We might raise questions internal to the practice, but such questions will usually be met with considerations about the usual pragmatic warrant for ascribing responsibility. External to the blaming norms, but still internal to larger aspects of the practice (or at least, the commitments of the responsibility system) are questions about whether the agent was the right sort of agent in considered circumstances. Here, the details turn on the theory of responsible agency, which is the subject of the next chapter. Finally, one can ask about the justification of praise and blame from a standpoint entirely external to the practice from, for example, the standpoint of what reasons we have to do something, all things considered. This is a question that a theory of responsibility, qua responsibility, may be able to shirk. Nevertheless, a teleological account has at least something to point to in its defense: the multifarious contributions its proposed norms have for the achievement of a valuable form of agency.

6. Modularity, non-exclusivity, and provisionality

I have been characterizing an approach to responsibility that takes its inspiration from one aspect of the classical MI picture. There are three further ideas I wish to couple with the agency cultivation model: *modularity*, *non-exclusivity*, and *provisionality*.

In light of the larger methodological commitment to a limited ethics approach, the present account should be understood as *modular*. That is, it can be integrated with different ethical theories without affecting the basic justification for the distinctive norms of responsibility. However, how we understand various elements of the account, and what external constraints structure and limit the account will vary by pairing. So, for example, if paired with consequentialism, we should look to the consequentialist theory of the good to inform the account of moral considerations. If paired with a Kantian ethical theory, moral considerations will presumably be understood in a different way, connected to the categorical imperative. Since the moral influence theory is not intended to be an account of right action, but rather a broadly modular account of moral responsibility, details about how to understand the content of moral notions invoked by the account will be subject to variation.[30]

A related but distinct aspect of my view is that it is normatively *non-exclusive*. A normatively exclusive account would maintain that this "higher-order" moral influence account is the sole way of justifying our responsibility-characteristic practices and attitudes. However, I see no reason to dismiss the possibility that there may be other, perhaps imperfectly overlapping, alternative justifications that independently vindicate or modify some subset of our responsibility characteristic practices and attitudes. If any of our reactive attitudes or responsibility-characteristic practices have other sources of justification as well, then so much the better. Multiple overlapping justifications can coexist peacefully, and indeed, prove to be mutually supporting in our moral practices. There would, of course, be interesting and complex issues in cases of conflict, but with respect to the general collection of our responsibility-characteristic practices, the present account should not be regarded as precluding alternative justificatory paths.

The rejection of normative exclusivity entails that my account is provisional. Discovery of additional, independent justifications for responsibility-characteristic practices and attitudes will potentially create conflicts where one justification counsels something that differs from the other. For example, an alternative account of the justification of the responsibility system fleshed out primarily in terms of a principle of fairness might, at various points, conflict with the account proposed here. We would then need to go in for further refinements in the account in light of this discovery.

There is a further reason for insisting on the provisionality of the present account. The justified blame norms are blame norms for now. However, as

---

[30] Again, I am supposing that many moral notions could survive in the absence of libertarian freedom. Certainly many, if not most, philosophers working in normative ethics seem to accept something like this point. And, many theories of justice seem to operate without presuming a notion of libertarian agency, although the matter is complicated. For discussion, see Samuel Scheffler, "Responsibility, Reactive Attitudes, and Liberalism in Philosophy and Politics," *Philosophy & Public Affairs* 21, no. 4 (1992): 299–324; S. L. Hurley, *Justice, Luck, and Knowledge* (Cambridge, MA: Harvard University Press, 2003).

our practices and the attendant psychology adjust to different circumstances, it is plausible to think that what blame norms are justified will also change.

I'm not suggesting that this will happen overnight, or with any frequency. On the contrary, I'm inclined to think that although our psychology is somewhat malleable, it is also fairly viscous. Although the present account takes our psychology as something of a theoretical primitive, it also countenances the possibility that the nature and disposition of that primitive may shift over time (*pace* Strawson). It is a picture on which there is a kind of mutual constitution between psychology, norms, and practices. Provisionality is simply a feature of the perpetually iterating nature of justified practices.

7. Answering the traditional objections

I have attempted to show how we might find some modest but not unimportant use for the idea of moral influence when it comes to the matter of justifying our responsibility-characteristic practices. As I noted at the outset of this project, the traditional picture of moral influence is held in sufficiently low esteem that any purported rehabilitation of this idea has to explain how those decisive criticisms of yore can be avoided. That is the task of this section.

Recall that the principal objections levied against traditional moral influence accounts were these: (1) that MI theories cannot adequately distinguish between responsible and non-responsible agents; and (2) that moral influence cannot be distinguished from other kinds of influence; (3) that MI theories cannot respect the distinction between being responsible and being appropriately held responsible; (4) that MI theories grossly mischaracterize how we praise and blame, and our concerns in doing so; (5) that MI theories cannot accommodate backward-looking moral concerns; and (6) that moral influence theories are inappropriately committed to a particular theory of normative ethics.

It should now be apparent that many of the objections simply do not apply to the agency cultivation model, in light of the more modest role it allows for moral influence. The details, however, are instructive.

Objections 1 and 2 are different aspects of the complaint that MI accounts are too course-grained to be adequate as theories of responsibility. The objections were potent when directed at traditional accounts. However, they are clearly inapplicable to the less ambitious role to which MI has been constrained in my account. Regarding objection 1, that an MI account cannot make suitable distinctions among agents, the answer is simple: My account does not rely upon MI to distinguish between responsible and non-responsible agents. That work is left to an account of responsible agency, which on my view is tied to a kind of moral considerations-responsive agency. Such an account, while compatible with the restricted use to which I put the idea of MI, does not itself depend on it. So, objection 1 is answered.

A critic could complain that such an account of responsible agency is not sufficient in the present context. After all, one might think that in light of these reflections on moral influence, a further condition holds on responsible agents: responsible agents must be influenceable. If they were not, it is hard to see how the account could get going. Were this reply correct, then we would be right back to the problematic idea that influenceability defines responsible agency, and that we have no way of drawing suitable distinctions between kinds of agents.

Notice, though, that agents who are responsive to moral considerations are influenceable precisely in virtue of their sensitivity to moral reasons. Indeed, it is the presence of this sensitivity that normally makes otherwise mere agents into *responsible* agents. So, not only does a Reasons account (at least of the sort I am suggesting) allow us some notion of the-agent-as-influenceable, the kind of influence that it countenances (i.e., action governance in light of moral considerations) permits us to draw the line in exactly the right place. Agents that cannot recognize or appropriately respond to such considerations are not in the ambit of responsibility, and those that can do those things, are properly subject to the norms of praise and blame.[31]

With respect to the other coarse-grainedness complaint, concerning MI's inability to distinguishing between kinds of influence, there is more to be said. Again, though, the reply hinges on the different labors assigned to the individual parts of a theory of responsibility.

---

[31] Again, I am bracketing cases of derivative responsibility where agents might not be responsible agents at the time of action but are nevertheless responsible on some tracing-related ground.

On the account I have offered, justified praise and blame involves the judgment that particular responsibility-characteristic attitudes (e.g., indignation) are licensed when directed at the target of evaluation.[32] In turn, this judgment presupposes that the evaluated agent is the right sort of agent to be a target for those reactions. So, on this account, the appropriateness of praise and blame is parasitic on the truth of the judgment that the target of praise and blame is a responsible agent. And, as we have seen, that is given by a theory of responsible agency and not a theory of the justification of the responsibility norms.

In contrast, other forms of influencing the behavior of agents have no such requirement that the agent be a responsible agent, and indeed no such supposition ordinarily built into them. In influencing a household pet, there is (ordinarily) no judgment that the pet is a responsible agent. Hence, the form of regard expressed in distinctively moral praise and blame is not present. So, even if some of the practices of moral influence are superficially indistinguishable from non-moral influence, the underlying attitudes and judgments are distinct.

What this makes clear is that judgments of genuinely moral praiseworthiness and blameworthiness have a distinctive cognitive content to them, a content that makes error possible. We can believe that the relevant capacities are present when they are not and we can mistakenly suppose that they are absent when they are present. What makes a genuine ascription of responsibility true is (i) the agent is a responsible agent and (ii) that the considered instance of moral influence corresponds to what a stable, justified responsibility system would prescribe or permit, given the facts about human psychology and given the aims of the responsibility system.

Even were we able to influence a cat's behavior in light of expressions of responsibility-characteristic attitudes and practices (such as moral praising and blaming), it would nevertheless fail to be genuinely moral praise or blame unless the praiser or blamer also believed that cats were responsible agents. Presumably, we sometimes make errors in the case of humans (and maybe, sometimes in the case of cats). All such cases show is that real praise and blame can arise from mistaken assessments of responsibility. And this is

---

[32] Here I focus on judgments of blameworthiness or praiseworthiness. The consequent blaming or praising attitude might be stymied for any number of reasons.

exactly what we should think. So, the second objection concerning coarseness is dispatched.[33]

The third major objection to traditional MI theories is that they cannot respect the important difference between whether someone is responsible and whether it is appropriate to hold someone responsible. Since agents can be responsible without it being appropriate to hold them responsible (recall the example of arbitrarily punishing only one person for his or her impolitic remark), any theory that collapses these distinct assessments fails to reflect an important feature of our thinking about responsibility. Traditional MI accounts appear to fail in just this way. They begin with an account of when we should hold someone responsible (when it is efficacious) and conclude that someone is responsible only when we should hold him or her responsible.

The account I have given permits a different response to this objection: whether someone is morally responsible depends on two things: (i) whether the evaluated agent is a responsible agent and (ii) the content of the relevant praise and blame norms for such agents in contexts of that sort. As I suggested earlier, though, this is consistent with a view that emphasizes that we can ask questions external to the responsibility system. We can ask whether a responsible agent ought to be held morally responsible in light of, say, considerations of justice, benevolence, prudence, and so on—even if that agent is both a responsible agent and indeed morally responsible.

One aspect of this picture is that it reflects a degree of modesty about the role that moral responsibility plays in our lives. Responsibility is important,

---

[33] Would practices of moral influence via praising and blaming constitute practices of *moral responsibility* without the presumption of responsible agency and the attendant stance or complex of characteristic attitudes and dispositions to judgment that follow from that judgment? I am inclined to think the answer is no. Something like this thought may be why some philosophers have thought that consequentialism is ill-suited to accommodate a concept of moral responsibility. Inasmuch as the theory places no special emphasis on recognizing the presence of our (perhaps distinctively human) capacity to recognize and respond to moral considerations, it looks like consequentialism cannot capture a core feature of moral responsibility. Of course, some contemporary forms of consequentialism are permissive about what counts as a value or an element of the good, and these accounts do not necessarily face this problem. If we include a shared recognition of our moral considerations-responsive humanity as something we value, then the objection can be sidestepped. These are delicate issues, and they connect to complex issues concerning consequentialist accommodation of side-constraints. If there is a way to get a "meaty" (or perhaps "meaty-like") notion of side-constraints in consequentialist form, then there may be no deep reason why this element of our responsibility practices—the characteristic form of agential regard manifest in the thinking someone is a responsible agent—cannot be suitably accommodated in a consequentialist framework.

but it does not and perhaps ought not override every other consideration in our lives. There are standpoints and concerns from which focusing on whether to praise or blame seems misplaced, even when there is a clear answer from the standpoint of moral responsibility. So, even if you thought that all-in moral considerations ought to be decisive in deliberation, it seems doubtful that the norms of moral responsibility (specifically, and by themselves) are the sort of thing that trump all other considerations.

The account's modularity is also relevant on this point. When engaged in the practice of praising and blaming, what we purportedly have reason to do depends on the background theory presumed. Although we can describe the general shape of a system of moral responsibility—its logic, as it were—particular cases will be decided by the integrated mesh of the norms of both responsibility and normative ethics.

To see how all of this operates, consider a concern that I have not yet directly mentioned, but is a familiar worry about consequentialist-style justifications: scapegoating. Suppose that we learned that the most effective, stable set of responsibility norms involved blaming some group of people who had done no wrong. So, for example, suppose that given a particular history and set of historical circumstances, the responsibility norms that most effectively yielded the right sorts of agents were norms that among other things, recommended blaming innocent members of some socially stigmatized group. If the account I have been developing permits this, one might think this is a significant strike against it.

There are, I think, two different lines of response appropriate here, one turning on the particular details of the package of views I favor, the other deriving from more general features of a modular account. I will pursue these lines of response in order.

First, notice how strange this result would be. It is easy to provide an abstract characterization of scapegoating, but it is difficult to see how a norm of praising and blaming that directs us to blame innocents would turn out to cultivate the requisite form of agency. The aim of the responsibility system, I have claimed, is to foster moral considerations-sensitive agency. I have also said that genuine judgments of praiseworthiness and blameworthiness contain a kind content to them, requiring that the target of the judgment be a moral considerations-responsive agent. These elements seems to preclude the kind of scapegoating scenario precisely because scapegoating an individual or group would be to fail to regard those agents in a way that is concerned with respecting and fostering the form of agency with which the responsibility system is concerned.

One might insist that this line of response is insufficient because any system-level justification of the sort I've emphasized is going to tolerate a certain amount of infelicity if the payoff is sufficiently large. It might be that scapegoating as a large-scale systematic practice is unlikely for precisely the reasons I specified. However, relatively localized instances of scapegoating might turn out to be called for if they entailed sufficiently big results for cultivating moral considerations-sensitive agency.[34]

To be sure, it remains an open question whether *any* account with this sort of two-tiered structure has resources for blocking effective collapse of the first-order norms in this way. These issues remain unresolved, and it would be a mistake to try to resolve them in any sweeping way here. That said, I'm inclined to think that the norms will have a broadly quality-of-will-oriented structure, and that a global trumping condition of "except when violating those norms will yield massive payoffs of the aim of the system" will not make it into the set of justified norms.

Here's why: one constraint on the justification of the norms is that they must be reasonably easily internalized and propagated across a diverse social world that expects local consistency in norms. If that's right, then a package of blame norms that include a universal trumping norm (i.e., blame whenever the payoff is high enough) that is at odds with the first-order requirements of the rest of the norms will be considerably more complicated and difficulty to implement, and thus, less justifiable than a system of blame norms that does not require learning, internalizing, and reliably implementing this norm. Such a norm would not be just one more norm. Instead, it would be a norm that requires agents to be prepared to radically re-evaluate the applicability of all the other norms at all times. That strikes me as a dubious candidate norm, given the constraints that plausibly govern a practicable system of norms.

Obviously, there is a lot more than can be said here, both pro and con. Fortunately, there is a second, independent line of response available here. It is roughly this: if you are a consequentialist, scapegoating is something you are already okay with or something you otherwise have resources to address; if you are a Kantian, you already have independent resources for blocking

---

[34] Thanks to Dana Nelkin for emphasizing this concern.

the permissibility of scapegoating. Either way, scapegoating is not a distinct-ive challenge for the account.

The key idea in this response is the idea of modularity, or the thought that this account is intended to be inserted into a more global account of ethical norms. So, ethical theories that do not centrally countenance fairness or that lack a notion of respect for persons will have few resources to rule out the permissibility of scapegoating in the context of responsibility. However, such accounts will already have to explain away or otherwise account for our convictions about the impermissibility of scapegoating. In contrast, if your theory of normative ethics holds, for example, that it is unfair to hold people to account for what they did not do, then that principle and its independent standing can constitute a fixed normative point around which the responsibility norms must conform.

Responsibility is only one set of normative concerns, and the end of the responsibility system is only one end among many legitimate concerns. Nothing in this account suggests otherwise, and I regard it as a virtue of the account that its normative structure can be made to conform to inde-pendent and antecedent commitments including fairness, proportionality, and so on. So, regardless of one's position on the general permissibility of scapegoating, the theory of moral responsibility can defer resolution of this matter to normative ethics.

Let's turn to objection (4) above, i.e., that MI theories grossly miscon-strue our responsibility practices, confusing a part of our responsibility practices (aiming to influence) with the entirety of our practices. On this objection, such a conception may commit us to a perpetually therapeutic or "detached" attitude towards praising and blaming. Whatever its virtue as a complaint against traditional MI accounts, this objection finds no purchase against the account I have offered. In particular, nothing I have said presumes that all individual acts of praising and blaming are undertaken with an eye towards influence, or that those acts of praise and blame have a structure any different than the critic contends.

What I have maintained is that the norms of responsibility are justified in light of the efficacy of those norms and the organic, diversely motivated collection of practices that those norms give rise to. Indeed, it is plausible to think that for creatures with psychologies like ours, that efficacy precisely depends on our being interpersonally engaged, feeling gratitude, resent-ment, and the like. A particular instance of praise or blame may not, in isolation, contribute to the aim of the responsibility system. Indeed, it may be a counterproductive but unavoidable aspect of a stable system (that is, it may be a practical spandrel). So, adoption of a permanent therapeutic standpoint is neither obviously desirable nor necessary. We need not abandon a commitment to the reactive attitudes. Instead, they provide some of the most basic mechanisms by which justified norms of responsibility come to be effective in the world.

As this account is prescriptive and undertaken in a revisionist spirit, it is no objection to what I have said to argue that our current practices fail to be those that are maximally effective at fostering moral considerations-sensitive agency. First of all, it is not clear that what is required is the maximally effective set of possible practices, as opposed to a system that is sufficiently effective given the current costs of being more or equally effective. Second, the objection is surely right in its substance: it would be surprising to learn that our current norms and practices (messy as they are) happen to be exactly those that are best at fostering moral considerations-sensitive agency. I am inclined to think that in responsibility, as well as in many other domains, there is room for a kind of moral progress.

On to the fifth objection, which holds that MI accounts have no place for responsibility-characteristic reactions (such as gratitude) that are backward-looking in their assessment. As P. F. Strawson pointed out, gratitude is among those attitudes that are particularly sensitive to the quality of will directed at us. That is, when others regard us with a good will, and in particular, when they act with good will towards us and we recognize it, we typically respond with gratitude. Gratitude thus helps mark recognition of a good will. Assuming a good will is at least sometimes reflective of moral considerations, it is reasonable to think that learning to track a good will can play a role in learning to track moral considerations. Perhaps more importantly, our reactions of gratitude can signal that we recognize that other agents are responding to what we regard as appropriately agency-guiding considerations. Of course, sometimes these considerations are extra- or non-moral, but inasmuch as gratitude reliably reflects appreciation of moral considerations-governed agency too, gratitude has all the license we can hope for. Similar remarks hold for other backward-looking attitudes: as long as they plausibly play a role in the social and intrapersonal economy of governance by moral considerations, there is no objection here.

I suppose it is at least a conceptual possibility that the experience of gratitude would interfere with the operations of an effective and stable system of moralized praising and blaming practices. As a widespread feature of actual human practices, though, this seems unlikely. Indeed, I suspect the most we would conclude from any purported discovery of this sort is that gratitude (as an attitude, not as a practice) is a practical spandrel—the kind of thing that some might wish we could get along without, but which we cannot.

Even if gratitude could be shown to interfere with the aims of the responsibility system, as seems very unlikely, it would have to turn out that there is *no* independent justification for gratitude. Indeed, this talk of *licensing* may strike us as artificial. If gratitude is a response that is deeply and irrevocably part of our nature as social beings it may need no licensing. If so, then it is one of those elements of our psychological landscape around which any plausible theory of responsibility must be contoured. And, in being such a thing, gratitude would present no difficulty for this account of responsibility. So, we would have to know that gratitude is unnecessary for some other aspect of our lives that is valuable to us, that no considerations external to responsibility favor it, and that it is not an irrevocable part of our nature. The same goes for any other backward-looking attitudes we might aspire to expunge.

We can quickly dispatch the sixth and final objection, which holds that MI accounts are problematically committed on the matter of the correct theory of normative ethics. As we have already seen, the present account is explicitly modular and intended to be compatible with a range of plausible normative ethical theories. So, this criticism does not apply to my rehabilitation of the spirit of moral influence.

What all of this should show is that the difficulties that beset traditional accounts of moral influence have less to do with the idea of moral influence per se than they have to do with overplaying the proper scope of the idea of moral influence. If the role of moral influence is limited to justifying the responsibility norms, then it can function as a sleek but powerful element in a larger theory of moral responsibility. That is what I have tried to provide with the agency cultivation model of the justification of the responsibility system.

8. Building better beings

It is time to survey the terrain we have traversed.

In the early parts of this chapter I considered some approaches to justifying the perpetuation of our responsibility characteristic practices. I argued that we cannot adequately ground the justification of moral responsibility in fixed features of our psychology nor in a simple teleology of our social practices.

It turns out that the right way to justify our responsibility practices is to start by thinking about the responsibility norms, and what would justify them and the practices that express them. On the agency cultivation model, we justify the responsibility norms, norms of moralized praising and blaming, in light of the role that the involved social practices plausibly play in cultivating a form of valuable agency, given various facts about the fixed and plastic features of our psychology. Teleology, psychology, and a special form of agency all end up having a role to play in the account.

What I accept from Strawson is this: our psychology provides the raw materials that structure the internal logic of the responsibility system, and in some cases, that psychology provides relatively fixed points or limits that will need to be accommodated by our responsibility practices. Moreover, I accept a broadly Strawsonian account of blameworthiness as tied to a kind quality of will, or the sort of concern due to others in light of moral values. We can now see why.

What makes the blame norms hang together, as it were, is that they can be characterized as focused on whether agents are demonstrating concern for morality. Moralized blame norms reflect assessments of whether agents are properly concerned about morality precisely because it is our becoming and being agents with such concerns that justifies our participation in and perpetuation of the responsibility system. Given a system of norms that is justified by its role in fostering a form of agents concerned with moral considerations, this should not be surprising. The blame norms are concerned with whether agents act with due concern, because the practices that reflect those norms tend to make us into agents who recognize and respond to moral considerations. So, Strawson was right about the shared *character* of the responsibility norms, even if he was wrong about the justification.

Indeed, the present account of the justification of the norms helps see how he was right about the character of those norms.

What I accept from the classical influence approach is the idea that we can justify responsibility-characteristic practices, including the business of holding one another responsible, in light of their effects. However, I also rejected a good deal of what was mixed into those traditional accounts, including the idea that moral influence implies a particular theory of responsible agency as susceptibility to influence, that praising and blaming are merely attempts by praisers and blamers to influence, that the level of significance for influence is tokenings of praise and blame, and the supposition that we could do without some account of internalizing the relevant norms.

Instead of thinking of the responsibility system as either an enforcer on behavior or the manifestations of a psychology we cannot shed, my suggestion is that we think of it as organized around fostering a distinctive form of agency. One virtue of this model is that it permits us to make sense of the temptation to think of responsibility as morality's henchman, enforcing the edicts of morality. Although our responsibility-practices and judgments may *appear* to function as a kind of coercive enforcement mechanism on behalf of morality, this is to conflate effect and aim. If we think of our responsibility practices, attitudes, and judgments as organized around the development and promotion of moral considerations-responsive agency, we can make sense of why responsibility is important, why morality and responsibility are important to one another, and why, even so, they each have their own proper internal normative structure.

These considerations also provide an answer to the challenge first mentioned in chapter 5: why is the agential ambit of moral responsibility marked out by the particular feature identified by one's account of responsible agency, and not some other feature? The answer is this: it only makes sense to demand adherence to norms of praise and blame if one has the capacity to regulate one's conduct in light of moral considerations. In the absence of such capacities, the thing that justifies praising and blaming (its role in cultivating a moral considerations-regulated form of agency) disappears. An appealing feature about this picture is that it is one on which the particular account of responsible agency and the justification of the responsibility-characteristic practices interlock. Given that the practice of praising and blaming is justified by its role in fostering responsible agency, it makes sense for those practices to be directed at agents in possession of capacities to guide conduct in light of moral considerations.

One might worry that things have still gone wrong in the following way. Suppose you thought that the salient feature of the morally critical dimension of responsibility practices is that they are concerned with moral reasons, either expressing them or, perhaps, recording how they stack up on some or another issue. (This much is at least consistent with a Reasons approach to responsible agency.) If so, then you might worry that praise and blame, on the present account, have the wrong role. Rather than being part of a reasons-marking practice, the present account treats them as blunt tools for manipulating particular kinds of agents. So, even if the norms of responsibility only apply to particular agents, the expression of praise and blame end up little more than tools of psychological manipulation. What we wanted, though, was an account on which the kind of influence exercised by praise and blame was less manipulative and closer to reasons-giving practices.

I can imagine disputing whether we should construe responsibility-holding practices of praise and blame more like a reasons-giving endeavor, as the objection suggests, than something like reasons-bypassing manipulation. However, nothing in the account requires that we regard the nature of blaming as coldly manipulative and devoid of some non-trivial connection to reason.

In the ordinary case, the way praising and blaming function is very much like a marking of morally salient considerations. It doesn't work by unfettered manipulation of behavior disconnected from any invitation to reflect on the involved moral considerations. On the contrary, moralized blame tends to push the target's attention to considerations that others perceive as morally salient. In this way, blame connects agents with psychologies like ours to moral considerations. Nothing in the agency cultivation model requires that we think of blame in any other way.

7

Responsible Agency

But conceptualism has lost ground: biological and social sciences no longer believe there are immutably determined entities that define given characteristics like those of the woman, the Jew, or the black; science considers characteristics as secondary reactions to a *situation*.

Simone de Beauvoir[1]

I am myself and my circumstances.

José Ortega y Gasset[2]

1. Where we are, where we are going

In the last chapter, I argued that the agency cultivation model provides a plausible justification of our holding one another responsible. The core idea of the agency cultivation model is that our responsibility-characteristic practices can be justified if the norms of moralized praise and blame suitably contribute to the development of a special form of agency. I took on board the idea that norms of a broadly Strawsonian sort—that is, norms emphasizing a demand for a kind of quality of will, or concern for what morality demands—can plausibly serve such a function. Among moral considerations-sensitive agents, the currency of such norms fosters moral considerations-sensitive agency. If this picture can be sustained, we have reason for insisting that nihilism about responsibility is too hasty. In particular we would have grounds for holding that there is a sound basis for thinking people can be responsible, even while acknowledging that

---

[1] Simone de Beauvoir, *The Second Sex*, trans. Constance Borde, and Sheila Malovany-Chevallier (New York: Alfred A. Knopf, 2010), 4.
[2] See José Ortega y Gasset, *Meditations on Quixote* (1st American edn.) (New York: Norton, 1961).

important aspects of our understanding of responsibility and its basis are somewhat at odds with some strands of ordinary convictions about these matters.

We are not there, yet. Suppose one accepts that the agency cultivation model could generate a warrant for holding one another responsible. Whether it *actually* generates that warrant importantly depends on whether the form of agency I gestured at—moral considerations-responsive agency—is indeed possible. Such an account requires two things. First, it requires some detail about the form of agency invoked by the account. Second, it requires that such a picture possesses sufficient resources to address worries that might be raised about the account.

Providing those things is the task of this chapter.

I will start by sketching something of a composite picture of responsible agency, one that takes its inspiration from various prominent Reasons accounts of responsible agency, but that is none of them in particular.[3] Instead, it is an amalgam of commitments that I take to have a degree of plausibility about them, and which will in broad outlines provide the foundations for the account I wish to develop. I will then consider some challenges to that account. In light of those challenges, I will offer a new account of responsible agency that addresses the worries that I take to beset some standard Reasons approaches to responsible agency.

2. An initial sketch of a theory of responsible agency

Let's begin by supposing that the form of agency that is of interest here involves at least two families of powers or capacities: (1) a relatively pedestrian suite of capacities for effective self-directed agency; and (2) a set of particular capacities that jointly constitute free will, understood as a distinctive power or capacity characteristic of responsible agency. I'll characterize the conditions in the former as *conditions of self-directed agency*, and the latter as *free will conditions*.

[3] For citations, see chapter 5, n. 5.

That free will, and thus, responsible agency involve some power or powers above and beyond bare agency and even relatively modest forms of self-direction should not be controversial. Of course, it depends on what one means by self-direction. I do not mean to help myself to anything especially contentious, and I certainly do not mean to invoke a robust picture of the self, autonomous agency, or the like. Among the features of agency I will take as implicated in self-directed (but not yet responsible) agency are such things as beliefs, desires, means–end reasoning, the ability to formulate and execute action plans, and the presence of ordinary epistemic abilities, including a general capacity for some degree of foresight regarding the consequences of actions.

There are interesting complexities to the matter of characterizing those other, not-necessarily-responsibility-generating parts of our agency. I will take up some of these complexities in the last chapter. Here, though, the particulars of differing accounts of more basic forms of self-directed agency are largely immaterial for present purposes. So long as a collection of familiar characteristics and powers are admitted to be present in the ordinary case, we have enough to proceed in constructing the outlines of a plausible Reasons account.

The ideas currently operative can be supplemented with a further idea, dating back to Aristotle. The idea is this: blameworthiness requires the satisfaction of both an epistemic and control condition. The epistemic condition derives from the familiar thought that if one could not have foreseen the effects of some action, we ordinarily do not regard the agent as blameworthy for that action. The control condition derives from the thought that if one could not control what happened, then again, one is not blameworthy. Since responsible agents are agents that can be blameworthy, it seems sensible to suppose that responsible agents must satisfy both an epistemic and a control condition.

The traditional control condition neatly maps on to the free will condition, but it is less clear where to put the epistemic condition. Is it a power embedded in responsible agency conditions, or is it a power of effective self-directed agency, or is it some further thing?

My view is that it is preferable to think of there being two distinct epistemic requirements at work here. One is a general one, the one just mentioned. The other is a more particular one. For the purposes of the present account, I will treat the general epistemic requirement (i.e., that

202 A THEORY OF MORAL RESPONSIBILITY

someone have reasonable foresight about outcomes) as a feature of self-directed agency, and not as something built into the free will requirement or as some third aspect of responsible agency.[4]

The second epistemic requirement is more obviously a free will-specific requirement. It is the requirement of recognizing moral considerations. As I've noted, I think it is helpful to think of these as distinct requirements, and on the present schema they occur in different places. The foreseeability requirement is treated as separate from the control element. The requirement for recognizing moral considerations is counted as internal to the control requirement, and as we will see, embeds in it a notion of freedom that proves important for some conceptions of control.

Some examples may help to sharpen the difference in these two epistemic requirements. In a particular situation, one might have a good grasp of the salient moral considerations that ought to play a role in one's deliberation, but all the same, one might have little grasp of the likely consequences of choosing one way rather than another. Such an agent would, presumably, satisfy the moral considerations epistemic condition but not the reasonable foresight condition. Similarly, we might imagine that an agent has a firm grasp of the likely consequences of various action possibilities while being altogether dead to the various moral considerations relevant to deliberation about what to do.

Going forward, my main interest concerns those capacities that constitute the free will (or the "control condition") part of responsible agency, so I will have comparatively little to say about the foresight condition I am locating in self-directed agency (see Fig. 1).[5]

I have already indicated that the species of Reasons account that is operative in the moral cultivation model is one that emphasizes that the

---

[4] I can't see how much turns on whether we think of the general epistemic condition as a third thing, separate from both free will and effective self-directed agency. Whether we constrict the operative background conception of self-directed agency so as to not include something like an ability to reasonably foresee the outcomes of various action possibilities, or whether we expand it to encompass such a power (as I am inclined to), the satisfaction of epistemic conditions will still turn out to be relevant for responsibility.

[5] Characterizing the foreseeability requirement is surprisingly difficult. For some ruminations, see the appendix to Vargas, "The Trouble With Tracing." For some specific proposals on how to understand the requirement, see Carl Ginet, "The Epistemic Requirements for Moral Responsibility," in *Philosophical Perspectives 14: Action and Freedom, 2000*, ed. James Tomberlin (Malden, MA: Blackwell, 2000); George Sher, *Who Knew? Responsibility Without Awareness* (New York: Oxford University Press, 2009). See also Fischer and Ravizza, *Responsibility and Control: A Theory of Moral Responsibility*.

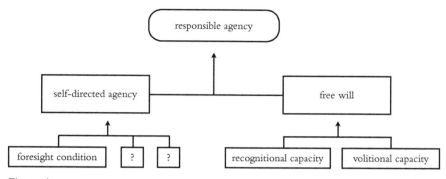

Figure 1

agent suitably recognize and respond to moral considerations. This is not a requirement on every Reasons account, but it is an important aspect of the account in progress, so some remarks are in order.

By "moral consideration" I mean a consideration with moral significance such that, were one to deliberate about what to do, it ought to play a role in those deliberations. I favor the language of moral *considerations* (as opposed to the more familiar language of moral *reasons*) mainly to avoid the suggestion of an account of responsible agency that is particularly bound up in a rationalist conception of agency (e.g., where reason is conceived of as something like an autonomous faculty that properly operates independently of the effects of affect).[6]

We can put this idea to work in the following way: what makes an agent properly subject to norms of moralized praise and blame is that he or she has the general capacity to suitably recognize and respond to moral considerations.[7] The "suitability" idea in the "suitably recognize and respond" clause is merely meant to mark the idea that the recognition and attendant response are not perverse (for example, only recognizing immoral reasons as a reason to do something). The notion of a general capacity is supposed to reflect the intuitive idea that normal adults have a capacity to recognize and

---

[6] What I have in mind by moral considerations includes things that we recognize as reason in as fully rationalistic a sense as you like, but also things that are largely or perhaps exclusively affective. If one is inclined to count the irreducibly affect-dependent as reasons, or at least reasons–candidates, then I have no objection to characterizing this as a reasons–responsiveness account. That said, my account is intended to be compatible with a wide range of plausible views on the ontology of moral considerations.

[7] Compare Wallace, *Responsibility and the Moral Sentiments*, ch. 6.

respond to moral considerations across a wide range of contexts. The phrase "in the paradigmatic case" is meant to allow for cases of derivative, or non-original instances of responsibility (e.g., cases where an erstwhile responsible agent turns him- or herself into a non-responsible agent).

There is a good deal appealing about this general characterization of responsible agency. It characterizes a form of agency that is plausibly valuable to have. The capacities it invokes are also familiar, trading on the idea that responsibility requires both recognitional and volitional powers in an agent.[8] Moreover, this form of agency is a good candidate to fill the role required by the agency cultivation model of moral responsibility. That is, it portrays a picture of agency and free will on which sensitivity to moral considerations is central, and for which norms of praise and blame that focus on quality of will might plausibly foster and sustain that form of agency. So: *if* we were agents who suitably recognized and responded to moral considerations, then it might make sense to think that we can justify some version of the responsibility system in the way I have described.

The trouble is that it is not obvious that we have cross-situational stable capacities to recognize and respond to moral considerations. Moreover, the sense of the involved notion of capacity is hardly obvious, either. So, more work awaits.

3. Against atomism and monism about free will

A plausible Reasons theory will need to look importantly different than the account I just sketched. The aim of this section is to explain why—that is, to make explicit what is problematic about such accounts.

Let *atomism* refer to the view that free will is a non-relational property of agents, that is, it is characterizable in isolation from broader social and physical contexts. Atomistic theories provide characterizations of free will or responsible agency that do not appeal to such relational properties as, for example, the normative status of agents with respect to institutions or

---

[8] Although the appeal to such powers plays a role in a wide range of work, including the criminal law, the most influential philosophical account of these powers (albeit with important differences from the account I have been sketching) is surely the one developed by Fischer and his sometime collaborator Ravizza. For representative work, see Fischer and Ravizza, *Responsibility and Control: A Theory of Moral Responsibility*; Fischer, *My Way*.

collectives. The characterization of responsible agency given in the prior section counts as atomistic.

I take it that many accounts of free will are atomistic in this sense. Such accounts specify some property—say, a real self, an uncaused event, the presence of reasoning capacities, or what have you—that, at least in principle, one could identify simply by looking inside the agent. If the relevant feature is there, then the agent has free will, independent of context.[9]

Atomism is often coupled with a view that there is only one natural power or arrangement of agential features that constitutes free will or the control condition on moral responsibility. This is a *monistic* view of the ontology of free will. Monistic views include those accounts that hold that free will is the conditional ability to act on a counterfactual desire. Identificationist accounts, which hold that free will is had only when the agent identifies with a special psychological element (a desire, a value, an intention, etc.) are also monistic. So are libertarian accounts on which one acts freely only when one acts in a specific non-deterministic fashion. In contrast, non-monistic (or pluralistic) accounts hold that there are multiple agential structures or combinations of powers that constitute the control or freedom required for moral responsibility.

The problem with atomism and monism about free will is that both seem to be at odds with the emerging picture of agency in the social, cognitive, and neurosciences. That is, if we suppose that the freedom or control implicated in assessments of moral responsibility is to be understood as a single, unified capacity that relies on or is constituted by a cross-situationally stable mechanism, then it seems unlikely that we have any such thing. What appears to us as a general capacity of reasons-responsiveness is really a cluster of more specific, ecologically limited capacities indexed to particular circumstances.[10]

---

[9] My point is not that atomism is an ineradicable feature of most contemporary accounts of responsibility, but rather, that: (1) atomistic presumptions are pervasive in the literature; and (2) the ubiquity of atomistic presumptions has kept us from appreciating some alternatives. Presumably, if push came to shove, at least a few philosophers would be happy to have their accounts read in non-atomistic ways.

[10] Manuel Vargas, "Situationism and Moral Responsibility: Free Will in Fragments," in *Decomposing the Will*, ed. Till Vierkant et al. (New York: Oxford University Press, forthcoming); John Doris, *Lack of Character: Personality and Moral Behavior* (New York: Cambridge University Press, 2002).

What this emerging picture suggests is that we cannot answer the question of whether an agent has free will simply by looking at the agent. What we need to know are facts about both the agent and the circumstances. On this picture, free will turns out to be a relational property, partly constituted by both agent and circumstance, and not the kind of thing that is settled entirely by the presence of, say, a mechanism of practical reasoning or a general cross-situationally stable capacity to recognize and respond to moral considerations.

One reason for doubting the standard atomistic and monistic picture of free will comes from social psychology. There is a body of compelling experimental data that suggests that contra traditional personality psychology and ordinary Western beliefs, we (at least we Westerners) frequently overestimate the role of individual dispositions in our explanations of actions.[11] That is, in a wide range of circumstances, it appears that the best explanation of why the agent acted one way rather than another appeals to features of the situation external to the agent, often in ways of which the agent is unaware.[12]

Such doubts about cross-situationally stable general capacities are widely accepted even among contemporary psychologists committed to an "interactionist" picture. This latter approach recognizes a somewhat greater role for agent dispositions in the production of action than is sometimes allowed for on the most demanding characterizations of the older situationist literature that brought our attention to the scope and subtlety of situational effects. However, it is notable that even on interactionist accounts, the

---

[11] Some prominent social psychologists have contended that the degree to which populations emphasize individual vs. situation in explanation and prediction varies across cultures. See Richard E. Nisbett, *The Geography of Thought: How Asians and Westerners Think Differently—And Why* (New York: Free Press, 2003). Recently, the idea that circumstances structure decision-making in subtle and under-appreciated ways has received wider attention in the popular press because of the visibility of Richard H. Thaler and Cass R. Sunstein, *Nudge: Improving Decisions About Health, Wealth, and Happiness* (New York: Penguin, 2009).

[12] For important philosophical discussions of this literature see Doris, *Lack of Character*; Maria Merritt et al., "Character," in *The Moral Psychology Handbook*, ed. John Doris (New York: Oxford University Press, 2010). For other relevant work, see Dana Nelkin, "Freedom, Responsibility, and the Challenge of Situationism," *Midwest Studies in Philosophy* 29, no. 1 (2005): 181–206; Eddy Nahmias, "Autonomous Agency and Social Psychology," in *Cartographies of the Mind: Philosophy and Psychology in Intersection*, ed. Massimo Marraffa et al. (Berlin: Springer, 2007); Joshua Knobe and Brian Leiter, "The Case for Nietzschean Moral Psychology," in *Nietzsche and Morality*, ed. Brian Leiter and Neil Sinhababu (New York: Oxford University Press, 2007); Doris and Stich, "As a Matter of Fact: Empirical Perspectives on Ethics."

role of individual dispositions remains considerably more limited than traditional personality psychology maintained. Perhaps the now standard view is that there are contexts where individual dispositions can be especially influential, but in a wide range of cases actions are disproportionately driven by circumstantial features that the performing agents do (and would) regard as deliberatively irrelevant.[13]

The literature on "stereotype threat" or "social identity threat" illustrates the startlingly localized and context-specific potential for degrading our rational capacities. Claude Steele, Joshua Aronson, and their colleagues have found that performance in a wide range of mental and physical activities is subject to degradation in light of subjects perceiving that there is some possibility of their being evaluated in terms of a negative stereotype.[14] So, for example, when there is an operative background assumption that women and blacks do less well then white men at math, the performance of women and blacks on math exams—a task that plausibly involves a species of rationality, if anything does—will drop when the exam is presented as testing native ability. These startling results disappear when the threat is removed, as when, for example, the exam is presented as testing cognitive processes and not purportedly native ability.

One can generate similar results in white males, by priming them with information about their stereotypically poor performance on math tests when compared to their Asian counterparts. When the threatening comparison is made salient to subjects, performance drops. When the threatening comparison is taken away, and the exam is explicitly presented as not susceptible to such bias, scores rise for the populations ordinarily susceptible to the threat.

---

[13] For an account that holds that, with respect to moral behavior, situations better predicts at a time and individual dispositions predicts over time, see Lawrence J. Walker et al., "Paradigm Assumptions About Moral Behavior: An Empirical Battle Royal," in *The Social Psychology of Morality: Exploring the Causes of Good and Evil*, ed. M. Mikulincer and P. R. Shaver (Washington, DC: American Psychological Association, 2011). There are, of course, important limitations to any empirical research, and it is not always clear what philosophical lessons we are warranted in drawing from research that tends to focus on behavior and less on how the agent understands the particulars of the situation. I take it that the important point here is simply that for any account that pretends to having broadly naturalistic bona fides, such an account cannot just help itself to the supposition that that we have some cross-situationally stable capacity to recognize and appropriately respond to moral considerations.

[14] See Joshua Aronson et al., "When White Men Can't Do Math: Necessary and Sufficient Factors in Stereotype Threat," *Journal of Experimental Social Psychology* 35 (1999): 29–46; Claude M. Steele et al., "Contending With Group Image: The Psychology of Stereotype and Social Identity Threat," *Advances in Experimental Social Psychology* 34 (2002): 379–440.

Remarkably, these results generalize to a variety of more and less cognitive domains, including physical performance.[15] One could resist the general lesson by arguing that (perhaps) there is a basic underlying capacity that is stable, and perception (whether conscious or not) of stereotypes affects the ease with those capacities are exercised. Notice, though, that this just defers the problem with atomistic views. Even if our basic capacities are stable across contexts, our abilities to exercise them vary by circumstance and this suggests that our situation-indexed capacities vary considerably.

I don't wish to rest the case against atomistic and monistic theories of free will entirely on experimental considerations. Armchair reflection suggests some reasons of its own for skepticism about there being a general capacity to recognize and respond to moral consideration.

Consider the recognitional element invoked in the initial account (Fig. 1). The moral considerations agents properly recognize are plausibly quite diverse in their nature. For example, some moral considerations may take the form of reasons understood in a robust sense, for example, something involving belief-like propositional content that could be articulated. Other times, perception of moral considerations will plausibly involve some complex process of visual recognition.

I, for one, would find it surprising if the same epistemic mechanisms are involved in recognizing such diverse things as the fact that someone is in emotional pain, that other persons are ends in themselves, and that one should not delay in getting one's referee report back to the editor.[16] Being able to perceive when a quiet friend is in need of consolation is unlikely to involve the same mechanisms as those involved in the exchange of reasoned philosophical arguments about duties. And, at other times, sensitivity to moral considerations may involve susceptibility to a nagging feeling, reacting to a dim hope, being able to imagine the situation of another, or

---

[15] Claude M. Steele, "A Threat in the Air: How Stereotypes Shape Intellectual Identity and Performance," *American Psychologist* 52, no. 6 (1997): 613–29. One remarkable result, discussed in this article, was that showing women TV commercials in stereotypically unintelligent roles before an exam leads to worse performance on math tests (393).

[16] The cataloging of the varied epistemic mechanisms of moral considerations will require empirical work informed by a more general theory of moral considerations, but there is already good evidence to suggest that there are diverse neurocognitive mechanisms involved in moral judgments. For a discussion of distinct mechanisms at the cognitive level, see Nichols, *Sentimental Rules: On the Natural Foundations of Moral Judgment.* For discussion of distinct mechanisms at the neurological level, see Jorge Moll et al., "The Neural Basis of Human Moral Cognition," *Nature Reviews Neuroscience* 6 (2005): 799–809.

attending to an inarticulate, largely inchoate suspicion about things. Just how any of this happens may vary from person to person and from situation to situation.[17]

Reflection on the plausible nature of moral considerations suggests that the epistemological powers required to recognize those considerations are themselves likely to be diverse. If all of that is right, it is difficult to see what non-trivial sense there is to be made of some general capacity to recognize (and suitably respond) to moral considerations.

So, for both empirical and armchair reasons, it seems preferable to have an account of responsible agency on which the crucial capacities proved to be more variegated than the picture presented at the outset of this chapter. Going forward, I will assume that the general thesis that our capacities are best understood as local and domain-specific.[18] However, given that free will plausibly involves such capacities, the characterization of our freedom in atomistic and monistic terms does not look promising. What we need is an account of responsible agency that allows for both pluralism about capacities across circumstances (so, no general cross-situationally stable capacity to respond to moral considerations) and pluralism about the mechanisms that constitute those capacities.

4. Capacity conundrums

In the previous section I raised worries about a conception of agency on which free will is understood as an intrinsic property of agents and on which the capacity to recognize and respond to moral considerations is regarded as a function of some single, cross-situationally stable mechanism or capacity.

In this section I focus on the recurring notion of free will involving a capacity. Notoriously, much of the free will debate founders on whether

[17] For that matter, it would be appealing to have an account that allowed for the idea that there might be non-standard paths to recognizing familiar moral considerations. Something like this possibility is suggested by the concern of many autistic persons for moral considerations. For discussion, see Jeanette Kennett, "Autism, Empathy and Moral Agency," *Philosophical Quarterly* 52, no. 208 (2002): 340–57; Victoria McGeer, "Varieties of Moral Agency: Lessons From Autism (and Psychopathy)," in *Moral Psychology, Volume 3: The Neuroscience of Morality: Emotions, Brain Disorders, and Development*, ed. Walter Sinnott-Armstrong (Cambridge, MA: MIT Press, 2008).

[18] John Doris and Dominic Murphy, "From My Lai to Abu Ghraib: The Moral Psychology of Atrocity," *Midwest Studies in Philosophy* 31 (2007): 25–55.

some or another proposed capacity is sufficient for freedom and responsibility. One traditional approach by conventional compatibilists has been to appeal to something like a conditional analysis of "can" (or other capacity-suggesting terms). On such an approach, to say that an agent has the capacity to do otherwise is to attribute a conditional power (or, perhaps, a conditional analysis of a categorical power): were one to decide to do otherwise, one would do otherwise.

The traditional conditional analysis was elegant and problematic in equal measure.[19] Although there continue to be interesting developments in that vein, I do not think the conditional analysis is workable in any of its standard forms. We need something different. Still, it is useful to start in the same place that gave inspiration to such accounts: ordinary usages of the idea of a capacity.

It is obvious that there are perfectly legitimate uses of "capacity" whereby one can have a capacity and fail to act in a way consistent with the full or best use of that capacity. Although I am not speaking in Spanish at the moment, there is a clear sense in which I retain the capacity to speak Spanish. And, although I may have overcooked the fish, I had and continue to have the capacity to not overcook it this coming Friday (indeed, I have undercooked it a number of times!).

What we have in mind with these sorts of capacity claims varies. Sometimes all we mean is something like "given what I know about the case, the following outcome(s) is (are) consistent with it." Other times we might think of capacities in something like the following way: "in cases relevantly similar to this one, things tend to go this way." And, often, talk of capacities is meant to describe some power one might have and can use under a wide range of conditions but not all conditions. For example, even when I'm sleeping, I plausibly retain a suite of capacities, including the ability to reason practically, to speak Spanish, to awaken at the sound of a crying child, and so on.

It would be strange to insist that I lose my capacity to speak Spanish every night and regain it every morning (Where did it go in the intervening time? How did I relearn the Spanish language so quickly?). There are, of course,

[19] For a useful overview of the difficulties faced by the classical conditional analysis, see Kane, *The Significance of Free Will*. For a critical discussion of "the new dispositionalism," see Randolph Clarke, "Dispositions, Abilities to Act, and Free Will: The New Dispositionalism," *Mind* 118, no. 470 (2009): 323–51.

things a dedicated denier of non-occurrent capacities could say. However, at least at the level of ordinary language, we can admit of having capacities without needing to deny that such capacities might go unexercised.

It should be clear that the notions of capacity invoked in the detection and self-governance requirements of responsible agency should be read as something akin to the capacity to speak Spanish. One can retain capacities of this sort without having the opportunity to exercise them, and one can retain these capacities even if we were to learn that the world was and is deterministic.

Try it: even if the world has been deterministic for its entire history, there is surely *some* sense in which I retain the capacity to speak Spanish even when I am not speaking Spanish; there is, of course, also some sense in which I would *not be able* to speak Spanish in some moment when I do not, were I determined not to. What I will argue is that the proper prescriptive notions of the capacities in question are akin to the senses we can recognize as operative when we say that I can speak Spanish in a deterministic world, even when I do not. On this approach, one can have a capacity to detect moral considerations and can appropriately regulate one's behavior in light of those considerations, without exercising that capacity in a given instance.

Here, though, is where concerns about the metaphysics of free will traditionally intrude. Even if it is reasonably clear that there are a variety of ways in which something might ordinarily and even truly said to have a capacity, some will surely insist that the notion of capacity required for ascriptions of moral responsibility is more demanding than the capacity to speak Spanish or the capacity to properly cook fish.

Consider a version of capacity talk that I will call the Garden of Forking Paths (GFP) picture of capacities. On the GFP model, the responsibility-relevant notion of capacity is very demanding, requiring that any assessment of capacities holds fixed *all* the background conditions in the considered case.[20] A capacity to do otherwise requires the availability of options given the exact same background conditions in the actual case (e.g., the actual past

---

[20] In what follows, I do not mean to suggest there is no room for alternative possibilities-requiring compatibilism. I simply want to make use of a model with stricter requirements. Also, a tip of the hat is in order for John Martin Fischer, as I believed it was he who introduced the GFP metaphor to the philosophical literature. His usage of it derives from the wonderful Jorge Luis Borges story "The Garden of Forking Paths" which can be found in Jorge Luis Borges, *Collected Fictions* (New York: Penguin, 1998).

and the actual laws). The core idea of the GFP model can be illustrated by asking whether you can walk through a garden via a different footpath than the one you are on. It all depends on the garden. In some gardens, the path branches with lots of ways to walk through the garden. In other gardens, there is only a single path. On the GFP model, capacity talk is construed along the lines of being in a garden with forking paths. In a deterministic universe, there is only one path, and thus, the only GFP capacities you have are those you exercise. In such a universe, there are no unexercised GFP-type capacities. In contrast, in an indeterministic universe there are multiple paths, and thus, unexercised capacities.

An important strand of incompatibilist theories of moral responsibility emphasizes the necessity of GFP-type capacities to do otherwise for moral responsibility. (Henceforth, talk of GFP-type capacities should be understood as a capacity to do otherwise that requires having alternative accessible futures given the same past and laws.) Here, though, the methodological work in Part I of this book can do some work for us. I am happy to acknowledge that there is no obvious reason to suppose that our talk of capacities is uniform across all contexts of action. In some contexts, we might well mean capacities in the GFP way of putting things. Indeed, I am sympathetic to the idea that at least with respect to a capacity for volitional control, the GFP model or something very much like it describes how many, perhaps most of us tend to think about a range of issues concerning human agency, including free will and moral responsibility. However, the kind of agency required to make sense of the GFP model of capacities is not required for moral responsibility, even if the GFP model is how we tend to think about things.

To make things explicit, I am dubious that there are adequate considerations for why—apart from the way we may happen to think of things—we *should* think of responsibility-relevant capacities in an especially demanding way. Reflection on the presumptive aim of the responsibility system provides one reason for favoring abandonment of the GFP model of capacity. Simply put, it is hard to see why such a requirement would be necessary for a system of responsibility-characteristic practices, attitudes, and judgments to foster considerations-sensitive agency. Even if there are other virtues to the possession of GFP-type capacities, it is difficult to see why, given the modest teleology of the responsibility system, such capacities would be required for moral responsibility. This suggests that the notion(s) of capacity at stake in the detection and self-governance requirements of responsible agency are ones that do not require a GFP model of capacity.

Fine and well, you may say—but what then are those capacities that are plausibly implicated in the agency cultivation model? Well, I've got a theory for you.

5. Responsible agency defined

On the account I favor, the powers that constitute free will are those that suffice to support moralized praising and blaming practices, so that such practices increase our acting on moral considerations and expand the contexts in which we do so.[21]

I'll start with a relatively uncontroversial characterization of the terrain. Given the presumption that free will is the capacity distinctive of responsible agency, we can say this:

For an agent S to be morally responsible for some act token A in context C requires that S is a morally responsible agent and the action is morally praiseworthy or morally blameworthy.

The present schema invokes several technical notions: the now familiar idea of a responsible agent and an account of what it is for an action to be morally praiseworthy and morally blameworthy. I've already signaled my acceptance of a broadly Strawsonian picture of the norms of blameworthiness. That is, responsible agents are morally responsible for an act when they act with ill will, or a failure of concern in light of morality. What is left is to say something about the form of agency to which the norms are properly brought to bear.

Here is my proposal for how we should understand that form of agency:

An agent S is a responsible agent with respect to considerations of type M in circumstances C if S possesses a suite of basic agential capacities implicated in

---

[21] Much of the machinery I introduce to explicate this idea can, I think, be paired with a different picture of the teleology of the responsibility system. The specific powers identified will presumably be somewhat different, but the basic approach is amenable to different conceptions of the organizing normative structure to the responsibility system. I leave it to others to show how that might go.

effective self-directed agency (including, for example, beliefs, desires, intentions, instrumental reasoning, and generally reliable beliefs about the world and the consequences of action) and is also possessed of the relevant capacity for (A) detection of suitable moral considerations M in C and (B) self-governance with respect to M in C. Conditions (A) and (B) are to be understood in the following ways:

(A) the capacity for detection of the relevant moral considerations obtains when:
  (i) S actually detects moral considerations of type M in C that are pertinent to actions available to S or
  (ii) in those possible worlds where S is in a context relevantly similar to C, and moral considerations of type M are present in those contexts, in a suitable proportion of those worlds S successfully detects those considerations.
(B) the capacity for volitional control, or self-governance with respect to the relevant moral considerations M in circumstances C obtains when either
  (i) S is, in light of awareness of M in C, motivated to accordingly pursue courses of action for which M counts in favor, and to avoid courses of action disfavored by M or
  (ii) when S is not so motivated, in a suitable proportion of those worlds where S is in a context relevantly similar to C
    (a) S detects moral considerations of type M, and
    (b) in virtue of detecting M considerations, S acquires the motivation to act accordingly, and
    (c) S successfully acts accordingly.

Furthermore, the notions of suitability and relevant similarity invoked in (A.ii) and (B.ii) are given by the standards an ideal, fully informed, rational, observer in the actual world would select as at least co-optimal for the cultivation of our moral considerations-responsive agency, holding fixed a range of general facts about our current customary psychologies, the cultural and social circumstances of our agency, our interest in resisting counterfactuals we regard as evaluatively irrelevant, and given the existence of genuine moral considerations, and the need of agents to internalize norms of action for moral considerations at a level of granularity that is useful in ordinary deliberative and practical circumstances. Lastly, the ideal observer's determination is structured by the following ordering of preferences:
  (1) that agents recognize moral considerations and govern themselves accordingly in ordinary contexts of action in the actual world;
  (2) that agents have a wider rather than narrower range of contexts of action and deliberation in which agents recognize and respond to moral considerations.

The account obviously invokes a number of complex and potentially troublesome notions, including talk of possible worlds and comparative proportions of worlds.[22] And, as I have noted in several places, the account's roughly cognitive and volitional requirements are features shared with various accounts. However, the way those requirements are fleshed out is novel. Here, they are understood in terms of the distinctive teleological justification advanced in chapter 6.[23] What results is an account whose metaphysics is structured throughout by the normative concerns that undergird our interest in responsibility.

In the sections that follow I will unpack some of the details of those capacities. Here, I'll briefly canvass some general features of the account.

First, the possibilities invoked in the above account are, by design, to be understood as constituting the responsibility-relevant capacities of agents. These capacities will ordinarily be distinct from the "basic abilities," or the intrinsic dispositions of agents.[24] Instead, they are higher-order characterizations picked out because of their relevance to the cultivation and refinement of those forms of agency that recognize and respond accordingly to moral considerations of the sort we are likely to encounter in the world.

Second, and relatedly, this is a picture on which the relevant metaphysics of our powers is determined not by the physical structures to which our agency may reduce, but instead by the roles that various collections of our powers play in our shared, normatively structured lives. The constituents of control are, on this account, plausibly constituted in a variety of ways.

Recall that on this account, free will is to be understood in terms of satisfying conditions A and B. Given that satisfaction of A and B might be attained in various ways in the natural world, it turns out that the

---

[22] The language of possible worlds is invoked as a convention, and not meant to commit us to a particular conception of possibility as, say, referring to concrete particulars. Relatedly, in characterizing the relevant capacities in this way, the capacities are not capacities of other agents, or idealized agents, or counterfactual agents. Rather, what responsibility-relevant capacities agents have *in the actual world* is settled by an idealized set of counterfactuals.

[23] I find a standard of "enhance and expand the frequency" of moral considerations-responsive agency to be the most appealing, but different conceptions of the teleology are possible, even on an agency cultivation model. For example, one might opt for a model that emphasizes protecting some form of agency, or that is concerned to, in some special sense, respect a privileged form of agency. Comparing the fruits of alternative approaches would require development of such accounts, which is again work better left for others.

[24] I borrow the term "basic abilities" from John Perry, although my usage is, I think, a bit different. See John Perry, "Wretched Subterfuge: A Defense of the Compatibilism of Freedom and Natural Causation," *Proceedings and Addresses of the American Philosophical Association* 84, no. 2 (2010): 93–113.

metaphysical realizers of free will need not be consistent or stable across contexts. Instead, free will is variably constituted, structured by the normative concerns of a justified responsibility system.

Third, responsible agency is to be understood as variably present across circumstances. There is no presumption of a universal, cross-situationally stable capacity to recognize and respond to moral considerations of any type. An agent might be a responsible agent with respect to some situationally relevant moral considerations but not to others. Accordingly, the licensing of praise and blame can only track those considerations to which the agent is a responsible agent.

6. Unpacking the machinery 1: detection

In this section, and the next, I aim to unpack and motivate some of the particulars of the preceding account of responsible agency.

Although the proposed definition of responsible agency is complex, that complexity is inexpensive, ontologically speaking. This picture of agency requires a construction—an idealization that is normatively structured—but it does not require us to postulate any entities or powers that are starkly at odds with a broadly naturalistic view of the world. What it provides is a prescriptive account of responsible agency that satisfies various desiderata outlined throughout this book.

Recall how we are to think of the detection condition:

(A) the capacity for detection of the relevant moral considerations obtains when:
  (i) S actually detects moral consideration of type M in C that are pertinent to actions available to S or
  (ii) in those possible worlds where S is in a context relevantly similar to C, and moral considerations of type M are present in those contexts, in a suitable proportion of those worlds S successfully detects those considerations.

This is a picture of the detection capacity that rejects the supposition that there is anything like a physically stable realizer (or even a non-normatively constituted functional arrangement) for the capacity to detect moral considerations.[25] It is a capacity which, because of its higher-order nature, can and likely does vary in its constitution across contexts. This entails that what counts as responsible agency can vary considerably across contexts even for the same agent. Across contexts, the responsibility-relevant capacity for recognizing moral considerations changes with no intrinsic change in the agent.

Notice that this account retains a natural way of accounting for the idea that an agent might be more or less sensitive to moral considerations of a given type. That is, we might say that an agent has greater sensitivity to a type of moral consideration if in a larger proportion of relevantly similar contexts the agent successfully detects such considerations. Presumably, some classes of considerations are, as a matter of course, more readily recognized than others. I take that considerations weighing against causing bodily harm may be more widely recognizable than say, considerations in favor of generosity when dealing with one's critics.

On the present account, detection of moral considerations need not be conscious, and the agent need not recognize that it is a moral consideration *qua* moral consideration that is moving him or her to act. Detection of moral considerations amounts to awareness of moral considerations, and that awareness need not be conscious or even necessarily explicable by the agent.[26] Moreover, we have already seen some reasons to think the mechanisms of this awareness are likely to be diverse in their nature and means of connection to the world, and, plausibly, variably constituted at cognitive and neurological levels.

What does matter is that it is a moral consideration that moves the agent to act either actually, or in the suitable range of counterfactuals. How and whether we judge the springs of our own action is less important than what in fact moves us to act. So, for example, the discovery that some or another agent misrepresents his or her motivations to him- or herself does not, by itself, strike against the agent's responsibility for the resultant outcome.

These virtues might look like trivial ones in light of the misgivings invited by those two prominent and suspiciously vague notions, "relevant similarity of context" and "suitable proportion of worlds."[27] Even in the

---

[25] It might be that the involved conditionals could be completely specified for all possibilities under all normative conditions, so that we could end up with a stable but grotesquely gerrymandered capacity and its realizer. This possibility is expositorily otiose, if metaphysically reasonable.

[26] For a defense of this idea, see Arpaly, *Unprincipled Virtue: An Inquiry into Moral Agency*.

[27] "Type of moral consideration" is not without difficulties of its own. But I will set aside this puzzle for now, because it does not seem to raise any interesting questions unique to this account.

best of circumstances, notions of context relevance and suitability of proportion are extremely slippery. Still, the present account gives us a reasonably firm grip on the matter.

Consider the notion of relevant similarity. We might imagine that the matter is settled simply by appealing to the agent, where relevance just is what is relevant to the agent. However, this conception of relevance is too flimsy a basis for supporting the normative practices involved in assessments of responsibility. The connection between an agent's powers and the customary broader social demands responsibility places upon agents (e.g., to cultivate awareness of considerations important to others) would be tenuous or broken if similarity of context were simply decided by the agent directly, or even by accidental, non-volitional elements of a particular agent's assessments. Moreover, one might imagine that subjective assessments of relevance might provide a strange inducement for agents to acquire extraordinarily fine-grained, self-indexed assessments of relevance. In doing so, the agent would insulate him- or herself from being appropriately held responsible. So, some non-subjective conception of relevance is required.

Even on a non-subjective conception of relevance, there remains a spectrum of possibilities, with extremely demanding conceptions of relevance on one end and extremely permissive conceptions of relevance on the other. For example, one could suppose that the relevant category of similarity is very coarse-grained, i.e., the bare fact that the context is actional or deliberative makes it the same context. But this makes the notion of relevance too expansive to do substantive work. For example, it would not permit us to distinguish between contexts when an agent is doggedly attempting to ascertain the moral considerations and contexts where, say, an agent was non-culpably extraordinarily time-pressured or subject to manipulation. All deliberative and practical contexts would count as capacity-supporting if the operative notion of similarity were sufficiently coarse-grained. According to such an account, it would very nearly always turn out that those agents were capable of detecting moral considerations, which is at least at odds with our inclination to think that sometimes people can fail to recognize considerations in one context but not another. So, the operative notion of relevance must pick out contexts in a more fine-grained way.

Consider now the alternative end of the spectrum of relevant similarity of context. We can imagine an almost maximally fine-grained specification of similarity in which deliberative similarity requires that an agent's deliberation have the same occurrent features and the same past, holding fixed the same laws of nature (in other words: a GFP-type capacity). On this conception of context relevance, in a deterministic world the contexts that would be deliberatively similar would always be exactly identical to the context under consideration. However, this extremely fine-grained conception of specificity is instructively implausible, too. Given that we are asking a question internal to a system organized around the aim of cultivating our responsiveness to moral considerations, a conception of relevance so narrow would be a hindrance to the attainment of the end of that system.[28] Under determinism, such a conception of the responsibility-relevant sense of capacity would require us to forgo the real benefits of responsibility, benefits that could be attained under a less demanding (and justifiable) conception of the involved notion of capacity. In short, there is no plausible reason, from the standpoint of the end of the responsibility system, for either an especially demanding or permissive conception of the responsibility-relevant capacity.

So: the governing conception of contextual relevance will be one where the granularity of distinctions between types of contexts will be neither too coarse nor too fine. It will operate with a moderate degree of granularity for similarity, of the sort likely to function well in everyday contexts of responsibility assessment. The notion of relevantly similar context will not be subjectively settled by individual agents or even jointly via some notion of relevance with conceptual currency in our community. Instead, the notion of contextual relevance will be settled by what is *actually co-optimal or better for fostering agency that recognizes and suitably responds to moral considerations in the actual world, in ordinary contexts of action* (given the existence of genuine moral considerations, facts about the granularity of norm that is most useful in ordinary deliberative and practical contexts, and holding fixed a complex range of general facts about our customary psychologies and the cultural and social circumstances of our agency).[29]

---

[28] I am here supposing that the notion of considerations makes sense in a deterministic world. There seems to be broad consensus that the existence of determinism would not preclude the existence of reasons, or the capacity of agents to respond to it. For some philosophical defenses of this idea, see Daniel Dennett, *Freedom Evolves* (New York: Viking, 2003): xiii, 347; and Fischer and Ravizza, *Responsibility and Control: A Theory of Moral Responsibility*.

[29] As a reminder, the "suitably" clause in the italicized bit is only mean to preclude perverse or accidental relations to moral reasons, such as when an agent always acts contrary to the ordinary moral significance of the consideration, or where the response is disconnected from the content or significance of the considerations.

This conception of the relevant notion of capacity provides a way of thinking about a range of science fiction thought experiments sometimes used by philosophers in the literature on responsibility. If currently science fictional cases play or come to play some role in the social circumstances of our thinking about the cases, this fact would presumably be of some consequence for what carvings of distinctions are relevant for the aims of the responsibility system. However, limit cases (such as Frankfurt cases and their ilk) are likely to create their own idiosyncratic classes of relevant similarity, i.e., Frankfurt case contexts might have their own rules about what counts as a capacity, quite apart from more ordinary contexts. Unless, of course, Frankfurt cases were the ordinary context. In sum, standard intuition pumps are typically of limited utility in understanding the features that would govern a normatively structured notion of capacity relevant to a responsibility system concerned with cultivating moral considerations agency, precisely because the circumstances of their intuition pumping are typically idiosyncratic.

Before turning to consider the notion of "suitable proportion of worlds" I should say something about the priority of elements embedded in the idea of "cultivating moral considerations-responsive agency." On this account, we can first think of the form of agency the system is directed at fostering as one in which agents actually recognize and appropriately respond to relevant moral considerations in the actual world. However, if we take seriously the aim of cultivating moral considerations-sensitive agency, and we think that form of agency is valuable, there is some pressure to think that the expansion of contexts in which such agency operates will be an end of the system as well, for fulfilling such an end expands the effective scope of a valuable form of agency. This suggests the secondary aspiration for our ideal observer: expanding the range of contexts in which agents have the desired relationship to moral considerations. So, this is a picture on which the aim of fostering moral considerations-responsive agency is tied first to supporting this form of agency in the actual world and, second, to expanding its scope of efficacy.

Turning to the notion of "a suitable proportion of worlds," as it pertains to condition (Aii) (the counterfactual condition) of the detection or recognition condition, the governing conception of proportion will not be fixed by our subjective estimation. Nor will it be fixed by some collective sense, whether implicit, explicit, or stipulative. Instead, the suitable proportion of worlds will be that proportion—whichever it is—which is at least co-optimal for a practicable system of judgments, practices, and attitudes shaped by the aims of the responsibility system.

Again, there are some distinctive and identifiable issues that emerge when considering the requisite proportion of worlds required for correctly attributing a capacity to detect moral considerations. First of all, we would do well to remember that non-ideality is the customary condition of our agency. As such, we cannot expect that the governing conception of considerations detection will be systematic detection of considerations in all worlds where there are relevantly similar contexts. That would be a requirement that none in the sublunary realm could hope to satisfy. From the perspective of a practicable system of responsibility, this outcome would be at odds with the point of it all.

A second extreme is possible, in the opposite direction. One might think that the existence of a single world is all the frequency required to settle the matter of whether an agent detects moral considerations. Such a construal of frequency would be very demanding on agents, for an unreliable and almost perfectly insensitive agent would still count as suitably sensitive to moral considerations on this account.

This demanding construal of the governing conception of proportion is implausible, in light of the normative work it must do and the consequences of such a demand on ordinary human agents. It is extraordinarily difficult for us to function as agents when our capacities are unreliable. Prediction, coordination, and the emotional backing that supports our willingness to be called to account for our behavior depend on a sense of confidence about the reliability of our capacities to detect those things that generate or express those demands. Thus, it is more plausible to think that a less demanding standard of sensitivity will be more effective at appropriately motivating agents and enjoining their compliance in a system of practices supporting the cultivation of moral considerations-responsive agency.

Notice, too, that the required degree of sensitivity might vary by context. Such variance would not be at odds with the idea that there is a fact about what degree of sensitivity is required in a particular context. Variance in the degree of sensitivity would, presumably, be partly or completely driven by the fact that a variable degree of required sensitivity in detection of moral considerations turns out to contribute to an at least co-optimal, practicable, responsibility system. My account is consistent with this possibility, but I am neutral about the likelihood of whether or not this kind of variance in sensitivity is indeed the governing conception.

The present approach will surely leave some unsatisfied. After all, it is more of a recipe for a substantive conclusion than a bold, decisive answer. However, the most obviously troublesome notions, including the notions of "deliberatively similar contexts" and "suitable proportion of worlds" can be understood in relatively clear ways. What I have endeavored to show is that the trouble raised by these notions has less to do with an inherent lack of clarity and more to do with their complexity, a complexity rooted in the ineradicably normative structure of the responsibility system. The ideal observer serves as a kind of tool for capturing that complexity, providing a construct that demarcates the conditions that are of interest to a responsibility system justified along the lines I have articulated.

None of this entails that at any given time we can know with absolute certitude that the conditions of responsibility have been met. In this, the account mirrors the predicament we find ourselves in when we are considering whether to hold someone responsible. We have a pretty good sense of what matters, and what information would help us arrive at the right conclusion, but we are not always in a position to know that information. Epistemic infelicities in actual practice are not novel. So here, at least, the relation between practice and theory seems about right.

7. Unpacking the machinery 2: self-governance

Let us now turn towards the self-governance, or volitional control condition on responsible agency. Note that the operative notion here is distinct from the more basic requirement of self-*directed* agency, which is not particular to responsible agency. Self-governance, as distinctive of responsible agency is:

(B) the capacity for volitional control, or self-governance with respect to the relevant moral considerations M in circumstances C obtains when either

   (i) S is, in light of awareness of M in C, motivated to accordingly pursue courses of action for which M counts in favor, and to avoid courses of action disfavored by M or

   (ii) when S is not so motivated, in a suitable proportion of those worlds where S is in a context relevantly similar to C

(a) S detects moral considerations of type M, and

(b) in virtue of detecting M considerations, S acquires the motivation to act accordingly, and

(c) S successfully acts accordingly.

I am skeptical of there being a single, unified thing that constitutes control across all circumstances, both internal and external to the context of responsibility. What counts as being in control of a computer mouse for a professional video gamer will be different than what counts as control for someone who picks up a computer mouse for the first time; a novice might be rightly said to have attained control of the mouse when he or she can effectively select among objects a hundred pixels wide. In contrast, in the context of competitive gaming, that coarse-grained a degree of selection might be rightly viewed as substantially out of control. Similarly, whether the physiological effects of three drinks of alcohol means one's driving is in or out of control is, of course, substantially a function of blood alcohol content. However, it is also partly a function of the minimal kinds of reactions and judgments we expect of drivers.

None of this complexity requires abandoning the idea that there can be facts of the matter regarding control. Still, when we turn to the matter of responsibility and how control intersects with it, we should accept the idea that there is not some uniform story to be told about control across all contexts.

First some clarifications, then the ramifications.

The clause in (Bi) regarding "in light of awareness of M" is meant to express the importance of a non-accidental relationship between the moral considerations and the action. The governing idea here is that the content of M must play a non-deviant role in the production of action. So, roughly, the fact that something counts as a harm to an innocent plays a non-deviant role in the production of action if it is the perception of harm and innocence (rather than purely content-independent elements) that contributes to some suitable responsive action in the considered agent (say, treating the injury of the innocent party).

The difference between cases in which an agent is governed in light of M and those in which M is recognized by the agent but has no proper connection to the production of action is brought out if we contrast it to a remote case of the sort that is of interest only to philosophers. Suppose Diego is a peculiar fellow who spontaneously provides bandages to the nearest person every Tuesday at noon, and does so as a kind of ritual disconnected from any impulse to help others. Suppose further that Diego recognizes considerations in favor of helping, but is always unmoved by such considerations. On a particular Tuesday at noon, Diego might recognize that the person nearest to him needs a bandage, but that consideration would play no role in his rushing to provide a bandage to that person. Rather, it would be the fact that it was the time of the ritual that did the work, and not the content of the consideration that there was a nearby person in need of aid. On the present account, Diego would not be a responsible agent with respect to considerations of type M in any circumstances, even if on any Tuesday at noon, he did recognize and (in some sense) respond appropriately to such considerations.

Having noted the need for a connection of content between the consideration and the course of action, henceforth I will dispense with this epicycle and simply presume that the requirement of recognizing and responding to moral considerations is understood to include a content requirement.

Now consider another shifty-sounding phrase in the definition: "accordingly pursue courses of action." This clause merely meant to capture the idea that the agent is moved to act in accord with the moral consideration. That is, this condition excludes cases of deviant *motivation*, where the motivation initially generated by the consideration is counter or orthogonal to the nature of the consideration. So, an agent would not be capable of the relevant form of self-governance if, the recognition that someone requires aid only and reliably gave rise to the impulse to make the needy more miserable.

The notions of relevantly similar contexts and suitable proportion of worlds are meant in the same senses as given before. That is, they are meant to pick out those contexts and sets of worlds that would be the co-optimal (or better) governing conception of contexts and proportion for a practicable responsibility system given the constraints of the psychological, social, and cultural conditions of our agency.

The capacity for self-governance is tied to the capacity for detection in an important way: whether one is self-governed in some or another context partly depends on whether or not the detection condition has been satisfied.[30]

---

[30] One might wonder whether what is at stake is a *capacity* for self-governance, or instead, self-governance, *simpliciter*? As long as we are in agreement about what the substantive requirements are, the rest is a matter of convention. Natural language seems to provide some slippage, with "capacity" referring to both powers manifested under actual conditions as well as powers manifested under

Self-governance is thus not some general capacity disconnected from the particulars of a capacity to detect relevant moral considerations. In the actual course of events one might fail to detect a given class of moral consideration and might nevertheless have the capacity for self-governance in light of moral considerations of the relevant type. If someone is great at recognizing considerations of loyalty, any shortcomings at detecting considerations of kindness would not impinge on self-governance in circumstances where only loyalty considerations are live. What is ruled out on this account is a case where an agent lacks the capacity to detect a given sort of moral consideration relevant to the circumstances of decision or action but where the agent is self-governing in light of that type of moral consideration.

One implication of rejecting a conception of self-governance as a general capacity is that we can acknowledge that a capacity for self-governance in one kind of activity need not translate to a similar capacity in an intuitively related activity. My ability to resist the impulse to make rude remarks to students and strangers need not mean that I am resistant to such impulses when with family members over the holidays. I'm told this point generalizes.

This variability of self-governance holds for neurological disorders, as well. Consider, for example, Tourette syndrome (TS). In some contexts it might have no impact on the suitability of an agent for the demands of moral responsibility. When it comes to helping someone apparently ill, the presence or absence of TS in a person will typically have no significance for the appropriateness of the demands of morality. In other contexts TS might be very significant for the capacity to govern one's conduct in light of moral considerations. It might, for example, make it impossible for the agent to preface a question with the standard niceties during the question period following a mediocre philosophy talk that has gone on too long.[31]

---

counterfactual conditions. I find it somewhat more natural to speak of a capacity for self-governance, but this is not meant to preclude cases of actual self-governance.

[31] I am ignoring some complexities here with how Tourette syndrome actually works, including issues surrounding the degree to which ticcing is under voluntary control. It is more accurate to characterize the syndrome as providing a strong desire to tic, a desire whose strength can grow unless satisfied by ticcing. However, the agent typically has a substantial degree of control over when such ticcing is performed, at least before the "pressure" to tic builds up a great deal. For a relevant philosophical discussion of Tourette syndrome and moral responsibility, see Timothy Schroeder, "Moral Responsibility and Tourette Syndrome," *Philosophy and Phenomenological Research* 71, no. 1 (2005): 106–23.

The circumstantialist picture of an agent's control, one which an agent's control can vary across context and relative to the involved moral concern with no variation in intrinsic features of the agent, is an important idea built into the core of the account. Different circumstances put pressure on our capacity for self-governance in a variety of ways, and what capacity we have for self-governance depends on our environment in various ways.[32] The power of a seed to grow into a tree is only a power it has in some contexts and not others. The challenge is to remember that this is true of persons, too, and that this generates the corresponding need to appreciate the circumstances that structure our powers.

The present account stands in contrast to the atomistic tendency in much of the Anglophone philosophical literature on responsible agency, a tendency to describe responsibility's requirements in a way that focuses exclusively on the agent. Responsible agency is treated as a set of properties that describe an agent in a vacuum, free of a context or environment. What I have been arguing, and what seems required by the standard picture in social psychology, is that we should instead conceive of the notion of self-governance or self-control as very explicitly tied to facts about agents in circumstances.[33]

Careful readers will note that the relevant capacity for self-governance is not characterized by a requirement that in the actual sequence the agent acted in the appropriate way. Instead, what is required is only that the agent has, or would have (in the specific sense of condition Bii), motivations of the right sort. This construal permits the possibility of weakness of will, for

---

[32] Circumstance sensitivity of responsibility attributions can, in principle, have numerous sources that we might characterize in terms of "context sensitivity": (1) variation might arise because contexts affect whether or not the self-governance condition is satisfied; (2) variation might arise because contexts affect whether or not the detection condition is satisfied; (3) variation might arise because moral demands might differ across contexts, thus affecting whether one can be rightly praised or blamed; (4) variation might arise because the degree of praise or blame is context-sensitive; and (5) context sensitivity might arise as a consequence of the notion of self-control itself having a variable meaning, for example, if in some contexts it picks out the conditions I have identified and in other conditions it does not. I am committed to contextual variation of varieties (1) and (2). I think varieties (3) and (4) are very plausible. I am open to (5) where it is construed as a point about the realizers for the normative structures identified in the account.

[33] I take it that what John Doris calls "collaborativism" is a version of circumstantialism that emphasizes the specifically social dimension of how agent capacities arise from features external to any particular agent. See John Doris, *Talking to Ourselves: Reflection, Skepticism, and Agency* (New York: Oxford University Press, forthcoming). The present account is largely friendly to that approach, but perhaps casts a wider net about what features of circumstances can properly be said to be implicated in talk of an agent's capacities.

these are cases in which the agent could have (in the responsibility-relevant sense) acted on the relevant moral considerations but failed to do so. Of course, if there is *no* world with relevantly similar contexts in which the agent ever acted in accord with the moral consideration, then we have already seen why, from the standpoint of the ideal observer, it would be odd to say that the agent should count as capable of governing him- or herself in light of the relevant moral considerations. Other defects of agency (phobias, for example) will plausibly exempt agents from responsibility, when they do, precisely by decreasing the frequency of worlds beyond the level required for self-governance in light of moral considerations.[34]

On many accounts of responsible agency it is difficult to see how an agent could be responsible in cases where action arises from processes that are, in the actual course of things, non-deliberatively undertaken.[35] However, the operative notion of capacity permits us to retain the commonsense idea that we can be responsible in cases of spontaneous action and in episodes of forgetfulness. One can retain the capacity to recognize moral considerations even when one does not. And one may also retain the capacity for self-government even when it is not exercised. The fact that the detection did not occur in the actual sequence does not show the absence of at least the responsibility-relevant capacity.

I have thus far written as though agents in any given context will be faced with moral considerations of only one type. However, in the course of ordinary, non-pathological deliberation about what to do, it is plausible to think that there may well be numerous moral considerations that are relevant to the choice. What then should we say about the interaction of responsible agency (in a context, relative to a kind of consideration) and blameworthiness?

Culpability concerning one type of consideration can rest comfortably with exemptions for culpability concerning other considerations. So, on this account, responsibility for some outcome is tied to the moral considerations

[34] This picture does not fully resolve the doubts about weakness of will raised by Gary Watson, but the idea of a principled demarcation of proportions of worlds required for responsible agency provides a framework of non-arbitrary standards for making sense of the idea that some defects of agency do undermine responsibility and that others do not. See Gary Watson, "Skepticism About Weakness of Will," *Philosophical Review* 86 (1977): 316–39.

[35] Considerations along these lines have been the inspiration for "attributionist" approaches to moral responsibility. See, for example, Angela Smith, "Control, Responsibility, and Moral Assessment," *Philosophical Studies* 138 (2008): 367–92.

and attendant self-government available to agents in the relevant circumstances. In turn, these assessments are tied to the particular considerations in play and available to the individual agent.

Now recall that the fact that an agent is a responsible agent (with respect to a consideration in a context) does not settle the matter of the agent's *blameworthiness*, that is, whether and to what degree blame of the agent is licensed. An agent might well be a responsible agent in some circumstance, owing to his or her possession of the appropriate sensitivity and responsiveness to some minor moral consideration, but not to others. And, at least with respect to that circumstance and the consideration in play, we look to the agent's quality of will. But the defect might be minor. The weight of the consideration, as a minor consideration, might not be much and the failure of good will that the agent demonstrates in ignoring it might be relatively minor. Moreover, this might be true even if the agent recognizes alternative considerations but lacks the capacity for self-governance in light of those considerations. So, the circumstance- and consideration-specific nature of responsible agency will preclude blameworthiness in an array of cases, restricting blameworthiness to those considerations to which the agent is alive and capable of self-governance. The resultant picture is one where blameworthiness is a somewhat more targeted affair than would be suggested by accounts emphasizing a general, cross-situationally stable capacity for self-governance.

Our blaming judgments will not frequently display such fine-grained sensitivity to the particulars of the case. Partly, this is because of the presence of a defeasible but (let us suppose) reasonably widespread presumption that ordinary adults possess the ability to recognize and appropriately respond to a range of familiar moral considerations across a range of ordinary contexts. In the normal course of things, there will usually be some motivation to talk as though responsible agency is not a circumstance- and consideration-specific capacity. What makes such talk often reasonable is that if our practices of moral education and participation in the responsibility system do anything, it is this: they ordinarily produce agents who will in fact be able to recognize a wide range of those considerations we regard as morally significant, and be capable of self-governance in light of such convictions. On my account, however, the *truth* of individual judgments turns on the presence or absence of the more local capacities of detection and self-governance.

8. Children and self-conceptions

The gradual ascent of children into ubiquitous responsibility happens in piecemeal fashion. Comparatively young children might well be responsible agents in very specific or local circumstances. Similarly, it might turn out that non-human species display similarly constrained conditions under which they are responsible agents. In the human case, it seems fair to characterize a good deal of parenting and acculturation as bent to the task of expanding the range of circumstances in which the targets have the capacities required for moral responsibility.

Initially, much of this happens via feigned attributions of responsibility. In contrast to genuinely holding someone responsible, moral education is typically undertaken in the way characterized by traditional moral influence theorists, that is, with the aspiration of influencing. There is no assumption that the target is a responsible agent. Indeed, the point of feigning praise and blame just is to get children to such a point where they have the capacities that are required for genuine praise and blame. In contrast, holding someone morally responsible assumes the relevant capacities are present and that the agent has failed to demonstrate the appropriate form of moral concern.

In both children and adults, the truth of whether an agent is a responsible agent in some context depends on the particular moral concerns at stake, and whether the agent can detect and self-govern in light of those particular concerns. The case of children might lead one to wonder whether it is an additional requirement of responsible agency, that agents *conceive of themselves* as beings who both can and are governed in light of moral considerations.[36]

For a self-conception requirement to be plausible, it couldn't be given an overly-intellectualist gloss, where the condition is only satisfied by creatures who have the thought "I am a being regulated by moral considerations." It would be more plausible to, for example, suppose there is a kind of dispositional or counterfactual condition that must be met in order to conceive of oneself in this way. So, for example, being willing to acknowledge that one is subject to the demand to take moral considerations into account, or that one's self-conception is in fact at least implicitly committed to this self-conception. What this requirement would do is to

---

[36] A condition like this one is tentatively suggested in Karen Jones, "Emotion, Weakness of Will, and the Normative Conception of Agency," *Supplement to Philosophy* 52 (2003): 181–200.

link susceptibility to moral considerations with a first-personal picture of agency, one where the agent is not merely the product of external forces but also an active element in its own right.

At least with respect to accommodating our phenomenology of agency, this requirement seems plausible. Such a requirement would also respect the idea that there is a role to be played by how an agent monitors his or her own sensitivity and responsiveness to moral considerations, and that a system that aims to cultivate considerations-sensitive agency will demand such powers if they are attainable. So, on the assumption that our conscious, deliberative agency is a causal contributor to what we do, then I am content to include this requirement.[37]

It seems to matter what agential powers are widely available to us. Given the aim of fostering our considerations-sensitive agency, we should expect that the borders of responsible agency will be drawn around whatever form of consideration-responsive agency is attainable among a suitably large portion of the moral community.[38]

9. Alternative possibilities

One appealing feature of this account of responsible agency is that it permits us to make sense of the idea that (at least sometimes) agents can do otherwise when acting. Once considerations-responsiveness is construed in terms of capacities, we get a natural way to map an interest in alternative possibilities onto the modal properties of the capacity to recognize and respond to moral

[37] I am sometimes tempted by the thought that if our conscious, deliberative self makes no causal difference in what we do, then it is difficult to see why a self-conception of moral considerations-responsive agency should be a requirement on responsible agency. I do not mean to deny that this discovery would be a blow to an admittedly prominent element of how we ordinarily conceive of our agency. My point is just that the distinctive normative structure of the responsibility system has considerable resilience, on this way of characterizing it.

[38] As I noted last chapter, considerations grounded in the particular presumed account of normative ethics will matter. The specific content of moral norms may play a role in deciding what counts as a suitable portion of the moral community. So, if only one of every 100 agents were capable of attaining a causally efficacious sense of his or her own considerations-responsive agency, considerations of egalitarianism and utility would plausibly cut against restricting responsible agency to that 1 percent. However, perhaps a suitably elitist perfectionist account of ethics could permit a notion of responsible agency that rare in its occurrence. Such considerations, and their degree of remove from ordinary convictions about responsibility and morality more generally, will entail different degrees of revisionism between the final account and folk notions of responsibility.

considerations. This mapping won't be a perfect match to ordinary talk of capacities, given that strands of the folk notion are entangled with a GFP-conception of alternatives, and other notions of capacity not yoked to the particular conception of the responsibility system that is operative here. However, given the aspiration of limiting the scope of the revision proposed by the account, it is something of a virtue of the account that it provides a way to accommodate the familiar thought that there are responsibility-significant possibilities regarding what could have happened, but did not.

To be sure, the account does *not* give us an account of alternative possibilities *simpliciter*. What it does give us is an account of responsibility-relevant alternatives. That's fine, because the ability to do otherwise is not what makes agents responsible. At best, it plays an evidential role in the discernment of the presence or absence of the relevant capacity.

Bracketing the usual background conditions involving self-directed agency, on the present account it is sufficient for original responsibility that an agent has done X, and where the doing of X involved recognizing and appropriately responding to moral considerations—regardless of whether the agent could have done otherwise. In cases where the agent acts in the right way from the right conviction, the matter of whether the agent could do otherwise is irrelevant. This is so, even if there are no alternative possibilities in the responsibility-relevant sense: the detection and self-governance conditions only require that the agent in fact recognize and appropriately respond to moral considerations. In cases where the agent fails in the actual sequence to recognize or respond, our interest in responsibility-relevant alternative possibilities is appropriate, but only as a kind of evidence about whether the agent possessed the relevant capacities. So, the role for responsibility-relevant alternative possibilities is somewhat limited.

On these matters, perhaps the chief advantage of the account is that it need not insist that this is how we actually think about responsibility and possibility. Rather, it is a prescription for how we ought to think about these things, given the normative function of the responsibility system.

10. Summary

When we say that someone is responsible, this claim entails that the agent is both a responsible agent (roughly, effectively self-directed and possessing

232 A THEORY OF MORAL RESPONSIBILITY

the twin capacities to recognize and respond to moral considerations) and that the agent has failed to act with the right quality of will.

My task here has been to characterize an adequate prescriptive, revisionist notion of responsible agency that can license the truth of such judgments in ordinary cases. I have sought to provide this account in the framework of a broadly Reasons approach to responsible agency, and to do so in a way sensitive to various doubts about whether we are indeed rational agents in the way required by the account. At the core of this account of responsible agency is the thought that any credible Reasons account will need to allow for the fact of our sensitivity to reasons being corroded or enhanced by features of the context of action.

On this account, free will is variably had in the same individual. That is, the range of moral considerations an agent recognizes in some or another context or circumstance will vary. In some circumstances agents will be capable of recognizing a wide range of moral considerations. In other circumstances those sensitivities may be narrower or even absent. When they are absent, or when they dip beneath a minimal threshold, the agent ceases to be a responsible agent in that context. We need not suppose that if someone is a responsible agent at a given time and context, that he or she possesses that form of agency at all times across all contexts. In some contexts I will be a responsible agent, and in others not. Those might not be the same contexts in which you are a responsible agent.

At the outset of this chapter, I noted that the present account was intended to build on existing Reasons accounts of responsible agency in a variety of ways.[39] Simplifying a bit, I take it that Wallace and I (in contrast to Fischer and Ravizza) agree on a requirement that responsible agents must be capable of self-regulation in light of specifically moral considerations. However, against Wallace, Fischer and Ravizza and I are in agreement about the need to spell out in some detail what the involved agential powers come to, beyond an appeal to a largely unspecified notion of a general capacity.

Focusing on the specification of the responsibility-relevant capacities, the most important innovation of the present account involves the character-

---

[39] In its general structure, the present account is perhaps most similar to Wallace's, on which accountability is understood in terms of "the power to grasp and apply moral reasons" and the "power to control or regulate behavior in light of such reasons." See Wallace, *Responsibility and the Moral Sentiments*, p. 157. My account also shares important features with Fischer and Ravizza's account. See Fischer and Ravizza, *Responsibility and Control: A Theory of Moral Responsibility*.

ization of the involved rational capacities. My account appeals to circumstantialist capacities set by normative idealizations. It rejects the idea of holding fixed some mechanism when comparing powers across contexts, and, as I will argue in chapter 9, it grants a considerably diminished role to the historical dimensions of agency.

An advantage of my approach, on which the capacities that constitute free will and responsible agency are only loosely connected to our intrinsic dispositions, is that it permits us to reconcile a picture of agency with the empirical and armchair considerations mentioned at the outset of this chapter. It does not presuppose that our capacities are stable across contexts, unaffected by circumstances. Moreover, it allows for a pluralist epistemology of moral considerations. Recognition or sensitivity to moral considerations is not a unified phenomenon, relying on a single faculty or mechanism. Moral considerations may be constituted by or generated from as diverse things as affective states, propositional content, situational awareness, and so on. Consequently, the corresponding epistemic mechanisms for apprehending these considerations will presumably be diverse as well.

There are a variety of ways to extend this approach to responsible agency. In the next chapter, I will consider the ramifications of this picture for thinking about the conditions of blame and the circumstances of responsibility more generally. I will then show how this framework gives us the resources to say what we need to about the idea of deserving praise and blame.

8

Blame and Desert

This chapter aims to fill in the details of the present account along two distinct axes. The first concerns exculpation in light of the way the way the norms of blame interact with the dynamic nature of the normatively salient aspects of our circumstance-structured agency. The second axis concerns desert, and the basis on which it makes sense to regard people as deserving moralized praise and blame.

I begin with exculpation and its connection to the quality of will account of the blameworthiness norms.

1. Exculpation and quality of will

In the Introduction, I made use of a distinction between excuses and exemptions. Each is the basis of exculpation in different ways. Exemptions indicate a failure to be a responsible agent. Excuses obtain when someone has free will, but fails to satisfy the further conditions for blame—in this case, ill will. Ignorance is the most common basis for excuse. The quality of will account of blaming norms has the resources to explain why: it is typically not a matter of ill will when one is ignorant.[1] If I don't know your foot is there and have no reason to think it might be, it is not a matter of ill will, or a failure of due concern about you in light of morality, when I accidentally step on your foot.

A distinctive feature of the present account of responsible agency is that a good deal of exculpation operates through the absence of responsible

---

[1] Again, the present focus is on original responsibility. Intentional cultivation of ignorance so as to avoid responsibility looks like the sort of thing that any plausible system of blaming norms would treat as blameworthy.

agency. That is, rather than presuming that exculpation should be overwhelmingly understood in terms of excuses, the present account suggests that exemptions (i.e., the lack of responsible agency) will play a comparatively larger role.

Consider ignorance. On the present account, ignorance *exempts* if the agent falls below the threshold specified for possessing the capacity to recognize the relevant moral considerations. An agent lacking the responsibility-relevant capacity to recognize moral considerations cannot be a responsible agent, thus blocking the appropriateness of blame. So, if ignorance entails a failure of the capacity to recognize moral considerations, then it will exculpate by blocking the presence of responsible agency.

On this picture, it may be less obvious how ignorance can *excuse*, given that being a responsible agent is a matter of having sufficient sensitivity to relevant moral considerations in contexts of the sort under consideration. For example, you might think that the failure to pick up on the fact that you are about to step on someone's foot is a kind of failure of responsible agency. That is, it is a failure to recognize the particular consideration in those circumstances that it would be wrong to step on this person's foot. If responsible agency really were so fine-grained in its specification, then I agree that it would not be clear how ignorance could ever excuse (as opposed to always exempting).

However, for reasons explicated in the last chapter—namely, reasons having to do with our cognitive and affective limits, the benefits of stable standards, and the resultant requirements for somewhat coarse-grained characterizations of capacities upon which to anchor morally influential practices—it seems unlikely that responsible agency would be so easily lost. As I noted there, what is plausibly at stake is the capacity to detect *kinds* or *types* of moral considerations in relative coarse-grained circumstances that do the work of defining responsible agency. It is not token-specific capacities in extremely narrowly construed circumstances that do the work. A characterization of the conditions of responsible agency that is so tightly specified to a context would lead us back to the problems with the GFP-type capacities. That is, with little justification, it would rob us of the valuable effects of praise and blame for little obvious benefit.

On the account given in the last chapter, what we should say about a (one hesitates to say) pedestrian case of accidentally stepping on someone's foot is: (1) that, presumably, the agent has the relevant capacities to detect and respond to the ordinary range of moral considerations (including reasons against pointless infliction of bodily harm) to count as a responsible agent; and (2) that possession of such capacities does not entail that such agents will always detect that such reasons are operative in some occurring context; but (3) that in this case, the failure to detect that there were reasons of the relevant sort present does not manifest ill will.

On this picture, the standards for blameworthiness (holding fixed satisfaction of the responsible agency standards) are more demanding than the standards for responsible agency. So, a failure to respond to considerations one could have (in some sense) anticipated does not always entail blameworthiness. Such failures only entail blameworthiness when they reveal a defect in the agent's level of concern as required by morality.

Here, it is natural to wonder what exactly the idea of a "defect in the agent's level of concern as required by morality" comes to. I've said very little about this matter, other than to point to it as a notion of how to generally characterize the norms of blameworthiness. Partly this is a matter of focus. I take it that the force of most scientific and philosophical threats to moral responsibility operates via a denial that we are the right sorts of agents to be held morally responsible. So, my account here has focused on explicating what sorts of agents are plausibly candidates for moral responsibility, and what the grounds are for justifying praise and blame. These issues can be answered in fairly detailed ways, without needing to settle what the general characterization of the first-order norms of moralized blame comes to.

That said, it is exceedingly difficult to say much that is informative about the norms of blameworthiness, apart from characterizing them as concerned with quality of will, or the agent's concerns in light of what morality demands. I am suspicious that much more can be said without invocation of a broader theory of normative ethics. This comparative paucity of detail might be thought to give rise to a worry about the role that the quality of will element plays in the account of responsibility. Here's the worry: it leaves it open to a critic to insist that on a "strict epistemic liability" picture, the quality of will story is mostly superfluous for understanding responsibility.

By a strict epistemic liability picture, I am imagining an account on which *any* failure to respond to a moral concern by a responsible agent automatically reveals a defect in the agent's quality of will. On this picture, there would be no room for excuses, and correspondingly, norms of blameworthiness specified independently of the requirements of responsible agency. Responsibility would hinge entirely on whether one is a responsible agent, and there would be no work left for the quality of will theory. This would be a picture on which agents can be exempt, culpably negligent, or willfully blameworthy, but never non-culpably ignorant.[2]

Although nothing in my general approach rules out this picture, it might seem to be a natural extension of the idea that exemptions can do a great deal of work, and that the standards for determining the capacities required for responsible agency are themselves centrally concerned with when an agent can recognize and respond to moral considerations.

Such a picture strikes me as a rather implausible implementation of the general framework of responsibility and exculpation that I have been advancing. Requirements of strict epistemic liability in responsibility would be extraordinarily difficult for creatures like us, at least right now. However, any revisionist proposal just is a proposal for creatures like us, right now. In our present circumstances, we are already generally committed to the notion that some failures of knowledge are non-culpable, even if there is some sense in which the agent could have taken steps to make him- or herself aware of the relevant considerations. So, repudiation of this standard would require a considerable escalation of cognitive and practical demands for blame-avoidance, and this would presumably reduce "buy in" to the system of responsibility norms. If blame avoidance (of the sort allowed by excuses) becomes extraordinarily difficult or impossible, we run the risk of discouraging widespread commitment to the practice of responsibility. So, a picture of quality of will that permits excuse by ignorance has both practical and theoretical virtues.

---

[2] Perhaps the most natural way to make sense of culpable negligence on the present account involves treating quality of will norms as sensitive to how easily the requirements for responsible agency are satisfied. On this way of thinking about negligence, there are two places where this breakdown might happen. First, there could be a moral considerations-linked element. The greater an agent's capacity for recognizing the relevant moral considerations in some circumstance, the harder it becomes to think that the agent manifested the appropriate level of concern when he or she fails to recognize or respond to the relevant class of consideration. Second, there is the reasonable foresight requirement on self-directed agency. In either case, culpable ignorance of the sort that generates negligence plausibly arises when a given agent's capacity to recognize what matters (whether likely outcomes or moral considerations) is sufficiently robust by the standards of the responsibility system, but he or she still fails to recognize what matters. This is not to say that culpable ignorance and negligence come to the same thing. I might be faulted for failing to know something I ought to have known, but I might have in any case been unable to do anything with that knowledge. In such a case, I would be culpably ignorant but not negligent.

This less radical picture of exculpation, which emphasizes the contingent features of our existing practices as a kind of consideration that weighs against a particularly dramatic revision of practices, might raise questions of its own about the role of the quality of will norms. Strawson thought that our concern for quality of will was an unchanging primitive, constitutive of the responsibility system. On my account, though, the quality of will picture gets its plausibility as a prescriptive theory of blameworthiness not as a description of what we do, but as a characterization of what sorts of practices make sense given the agency cultivation model and our current arrangement of our psychological dispositions, inherited social practices, and the like. Given that I've maintained that our psychology and responsibility practices are somewhat more malleable than Strawson's remarks suggest, a critic might wonder whether the quality of will account is a fixed point in the present theory of moral responsibility. If it is not, then it might come at little or no cost to dispense with it.

Last chapter, I acknowledged that some of the psychological elements that drive both a concern for quality of will and also structure the internal logic of the responsibility system may well be psychological primitives, immune to transformation, just as Strawson claimed. However, it also seems relatively clear that we can attenuate some of our attitudes without thereby abandoning the entire framework of interpersonal concern.[3] This degree of flexibility suggests the possibility that something other than quality of will might serve as a better account of blameworthiness, at least for some group with a different arrangement of psychological dispositions, inherited norms, and the like.[4] Alternately, perhaps such transformations will arise for us over the course of gradual changes in the mutually constituting structures of our psychologies and norms.

I am inclined to accept the core element in both thoughts: while the quality of will characterization of the blaming norms seems plausibly effective for us here and now, it is conceivable that things could be different. Although the present account provides us with adequate warrant for rejecting responsibility nihilism, it is not a warrant in perpetuity. Over time, given changes in our social world, changes in what we rightly find

[3] This latter thought, of relatively localized attenuations of elements of what Strawson regarded as the "participant stance," plays an important role in the work of various responsibility nihilists. See, for example, Pereboom, *Living Without Free Will*; Honderich, "After Compatibilism and Incompatibilism."
[4] If so, this would suggest a form of relativism about responsibility (see chapter 4, § 5).

praiseworthy and blameworthy are to be expected. Those successors to our current practices of responsibility may be structured by concerns that seem alien, bizarrely tender-minded, or perhaps unforgiving in odd ways. However, so long as it remains a framework for regulating moralized praise in blame in a way connected to a concern for morality, it seems to me that we will rightly have reason to take seriously the thought that it is a system of moral responsibility.

Thus far, I've been focused on how exculpation for things like accidents are handled, given the quality of will account. Perhaps a more challenging issue for traditional quality of will accounts include such things as cases of agents under coercion or duress, wartime atrocities by otherwise ordinary agents, or peculiar situations in which agents can act in unexpectedly hostile ways. The present approach has good resources for addressing some of what is challenging about these cases.

Consider a case where someone is coerced into participating in some heinous crime. At first blush, it seems that culpability need not hinge on whether the agent acted with a suitable quality of will. It also hinges on whether there was a breakdown in responsible agency along the way. Plausibly, duress works precisely by making it much harder to govern ourselves in light of considerations that run afoul of the coercer's will, and sometimes that difficulty will be sufficient to push the agent beneath the standard of responsible agency.[5]

Of course, it does not follow that any instance of coercion or duress constitutes an eradication of the relevant capacities for self-governance. There are cases of remarkable agents who act in ways demonstrating considerable moral resoluteness in the face of what might typically be self-governance-undermining pressures. Still, the present picture gives us resources considerably beyond the traditional Strawsonian approach for explaining the familiar thought that there are cases where an agent is acting with manifestly ill will (say, a colonel ordering the deaths of tens of innocents) but where something else (say, the colonel facing the threat of

---

[5] My interest here is how the present account, which emphasizes broadly Strawsonian norms of blame, can account for cases that are otherwise difficult to explain under a quality of will account. That said, it is plausible to think that under a revisionist account that adopts an agency cultivation model for the justification of the responsibility norms, duress may not function as frequently as an excuse as we like. Or, at any rate, the prominence of duress as an excuse will partly depend on the effects of different possible duress norms.

her husband and son being executed if she does not comply) undercuts some of the force in a way that does not presume the absence of ill will.

Such cases—action under duress—are complicated for a variety of reasons, not the least of which is that reasonable theorists can disagree about whether these cases are ever exculpatory, that is, whether immoral coercion ever justifies compliance. Even bracketing those disagreements, it seems reasonable to expect disagreement about whether any given coerced agent ought to have acted one way or another in light of the coercion. So, for example, in the case of the colonel just given, we can expect reasonable disagreement about whether the colonel's special relationship to her family gives her reason to kill a greater number of innocents to spare the lives of her family members. And, we might disagree about how great the threat to the colonel or her interests must be to license wrongdoing on her part, and if wrongdoing is licensed, just what degree of wrongdoing is licensed.[6]

Partly, these disagreements reflect the imperfect relationship between the justified norms of responsibility and our understanding of them. However, part of the disagreement is more specific to the particular fact that the relationship between ill will and coercion is complex. Failing to act in accord with a consideration of minimal moral significance plausibly demonstrates less ill will than failure to act in accord with some consideration of great moral significance. The variety or number of moral considerations that speak in favor of the course of action also plausibly matters. If I recognize a diversity of moral considerations opposed to some course of action, other things being equal, I demonstrate more ill will in acting contrary to them than I do in acting in some fashion that runs afoul of only a single moral consideration. The degree of difficulty matters as well. I demonstrate less of a defect of will in caving in to some extraordinary tempting bit of immorality than I do when I give in to the most pedestrian and minimally appealing vice.

---

[6] In at least some cases—perhaps not the colonel—exculpation or mitigation by coercion will not work by showing that the agent lacked ill will. In the full exculpation case, it will work by showing that the agent was not a responsible agent with respect to the relevant moral considerations in those circumstances. In the mitigation case, it will work by raising the prospect that although the agent might have had the relevant capacities to recognize and respond to moral considerations, exercising those capacities was especially difficult in those circumstances. Alternately, it might work epistemically: given what we know, we may be somewhat uncertain as to whether the agent has the relevant degree of control required, and so we attenuate the strength of our blaming judgment in light of our uncertainty. A virtue of the present account is that it gives us a multi-dimensional set of factors for understanding how mitigation might work, and it does not saddle us with the need to insist that absence of ill will does the vast majority of exculpatory work.

What the present account should make vivid, however, is that even if we accept an account of responsible agency in terms of moral considerations responsiveness, and even if we accept a general characterization of the norms of blame in terms of ill will or the concern owed to agents in light of morality, it is no small thing to untangle the relationship of these matters in particular cases. Even if we understand the general structure of responsibility, it does not guarantee that we have ready access to the right answer for every particular case we encounter.

2. The costs of holding responsible

The foregoing considerations, which emphasize the non-static nature of blame norms and responsibility capacities, can raise the question of whether it could ever turn out that adherence to norms of blame might simply be too psychologically or socially costly for agents like ourselves. The benefits of a responsibility system don't come for free. Indeed, it is clear from both the armchair and experimental evidence that the practice of holding one another responsible is, in various ways, costly for agents who participate in and perpetuate such practices.[7]

Sociological research on major disasters suggests at least one context where this might hold. Consider the following:

University of South Alabama sociologist Steven Picou documented significantly higher rates of anxiety and depression in Alaska fishing towns after the Exxon Valdez oil spill. He expects the same in the Gulf [after Hurricane Katrina], because of what he calls a "corrosive social cycle."

"See, there's an all-clear that's signaled after a natural disaster, and you know when it has ended," Picou says.

That gives communities closure, and people tend to pull together in recovery. But with a man-made disaster like an oil spill, Picou says, the effects unfold over time, and it's more common to see communities tear apart. People get caught up blaming the company and fighting for a piece of the compensation pie. In Alaska, Picou says, the legal battle with Exxon became like a second disaster for the people.

---

[7] See Shaun Nichols, "After Incompatibilism: A Naturalistic Defense of the Reactive Attitudes," *Philosophical Perspectives* 21 (2007): 405–28.

"And by 2000, what we found was that the primary source of stress relating to the spill was being a litigant and not being a commercial fisherman," Picou says.[8]

The implication of this work is that practices of holding responsible—including judgments and attitudes of blame—constitute "a second disaster" for those who are inclined to participate in responsibility-characteristic practices. If so, then we might wonder whether, even on the present approach to moral responsibility, it turns out that at least in some cases, we are better off abandoning the framework of the responsibility system.

I don't see any way to rule out the possibility that there will be circumstances where the costs of blaming and ongoing participation in the responsibility system become, on some reasonable measure, too high. As a consistent feature of the world, however, this is rather unlikely. The more plausible lesson is this: sometimes blaming will be (locally) very costly, and perhaps even costly enough that it makes sense to maintain that one should not blame those who deserve it. In such cases forgiveness or even ignoring the transgression may, all things considered, be the better route.[9]

Under conditions where strong blame is warranted, and where it is costly to sustain those emotions, dispositions, and the resultant practices, forgiveness may have a special appeal, even in the face of ongoing intransigence. Whatever else is true about forgiveness, it does have the effect of working as something of safety valve on the costs of blame. Importantly, it does this without turning a blind eye towards the moral significance of the transgression. Done properly, forgiveness works in light of full awareness. Consequently, it does not undercut the aim of the responsibility system so much as it presumes it. On an interpersonal level, it seems to me that there is much to be said in favor of forgiveness and the way it relieves the burdens of blame. Moreover, it permits a restoration of the social order. A degree of readiness to forgive might be salubrious for both individual and community.

---

[8] Julie Rose, "Weathering Emotional Storms Over Gulf Oil Spill," *All Things Considered* <http://www.npr.org/templates/story/story.php?storyId=128334355>, accessed July 19, 2010. For the empirical data related to these claims, see J. Steven Picou, "When the Solution Becomes the Problem: The Impacts of Adversarial Litigation on Survivors of the *Exxon Valdez* Oil Spill," *University of St. Thomas Law Journal* 7, no. 1 (2009): 68–88. Relatedly, see DeMond Miller et al., "Assigning Blame: The Interpretation of Social Narratives and Environmental Disasters," *Southeastern Sociological Review* 1 (2000): 13–31.

[9] It may also be helpful to recall the point made in chapter 4, that there may be good reason to refrain from blaming even when someone deserves blame.

However, in a world heavily structured by institutions and multi-national organizations that wield more power and influence than any individual, and that do not operate as individuals do, the calculus becomes more complicated. Individual moral outrage and ongoing participation in blaming practices directed at such institutions and organizations, sustained without a willingness to forgive, may come at tremendous cost in just the ways the above-mentioned sociological work suggests.

This isn't to say that we should simply accept the conclusions of sociologists. Drawing philosophical conclusions from empirical work is always a tricky business. For example, the above-cited research focuses on the psychological and physical health costs of participating in litigation, which is something distinct from assessments of moral responsibility and participation in the associated practices. So, it may well be that the stress is a result of particular features of the U.S. legal system. And, of course, there are other disanalogies between the legal circumstances that are Picou's focus and ordinary practices of blaming. In his studies, the interlocutors are corporations versus individuals and families, rather than the individual-to-individual relationship more customary of ordinary moral blame.

Still, it surely seems right that there might well be cases in which various considerations weigh against the benefits of blaming, or even more general participation in the responsibility framework. As important as responsibility is, it does not obviously trump all other considerations or concerns that can matter to a human life. Nevertheless, there is a point here that should not be lost amongst the concessions. The point is this: the willingness of individuals to blame is plausibly a prerequisite on collective action. Such action is, I suspect, the only way to reshape institutions and collective organizations that do not themselves have anything like our ordinary capacities to recognize and respond to moral considerations. If all of that is right, then we have returned to the inspiring and depressing fact that we collectively shape the forces that make us individually responsible. Opting out of participation in the responsibility system may cause us to relinquish one of our most important tools for reshaping the social world.

3. The ecology of responsibility

An important consequence of the present picture of responsible agency is that blameworthiness is a matter of a web of contingent empirical and normative features. In this section, I'll try to pull together some of the strands developed in the preceding sections in a way that suggests that the theory of moral responsibility may have as much to do with political philosophy as anything else.

Consider a *Borat* case.[10] Borat cases occur when one visits (or is visited by someone from) a significantly alien culture. In such cases, either or both the alien and those visited by the alien may be unsure to what extent the other recognizes norms and considerations one recognizes as customary and salient, from context to context. Here in the West, in such cases there is often tolerance of behavior we would ordinarily regard as blameworthy when we encounter sufficiently alien agents. (I restrict my remarks to the West out of familiarity; I also acknowledge that there have been and will continue to be cases in which aliens in the West are obviously not met with such tolerance.)

The account I have offered suggests two explanations for why such tolerance can be justified when it occurs. One explanation appeals to the standard of blameworthiness. As we have seen, the question of blameworthiness depends on whether the considered person is a responsible agent, and if so, whether that agent demonstrates the requisite degree of moral concern. In Borat cases, the fact of cultural difference pushes us to doubt whether or not actions that would ordinarily strike us as blameworthy indeed demonstrate a failure of due concern. The fact of the robust cultural gap, coupled with the presumption that ordinary agents do not act with an aggressively ill will in alien contexts, gives us caution. What looks like ill will might be no such thing at all, for either party might misunderstand the will of the other.

The present account suggests a second way we might justifiably be cautious about blame. Recall that a distinctive feature of the present account is that one may be a responsible agent in one context and not another. We might take this thought and apply it here: we could think that (in the case of an agent in alien circumstances) the agent fails to be responsible in those circumstances.

In such cases, our ordinary license to blame might be stymied by the sense that there is a non-typical awareness of the relevant moral considerations. So, agents in alien circumstances may find themselves with diminished capacity to recognize locally salient moral considerations. In such cases, blameworthiness is blocked, when it is, not by an absence of ill will so much

---

[10] George Fourlas suggested the label in light of this sort of thing playing a prominent role in the movie *Borat: Cultural Learnings of America for Make Benefit Glorious Nation of Kazakhstan.*

as it is blocked by the fact that in that circumstance, the agent is not a responsible agent with respect to that consideration.

The mere fact of a non-standard relationship with moral considerations regarded as locally salient needn't always entail exculpation. For example, consider a particular agent who is both largely alien to a local context but has an exceptionally good track record of moral concern. If he or she takes pause at some local behavior, we might regard this as a reason to search for moral fault in our own practices, norms, and judgments.

Parallel remarks presumably hold for failures on the self-governance side of the equation. We might think the other party recognizes the consideration, but has not been "trained up" with the resources to respond to these considerations as we judge fit.[11]

What is implicit in either failure of responsible agency is the thought that distinct forms of acculturation provide agents with differential capacities to recognize and respond to moral considerations in different contexts. This is an important point, and one that intersects with a larger body of literature that attempts to understand the nature of human agency embedded in social and cultural contexts.

In a growing number of the sciences, researchers now countenance the idea of local cultural narratives that provide a kind of *script* or framework of culturally structured inferences and behavior that guide complex behavior and give rise to particular experiences. For example, recent work on chronic back pain has found it helpful to invoke a notion of social narratives to understand how and why the experience of back pain sometimes persists long after the underlying physiological problem seems to have been addressed.[12] And, social science data are filled with local practices constructing rich and intricate behaviors that can appear altogether alien and flatly irrational to the casual outside observer.[13] These data have begun to make their way into a variety of philosophical accounts of various stripes.[14] The

---

[11] My sense is that, as a matter of actual practice, we are less forgiving about self-governance failures than we are about epistemic failures. Perhaps this reflects an implicit presumption about internalism about reasons. If the agent recognizes some consideration, we might think (rightly or wrongly) that ipso facto, that agent should have some propensity to be self-governed in light of it.

[12] For a literature review, see Robert J. Gatchel et al., "The Biopsychosocial Approach to Chronic Pain: Scientific Advances and Future Directions," *Psychological Bulletin* 133, no. 4 (2007): 581–624.

[13] A classic account can be found in Philip L. Newman, "'Wild Man' Behavior in a New Guinea Highlands Community," *American Anthropologist* 66, no. 1 (1964): 1–19.

[14] See, for example, Ian Hacking, *Rewriting the Soul: Multiple Personality and the Sciences of Memory* (Princeton, NJ: Princeton University Press, 1995); Ron Mallon, "A Field Guide to Social Construction," *Philosophy Compass* 2, no. 1 (2007): 93–108; Kwame Anthony Appiah, *Cosmopolitanism: Ethics in a*

literature is too diverse to summarize in more than a cursory way, but here's the basic upshot to much of it: culturally laden conceptions of agency structure our in-fact capacities.

How we conceive of our agency, and the powers we take agents to ordinarily have, will play some role in whether or not we are responsible agents in a given context, because of the power of such narratives to structure our agency. By promulgating narratives of control in those circumstances that test our control, we might (at least sometimes) make it the case that agents come to have enough self-control to be responsible agents. Similarly, by promulgating narratives of incapacity, of the inevitability of caving in to nigh-irresistible desires and temptations, we run the risk of self-fulfilling narratives here too. This is presumably true of both our basic abilities as well as higher-order capacities of the sort identified by this account.

Matters here are obviously complex. Some desires may well be insuperable in particular circumstances, quite apart from the particular cultural narrative within which they are placed. My point is that once we look beyond intrinsic features of agents to the wider set of relations that structure the various capacities that are of interest to us, what we find is that moral ecology matters.

By *moral ecology*, I mean the circumstances that support and enable exercises of agency in ways that respect and reflect a concern for morality. We've already seen one way in which moral ecology matters: if the standard picture in social psychology is right, we are considerably more sensitive to the influences of circumstance than we suppose, and these differences have consequences for the shape of our dispositions and decision-making. What the foregoing points to is another element in that ecology: narratives, scripts, or cultural frameworks—whether internalized or merely part of the web of expectations we are aware of as structuring the available decision paths—have consequences for our capacities, especially when those capacities are higher-order functions, structured by normative interests.

World of Strangers (New York: W. W. Norton, 2007); Sally Haslanger, "Changing the Ideology and Culture of Philosophy: Not By Reason (Alone)," *Hypatia* 23, no. 2 (2008): 210–23; Ron Mallon, "Making Up Your Mind and Explaining Yourself" (Unpublished manuscript: In progress). For discussion of how self-conception and effort intersect with various concerns about free will, see Carol S. Dweck and Daniel C. Molden, "Self-Theories: The Construction of Free Will," in *Are We Free? Psychology and Free Will*, ed. John Baer et al. (New York: Oxford University Press, 2008).

So, societies, states, and cultures all structure our actual capacities. Being raised in an anti-racist context presumably plays a role in enhancing sensitivity to moral considerations tied to anti-racist concerns. Similarly, being raised in a sexist, fascist, or classist culture will often shape a person's dispositions to ignore egalitarian concerns. Moral ecology matters, and it is among the various inputs to which a justified system of responsibility must be sensitive.

There are two features about this picture that I wish to highlight. First, the complex relationship between our dispositions, social contexts, and normatively significant circumstances is unlikely to be stable in perpetuity. Given that the responsibility system interacts with these facts, and given that the boundaries of responsible agency are partly structured by these facts, we have reason to think that any equilibrium point a society achieves is only temporary. As changes in the moral ecology unfold, changes in moral psychology seem likely to (eventually) follow.

This picture is consistent with the view that the *basic* emotional architecture of humans is the same everywhere and everywhen. What it requires is only that the more particular emotions and experiences that are shaped by culture and practices are historically bounded. Those more malleable elements of psychological endowment may change over time, whether because of broader cultural changes or changes wrought by transformations in how we think about the conditions of responsibility. In turn, this would reshape the various inputs to the responsibility system. If that is right, it isn't just the justified norms of praise and blame that can change. Rather, the forms of agency we possess are themselves subject to change. If that is right, then the picture here of responsible agency and free will is less a picture of some atemporal metaphysical facts than it is a picture of socially embedded and normatively structured properties that change over time.

The idea of moral ecology and its interaction with responsibility presses on us a new set of questions. Perhaps the most salient is this: will we remain, as we largely have been, passive to that ecology, or will we will instead undertake attempt to systematically shape our moral ecology? To ask this question is to ask whether we should undertake a program of *moral architecture*, or an intentional plan of constructing a social world conducive to responsible agency and moral conduct.

To raise such questions invites objections that one is engaged in utopian idealism, disconnected from real-world constraints on how we organize ourselves.[15] There are also the dystopian versions of these accounts, which are quick to emphasize the risk in such projects. Those risks are usually portrayed in terms of a loss of freedom, human dignity, and the bypassing of any exercise of rational agency.[16]

From the standpoint of serious, philosophical reflection on moral responsibility, any proposal for a program of moral architecture will need to navigate between utopianism about what is possible and dystopianism about what necessarily follows. I have little to say about whether and how we should proceed, beyond noting that it is unlikely that we will perpetually foreswear attempts to design our moral ecologies. We can, of course, endeavor to let our moral ecology unfold without any guidance from us. However, there are substantive questions here about whether we ought to, given that we can shape our moral ecology. For example, we can ask whether societies or states have a moral, practical, or political obligation to endeavor to shape the circumstances of actors in ways that insulate them against situational effects that degrade their (moral or other) reasoning.[17]

The present account does not pretend to answer those larger questions. Whether and how we might undertake design of a moral architecture is beyond the scope of this book, and as I suggested, it is arguably a question in political philosophy. However, it seems plausible that once we are widely aware of the circumstance-dependence of our responsibility, we have obligations to build the moral infrastructure required to support our moral considerations-responsive agency. If we don't provide that infrastructure, we may begin to undercut the entitlement to blame and the benefits we derive from it.

An important result of this account is that these questions press themselves upon us. On standard atomistic accounts of responsibility and free will, such questions rarely arise. Thinking about the relevant features of responsible agency as given entirely by features "under the skin" as it were, gives us no reason to take a hard look at everything outside of it. It is only when we see start to see our agency as something structured by and

---

[15] A classic target of objections in this vein includes B. F. Skinner, *Walden Two* (New York: Macmillan, 1948).

[16] The classic text here is Aldous Huxley, *Brave New World* (New York: Perennial, 1942).

[17] We can also ask whether there are particular cultural frameworks that better serve our ends than others.

systematically a part of a larger fabric of capacity-constituting circumstances that we will begin to take seriously the matter of our moral ecology.

4. Desert landscapes

I now turn to a matter that might initially seem quite disconnected from heady issues about the social circumstances that produce our culpability: desert for praise and blame. This is an important issue in two ways. First, as we will see, desert has an important social role that goes underappreciated in standard accounts of responsibility. Second, and independently, providing a satisfactory account of responsibility is especially pressing for any account that appeals to effects to justify the responsibility norms. Here's why: such accounts are sometimes regarded as lacking the resources to say why people can deserve blame. That is, one can allow that it is perhaps useful to blame, and that it has an important role to play in our becoming agents of a particular sort. Nevertheless, the critic can protest, these things do not constitute an adequate basis for desert.

Having some account of desert in this domain is of interest to more than free will junkies.[18] It is, however, notoriously difficult to see what could possibly unify such diverse claims as: "Both the Mona Lisa and the Niagara Falls deserve our admiration," "I will work hard to deserve the promotion you just gave me," "Chris deserves respect in virtue of being a rational being," and "The East Bakersfield Blades deserved the State Championship."[19] Whatever it is that serves as the basis of desert, or the grounds on which something is deserved, it seems likely to be nearly as varied as the ontologies of those objects that can be said to deserve something. The bewildering variety of uses of desert aside, there is plausibly some uniformity to the structure of desert attributions in the case of agents being said to morally deserve something. In such cases, desert is usually construed as a three-place relation between a person, the desert basis (or the things in

---

[18] For example, contemporary theories of political liberalism have been portrayed as dissatisfying to critics in part because of the limited role that desert plays in such accounts. However, if we do not ever deserve praise or blame, this concern evaporates. See Scheffler, "Responsibility, Reactive Attitudes, and Liberalism in Philosophy and Politics." The possibility of our deserving blame also connects to debates about whether political orders need to reflect pre-institutional notions of desert—that is, notions of desert that do not depend on social institutions or arrangements of convention.

[19] On the "promissory" notion of desert where one acts to deserve something already received, see David Schmidtz, "How to Deserve," *Political Theory* 30, no. 6 (2002): 774–99.

virtue of which one is deserving), and the thing deserved.[20] Call this a schema for *agentic moral desert*.

This schema suggests that the present account of moral responsibility gives us the following picture of deserving blame: a person deserves blame in virtue of being a responsible agent and doing something morally bad in a way that manifests bad quality of will.

Is this a plausible picture of the desert base for moral blame? I think so, but there is a line of objection that merits consideration. It objects to the fact that the blame norms are, on my account, justified by their effects. Here is the objection:

It may be the case that we can show that norms of praising and blaming are justified, and that our participation and perpetuation of blaming practices serve some end that we value or are even perhaps implicitly committed to. However, these facts do not suffice to show that blame is deserved. We might have good reason to praise and blame in light of effects, but justification on the basis of effects offers the wrong sort of reason for saying that praise and blame are deserved. If blame is deserved, it cannot be, even indirectly, on the basis of effects. Rather, the basis of desert must somehow be tied to the agent and the wrongdoing, and nothing else.

My aim in the rest of this chapter is to address this objection.

I'll begin by considering an alternative account of the desert base, on which the above complaint does not obviously arise. I'll then argue against that account and use considerations that arise in the context of that account to give us reasons to reject the above criticism. Finally, I'll consider how the criticism can be addressed in its own terms, even though I reject the presumptions that give rise to it in the first place.

5. Basic desert as diagnostic

My account of blame's desert base is something that we might characterize as "post-institutional," or more accurately "post-social," given that a number of its features arise out of facts about sociality.[21] On the criticism

---

[20] See Serena Olsaretti, "Introduction: Debating Desert and Justice," in *Desert and Justice* (Oxford: Oxford University Press, 2003).

[21] I'm inclined to think that one problem with the label "post-institutional" is precisely that it lends itself to be associated with a view on which desert depends on political or intentionally organized institutions, which is manifestly *not* my view.

we are considering, there is something illegitimate about appealing to systemic socio-normative considerations in providing an account of the basis of desert.

It is constructive to consider what it would take to not run afoul of this criticism. Surprisingly, there are relatively few explicit accounts of the basis for deserving blame.[22] There is, I think, a fairly widespread tendency to suppose that one deserves blame to the extent to which one is responsible for some outcome.[23] So, libertarians presumably think that one cannot deserve blame unless one was suitably indeterministic at some appropriate prior moment. Conventional compatibilists point to the conditions given by their accounts, and so on. What we rarely see, however, is an account that articulates the particular notion of desert that the theorist takes his or her account to have secured.

One admirably forthcoming exception to this generalization is Derk Pereboom. He has specified the notion of desert that is operative in his own discussions of free will and moral responsibility, a notion he thinks is operative in the larger literature.[24] Here's how Pereboom characterizes the relevant notion of desert:

for an agent to be morally responsible for an action in the sense at issue is for it to belong to him in such a way that he would deserve blame if he understood that it was morally wrong, and he would deserve credit or perhaps praise if he understood that it was morally exemplary, supposing that this desert is basic in the sense that the agent would deserve the blame or credit just because he has performed the action, given understanding of its moral status, and not by virtue of consequentialist considerations.[25]

---

[22] My focus here is primarily on blaming reactions, and less on blaming judgments, to use the language introduced in chapter 4.

[23] This idea has considerable currency in the larger literature on desert. See Owen McLeod, "Desert," in *The Stanford Encyclopedia of Philosophy (Spring 2009 Edition)*, ed. Edward Zalta <https://leibniz.stanford.edu/friends/members/view/desert/>.

[24] Neil Levy has suggested that he believes that Pereboom has captured the relevant notion of desert. See Neil Levy, "Review of Four Views on Free Will," *Metapsychology Online Reviews* 11.40 (2007) <http://metapsychology.mentalhelp.net/poc/view_doc.php?type=book&id=3851&cn=394>. And (albeit before cautioning that this consensus may be too quick), McKenna writes that "My impression is that Kane, Fischer, and Vargas are all in agreement that the controversy is focused on basic desert entailing sense of moral responsibility," in McKenna, "Compatibilism and Desert: Critical Comments on Four Views on Free Will," p. 12.

[25] Fischer et al., *Four Views on Free Will*, p. 197.

The "basic-ness" of the account is composed of two things: the moral significance of the action and an agent who knowingly and intentionally performs the act. It also invokes an exclusion principle: the notion of desert is not one that can be generated by consequentialist considerations.[26]

It is important to recognize that "basic desert" is something of a technical term. It picks out a particular substantive conception of desert. It is not simply a term that refers to whatever notion of desert we happen to be invoking in responsibility ascriptions. Of course, if Pereboom is right, it is that, too.

But why think that basic desert is the notion of desert at stake in ascriptions of moral responsibility? Pereboom simply asserts that it is. I take it that in doing so, he means to signal that his account is intended to capture our commonsense views about the notion of desert at stake in desert-imputing responsibility ascriptions.

(An aside for insiders: Although Pereboom says very little in direct support of his account of basic desert, perhaps Pereboom could point to something like his "Four Case Argument" as some reason to think ordinary desert arguments are desert imputing.[27] I'll say more about the Four Case Argument next chapter. But there are at least three things that I can say about its potential use here: first, as that argument stands, it does not make an explicit appeal to basic desert. Second, as a matter of folk reactions to the argument I find that people are seldom persuaded by it, so even if it did appeal to basic desert it is not clear that Pereboom's intuitions here are widely held. This is consistent with my previous remarks about the variable extent to which sourcehood or origination intuitions are at work in folk conceptions of free will. Third, the issue here is ultimately prescriptive, and so what we need to know is *why* we should accept that basic desert is a conceptual requirement, as opposed to a contingent but widely had belief. I don't see how the Four Case Argument can distinguish between these possibilities. But this is all too quick, so let's just bracket this matter for now.)

---

[26] In a more recent formulation ("Hard Incompatibilism and Its Rivals," *Philosophical Studies* 144 (2009): 21–33) Pereboom has also excluded the possibility of contractualist considerations generating basic desert (22).

[27] The Four Case Argument starts with a case of direct, intentional manipulation of brain states of some agent, and proceeds to progressively replace that manipulation with ordinary causal forces. Pereboom contends that the argument shows that (bracketing some important caveats) ordinary causal forces rule out free will and moral responsibility.

BLAME AND DESERT 253

Let us suppose that we accept the presupposition that the relevant notion of desert is whatever it is that we have in mind in our ordinary attributions of moral responsibility. This would take us back to doing a bit of diagnostic work. We might yet hold out for a revisionist theory of desert. I don't think that's necessary, though. What we find, I believe, is that Pereboom's picture imputes more requirements than are plausibly in common sense.

Consider an ordinary case of judging that someone deserves blame. Suppose we judge that Fitzgerald deserves Jackie's blame for having an affair with Marilyn. On Pereboom's account, we are purportedly committed to (A) the "basic"-ness of Fitzgerald's deserving Jackie's blame—i.e., the desert base—is settled by features of Fitzgerald and the moral qualities of his action, and (B) a desert base that cannot appeal to consequences, even indirectly.

But why think all of that? I find it more plausible to think that when we judge that Fitzgerald deserves Jackie's blame what we are mainly committing ourselves to is the idea that Fitzgerald has done something wrong, and that in light of that violation, blaming is called for.[28] In making this judgment, we need not have any view one way or another about the particular details of *why* that blaming is called for. We must, of course, think that the blaming is in some way sanctioned or justified. However, it seems strange to suppose that we have worked out views about just how that sanctioning or justification would go. For ordinary practical purposes, all we need to know is that the agent has done something wrong and that something about that wrongdoing licenses blame. What that something comes to is, I think, not anything about which we have formed thoughts or strong convictions. Indeed, from the standpoint of our ordinary discourse and practical life, what is important is confidence that we are correct and justified in our first-order judgments. The justifiers and their precise nature are ordinarily of secondary and considerably lesser importance.

It would obviously be helpful to have empirical data to lean on, as we had when considering incompatibilist intuitions in chapter 1. In the absence of targeted work of the sort experimental philosophers have been producing, what empirical data there are on these issues are suggestive. It looks like people's attitudes about something related—punishment—are mixed, with case-based judgments leaning retributive and consideration of general

---

[28] Perhaps there is a further norm here, one concerned with when violations are to be responded to with blame. For our purposes, nothing turns on this possibility.

principles favoring deterrence.[29] I take it that appeals to deterrence suggest some degree of willingness among the folk to entertain the suitability of some consequences in the basis for punishment. Moreover, the fact of fragmentation in responses across kinds of cases suggests that there is no easy claim to univocality in folk notions of desert.

A different reason for thinking the shallowness thesis is right, apart from reflection on cases and limited experimental data, is the continuity of shallowness across our larger class of moralized judgments. I might, for example, think some arrangement is unjust or just without having a worked-out conception of what justice comes to. You and I might concur with your assessment of a colleague being vicious and unkind without either one of us having a specific theory of what those properties consist in. Such thoughts do not require a worked-out conception of what the moralized notions come to.

A critic could object that the fact of disagreement can indicate the presence of particular conceptions of some element of morality. When we disagree, the robustness of our disagreement seems to depend on there being at least some agreement about a conceptual core. That is, disagreement about the substantive commitments seems to presume some consensus about the concept at stake—otherwise we would be talking about different things.

This sort of argument, however, seems to break in the direction I have been pursuing. Plausibly, any widely shared conceptual element in normative notions tends to be no more robust than is required to permit concept acquisition and use. This is why the task of a philosophical theory of justice, desert, or what have you, is typically to flesh out the best conception or substantive account of the property or thing that our concept attempts to pick out. This is why normative theory is so rarely satisfied with simple forms of conceptual analysis. We can't hope to understand justice, goodness, and so on simply by appeal to the linguistic or conceptual overlap of community, for that overlap tends to be compatible with a wide range of substantive differences about these important notions.

---

[29] Kevin M. Carlsmith et al., "Why Do We Punish? Deterrence and Just Deserts as Motives for Punishment," *Journal of Personality and Social Psychology* 83, no. 2 (2002): 284–99.

Here, Pereboom—or, perhaps, a Pereboomian—might take a different tack. The Pereboomian might argue that desert-imputing judgments of responsibility are not shallow for everyone in the way I have suggested. Perhaps at least some of us have conceptions of desert with the particular commitments stipulated by Pereboom. This would be to take a page from the playbook I was using in the discussion of libertarianism: in this case, the idea would be that there is one strand of the folk notion that has the particular constraints of basic desert as Pereboom has characterized it.

I am skeptical about the plausibility of this move in this context. First, the evidential basis here looks rather different. In the case of characterizing the folk metaphysics of responsibility, there is a variety of data I marshaled in making the case that there is a non-trivial element of ordinary thinking committed to the particular metaphysical commitments of libertarianism. Second, this move appears to be vulnerable to the reply I did go on to make: such elements are plausibly connotational and not obviously the sorts of things we need to build into our theory.

In general, the fact that some people have more elaborate commitments regarding the specific normative structure of some moralized notion does not mean that those elements are built into our shared concept or the patterns of inference ordinarily made in light of the concept. As we have already seen, the possibility that we can change our minds about the truth-makers of various normative notions suggests that, ordinarily, the strict conceptual content implicated in a moral judgment is comparatively minimal, even in the case of desert.

Recall the example of the transition from a view that morality requires God's existence to a view that there can be a God-independent foundation for morality. Whatever one thinks about the warrant for this phenomenon, conceptual shallowness is part of what made it possible. That is, when one's moral vocabulary comes to be coupled with substantive ontological commitments (such as "God's will is the truthmaker for moral claims"), those commitments can be jettisoned or transformed without losing moral judgments as such, precisely because most ground-level moral judgments are not themselves conceptually deep. Shallowness in conceptual content is consistent with a range of more detailed commitments about the conceptualized thing, and those commitments can change for any number of reasons (including theoretical reflection, education, or general processes of acculturation).

The idea of conceptual revision in any domain gets its power from the thought that just because some people have robust content associated with a shared concept does not mean that this content is part of the shared concept, or even essential to their own thinking. If we have a notion of desert that is conceptually shallow, then the presence of substantive commitments that run deeper in some or even a large part of the population (e.g., an exclusion condition that rules out specific kinds of justification for desert judgments) would not show that those deeper commitments are part of the concept.

Here's the bottom line on the diagnostic interpretation of basic desert. There is little evidence that ordinary desert ascriptions are especially deep in any uniform way to support the "basic desert as folk desert" reading. What seems more likely is that ordinary desert attributions can tolerate a range of different pictures about the basis of desert. On the picture I am suggesting, ordinary responsibility judgments are insufficiently rich in content to commit us to a specific theory of desert. Of course, free will skeptics will want to plump for a more demanding construal of desert, and conventional compatibilists will advocate a less demanding construal of desert conditions. In either case, however, these are matters on which philosophical argumentation takes us beyond the materials and commitments we find in ordinary uses of desert.

None of this is to suggest that such accounts are ultimately spurious. The deeper matter is what our prescriptive account of desert should be. More and less demanding accounts of desert can be consistent with a relatively shallow folk notion of desert. Basic desert might yet carry the day as a prescriptive account. If my shallowness hypothesis is correct, however, the proponent of a basic desert has no automatic license for inferring basic desert from ordinary, everyday ideas of desert.

Folk commitments about desert do little to restrict the range of viable prescriptive accounts of desert. While one could propose an account that insists that ordinary desert-imputing judgments of responsibility do not appeal to consequentialist or contractualist or other considerations (as Pereboom does), nothing in ordinary discourse requires us to do so. So, if there is some special pressure to characterize desert as Pereboom has done, then we need an account of what those *philosophical* pressures are, for nothing in ordinary responsibility judgments seems to commit us to his particular conception of desert.

6. Basic desert as prescriptive

I've argued that there is no particularly compelling reason to think that ordinary ascriptions of responsibility specifically invoke basic desert. Instead, the shallowness of such judgments simply underdetermines what theory of desert we should accept, given coherence with the relatively minimal elements in ordinary attributions of responsibility.

Here, however, the proponent of the basic desert model might grant the foregoing and instead maintain that basic desert is only intended as an account of the truth conditions for ordinary claims, quite apart from whether ordinary judgments require or presume an explicitly basic desert-style conception of desert.[30] On this proposal, the ostensive virtue of basic desert is not that it captures our in-fact cognitive content in responsibility ascriptions, but rather, that it offers *the correct account* of the in-fact basis of desert for our judgments of responsibility, independent of whatever it is that we think we are referring to. (So, we are now shifting to the matter of prescriptive theorizing.)

Such a proposal would raise a number of puzzles, in both its "basic-ness" and its exclusion of consequentialism. To begin with, it is not clear how the consequentialism exclusion is meant. Is it meant to exclude any appeal to teleological reasoning (for example, an appeal to the virtues of backwards-looking blaming practices with respect to cultivating desirable forms of agency), or simply any justification exclusively grounded in a consequentialist normative ethics? I suspect it was formulated with the latter in mind, but perhaps some proponents of basic desert intend the former as well.

Still, why should we accept the exclusion of consequentialist normative ethical accounts, or any other approach to accounting for the desert base? I don't find consequentialism especially appealing as a global theory of normative ethics, but I can't make out the basis for its exclusion here.[31]

---

[30] Compare: we might, for example, someday discover that God does exist and perhaps he will communicate to all of us that morality does indeed depend upon His will. Were this to happen, what we would have discovered was that the old volitionalist view of metaethics was not essential to the concept but instead an accurate description of the truthmakers for moral claims. The intelligibility of this thought experiment is evidence that denotation and connotation come apart, even in the matter of morals.

[31] Reminder: one can accept that the responsibility system has a teleological structure, as I have argued, without being committed to consequentialism.

Notice that the proponent of the view under consideration cannot motivate the appeal to the no-consequentialism restriction by citing the counterintuitiveness of consequentialist theories, or by appealing to the idea that such a constraint is grounded in our ordinary concept of the responsibility-relevant notion of desert. First, consequentialists have familiar replies to the charge of counterintuitiveness, including the thought that what is at stake is the true theory of morality and not the folk notion, that reflective equilibrium favors the account, that consequentialist considerations can explain the concern we have for such things, and so on. Counterintuitiveness is a kind of cost for the consequentialist, but it is not special to this case and hardly decisive. Second, here the supposition is that basic desert is not intended as an account of our ordinary concept, but instead as an account of what we properly mean to refer to, after successful theorizing about the nature of the responsibility-relevant notion of desert. As such, we are beyond simple appeals to our ordinary concepts.

What then might the basis be for excluding consequentialist accounts of the basis of desert? The matter of the true account of normative ethics is hardly uncontroversial, and it may turn out that some consequentialist account could be the true account of morality. Perhaps basic desert proponents are intending the exclusion condition to reflect a commitment to some or another substantive account of normative ethics. If so, then we deserve to know what those accounts are, and to have the opportunity to evaluate that package of commitments against the alternatives. Until then, however, we should reject exclusion conditions that are partisan about normative ethics or the foundations of normative and evaluative notions. All of which is to say, it is very difficult to make out the grounds for the no-consequentialism condition.

Now consider the condition of basic-ness. As formulated, basic desert stipulates that the desert base is limited to the moral valence of the act and the agent. Interestingly, this claim is compatible with some possibilities that are at odds with the spirit of "basic-ness" purportedly given by basic desert. For example, it appears that the account is compatible with any view on which an action's moral status may hinge on contextual or circumstantial properties. If basic desert is compatible with the possibility that the moral valence of actions is sensitive to circumstance or context, then I see no reason why it could not turn out that the desert basis of responsibility ascriptions includes complex social and normatively structured facts—including those specified by contractualist accounts or sophisticated forms of multivalue consequentialism.

This possibility, of countenancing complex social and normatively structured facts as part of the desert base, is important for two reasons. First, it suggests that if we bracket the exclusion condition there are independently good reasons for letting in a broader range of contributors to the desert base. If so, then the objection against my account's treatment of the basis of desert is something of a non-starter. Second, this possibility of a broad, socionormatively structured desert base suggests that what is presented as basic is not very basic at all, i.e., the desert base might well hinge on morality-constituted facts about social position, contexts of action, institutional arrangements, and the like.

I see no reason why it could not or should not be that such facts play some role in desert. Perhaps it is a lingering atomistic prejudice to think that we should understand the basis of desert in terms of intrinsic features of the agent and intrinsic features of the moral status of the act. If it is, then there is no reason to accept "basic-ness" as a constraint on our prescriptive account of desert.

Even in ordinary discourse, it is not uncommon to hear appeals to relatively broad bases of desert, bases that involve a range of considerations that might appear on the face of it to be rather distant from the particulars of the claim. So, for example, if I claim that the East Bakersfield Blades deserve to win the city football title despite their complete defeat at the hands of the West Bakersfield Vikings in the playoffs, I might adduce a wide range of considerations in favor of the conclusion. I might, for example, argue that the Blades are a better team but that they were hampered by a bout of food poisoning. Or, I might insist that the refereeing was unfair. Or, I could appeal to the thought that the Blades tried harder, or that as a collective team their effort and spirit was greater than the dispirited but more imposing Viking players.

Some of these considerations might move you or they might not. One might object that the diverse considerations raised on behalf of the Blades confuses the epistemic role of social practices and extra-agential elements with the metaphysical basis of desert. On this matter, it helps to distinguish two views about extra-agential features and their relationship to desert. We can think of social practices (and other more-than-an-individual-agent considerations) as *discerning* antecedent desert facts, or we can think of them as *producing* or determining those facts.

Consider an election. You could think that an election produces some fact about who deserves to win. So, for example, whether Nebuchadnezzar deserves to win the election against Saladin depends on the election rules. If they are followed, and Nebuchadnezzar wins, then Nebuchadnezzar deserved to win over Saladin. In this case, the election produces the desert facts. However, we could think that the role of the election is not to produce some desert fact, but is instead only a procedure for trying to determine some antecedent and independent fact about desert. On this model, elections are merely tools for tracking prior facts about, say, who is best suited to lead. And, we might think, it is that fact—the fact about the best leader—that settles who deserves to win. Because we don't have good independent access to that fact, we use elections as a tool for discernment, not as tool for production of desert. On this model, Nebuchadnezzar deserves to win only if he is indeed the better leader; indeed, he might deserve to win even if he in fact loses the election to Saladin.

In reply to social practice or other extra-agential examples of desert, the Pereboomian might object the proper view of such things is that they discern desert, and do not produce desert. As such, appeals to the fact that the election went one way or another, or examples turning on group social practices like team sports, will do nothing to make plausible that the basis of deserving moralized blame is rooted in social institutions or practices.

There are at least two things that can be said in defense of the picture I have offered, where socio-normative considerations can serve as part of the basis of desert. First, notice that even on a discernment model, what is plausibly discerned can sometimes include broadly socio-normative features of the world. Adherence to the discernment model does not block the possibility that what is discerned is a basis for desert that has its roots in features that are partly external to the agent and the act. Second, morality itself is plausibly grounded in facts about our sociality, so it should not be surprising if the basis of moral desert claims is tied to facts whose constitution admits of relatively broad socio-normative features. After all, morality is in some sense the shared, normatively structured, cooperative activity par excellence.

So, even if we grant that there are cases where socio-normative institutions and the like play a merely discerning role, this would not block the result that what are discerned are socio-normative properties that ground desert in more than features of the agent and the act.

If all of that is right, however, this dialectical situation puts a special pressure on those who wish to insist that moral desert for blame can only have a narrow basis, emptied of appeal to relational or social properties. In short, the Pereboomian needs to give us a reason for thinking that we cannot make do with any broader notion of desert than basic desert. Given that at least sometimes extra-agential considerations seem to be desert-determining, there is not yet any good reason to accept as a prescriptive theory the basic desert account of deserving moral blame.

7. The social self-governance model of deserving blame

If all of this is right, then basic desert's initial appeal fades under scrutiny. What then of the initial criticism that the present account depends on the wrong sort of basis for deserving blame?

On the one hand, I'm not sure there is much more I need to say. The objection about the purportedly overly-broad desert basis, a basis that appeals to indirect effects of quality of will norms, seems undermotivated. On the other hand, the may be more that can be said on behalf of the wrong-reasons intuition I portrayed as the motivation of my critic.

A critic could think my account gives the wrong reason for the basis of desert, if he or she thought that the desert basis had to be tied to something like libertarian free will or some impossible notion of agency. In so, we can simply reject the requirement that we capture that notion of desert, perhaps doing so on familiar revisionist grounds. Of course, the responsibility nihilist might insist that in doing so, we will have just rejected the core of moral responsibility. But that pushes us back to the familiar issues about whether and on what basis we decide that we are still talking about moral responsibility, and whether and on what basis some proposal for a desert basis counts as a desert basis and not some other thing. There is little promise of progress to be had here, apart from trying on the non-skeptical ideas for size and seeing how far they go if we earnestly endeavor to consider them as alternatives to those notions we dismiss.

Nevertheless, my approach has further resources for supplementing the operative picture of the desert basis for blame. The supplementary picture

I have in mind is this: blaming reactions, which both presume and express recognition of responsible agency, are especially fitting in the case of wrongdoing. What makes them fitting is that they engage our considerations-responsive capacities in a distinctive way, reproducing on an intimate scale the larger aspirations of the responsibility characteristic system. Once we understand how this works, it becomes harder to think that blame is not deserved.

Christopher Bennett has offered an account of the reactive attitudes that helps to illuminate these matters.[32] There are two parts to the account: what goes on when the blamer blames, and what happens when the blamed party accepts the blame.

As Bennett sees it, blaming reactions (especially in the form of social estrangement) have two aspects. One aspect is *expressive* or *symbolic*. Blaming expresses our dissatisfaction with what the agent has done. (In this mode, it is backwards-looking.) In the terms of my account, it expresses our discontent with the blamed agent's quality of will. The social estrangement that ordinarily follows from blaming judgments—the blamed person's being subject to stigma, scorn, or other forms of interpersonal alienation—expresses or symbolizes the blamer's disapproval. The second aspect is *communicative*. It doesn't just express our dissatisfaction, but it is ordinarily intended to communicate that dissatisfaction to the agent. In blaming we attempt to communicate to the agent our conviction that he or she has rejected our shared norms of conduct.

Those are the two aspects of the blame that are significant on the blamer's side of blaming practices. For my purposes, the really important part of the account emerges on the significance of blame for the blamed, in particular, when the blamed accepts blame. In the ordinary case, when an agent is subject to the characteristic range of blaming practices (e.g., "getting the cold shoulder"), this fact triggers in (pro-social creatures like ourselves) a characteristic suite of emotions. Paradigmatically, acknowledgment of blame (unless one altogether rejects its grounds), elicits in the blamed feelings of guilt, social estrangement, and sorrow.

These effects are not merely emotional byproducts of blame. On Bennett's account, they are absolutely crucial elements to what makes blame

[32] Christopher Bennett, "The Varieties of Retributive Experience," *The Philosophical Quarterly* 52, no. 207 (2002): 145–63.

deserved. The experience of feelings of guilt that constitute acceptance of blame "represents a form of moral progress, a moral re-awakening."[33] Blaming has a cost to those subjected to it. For social creatures like ourselves, this constitutes a loss of status and a form of estrangement from our communities. Guilt and the process of repentance have restorative functions: they provide us with the impetus to undertake courses of action that repair or restore that status. In their absence, genuine acknowledgment of wrongdoing is difficult. The ordinary path by which an agent apologizes and dissociates him- or herself from the act involves the experience of guilt. Such dissociation is an important part of re-constituting the perception of others that we act with the required quality of will.

Recasting this idea in terms of the present account, acceptance of blame (via the concomitant experience of guilt) provides a path to improved self-governance in light of moral considerations. That is, blaming is ordinarily deserved because, in creatures like us, blaming plays a crucial role in our ability to self-regulate. Without blame, guilt cannot benefit the wrongdoer. Were we to opt out of blame, as the responsibility skeptic would have us do, we would thereby remove one of the vehicles by which others around us (and perhaps ourselves) undertake moral improvement. In short: in the ordinary case, a responsible agent's experience of guilt and repentance is beneficial *to the agent*.

Let's call this general approach *the social self-governance model of deserving blame*, or for short, the *social self-governance model*. I find a social-self governance model persuasive, although there are some important particulars on which I diverge from Bennett's account.

First, Bennett thinks the process of repentance is needed for the blame to be "complete." I'm unsure what exactly this means, but at times he seems committed to a view where blame actually requires acceptance for it to be fully blame. For example, he writes that "As with sex, blaming is an activity that superficially appears to consist in one person doing something to another—and indeed abortive or perverted forms of blame can be like this. On a deeper understanding, though, they both involve something that can only properly be done together."[34] I'm not entirely sure how to

---

[33] Bennett, "The Varieties of Retributive Experience," p. 156.
[34] See Bennett, "The Varieties of Retributive Experience," p. 153.

evaluate the propriety claim in either case, but it seems to me a blaming reaction is what it is regardless of its effect.

Perhaps Bennett is running together two things for rhetorical effect: the nature of particular blaming reactions with the collective practice of blaming. It might be that what he is pointing to is this: particular blaming reactions may not have the uptake he highlights, but if we wish to understand the deeper nature of the practice, that uptake is crucial for making it the case that blaming is deserved.

I agree that justified blame fails to serve its corrective function when it is not accepted. And, if there were a community that *never* accepted blame, then it is hard to see how blame could play much role in cultivating the relevant forms of agency. In such a community, blame would not be deserved. But this simply pushes us back to the place where we began: for blame to be deserved, it suffices that a system of praising and blaming really does contribute to the cultivation of moral considerations-responsive agency. In such a context, however, justified blaming reactions directed against responsible agents are what they are (complete, whole, etc.) regardless of whether the other party is playing along.

A second point of divergence concerns Bennett's claim that the reactive attitudes are essentially retributive. For present purposes, I don't see that much turns on whether we characterize those attitudes as retributive, so long as we agree that they play particular roles in the expression and reception of blame—although this does not mean that Bennett is wrong.

A third point on which my version of the self-governance model diverges from Bennett's: Bennett holds that our participation in blame betrays a commitment to the thought that it is "non-contingently a good thing that those who have done wrong should undergo certain forms of suffering."[35] I'm not convinced we need to think that we are committed to anything that strong.

One simple reason is that there can be agents that have done wrong but are not responsible (e.g., in the case of person who acts badly in circumstances where that person is not plausibly a responsible agent). So, at least *some* cases of wrongdoing don't bring with them any obvious requirement of suffering. A second reason for caution about endorsing the apparent necessity claim about the goodness of some forms of suffering: I don't see why one's participation in blaming reveals a commitment to anything more

---

[35] Bennett, "The Varieties of Retributive Experience," p. 147.

than the thought that responsible agents ordinarily deserve blame, that the blamed agent's deserving blame partly depends on whether it is ordinarily good for the blamed to be blamed, and there is good reason to think we are in the bounds of ordinary cases. Although there might be independent reasons to embrace either, for present purposes neither the necessity claim nor the strict tie to wrongdoing is required for the truth of ordinary desert-imputing responsibility ascriptions.

A fourth and related point: Bennett seems to think that the *benefit* of blame is non-contingently had. But again, we need not stipulate this much. We have all we need if we hold that blame is beneficial *to the extent to which agents are moved to improve their behavior.* Perhaps blame's benefit for the blamed can vary.

In sum, on the version of the self-governance model I favor, the deservingness of blame reactions is tied to features intimately connected to their significance for the blamed. If one were disposed to lofty-sounding formulae, one might even say that this model gives us a plausible picture of why our engagement with responsible agents in blaming-characteristic forms is fundamentally a way of respecting their responsible agency. In blaming, we respect the distinctive form of agency that marks us out as free and responsible, and we do so in a way that recognizes the ongoing challenge of being morally self-governed.[36]

8. Enough desert for one sitting

I've introduced a picture on which blame is deserved partly in virtue of the good it can bring to agents subject to it, and in virtue of what our willingness to blame communicates about our respect for responsible agents. Although I still reject the requirement for a desert base as narrow as the one expressed in the

---

[36] I'm tempted to say that it would be unfair to not blame. Concerns about fairness can intersect with a number of aspects of responsibility, and elsewhere I have argued that it is a mistake to frame the conditions of being responsible in terms of the fairness of holding responsible. See Vargas, "Responsibility and the Aims of Theory: Strawson and Revisionism." Throughout this book, I have largely avoided focusing on considerations of fairness, mainly because its significance varies in light of one's commitments to matters in normative ethics (e.g., as just another concern among many normative concerns, or as a special or even overriding concern). What the social self-regulation picture suggests, though, is that fairness concerns do not automatically count against letting effects matter for desert. In this case, it is precisely because of effects that it would be unfair not to blame.

account of basic desert, the social self-governance model provides good reasons to think blame is deserved (at least when responsible agents have acted wrongly in a way that manifests an insufficiently good will).

Part of the appeal and power of this approach to desert is that it fits as well as it does with the other elements of the account. It illuminates the mechanics of *how* praising and blaming achieve the effects that they do achieve, and the distinctive roles that such practices play for the blamer and the blamed, in such a way as to make sense of the idea that agents really due deserve blame.

It is a picture that dovetails with some of the key elements of the teleological picture, in that it shows how we can be justified in our responsibility-characteristic judgments and practices, it helps illuminate why specifically moral considerations-responsive agency matters, and it shows why quality of will should be significant to us over and above morally attractive effects of action. We can think both that blaming can be justified, and that in contexts where it is, that agents will typically deserve that blame. If that's right, then we have all the grounds we require to accept the claim that responsible agents can sometimes deserve moral blame.

9

History and Manipulation

1. Three claims

I have argued that responsible agency requires a capacity for detection of moral considerations and self-governance in light of these considerations. Where these conditions are met, we have a responsible agent. What happens, however, when they are not met? In particular, we might wonder about both agents that culpably work themselves into states where they lack the capacity to respond to moral considerations, as well as cases where the structures characteristic of responsibility are implanted in agents. These are the issues I address in this chapter.

I will argue for the following claims: (1) agents can be responsible even when they lack those powers characteristically sufficient for moral responsibility; (2) history matters, but less frequently than we might have supposed prior to revision of our folk commitments about free will and moral responsibility; and (3) our intuitions about manipulation cases are not especially reliable, and there is some reason to accept what might otherwise look like counterintuitive results about a small subset of manipulation cases.

2. Three approaches to the question of history

Consider several possible views on the role that an agent's history may play for a theory of responsibility.

On one view, all that matters is that the agent satisfies some necessary and sufficient non-historical conditions on moral responsibility. On such an account, whether an agent is responsible or not does not depend on facts about the agent's history. If we wish to know whether an agent is responsible, we simply check the occurrent structures of the agent. Call such a view an *essentially structural* view of moral responsibility.

The following is one example of how such accounts work. On a simple "hierarchical theory," a suitable agent is morally responsible if and only if he or she has a desire to act upon the desire that is his or her will. In Frankfurt's classic example, an unwilling addict who gives in to her overpowering urge to take a drug could not be said to want the drug-taking desire to be her will, and thus, is not a responsible agent. By contrast, a willing addict counts as responsible because he both wants to take the drug and he wants the desire to take the drug to be his will. However, in neither case does the history of the agent matter for responsible agency. Rather, what matters is the occurrent desiderative structure of the agent. So, on this kind of view, what matters is the structure of agency, not its history.

Now consider a polar opposite of the essentially structural view. On such a view, there is always some historical condition that must be satisfied for an agent to be morally responsible. On such views, it matters *how* the agent came to have whatever structural features he or she possesses. The guiding motivation for this sort of approach is the thought that some histories undermine responsibility, no matter the arrangement of occurrent structural properties. Call such views *essentially historical* views of moral responsibility.

Between essentially structural and essentially historical views, we have a class of views that we might characterize as "semi-structural," or equally, as "semi-historical." To avoid confusion or discontent with one label over the other, I will refer to such accounts as *mixed*.[1] On a mixed view, in some cases structural conditions will be sufficient, but in others, there will be some historical requirement. Whether there is anything that makes such a view more than an unprincipled (if convenient) disjunction, is a matter I will address further on.[2]

There are two points I'll note here about these options.

---

[1] In previous work, I characterized a particular view as *semi-structural*. However, the mixed label is a better characterization of the category than the earlier label. For those who have a mixed view on which historical features are what typically satisfy the conditions for responsibility (but on which there are rare cases where purely structural features can be sufficient for responsibility), the label "semi-structural" will seem very misleading. Thanks to Al Mele for this point.

[2] Depending on whether the mixed view has some unified story to it, it might turn out that it makes sense to think of a given mixed account as "variantist" about responsibility, that is, as allowing for variable conditions on moral responsibility. I take it that if there were a strongly principled story to be told about what unifies the conditions, the account's variantist credentials would be less compelling.

The first point is that both structuralist and essentially historical views can be made more plausible by adding some epicycles. For example, proponents of the essentially historical approach can insist that there might be limit cases in which the relevant historical condition is satisfied contemporaneously with some set of structural conditions. If, for example, my being a responsible agent requires both that I act from my values (a structural condition) *and* that I have taken responsibility for the values I have (a historical condition), there may be cases in which I take responsibility for my values and simultaneously act from my values.

On the other side of the spectrum, the structuralist might allow that some structural features are temporally extended, and their presence might not be properly characterized in terms of time-slice features. Deliberation is one example. On this amendment, a historical condition understood in terms of the temporally extended process of deliberating or being responsive to one's values, say, is not what separates the structuralist from the historicist. Rather, it is the issue of whether or not a particular pre-deliberative (or pre-process-of-decision elements and/or processes) requires a particular history.[3]

Moreover, a structural theorist need not claim that history is always irrelevant to the assignment of responsibility. That is, it may be that the only way we can learn about the structure and powers of an agent is by attending to the agent's history. History can, as a practical matter about the epistemology of responsible agency, play a role in how we evaluate the capacities of an agent. However, the practical importance of history is ultimately parasitic on the ontological issue we are trying to settle.

The basic upshot is this: even if we don't find the purest forms of these approaches to be very plausible, something very close to each of these "pure" types can plausibly address some of the more obvious potential sources of discontent.

---

[3] Zimmerman labels these "process-historical" and "source-historical." The former refers to the temporal extendedness of certain structural features and the latter refers to what I have in mind by historical theories. See David Zimmerman, "Reasons-Responsiveness and Ownership-of-Agency," *Journal of Ethics* 6 (2002): 210. What I identify as structural and historical theories, Fischer and Ravizza call "mesh theories" and "historical theories," in Fischer and Ravizza, *Responsibility and Control: A Theory of Moral Responsibility*, pp. 183–4. Mele gives a related distinction as "internal and external conceptions of psychological autonomy." See Mele, *Autonomous Agents: From Self-Control to Autonomy*, pp. 146–9.

The second point worth mentioning about the classification I have offered is this: these approaches are not just the mythological constructions of a taxonomically minded philosopher. Influential defenders of diverse accounts of moral responsibility have held the polar accounts. Harry Frank-furt's early account of free will and moral responsibility is perhaps the clearest version of a structural account.[4] If we invoke the emendation concerning temporally extended historical properties, then Gary Watson's account is plausibly a structuralist account.[5] On the other side, Fischer and Ravizza argue that an agent's responsibility depends, in part, on the agent having "taken responsibility" for his or her reasons–responsive mechanism (1998: 210).[6] What makes the account essentially historical is that regardless of whatever reasons–responsive mechanism is in play, and regardless of how responsive that mechanism is to reasons (yes, even with a God-like sensitiv-ity to reasons), the agent still has to have taken responsibility for that mechanism at some appropriate time in the past.[7]

3. A cautionary note

The essentially historical and essentially structural views are not simply another facet of the incompatibilist/compatibilist dialectic. Some philoso-phers have suggested there is a conceptual pull between historicism and

---

[4] Frankfurt, "Freedom of the Will and the Concept of a Person." See also Dworkin, *The Theory and Practice of Autonomy*. However, Mele has highlighted some complexities in interpreting Dworkin's account as structuralist. See Mele, *Autonomous Agents: From Self-Control to Autonomy*, p. 148.

[5] Watson, "Free Agency."

[6] See Fischer and Ravizza, *Responsibility and Control: A Theory of Moral Responsibility*, p. 210.

[7] A brief aside for fans of Fischer-ania. There is an interesting issue here that ties into how Fischer wants to individuate mechanisms. I take it that Fischer and Ravizza hold that the agent must think of his actual dispositions, habits, and reasoning mechanisms that lead to his various deliberations, choices, and actions *as his own*. In cases where manipulation has occurred, Fischer has claimed that the agent is not typically taking responsibility for the right *kind* of mechanism (that is, a manipulated mechanism)—unless, of course, the agent is told of the manipulation. See John Martin Fischer, "Précis of *Responsibility and Control: A Theory of Moral Responsibility*," *Philosophy and Phenomenological Research* 61, no. 2 (2000): 441–6. However, if ownership can be accounted for by (for example) simply having a certain structure of agency, none of the preceding is yet sufficient to warrant the claim that responsibility is "essentially historical." That is why the business about *kinds* of mechanisms seems to matter. If the kind of mechanism has to do with its causal history, then it looks like history can sneak in the back, as it were. But in another place Fischer and Ravizza seem to back off of a similar strong degree of knowledge when they claim that "we have in mind a way of individuating mechanisms which does not require that the agent know everything about the causal origins of its inputs or its inner working." See John Martin Fischer, "Replies," *Philosophy and Phenomenological Research* 61, no. 2 (2000): 476.

incompatibilism on the one side, and on the other, structuralism and compatibilism.[8] However, most compatibilists who have clear commitments on this issue seem to be essentially historical theorists.[9] So, it would be a mistake to assume that the history/structure disagreement is just another facet of a more fundamental disagreement between compatibilists and incompatibilists.

For example, all the views about history I have canvassed either already exist or could be reproduced in incompatibilist terms. We might imagine Sartre or someone with an Epicurean-like view to be a structural libertarian. Laura Ekstrom's libertarianism includes a negative historical condition that, like Mele's account, suggests at least a mixed view, if not an essentially historical account.[10] Kane's account has historical elements (for example, the requirement of "ultimate responsibility") but if one can at least sometimes be non-derivatively ultimately responsible for a choice at some moment, then the account is also a mixed one. And, at least one formulation of Galen Strawson's pessimistic incompatibilism seems to be mixed; he maintains that a responsible agent's will needs either to have a structure of self-causation or when it does not, it needs to be the downstream product of a self-caused will.[11]

Revisionists might be tempted to suppose that conventional compatibilists who endorse an essentially historical account of responsible agency are simply unaware of the work that suppressed incompatibilist intuitions are doing in their thinking about responsibility. However, we would need compelling evidence to ascribe this degree of confusion or even self-deception to so many philosophers. Reliable empirical work could be helpful if it provided some tools for determining the extent to which historical intuitions are indeed widespread, and the extent to which they are connected with various possible metaphysical commitments relevant to concerns about

---

[8] For example, Fischer has thought that "one reason why Harry Frankfurt has so frequently reiterated the view that responsibility is not a matter of history is precisely because he is afraid of falling into the clutches of incompatibilism." See John Martin Fischer, "Chicken Soup for the Semi-Compatibilist Soul: Reply to Haji and Kane," *Journal of Ethics* 4, no. 4 (2000): esp. 407. See also John Martin Fischer and Mark Ravizza, "Responsibility and History," in *Midwest Studies in Philosophy*, ed. Peter A. French et al. (Notre Dame: Notre Dame University Press, 1994), p. 444. Richard Double, who is not a compatibilist, has made similar remarks. See Double, *The Non-Reality of Free Will*, pp. 56–7.

[9] For evidence of this point, see Zimmerman, "Reasons-Responsiveness and Ownership-of-Agency."

[10] Ekstrom, *Free Will: A Philosophical Study*, pp. 245–7.

[11] Strawson, "The Impossibility of Moral Responsibility."

moral agency. In its absence, it seems to me that we should adopt the picture I suggest above, of treating the history and incompatibilism intuitions as at least prima facie distinct.

4. In the mix

Here, I want to say a bit about the motivations for adopting a mixed theory, and to connect it to my account of moral responsibility.

Consider the following example.

A local platoon commander has ordered his soldiers to round up twenty innocents. After they are rounded up, he asks a visiting guest to shoot one, and if he does so, he will release the other nineteen. When the guest declines, the commander turns to two of his best aides, Ian and Phineas, and asks them to kill the twenty innocents by the next morning.

One aide, Ian, decides he has to get drunk to be able to follow the commander's order to slaughter the defenseless civilians. Only then will he be sufficiently numb to the horror of it all to go through with it. He eventually succeeds in getting sufficiently drunk such that he becomes numb to moral considerations generally. He goes on to carry out the orders, killing half of the civilians.

The other aide, Phineas, has the misfortune of having suffered a head injury some time prior to receiving the order to kill the natives. The head injury results in brain damage of a sort that destroys some of his capacities to recognize reasons. He is no longer sensitive to moral considerations, at least in contexts of military commands. However, this impairment has left his other faculties intact.[12] Phineas straightaway fulfills his assignment, killing half of the natives.

On a mixed view of things, Ian is responsible. In contrast, his colleague Phineas is not. Phineas is not a responsible agent, but through no fault of his own. Therefore, he cannot be appropriately held to the norms of responsibility. There might be good reason to, in a sense, quarantine him. However, genuine moral praise and blame are inappropriate in his case.

My account of responsible agency is mixed.

---

[12] Phineas is very loosely modeled on the real world example of Phineas Gage. The case of Phineas Gage is engagingly described in Oliver W. Sacks, *The Man Who Mistook His Wife for a Hat and Other Clinical Tales* (New York: Summit Books, 1985).

One reason why derives from the general approach: I have focused on providing conditions that are ordinarily sufficient for moral responsibility and plausibly obtained with some frequency in the ordinary course of things. Those conditions are structural, given what I have thus far said. However, it is compatible with all of that that there may be historical conditions that independently suffice for free will and moral responsibility.

A second reason to make a concession in the direction of history comes from so-called "tracing" cases. A common feature of responsibility practices involves tracing responsibility for an action past the immediate structure of agency back to some earlier point in the agent's history. Drunk driving is one example. We hold someone responsible for the results of drunk driving not because of the kind of agent they are when they get behind the wheel, but rather, because of the kind of agent they were when they started to drink, knowing that drinking impairs judgment and coordination, and so on. That is, even if the agent does not satisfy the structural requirements for responsibility at the time of action, we can trace responsibility back to a prior state where the agent did satisfy the structural conditions in a way that generates responsibility for the later actions. So, even if the structure of agency is important, this does not rule out the need to acknowledge that a certain kind of history may be required for responsibility.

A dedicated structuralist could reply in various ways. For instance, the structuralist could argue that we ought to hold the considered agent responsible only for being drunk, but not responsible for any of the consequences that follow from the drunkenness. Though clearly a departure from ordinary moral thinking, this approach would carry the benefit of avoiding some of the problems that go under the heading of "moral luck" (e.g., that we would treat worse a drunk driver who got "unlucky" and killed someone while drunk driving as opposed to another drunk driver who got lucky and didn't kill anyone).

However, there are good reasons to hold drunk drivers responsible for more than their drunkenness. At the very least, typical agents who end up driving drunk at some point knew (or culpably didn't know) that they were creating conditions under which horrible results have a considerably higher likelihood of happening. Consequentialist and Kantian explanations may augment this idea by emphasizing, in the consequentialist analysis, the beneficial consequences of holding agents responsible for the consequences of their drunken driving, or in the Kantian analysis, the failure of the drunken driver to show suitable respect for oneself and others by failing to recognize the hazard one has become. Of course, more would need to be said to address the further issue of moral luck. However, it seems to me that at least prima facie, there is some pressure in favor of either a mixed or essentially historical approach.

There is some further complexity lurking. Consider, for example, an agent who knowingly undermines his or her capacity to detect moral considerations with an eye towards enabling immoral behaviors, as Ian did (or, presumably, as some high school and college students do on any given Friday night). It may make sense to treat this sort of case differently than a case in which someone knowingly takes steps that undermine his or her capacity for sensitivity to moral considerations as, say, a release from the pressures of daily life but without an eye towards enabling downstream mischief. How we sort out these differences is something I will not pursue here, beyond noting that one salient difference in these cases concerns the quality of will that is demonstrated by these agents.

Do any of these considerations favor a mixed case over an essentially historical account? Not by themselves. But we can also ask the question in the other direction: do any of these considerations favor an essentially historical count? And again the answer is no. However, in the present dialectical context, this result seems to favor the mixed theory, if only because the account of responsible agency with which we started is structuralist.

Nothing in the very idea of responsiveness to moral considerations suggests a historical requirement. The only reason to build out from the structuralist substrate of the present account of responsibility would be in the comparatively limited way suggested by cases in which agents culpably lack responsible agency. In the absence of some argument for a more systematically historical requirement, a mixed account is all we need.

5. An indirect argument for the essentially historical view

Proponents of the historical view might reply with an indirect argument. Fischer and Ravizza have suggested one. They argue that tracing examples at least show that there are certain contexts in which moral responsibility ascriptions do not supervene on responsiveness profiles, but depend crucially on history. This can make it at least plausible that in general such ascriptions depend on history, especially in light of the fact that it may seem odd that history matters only in certain cases (where there is a lack of responsiveness) but not in others (where there is responsiveness). On what basis could it be though that there would be this sort of asymmetry in the relevance of history?[13]

These remarks suggest that unless we have a principled explanation for why we care about some history and not others, the mixed view appears to historical theorists as adding ad hoc epicycles to a troubled structural picture.

I don't think this argument works. First, notice that indirect argument is likely to do little to change the mind of antecedently convinced mixed theorists. Proponents of mixed accounts can object that historical theorists' insistence on symmetry in the importance of history is undermotivated. Moreover, the fact that we sometimes care about history no more supports the plausibility that we always care about history than it supports the plausibility that we only sometimes care about history. So, mixed theorists will remain unmoved by the arguments of their essentially historical-minded friends.

Second, at least the present account has some explanation of why history matters sometimes and not others. So, historical theorists cannot charge the present account with failing to have a principled explanation of why we should care about some history and not others. However, it is unlikely that mixed theorists will convince antecedently convinced historical theorists, either. There is, however, another line of argument available to the proponents of the essentially historical view of responsible agency.

6. Manipulation

It is at this stage that manipulation arguments take center stage.

Consider *Andrés*:

Andrés is walking down the street when he sees a woman he finds attractive. He is immediately struck by the impulse to wolf-whistle at her. Although he grew up in a

---

[13] Fischer and Ravizza, *Responsibility and Control: A Theory of Moral Responsibility*, p. 473.

place where such behavior is common, he also knows that this is something that is not to be done. And, indeed, he vaguely feels like there is probably a good reason for thinking that wolf-whistling, cat-calling, and other related behavior are immoral—or at least really impolite. Nevertheless, he shrugs his deliberative shoulders and lets out a long, slow whistle at the woman he's noticed.

Let us suppose, plausibly enough, that this bit of wolf-whistling is morally objectionable. Let us also suppose that Andrés satisfies Frankfurt's conditions. That is, his whistling issues forth from a desire to whistle, where he also has a second-order desire that his desire to whistle be his will. Let us also suppose that he satisfies the conditions for moral responsibility adumbrated in Part II of this account: he is able to recognize and appropriately respond to moral considerations. Supposing he is self-governed, these facts are enough to make Andrés a responsible agent.

Now suppose, though, that we also learn one more set of facts about Andrés.

Whatever his inclinations, Andrés normally behaves like a perfect gentleman. Even if he occasionally has the desire to whistle at a beautiful woman, he is always able to squelch it. Unbeknownst to him, however, Andrés has been subject to a dastardly neurological intervention from a crack team of sexist neurosurgeons. The intervention is designed to generate a range of sexist behavior, including cat-calling, whistling, and various other forms of behavior that Andrés ordinarily eschews.

Here, the details of the intervention matter in subtle ways.

Consider what we might say if we learned that his will had the particular structure it did because a nefarious neurosurgeon (of the sort that roams the free will literature) was somehow able to secretly implant the relevant desiderative or valuational structure into his mind immediately before the attractive woman walked by. On this picture, the entire volitional structure is imposed, and imposed in some way that guarantees the sexist behavior. If so, then it seems that Andrés comes to whistle in this instance *because of the work of the manipulator*.

I trust that for most readers, this will not seem like a case of responsibility. The intuition at work here seems to be this: if the entire desiderative and valuational structure of some agent in a context is replaced in wholesale fashion, and engineered to produce a particular outcome, that agent is not morally responsible. So, it is a problem for any account on which moral responsibility is understood in terms of coherence between an agent's will and the agent's then-occurrent structure of desires and/or values. And more importantly, it seems to show that history matters both in cases where the relevant structure is not present (as in drunk driving cases) and in cases where the structure is present (as in *Andrés* cases). It therefore appears that the essentially historical approach, and not a mixed theory, seems to be the right view.

Not so fast. On the account of responsible agency developed in this book, what we look for are Andrés' capacities to recognize and self-govern in light of moral considerations. This means the details of the intervention matter. Suppose that the neurosurgeons merely give Andrés very weak and far from compelling desires. Moreover, suppose his capacity to recognize and respond to moral considerations remains intact and functional in the ordinary way. My intuition is that this manipulation would not suffice to undermine the kind of control required for moral responsibility. And, this is consonant with the theory. The addition (or substitution) of desires with this content and strength don't disrupt the kind of control that suffices for moral responsibility. If you think it does, then you should think the same thing about any food advertisement that makes you hungry.

Suppose, however, that the neurosurgeons implant extraordinarily strong desires—desires that are altogether irresistible. Here my intuition is that this would undermine the kind of control required for moral responsibility. And again, this is consonant with the theory. Where desires are irresistible, Andrés would lack the ability to govern himself in light of moral considerations that tell against both gender-based harassment and more general prohibitions against annoying or intimidating innocent strangers. If you like, we can say that he lacks the ability to do otherwise in the sense relevant to moral responsibility.

More interesting cases arise with desires that are strong but not irresistible. Presumably, there will be cases where the desire is strong, but not sufficiently strong to disrupt control. Similarly, there will be cases where the desire is sufficiently strong, even if not exactly irresistible, and this will be sufficient to disrupt responsibility-relevant control.

All of this seems right, given the prescriptive theory we have on the table. If we take seriously that the distinctive form of agency with which moral responsibility is concerned is one that emphasizes the capacity to recognize and appropriately respond to moral considerations, then the mere fact of implantation alone does not seem to change whether one is a responsible agent in a given set of circumstances.

Here, the circumstantialist conception of agency may do some work in massaging our intuitions. Notice that on the present account, a given bit of manipulation need not have global effects. It isn't as though changing Andrés' disposition to leer and whistle will necessarily make him incapable of recognizing and responding to someone injured in a car accident. However, if there is some more global damage to his ability to recognize and respond to moral considerations—perhaps the manipulation gives him acquired psychopathy—then the account has a straightforward explanation for a more global exculpation.

The basic upshot is this: if the manipulation leaves the agent's relevant agential structures intact (in the most plausible case, those structures that constitute the capacities to recognize moral considerations and to self-govern in light of them), then what is left is still a case of responsible agency. On the other hand, if the manipulation destroys or impairs those structures, then there is less reason to think that responsible agency has survived the manipulation in those circumstances.

This position will strike some readers as counterintuitive. Others will, I hope, find it perfectly plausible. Be that as it may, I think we can go some distance to explaining why one might not be persuaded by the argument thus far. Here's the thought: one's reaction to manipulation cases is partly structured by: (1) whether one operates with an *internalist* conception of reasons; (2) whether one imagines manipulation cases as *replacing* control structures; and (3) how one thinks about *personal identity*.

First, our view of the nature of reasons may affect how we think about a post-manipulation agent.[14] If one is an externalist about normative reasons (i.e., normative reasons do not depend on the agent's motivations), then changing the structure of an agent so that the post-manipulation agent is strongly responsive to reasons, may leave one inclined to think the agent is still a responsible agent because the ends of the agent are fixed by something external to the agent. In contrast, on an internalist picture of reasons, where one's reasons are at least partially fixed by contingent features of the agent, there may be greater temptation to think that manipulation of the agent

---

[14] This is a point Bratman has made. See Michael Bratman, "Fischer and Ravizza on Moral Responsibility and History," *Philosophy and Phenomenological Research* 61, no. 2 (2000): 453–8.

(and thus, her reasons) undermines responsibility even if the manipulated agent is responsive to her manipulated reasons.

Second, it may also make a difference whether we describe the relevant agential structure as *persisting* through pre- and post-manipulation agents or whether the pre-manipulation agent's structure is *replaced* with another structure. My bet is that most folks would be less willing to ascribe responsibility in cases where the relevant agential structure was replaced than in cases where the relevant agential structure was intact, but just subject to manipulated inputs. (Although notice that this too intersects with the view one takes on the nature of reasons.) As I described the second class of *Andrés* examples, the manipulation was one where the control structures persisted.

In light of this, proponents of essentially historical views might wish to seize upon the intuitions generated by replacement cases. So: imagine Andrés remains moral considerations-responsive, but that all of his responsibility-constituting control structures (i.e., his various circumstance-specific capacities to recognize and respond to moral considerations) are replaced with new control structures that are sufficiently responsive to moral considerations to count as constituting responsible agency. However, these new structures make him far more disposed to leer, cat-call, wolf-whistle and so on. This, the historical critic will claim, shows that the present account cannot be right. After all, on the present account, Andrés would be a responsible agent but surely such wholesale replacement of his capacities would undermine responsibility.

I agree that such replacement would plausibly undermine Andrés' responsibility. Replacement would do so by undermining the identity of the agent. On this view, the post-neurosurgical intervention agent is responsible but not Andrés. And, as far as I can tell, there is no obvious reason to think this is a less adequate outcome to our theorizing than holding that it is the same person post-intervention, but non-responsible.

Let's back up. We've now arrived at the third variable that affects how we think about these cases: one's theory of personal identity over time. If one operates with a psychological conception of personal identity, where one's identity over time (or perhaps just one's continuity) is secured by overlapping psychological ties, then the more dramatic the manipulation the more likely it is that we will have disrupted identity or continuity conditions.

How to tell that story is tricky. However, on one way of cashing out the details, you might suppose that an agent's control structures—those features

that underwrite the ability to recognize and respond to moral considerations, play some role in the constitution of an agent's identity. Why? Well,
the normal constitution of those control structures involve taking a stand on
what considerations should rightly move one to act, and the psychological
elements of such stances are plausible constituents of personal identity over
time.[15]

   The main point here is just that if one accepts a psychological account of
personal identity, then there are resources that can be brought to bear on
this matter. When the case is a wholesale replacement of those control
structures, as in the Andrés case, it is not implausible to maintain that such
replacement is identity-disrupting precisely because those structures typically play an identity-constituting role. We might argue about whether
disruption of those structures is sufficient for disrupting identity. It depends
on the details, and worries about greater and lesser degrees of continuity
loom in the background.

   We might wonder, though, about more targeted replacement of control
structures. Surely it would not be identity-disrupting if we swapped out one
very local control structure in an agent. So, for example, let us suppose that
Andrés retains his normal gentlemanly dispositions in all social contexts
except at particularly raucous hockey games. In such circumstances—and
only in such circumstances—he is uncharacteristically prone to cat-calling.
What then?

   Notice that such a replacement would involve some disruption of self-
governing policies, but not enough to plausibly disrupt personal identity.
Here, I'm inclined to tell you how good the bullet tastes.

---

[15] In the Appendix, I offer some details about how I think of these issues. If those resources were
already on the table, I'd say the following. Start with the idea of a particular policy one might have in
one's psychic economy, concerning how much weight one gives particular considerations in deliberation. Such policies can play two roles. First, they structure the agent's capacity to recognize moral
consideration. Second, these policies are plausibly identity-constituting elements, given their temporally
extended nature and the way they structure agential activity over time. Here is the kicker: in replacement
manipulation stories, stories on which the neurosurgical intervention replaces the moral considerations-
responsive structures, the neurosurgical intervention disrupts those psychological elements that have a
special role to play in constituting identity. The more systematic the disruption of those ties (for example,
in wholesale replacement of values and desires) the more plausible it is to say that the post-neurosurgi-
cally modified agent is not the same agent. Alas, unless you've already read the Appendix, you'll have to
take my word for it. Or, you could go read Michael E. Bratman, "Identification, Decision, and Treating
as a Reason," in *Faces of Intention: Selected Essays on Intention and Agency*, Cambridge Studies in
Philosophy (Cambridge: Cambridge University Press, 1999); Michael Bratman, "Agency, Time, and
Sociality," *Proceedings and Addresses of the American Philosophical Association* 84, no. 2 (2010): 7–26.

It seems to me that were we to find ourselves with Andrés at that game, and we witnessed the unfolding of a wolf-whistling sequence of events in real time, and in full information about what had been done to him, we might still lean in as he inhales for that whistle. What we might say is this: "Get a grip. I know you feel like making a scene here, but I also know that you don't have to. Contain yourself and don't be a jerk." We might go on to point out to him that this is uncharacteristic of him, and that if he thinks such behavior is inappropriate at the opera, at water polo games, and NASCAR races, then he ought to think it is true at the hockey rink, too.

In having this reaction, we would recognize that, although there is some sense in which in this isolated set of circumstances he is not himself, he is still in control of himself in the sense required for moral responsibility. He recognizes considerations to not whistle and he can govern himself in light of those considerations. Moreover, that uncharacteristic disposition that he finds himself with should be amenable to the usual sources of internal criticism. Given the very targeted intervention of the neurosurgeons, we have no reason to think that Andrés cannot be reflective about his impulses, and recognize that there is something outlaw about his disposition. If we swear off holding him responsible, we rob him of some of the resources he would otherwise have for bringing those self-critical, self-governing capacities to bear. Indeed, the social self-governance model of deserving blame independently tells us that much. So, I think he deserves our engagement with him in responsibility-characteristic ways, and I am inclined to think it is no real cost at all to think that he is indeed morally responsible.

Perhaps some of this moves you. Perhaps it does not. If it does not, then I can only add one more thing to dissuade you from thinking that my admission on this matter is a significant cost. It is this: we are envisioning a completely science fictional scenario that, for all we know, is altogether impossible. Remember, it requires that we could do targeted replacement of highly context-specific considerations-responsive capacities via neurological manipulation. Perhaps some day we will have that power. Still, it seems to me a very small cost to pay—if it is any cost at all—that the present account generates some counterintuitiveness in a very remote, perhaps impossible circumstance. Which, all things considered, is not bad for a revisionist theory.

Let's take stock of where we are, so far. I began with what appeared to be a structuralist account, one that understood responsible agency in terms of the presence of particular capacities that have no interesting requirement of a particular history. However, I noted that tracing cases give us some reason for moving away from an essentially structural picture to a mixed account. This was not meant to be a point about the preservation of our intuitions but rather about normative considerations in the context of prescriptive theorizing. We have a good reason to care about an agent's history in cases where responsible agency is absent because the history determines whether the agent is both (1) an appropriate candidate for the system of practices that tend to encourage the preservation of responsible agency, and correspondingly; (2) whether the agent is owed our expression of concern and the possibility for improved self-governance that blame brings with it.

I then considered whether manipulation cases push us to a fully historical account of responsible agency. I argued that they do not. More dramatic manipulations will raise concerns about the continuity of the person than less dramatic manipulations. Less dramatic manipulations do not (to my mind) undercut what is appealing about the general approach I have taken to responsible agency.

In sum, if there is a lesson here, it is this. These issues are delicate, complex, and interconnected. These facts entail that there are no quick and easy lessons to be learned from manipulation cases. Nevertheless, careful reflection on these cases suggests that the present account can say all it needs to about the obvious problem cases.

7. CNC/Brave New World cases

In the remaining three sections of this chapter, I consider what guidance the foregoing picture gives us with respect to some other manipulation-related arguments in the literature. In this section, I focus on so-called *Brave New World cases*.

Consider Brave New World cases, or "covert non-constraining control" (CNC) examples. As in Huxley's novel, agents in these cases are raised or engineered to prefer their available choices.[16] Such agents are systematically

---

[16] Huxley, *Brave New World*.

and subtly manipulated so that their reasoning capacities are intact, but at least intuitively, the agents are not responsible. Incompatibilists often emphasize the difficulties compatibilists have in either denying the apparently widespread intuition that, in Brave New World cases, agents are not responsible, or (if they do accept the intuition that they are not responsible), in accounting for the relevant difference between Brave New World cases and determinism.[17] Given standard forms of compatibilism, neither horn of the dilemma seems attractive. On one horn, it is difficult to dismiss Brave New World cases because too many people seem willing to say they are not cases of responsibility. On the other, it is a not insignificant challenge to explain the difference between determinism (or even ordinary causal interactions with the world) and the systematic, covert manipulation that takes place in Brave New World-style examples.

Here, we have an answer that splits the difference. We can say that the intuition (inasmuch as we have it) that Brave New World agents are not responsible is likely an artifact of historical impulses in ordinary thinking about responsibility. However, once we get clear on what is normatively salient in our collection of history-oriented impulses, and that a history of manipulation does not, by itself, make you an inappropriate target of the responsibility characteristic practices and attitudes, the relevant difference for responsibility is the presence or absence of responsible agency. If responsible agency is present in a Brave New World case, the agent ought to be counted as a responsible agent because she has the capacities required by the agency cultivation model. Of course, where responsible agency is not present, the standard interest in history comes into play.

So, Brave New World cases fail to show that there is no difference between determinism and the kind of agency that can provide the normative basis for responsibility-characteristic practices, attitudes, and beliefs. Rather, what they show is the problem with the pervasive assumption that our ordinary intuitions about responsibility do a good job of tracking what is, in fact, normatively justifiable.

---

[17] See Robert Kane, "Non-Constraining Control and the Threat of Social Conditioning," *Journal of Ethics* 4, no. 4 (2000): 357–60; Pereboom, *Living Without Free Will*; Zimmerman, "Reasons-Responsiveness and Ownership-of-Agency." They agree about the historicist pull of these kinds of cases, although they disagree about the prospects for libertarianism and compatibilism.

8. Pereboom's "Four Case Argument"

In his defense of hard incompatibilism, Derk Pereboom has made intriguing use of multi-stage manipulation argument. In this section I consider what my account of responsible agency can say about this argument.

The aim of Pereboom's argument is to show that for any agent satisfying compatibilist conditions of free will and moral responsibility, there is no principled, responsibility-relevant distinction we can make between a case of direct neurological manipulation and other cases of external causal influence, including determinism. Since direct neurological manipulation is presumably *not* a case of moral responsibility, and there is no principled distinction between the cases, Pereboom concludes that we should think that there is no responsibility in any of the cases, including the final case, which describes agency operating in a deterministic physical universe. The key to the argument is incremental variation, starting with an apparent case of non-responsibility. Here are the cases:

Case 1: Professor Plum was created by neuroscientists, who can manipulate him directly through the use of radio-like technology, but he is as much like an ordinary human being as is possible given this history. These neuroscientists manipulate him to undertake the process of reasoning by which his desires are brought about and modified. They do this by pushing a series of buttons just before he begins to reason about his situation, thereby causing his reasoning process to be rationally egoistic. Plum does not think and act contrary to character since his reasoning process is often manipulated to be rationally egoistic. His effective first-order desire to kill White conforms to his second-order desires. The process of deliberation from which his action results is reasons-responsive; in particular, this type of process would have resulted in his refraining from killing White in some situations in which the egoistic reasons were otherwise. Still, he is not exclusively rationally egoistic, since he typically regulates his behavior by moral reasons when the egoistic reasons are relatively weak—weaker than they are in the current situation. He is also not constrained in the sense that he does not act because of an irresistible desire—the neuroscientists do not provide him with a desire of this kind.

Case 2: Plum is like an ordinary human being, except that a team of neuroscientists has programmed him at the beginning of his life to weigh reasons for action so that he is often but not exclusively rationally egoistic, with the consequence that in the circumstances in which he now finds himself, he is causally determined to undertake the reasons-responsive process of deliberation and to possess the set of first- and second-order desires that result in his killing White. Plum does have the general ability to regulate his behavior by moral reasons, but in his circumstances the egoistic reasons weigh heavily for him, and as a result he is causally determined to murder White. Nevertheless, he does not act because of an irresistible desire.

Case 3: Plum is an ordinary human being, except that he was determined by the rigorous training practices of his home and community so that he is often but not exclusively rationally egoistic (exactly as egoistic as in Cases 1 and 2). His training occurred when he was too young to have had the ability to prevent or alter the practices that determined his character. As a result, Plum is causally determined to undertake the reasons-responsive process of deliberation and to possess the first- and second-order desires that result in his killing White. He does have the general ability to grasp, apply, and regulate his behavior by moral reasons, but in these circumstances the egoistic reasons are very powerful, and so the training practices of his upbringing, together with the background circumstances, deterministically result in his act of murder. Still, he does not act because of an irresistible desire.

Case 4: Physicalist determinism is true, everything in the world is completely physical, and Plum is an ordinary human being, raised in normal circumstances, who is often but not exclusively rationally egoistic (just as egoistic as in Cases 1–3). Plum's act of killing White results from his undertaking the reasons-responsive process of deliberation, and he has the specified first- and second-order desires. He also possesses the general ability to grasp, apply, and regulate his behavior by moral reasons, but in these circumstances the egoistic reasons weigh very heavily for him, and as a result he is causally determined to murder White. But it is not due to an irresistible desire that he kills her.[18]

Pereboom's argument is straightforward: if we think the first case—a case of direct neurological manipulation—is not a case of responsibility, then we should say the same thing about the other cases (including neurological and social "programming"), right up to the last case of ordinary determinism. Since we do think that an agent is not morally responsible if directly neurologically manipulated, then we should say that if determinism is true, no one is responsible. And, if we say the latter, then we should say that compatibilists are mistaken: determinism and moral responsibility are incompatible.

I am inclined to think that Pereboom's Four Case Argument illustrates a prima facie problem for our commonsense conceptions of freedom and responsibility. However, it is not especially problematic for the account

[18] Fischer et al., *Four Views on Free Will*, pp. 94–7.

I have offered, which explicitly discounts intuitions grounded in implausible conceptions of agency. What is needed is a principled account of where to draw the line, and the present account gives us that much.

I should acknowledge at the outset that Pereboom's cases are, for my purposes, underdescribed. Some reconstruction is therefore required. To foreshadow: his characterization of the cases wasn't designed to address an account of the sort I offer, which appeals to circumstantialist, pluralist capacities picked out by a normative, idealized construct. The properties that matter for my account aren't those that appear in conventional atomist, monist Reasons accounts or traditional identificationist accounts, so it is not always clear how to most charitably reconstruct Pereboom's argument.

Let's start with the comparatively easy cases. At least Cases 3 and 4 look like instances where the agent is (on my account) a responsible agent. That is, so long as the agent really does have the basic structure of responsible agency (including the capacity to detect and appropriately respond to moral considerations) we have moral responsibility. As I noted above, given the presence of capacities sufficient for moral responsibility, it is irrelevant how the agent came to have those capacities. So, I think Pereboom can grant that this is what I *should* say about those cases. The pressure of the argument comes from where one draws the line between responsibility and non-responsibility in Cases 1 and 2, and whether we have the resources for making that distinction a principled one.

(Note that the form of my argument does *not* work by starting from the presumption that Cases 3 and 4 are intuitively cases of responsibility. Given various strands of folk thinking, I'm happy to allow that for many people they may not be. Instead, the argument moves the plausibility and theoretical virtues of my independently motivated account of responsibility to the question of whether it is capable of providing a principled explanation of why we should handle the particular cases of Pereboom's argument in one way rather than another.)

Given an antecedent commitment to my account of responsibility, Case 2 is a good candidate for moral responsibility. However, it is also here that we begin to see how an ambiguity emerges in how we should interpret the case. If we think the case is best interpreted as one on which the agent lacks the particular higher-order capacities I've identified with responsible agency, then we should think Case 2 is not a case of moral responsibility. However, if we presume that the agent has the responsibility-relevant capacities stipulated by my account—and I think we should—then there is no reason not to treat this as a case of responsibility.

This might seem surprising. However, it is less surprising if we recall *why* these capacities are responsibility-generating. If we focus on the role of the capacities in a system of responsibility, how they license praising and blaming, and how participation and promulgation in this system of practices characteristically is of benefit to both the individual agent and our collective interests in a valuable form of agency, then it should seem less surprising that an agent with these capacities is responsible in Case 2.

Of course, to the extent to which we have lingering incompatibilist inclinations, and/or lingering essentially historical inclinations, we may yet feel some residual tug of our pre-philosophical commitments. But such reactions are roughly on a par with our folk dispositions to think about the motion of objects on the basis of something like Aristotelian impetus theory or, more controversially, our disposition to treat in-group members as obviously more morally significant than out-group members. The point is that once we get clear on an independently plausible prescriptive account of the matter, lingering intuitions about particular cases are of limited import and generally not the sorts of things sufficient to trump a theory that disavows the project of vindicating every intuition.

So, Case 2 is plausibly an instance of moral responsibility.

Let's now focus on Case 1. I am inclined to think that the most natural reading of the case is one in which the agent is *not* morally responsible *precisely because of the intervener*. However, the details matter, and this is where we run up against the limits of the description provided by the case. I believe there are reasons for reading the case in different ways, and depending on how we fill in the details, we generate different answers to the question of whether an agent in Case 1 is properly held responsible.

For my purposes, what matters most is *how* the manipulation is brought about. Pereboom writes that they manipulate Mr. Plum "by pushing a series of buttons just before he begins to reason about his situation, thereby causing his reasoning process to be rationally egoistic. Plum does not think and act contrary to character since his reasoning process is often manipulated to be rationally egoistic."[19] But how exactly does this manipulation process operate?

---

[19] Fischer et al., *Four Views on Free Will*, p. 94.

One way the manipulators might do their manipulation is by merely altering the inputs to the agent's deliberations, leaving the mechanisms of reflection intact. This is, I think, Pereboom's preferred way of thinking about the case. If so, then we have a case much like the *persistent* version of the case of Andrés, for the manipulation works by affecting the inputs, but intuitively leaving the reasoning capacity or deliberative mechanism(s) untouched. However, as we've seen, there is independent reason to regard such cases—ones on which the responsibility relevant capacity in the involved circumstance persists across the manipulation—as plausible candidates for moral responsibility. I'll come back to this idea in a moment, but I want to say something about the other way we might fill in the details of the case.

There is an alternate description we might give of the case. On this description, the manipulation amounts to something closer to micro-management of the reasoning process itself, whatever that comes to. The precise details depend, presumably, on the relationship of neurological processes to reasoning and the way we characterize reasoning, or more accurately, moral considerations-responsive processes. At any rate, the basic idea is this: on this way of characterizing the intervention, neuroscientists leave Plum's desires untouched, and they only manipulate the nature or structure of the reasoning or the considerations-responsive process. Call this *input-independent* manipulation, for it works by affecting something about the nature of reasoning or considerations-responsive mechanisms, leaving untouched the agent's desires, values, and the like.

I do not know if this latter possibility is genuinely coherent. Nor do I have much sense of whether such input-independent manipulation is in fact possible given the limits of a future neuroscience and given the facts about our neurological architecture. Whether we think such manipulation is possible will at least partly turn on our picture of reasoning and/or deliberation. I have nothing original to say about these matters, so let us grant the possibility that input-independent manipulation is possible. If this is what is going on in Case 1, then what should we think about the responsibility of agents subject to input-independent manipulation?

If this is how the manipulation operates in Case 1, then we should think it is unlikely that Plum is responsible in Case 1. To see why, I'll start with what looks like both a non sequitur and a seemingly innocuous aspect of how Pereboom characterizes the case. I have in mind the frequency and scope of the manipulation. In Pereboom's words, "Plum does not think and act contrary to character *since his reasoning process is often manipulated to be rationally egoistic.*"[20] Let's focus on that final clause.

On an identificationist account of responsibility, I'd be inclined to contest Pereboom's characterization. Surely it is more plausible to think that such manipulation, if it is required to regularly sustain egoistic reasoning of the sort described in the case, is more akin to a "mask"— something that obscures the manifestation of Plum's actual character, rather than something that constitutes a legitimate change in Plum's character. Alternately, if we suppose that being subject to frequent manipulation of this sort has actually changed Plum's character so that the rationally egoistic reasoning proceeds in these circumstances without the support of the intervener, then it would be plausible to say that in such circumstances Plum indeed acts from his character. However, absent occurrent manipulation, it is far less obvious that we should conclude that Plum is not responsible. So, it seems to me that Pereboom faces a dilemma: either Plum does not in fact act from his character, or else he does but then he is arguably intuitively responsible.

But I do not embrace an identificationist account of moral responsibility. What I need is a reply that makes sense in the context of a broadly Reasons account of responsibility. In that context, one thing that is interesting about the particular way the regular but circumstance-localized manipulation operates, is that it blocks a reply I suggested in *Andrés*, i.e., that wholesale replacement of values or desires is plausibly identity-disrupting. So, another answer is required. Fortunately, the fact of regular manipulation provides grist for a different sort of reply.

Recall that we have rejected atomistic conceptions of control. This thought does some work for us here. What a non-atomistic picture of control presses upon on us is the thought that control is not an intrinsic property of agents, but a function of *agents in circumstances, given the ends of the responsibility system.* In light of this conception of how the responsibility-relevant capacities are picked out, I don't see how or why the ideal observer (recall: the observer is part of the construction that settles facts about the relevant notion of circumstance-indexed capacities) would treat agents in contexts of selective and deep manipulation as having

---

[20] Fischer et al., *Four Views on Free Will*, p. 94.

responsibility-relevant control. How could this possibly serve the ends of us respecting the relevant form of agency? How would countenancing eligibility for blame in selectively and maliciously manipulated agents support the cultivation of the relevant forms of agency?

The entire point of the manipulators in the examples is to disrupt the otherwise ordinary functioning of some agent, and to do so in a way that renders that agent's pattern or responses and dispositions different than they would otherwise be. As such, these are precisely circumstances in which it is plausible to think of such manipulated agents as lacking the capacities that circumscribe the scope of deserved praising and blaming. Agents of that sort would not plausibly generate the customary systemic benefits of interest to the responsibility system, and they could not plausibly create demands on us to contribute to improved self-governance, given the power of the manipulators.

(And again, notice that this is *not* a point about what strikes us as intuitive. Rather, it is a point about how, given the present picture of moral responsibility, we ought to distinguish between the various cases presented in the Four Case Argument. If the input-independent manipulation is such that the resulting capacities cannot support such practices and desert-generating entitlements, then *that* fact will be our reason for treating it as a case of non-responsibility.)

In short, I am inclined to think that if we read Case 1 as invoking an input-independent picture of moment-to-moment manipulation, then this would disrupt the presence of capacities that properly constitute responsible agency.

But perhaps there is a way to render input-independent manipulations in some difficult-to-conceive of fashion that does not run afoul of the various constraints on the circumstantialist conception of responsibility-relevant capacities. This would push us back in the direction of the initial way I suggested characterizing the case, as one in which despite the presence of the manipulators, Plum in fact retains the capacities required for moral responsibility. If the manipulation is characterized in a way that plausibly permits this by my theory's lights, then I think we should think that the agent is indeed genuinely responsible, however counterintuitive it might seem relative to our pre-revised commitments.

I recognize that this may sound incredible, especially if one is not yet sold on my account of responsibility. But recall the lesson learned from reflection on *Andrés*. If an agent is sufficiently capable of recognizing and responding to moral considerations *in that context*, then we have an apt candidate for deserving praise and blame. Indeed, as I noted, we might be said to owe the agent our blame, lest we rob what control remains for the manipulated agent. If, however, he lacks these capabilities, then he is not a responsible agent. (And notice: in no part of this explanation is determinism relevant!)

Perhaps we can identify another interfering intuition that we should reject. Some (perhaps you) may be reluctant to think of Plum as responsible in Case 1 because he is subject to the effects of malicious influence by another agent, and if they are responsible for what he does, then Plum cannot be responsible. Assuming that the manipulators are responsible agents, it is surely the case that such agents act with ill will, and are consequently blameworthy for what they do. But responsibility is not a zero-sum thing. As Frankfurt has pointed out, an agent can be fully responsible without being solely responsible.[21] Even if the manipulators bear some responsibility, so long as Plum has the relevant capacities of moral considerations-responsiveness, then he is responsible for what he does.

Rather than trying to directly combat whatever intransigent intuitions might remain, I'll take a different tack. I think we can enhance the plausibility of the line I take by considering a somewhat different example. Consider the case of *Professor Foggybottom*.

In the not-so-far-flung future, custom-built cognitive enhancement modules become available. They are like spectacles—they come in varied powers and can be put on and removed as one likes. (The details of how don't matter. If you like, imagine it works via a magnetic baseball cap; or, if you prefer, via a hardware piece that interfaces with standardized cortical implants. Or, you know, brain-wave WiFi.) Some enhancements ramp up the user's epistemic powers. Others enhance willpower, the ability to sustain concentration for longer periods of time, the capacity to recall propositional information, and so on. And, of course, one can get these enhancements bundled together in one small package.

August Full Professors, especially those at elite universities, find these implants invaluable in the face of their gradually diminishing natural powers. Philosophy professors, especially, make extensive use of such devices. Fortunately, the greater earning power of senior figures permits them to buy more expensive devices that

---

[21] Harry G. Frankfurt, *The Importance of What We Care About: Philosophical Essays* (Cambridge: Cambridge University Press, 1988), p. 25 n. 10.

keep them ahead of the enhancement-happy whippersnappers eager to gain some share of the finite professional attention that is available in the high-status sectors of the profession.

Professor Foggybottom, a very distinguished and influential figure in the contemporary scene, is an avid user of the top-of-the-line multifaceted cognitive enhancer. Like his favorite pair of spectacles, it provides an extremely powerful enhancement of his acuity. It is so powerful, that when he uses the device, he's just as quick, just as capable of following a complex formal argument, just as subtle in generating counterexamples as he ever was—even when he was a young whippersnapper using the best early versions of the cognitive enhancer.

One day, during the middle of a question and answer period after a customarily brilliant talk, his device suffers a malfunction and stops working. For most users of these devices, this would be a potentially catastrophic thing if it occurred in the middle of a question and answer period. Professor Foggybottom doesn't have to worry, however. His device has a special backup system. When the main system fails, the device contacts headquarters, and a crack team of cognitively enhanced technicians immediately begins doing either of two things. One, they process his cognitive inputs with their own well-functioning, cognitively enhanced minds, returning the results to him. Or two, accessing a large database of information about philosophy he is known to have read, including the latest journal articles, the technicians feed Foggybottom that information for him to process in his unenhanced state. In doing so, they are more reliable than his memory would be on its own.

Finally, in some cases, when the backup system is operating, what happens is a multi-directional exchange of information, with: (1) the professor sending inputs to the reasoners that are processed and sent back in light of their own enhanced cognitive mechanisms; while (2) simultaneously receiving inputs from the databases that provided redundant and efficient delivery of information that he has but is slow to access; and (3) also deliberating on his own about the considerations that occur to him and that are provided by the tech crew working backup on his cognitive enhancer.

There are lots of questions we might raise about Professor Foggybottom and his world. For example, we might wonder whether anyone using cognitive enhancements deserves credit for their philosophical achievements produced while making use of such devices. To facilitate reflection, let us assume the following: in Foggybottom's world, at least the philosophers hold that people are properly given credit (negative or positive) for what they say or do when acting with a functioning cognitive enhancement module. Why? In most cases, philosophers seem to arrive at this conclusion in light of reflecting on their earlier experiences with caffeine and the like. What they conclude is that, hardware aside, the use of such devices is not significantly different than some really excellent coffee. The modules simply provide a hardware-based enhancement of existing capacities, and the agents with such hardware remain in control of what they say and do in all the usual ways. What the modules do is simply provide them with enhanced degrees of capacities they already possess in some quantity. So, in their world, the products of those enhancement-involving capacities— talks, articles, and so on—are regarded on equal footing with comparable products produced devoid of such enhancement. After all, they say, the journals don't distinguish between papers written with and without what are comparable cognitive benefits, such as caffeine, adequate sleep, Ritalin, a robust collection of university journal subscriptions, or smart colleagues.

Back to Foggybottom, then. In this world, Foggybottom will get credit for his customarily excellent, if slightly atypical performance at the talk, even if everyone recognized that his module suffered a failure in its primary system. Why? Well, nearly everyone in that world thinks that so long as the dysfunction of the primary system of the module did not disrupt the speaker's native (and let's presume) considerations-responsive mechanisms, the speaker retains the capacities in virtue of which credit (positive or negative) makes sense. So, even with full information about the breakdown in Foggybottom's mental spectacles, and his ensuing (if unknowing) use of a redundant but comparably effective pair, he's above the threshold for intellectual credit, given that he had intact all the requisite capacities to govern his behavior and make considerations-responsive decisions.

Now, finally, I can say why I've taken you on this lengthy detour. If we understand the manipulation to keep Plum's capacities to recognize and respond to moral considerations above the baseline, then I can't see how Pereboom's Case 1 is interestingly different than the case of Professor Foggybottom. Neither Plum nor Foggybottom are aware that their respective customary deliberative mechanisms have given out, and that an alternative system is in play. Moreover, in both cases, the alternative system is not completely alien to actual patterns of reflection and deliberation in either agent. And, as such, the products of such systems, however external to the agent, are for the purposes of assigning credit and participating in the relevant social practices, to be attributed to the involved agent. It is just that in Foggybottom's world this is a familiar enough phenomenon and in our world, we are less cognizant about mechanisms that alter our cognitive capacities without eradicating our responsibility.

In both cases, so long as the requisite capacities are above the relevant threshold, the fact of real-time, active participation of other agents in sustaining the functioning of those systems means that Foggybottom and Plum remain within the net of relevant evaluative practices. Of course, *if* the alternative operative system disrupts the possession of the baseline capacities for critical appraisal of what they do, then this is another matter. But there is nothing unprincipled in acknowledging this possibility.

To sum up, if we regard Pereboom's Case 1 as an instance of non-responsibility, then the real-time manipulation must disrupt the moral considerations-responsive capacities. But then we have a reason for thinking that Case 1 is relevantly different than Case 2. If we think that despite the manipulation, Plum retains the relevant capacity for recognizing and responding to moral considerations, then we have a warrant for thinking that it is a bizarre but nevertheless genuine case of moral responsibility. In short, however Pereboom precisifies the case, we have principled reasons for handling it in detail-specific ways.

Of course, this is a theory-driven answer, and not a folk-intuitional answer. But in this context, that strikes me as an advantage over an argument whose force depends very significantly on arguably error-laden intuitions.

9. Do Mele and I substantially disagree?

I wish to conclude by considering of how my account is similar or dissimilar from an aspect of Al Mele's prominent account of responsible agency.

In early work, Mele argued that moral responsibility requires that the agent's capacities must have been acquired in a compulsion-free way. The relevant notion of compulsion is this: the acquisition of the relevant features of the agent (S's pro-attitudes) is brought about in a way that "bypasses S's capacities for control over his mental life; and the bypassing issues in S's being practically unable to shed [the relevant pro-attitude(s)]; and the bypassing was not itself arranged (or performed) by S; and S neither presently possesses nor earlier possessed pro-attitudes that would supply his identifying with [the relevant pro-attitude(s)], with the exception of the pro-attitudes that are themselves practically unsheddable products of unsolicited by-passing."[22]

Is this an essentially historical account, or is it a mixed approach? Previously, I was inclined to think that it was an essentially historical account, because it uniformly appeals to a no-compulsion constraint. Since any occurrent agential structures might have been installed from the outside, as it were, it looks like the no-compulsion requirement always gives us a reason to look to the agent's history. However, threads of Mele's early account also suggested to me the following possibility: he could allow that possession or rare or exceptional agential powers might be sufficient for responsibility.

In the context of discussing a case like *Andrés*, I wrote the following:

If Mele thinks that the paradigmatic or model agential structure required for responsibility is one in which an agent's relevant desires are sheddable, then what I have been calling his "negative historical condition" is really the tracing condition of a [mixed] account. On the other hand, if Mele does not think that there is any such requirement on the basic agential structure of responsibility, then his theory does count as a genuinely historical one. A case that is worth thinking about in this context is one where an agent has only sheddable desires—if Mele thinks that these structural properties (plus whatever other structural properties he thinks are required for responsible agency) are enough to make the agent a responsible agent, then on my way of thinking about these things, he is a mixed theorist. Given his stated account of compulsion, I am inclined to think that this is what he should say.[23]

In subsequent work Mele considered a case that resolved this matter—or at least, it strongly hints at how my taxonomical puzzle should be resolved.

The relevant example concerns an agent he names Mabel. Mabel is an agent with "the marvelous ability to produce in herself any conceptually possible system of values from moment to moment" and thus, "can undo the effects of value manipulation at any moment."[24] Mabel seems potentially capable of satisfying conditions of responsibility in a non-historical fashion.

---

[22] Mele, *Autonomous Agents: From Self-Control to Autonomy*, p. 172.

[23] See Manuel Vargas, "On the Importance of History for Responsible Agency," *Philosophical Studies* 127, no. 3 (2006): 376 n. 18.

[24] Alfred Mele, "Moral Responsibility and History Revisited," *Ethical Theory and Moral Practice* 12, no. 5 (2009): 468.

So, even though agents like us ordinarily lack Mabel's marvelous power, it seems possible to satisfy conditions sufficient for responsibility without appeal to some historical property.

If I have understood things rightly, then Mele and I are both mixed theory proponents. However, our accounts come down on rather different parts of the continuum of mixed theories. Where I am inclined to think that conditions sufficient for moral responsibility can ordinarily be satisfied without requiring satisfaction of some historical condition, Mele holds that responsibility ordinarily requires satisfaction of some historical condition, even if in exceptional cases there might be agential structures sufficient for responsibility. The source of the disagreement is located in our different conceptions of responsible agency.

What I focus on in the remainder of this section is whether there are any reasons specific to the matter of history that, apart from our larger theories, should push us in the direction of his more history-demanding account or my less history-demanding account. To answer this question, we should look to Mele's reply to my earlier account of these matters.[25]

Mele focuses on two ideas. The first concerns a claim I made in earlier work that the history/structure debate was an instance of a "dialectical stalemate" (Fischer's term for a case in which antecedently convinced parties of differing convictions lack the resources to move each other from their respective positions). Mele notes that it is far from clear that there is a general stalemate in this domain, and that even if it is such a stalemate, that what matters is not the fact of disagreement but the quality of the arguments.[26] Mele is right; there is an interesting disagreement here, but it is not obvious that we are anywhere near a stalemate.

The second and more important matter concerns the significance of intuitions about these cases. Particularly important in Mele's discussion is the question of what we should say if some majority of persons (whether philosophers and/or the folk) have a strong intuition that agents who act from engineered values are not morally responsible. I think Mele and I are in agreement that what we should say depends on what we think about *why* people have what intuitions they have. I suspect we disagree on the why, however.

---

[25] Mele, "Moral Responsibility and History Revisited."
[26] Mele, "Moral Responsibility and History Revisited," p. 472.

Let's look at the cases that figure prominently in Mele's discussion.

One Good Day
Consider Chuck. Chuck wholeheartedly enjoys killing people. He used to feel guilty about this, but he (freely and responsibly) undertook a program of self-(dis) improvement that, over the years, successful expunged all feelings of guilt or mercy. Indeed, he hardened his heart sufficiently so that he had no values at all that could motivate a charitable deed; anything he did that appeared charitable was always in the service of some nefarious end.

Now consider Beth. Beth is an exceptionally sweet person, and always has been. Her character—or collection of values—leaves no place for desires to bodily harm others. Moreover, she was significantly responsible for having the character she had.

Over night, without Chuck's consent, some manipulators "erase his bad values and replace them with good ones that match Beth's. Shortly after he awakes, he starts working with a local Habitat for Humanity crew in the neighborhood. When the work day ends he drives around town for an hour and buys several boxes of Girl Scout cookies from every Girl Scout he sees—about 50 boxes in all. Then he delivers the cookies to a local homeless shelter. His motives are pure, as Beth's are when she does her charitable deeds."[27]

Mele thinks that Chuck is not responsible for his good deeds in *One Good Day*. Presumably, he also thinks that were the same value-transformation to be performed on Beth (so that she now has Chuck's values) she would not be responsible for those murders, no matter how grisly. In contrast, the view I have been defending seems to entail that Chuck and Beth would be responsible for their actions in their altered states, for I have no clause that rules out such value-transformations.

The question is whether intuitions of the sort Mele has should shape the account I have offered, or instead, whether we should reject such intuitions as erroneous or otherwise not-to-be-countenanced on our prescriptive theory of moral responsibility.

I've already said a fair amount in §6 of this chapter about why I think that if we carefully reflect on the nature of moral responsibility and the particulars of manipulation cases we should conclude that dramatic manipulations that are identity- and moral-considerations-responsiveness-preserving should not count as undermining responsibility. To motivate this picture,

---

[27] See Mele, "Moral Responsibility and History Revisited," pp. 464–5, 471.

I appealed to the general explanatory power of my account and to considerations rooted in the function of blame in the blamed agent's striving for
moral self-governance.

What can be said in favor of Mele's view? Here is what he writes:

it is fair to ask me why I believe that the intuition that Chuck is not morally
responsible for his good deeds is not misleading. A short answer harks back to my
radical reversal suggestion. It is that the following collection of facts suffices for
Chuck's deserving no moral credit for his good deeds in One Good Day: his pre-
transformation character was sufficiently bad that charitable deeds were not even an
option for him; he was morally responsible (to some significant degree) for that
character; the facts about his history that accounts for his moral responsibility for
that character; and the facts that account for the good deeds at issue.[28]

That's helpful. Notice, though, that apart from the final fact he cites (I'll get
to that in a moment), the explanation Mele offers for his intuitions is not
obviously an explanation of the intuition that post-transformation Chuck is
not responsible. Instead, it is most plausibly an explanation of a different
intuition: the intuition that Chuck was responsible for the bad things *when
he did them*. In other words, the considerations marshaled are about *pre-*
transformation Chuck, and not telling one way or another about *post-*
transformation Chuck.

Why do I say this? Well, none of the things he points to make any
reference whatsoever to post-transformation Chuck. They are all about
how pre-transformation Chuck came to be a bad dude. What we need,
though, is some reason for thinking that those considerations about pre-
transformation properly explain anything about the post-transformation
Chuck. (I say "properly" because we can acknowledge that we might
have them in the post-transformation case without thinking there is anything besides habit or prejudice fueling them. I trust Mele agrees, which is
why he is offering them as reasons for taking this intuition as theory-
guiding.)

What about the final consideration Mele cites in favor of his intuition that
Chuck is responsible? It is this: "the facts that account for the good deeds at
issue." But we agree about those facts. What is at stake is whether they tell
us anything about Chuck. Mele thinks they do, i.e., that they undermine

---

[28] Mele, "Moral Responsibility and History Revisited," p. 473.

responsibility. However, what we are looking for is some explanation of *why* these facts undermine responsibility. So, I think the only considerations Mele provides for the accuracy of his intuition turn out to be the intuition itself.

Perhaps I'm misreading Mele. Perhaps we should read this passage as indicating support for a much broader historical requirement than I attribute to him. That is, we might think that what Mele is pointing to is some requirement that one can only be morally responsible if one is responsible for one's character. But as I understand his account, this is a sufficient but not necessary condition on moral responsibility.

I am prepared to acknowledge that we have historical intuitions of the sort Mele relies upon, and I am inclined to think they are generated by an unwarranted conviction we have about the requirement that we be ultimate sources of our own actions. The diagnostic account I've given, and the argument for revisionism in Part I of this book provides a natural explanation of the intuition. The question is whether the conditions I've given are sufficient for moral responsibility. I don't see any considerations in Mele's discussion that give us reason to think not.

Here's how matters stack up: Mele and I both think that structural conditions can be sufficient for responsibility. He thinks it is achieved in the Mabel case, but that such cases are rare. My account, however, emphasizes capacities to recognize and self-govern in light of moral considerations, which are more readily had. So our disagreement on this matter is largely a function of our distinct accounts of moral responsibility, and (I think) less a function of distilling any real insights from the history question in isolation of broader commitments.

Mele's own theory of responsibility emphasizes what he characterizes as "psychological autonomy."[29] This is hard to have, on his account, if one has a history like Chuck or Beth's, for such cases undercut the psychological autonomy that Mele puts at the foundation of his account of moral responsibility. In contrast, I'm inclined to think that the matter of moral responsibility is separable from questions of psychological autonomy. Indeed, I'm inclined to think that dramatic values-transformations are indeed violations of psychological autonomy, or at least one plausible conception of how to understand the protean term "autonomy".

[29] Mele, *Autonomous Agents: From Self-Control to Autonomy.*

However, I'm unpersuaded that *One Good Day* works against the account I offer, for several reasons. First, radical transformations of value, especially on the order of *One Good Day*, invite questions about personal identity. In what sense is Chuck the same person pre-and post-transformation? Given the role of values and treating things as reasons in constituting the various Lockean ties that make up identity over time, I think there is ample room for skepticism about whether identity holds up across such transformations. Second, *One Good Day* is a case about praise and this raises some puzzles of its own when used as a probe. Although I won't try to make the argument here, I think we're pretty bad about knowing when and how to praise.

But suppose that this latter concern is not operative. Then, I'm inclined to think (surely, in the grips of my theory) that if Chuck really is recognizing moral considerations and self-governing in light of them, he really is praiseworthy *for just that reason*. If all that is right, I even have a straightforward diagnosis for our reticence to view Chuck as praiseworthy. It derives from the fact of his having done those terrible things in the past, and his not feeling guilty (even now), coupled by his continuing failure to make right for his wrongs.

Mele could build in to the example the claim that Chuck does not remember these loathsome deeds. But notice: if he does modify the example in that way, it only enhances the plausibility that the transformation is identity severing. In contrast, if he does remember his vile deeds, then his failure to repent in some plausibly connected way (buying Girl Scout Cookies looks like the wrong way) underscores that he is not indeed being governed by moral considerations in the responsibility-constituting way.

I think our intuitions are a somewhat better guide if we keep these thoughts in mind and go on to consider the inverse of the *One Good Day*. Suppose Beth wakes up on One Bad Day. Further, let us suppose that she has the capacity to recognize and self-govern in light of moral considerations in just the way I have outlined. She simply values the grisly taking of life more than she values moral considerations against life-taking. So, she goes out and proceeds to rape, torture, and murder the neighbor she thinks she can most easily get away with harming.

My intuition is that Beth is responsible. And that's my intuition even if the next day she is back to being good ol' Beth. I think that at least on the day she is evil, that she really is responsible for those evils.

We might wonder what happens to our intuitions if Beth switches back to Good Beth after One Bad Day. I suspect that she would feel incredibly guilty, and she would rightly wonder what came over her. And, I think we could ask some difficult-to-answer questions about whether she really was the same person from one day to the next. And, I think what we should say about apologies, repentance, and forgiveness in such a case would be incredibly complex. Whatever else is true, our ordinary responsibility practices seem ill-adapted for engaging with agents of the sort we are imagining Beth to be.

Here's what I'm relatively confident about, though: on her Bad Day, when Beth looks up from the gristle of bone and human meat underneath her, and we ask her "why?" she'll say she wanted to, that she knew what she was doing, that she was in control, and that she could have done differently, and that she decided not to. And, in all the ways that matter to moral responsibility, she would be telling us the truth.

Recall that I've offered an account on which, for an agent to be responsible for doing something blameworthy, he or she has to have a capacity to recognize and appropriately respond to moral considerations. In the absence of this capacity the agent simply isn't the right sort of being to deserve praise or blame. Beyond pointing to my theory, I don't know what to say to convince you if you don't share my intuition about how to think about *One Bad Day*. Regardless of how Beth came to be that way, it seems to me that she had the sort of control that is required for moral responsibility, and boy, did she act with ill will.

Mele concludes by noting that my approach can seek to accommodate very widely shared strong intuitions and "Should it turn out that the intuition that Chuck is not morally responsible for his good deeds in *One Good Day* is of this kind, Vargas might deem it reasonable to modify his position on moral responsibility accordingly."[30] But I don't yet see that we have sufficient reason to think that those intuitions—however widespread they may be—are reliable or truth-guiding. Nevertheless, I remain willing to be convinced otherwise.

---

[30] Mele, "Moral Responsibility and History Revisited," p. 474.

10

Some Conclusions

When I began the presentation of the prescriptive account, I claimed that there were a variety of theoretical burdens that the proposed account would have to satisfy if it were to constitute an adequate revisionist account of moral responsibility. Among those burdens were the satisfaction of standards of naturalistic plausibility and normative adequacy. The latter entailed some explanation of how the normative elements characteristic of responsibility were to be addressed.

I have said nearly all I am going to say about the substantively normative issues. In this chapter, the main concern is to address some remaining metaphysical and methodological issues. I start by reconsidering the question of naturalistic plausibility. I then address what the present account allows us to say about the scope of moral responsibility, and in particular, what it allows us to say about non-moral instances of responsibility. Finally, I conclude by reconsidering the question that has been at the heart of this project: are we really responsible?

1. Naturalistic plausibility revisited

Way back, in chapter 2, I argued that any prescriptively libertarian account ran afoul of a reasonable standard of naturalistic plausibility. One element of my rejection of libertarianism was that there are no truth-relevant considerations that speak in favor of the crucial posits of a libertarian account. However, a critic could object that, for all I've said, the same is true of the present account. That is, even if the present account of considerations-responsive agency is compatible with what we know about the natural world, there is no evidence in favor of it.

This is an important objection, but I think it can be overcome.

First, recall that the standard of naturalistic plausibility admits of several construals, and one is comparative. As I noted when I introduced the standard, contemporary prescriptively compatibilist theories will nearly always be comparatively more plausible than libertarian theories, given that libertarian accounts are forced to postulate a more demanding ontology of agency, one that requires indeterminism to occur, and to occur in particular places and not others. So, the present account's prescriptively compatibilist credentials do important work.

Second, on the threshold interpretation of the requirement, there is some evidence in favor of our plausibly being responsive to considerations. In a recent review of the status of the neuroscience of volition, Adina Roskies argues that while work on the neural basis of decision-making has nothing to contribute to traditional philosophical debates about freedom, it is nevertheless illuminating in understanding the nature of decision-making for it "provides a relatively comprehensive model of a decision process in that it incorporates all the basic elements we would intuitively expect—representations of options, value, evidence, a dynamical characterization of the evolution of the system over time with changing inputs, and even confidence" (120).[1]

As part of her discussion of the state of research on neuron-level encoding of information in primate brains, she makes some particularly intriguing remarks. She starts with the idea that there is growing evidence that there are populations of neurons that represent propositional content in monkey brains. From this she argues that

It is not difficult to imagine that different neural populations can represent other propositions, and although we currently lack a general framework for conceiving of how propositional content is represented in the nervous system, we know that it can be because we do represent it. Once we can conceive of the neural representations of abstract propositions, it is but a small step to think of them as representing reasons or considerations for action, and their relative firing rates a reflecting the weight given to reasons for decisions or action. (119)

If Roskies is right, there is some reason to think that we find a neurological basis for some reasons-recognition in primate brains. And, as she notes, this suggests that there may be a more general phenomenon at work here.

---

[1] Roskies, "How Does Neuroscience Affect Our Conception of Volition?"

Of course, the generalization of this phenomenon outside of relatively circumscribed experiments, and the subsequent generalization of the phenomenon to the human case, is speculative. Still, the evidence is suggestive and indicates that at least some of the functional structures to which the present account appeals plausibly have relatively direct instantiations in our neural equipment. One might even say it is an inference to the best explanation of how we do what we do, given what we know about the brain.

Stepping back, the conclusion that we find *some* neurological data that suggest that at least in limited cases there is neurological encoding of representations of reasons should strike us as relatively unsurprising. Given broadly physicalist presumptions, unless one were committed to the view that we *never* act on reasons, or that there is no sense to the idea of us being creatures who are responsive to considerations, this is exactly what we should expect.

Although wholesale reasons–skepticism is not unthinkable, it would be a radical departure from the kinds of views widely held in the social and cognitive sciences. Even among views that argue that our ordinary conscious explanations of our actions betray a good deal of confabulation, only the most wild-eyed proponents of such views go on to assert that as a whole we never represent or respond to considerations. As we have seen, the main question is whether we are considerations–responsive enough to make it plausible that we are responsible agents, at least sometimes. My circumstantialist account of our capacities answers in the affirmative.

Of course, a critic might object that we are still short of what we need, for the likely fact that we recognize and respond to considerations does not yet show that we recognize and respond to moral considerations. It is true that none of the foregoing demonstrates the existence of responsiveness to specifically moral considerations. Indeed, for all that has been said it might turn out that moral nihilism is true, and that there are no such things as moral considerations.

While it is true that the account has not shown that there are, in fact moral considerations, it need not do that much. The account was not intended to defeat any possible source of responsibility nihilism. Rather, the intent has been to show why, given some widely accepted assumptions (including the assumptions that there are moral considerations), we are plausibly agents capable of blame–licensing activity.

2. Extending the scope of the account

Here, I turn to a different issue: the extent to which the basic framework of my approach to moral responsibility can be generalized to what might be thought of as other forms of responsibility.[2]

Consider the fact that we are sometimes inclined to think that someone can be responsible (in some to-be-determined-sense) for an extraordinary act of apparent athletic skill. Whether the considered athlete is indeed responsible (in that to-be-determined-sense) turns on how the act was performed. If the feat was accidental, it strikes us as less to the credit of the agent than an otherwise identical feat that was not accidentally performed. These thoughts might motivate the following view: if the agent is responding to considerations relevant to the sport or athletic endeavor, then it is proper to credit the athlete with the extraordinary act. We might admire the maneuver regardless of whether it was intentionally performed or not. However, if we regard the play or score or maneuver as a freak event and not done in response to considerations proper to the activity, there is some impetus to withhold a form of praise or regard, one that we reserve for what we might think of as "genuine" expressions of agency.

Now consider the production of a piece of art—a painting, let's imagine. Although there are surely some who contest the following thought, it is a recognizable enough view to think that whether an artist deserves praise for his or her art is at least partly a function of some engagement or response to aesthetic considerations—be they immediate concerns about beauty, philosophical motivations about the use of form or color, or intentional bending of convention, genre, or tradition. The splotches on the floor of Jackson Pollock's workshop might be indistinguishable from his canvases, but the collateral effects of the painting do not themselves ordinarily constitute more than a curiosity.

(Of course, art being what it is, one can imagine that an artist might seek to comment on the limits of the artistic tradition precisely by presenting the detritus of the workshop as itself an object of art; but this only reinforces my point about the necessity of some form of agency mediating the production of art, and the fact that some (but not all) forms of artistic credit track this fact.)

---

[2] Thanks to Matt King for a helpful conversation about these issues. For a different take on these issues, see Matt King, "The Structure of Responsibility" (Ph.D. Dissertation, University of Maryland, 2008).

I am not claiming that either the athletic or artistic cases are instances of *moral* responsibility. The athlete might be responsible for the spectacular manner in which he or she scores, but there is nothing moral about it (let us suppose). And, let us suppose, that the placement of a particular splotch of paint is morally inconsequential. What then should we say about such cases?

I am inclined to think that these are cases of responsibility in some sense— just not responsibility in the moral sense. This suggests that responsibility more generally might be understood as a family of notions, the members of which can be distinguished by the types of considerations they involve. Roughly, whether someone is rightly praised for a work of art is a function of whether she or he recognized aesthetic considerations in the production of the piece and regulated him- or herself in light of it. Similarly, whether someone is blamed for failure on the field of some athletic contest is at least partly a function of whether the agent was capable of recognizing and responding to considerations indexed to the athletic context. In neither case are such appraisals necessarily moral, although they might be that, too.

Such overlapping modes of appraisal are familiar phenomenon in real life, even if we don't ordinarily think of them as such. The player who throws the game, the movie director who lauds the dictator, and the writer who is an apologist for human rights abuses can trigger overlapping and sometimes dueling reactions. Sometimes our moralized reactions swamp the other form (s) of appraisal; sometimes the moral reaction is blunted by our enthusiasm for the rousing chorus or the success of the party. The world is complex.

In focusing on the role of considerations-responsive agency in such examples I do not mean to suggest that there cannot be other systems of appraisal internal to that practice. There may well be modes of evaluation proper to various practices in which appeals to epistemic and self-governing capacities play a more limited role. Some practices may have role responsibilities that have a strict liability structure to their performance. You might think, for example, that in American football the left tackle's job is to protect the quarterback's blind side, no matter what. Such considerations will structure our evaluation of the praiseworthiness and blameworthiness cases in ways that won't neatly map on to the case of individual moral responsibility. Nevertheless, a wide range of agential assessments are intelligibly and rightly sensitive to the operation of domain- and interest-specific considerations in agential self-governance. Moral responsibility is arguably the most important of these. It is not, however, the only one.

3. Limiting the scope of moral responsibility

The picture I presented in the last section proceeded partly on the basis of the thought that there are actions that normal human adult agents can undertake in which moral responsibility does not apply, but in which other forms of responsibility might plausibly obtain. On this picture, one cannot be morally responsible for behavior that has no moral significance. So, for example, it would be inaccurate to claim that someone is morally responsible for, say, putting on slippers in the morning (supposing there is no moral significance to the act of putting on the slippers). There is no reason to deny that a person can be *causally* responsible for putting on slippers. However, in the absence of an act being morally significant, one cannot be morally responsible for it.

That's what my account says, anyway. This is not a universal conviction among theories of responsibility. For example, John Fischer's distinguished account of responsibility accepts the idea that an agent may be morally responsible for behavior without moral significance, or what Fischer calls "morally neutral" behavior.[3] So, there's a disagreement here.

Apart from intrinsic interest, the matter is methodologically important, for it is connected to the question of whether either account relies on a plausible picture of the work of the concept. I have claimed that the work of the concept has to do with regulating inferences about differential moral praiseworthiness and blameworthiness, but Fischer's account suggests that this isn't right, for on his account the ambit of the concept of responsibility is much wider. So, in what follows, I offer reasons to favor the more restricted conception of responsibility implied by my account.

Let's start with the idea that, ordinarily, when normal adults put their slippers on, they typically retain capacities to recognize and respond to a wide range of moral considerations. Nothing in my account conflicts with this thought, and I take it that Fischer's account agrees on this much. That is, we can both allow that the average slipper-attiring agents are responsible agents in the terms of our respective accounts. If so, then we might characterize the point of disagreement as this: I think that to describe morally responsible agents as *morally responsible for putting on the slippers* inaccurately extends

---

[3] For statements of the view, see Fischer and Ravizza, *Responsibility and Control: A Theory of Moral Responsibility*, n.11, p. 8; Fischer, *My Way*, p. 233.

the scope of moral responsibility—or that it at least greatly misleads—and Fischer does not.

On my account, we should reserve the phrase "is morally responsible" for cases in which moral praise and blame can arise—i.e., in cases where there is both responsible agency and something morally salient involved in the action. Fischer prefers to allow a much more permissive usage of "is morally responsible" that picks out cases of "bare" responsible agency *and* cases of responsible agency plus blameworthiness.

Two considerations rooted in ordinary usage speak in favor of my approach. First, if I am right that there is something odd about describing agents as morally responsible for actions that lack a moral valence, then my approach does better at preserving our linguistic practices as we find them. Of course, it is open to Fischer to reply that in this way, perhaps, his account is revisionist, but despite that shortcoming, it accurately reports the true nature or conditions of responsibility. However, I take it that the force of such a reply would hinge on more global comparisons of Fischer's account with alternative theories. Moreover, the revisionist move on this front strikes me as at least a cost to be registered in contrast to an account that entails no such revision in *that* way. (Of course, for a theory like mine that entails revision in a different way, such considerations may ultimately be offsetting, even if they aren't operative here. Again, more comprehensive evaluation of the theories would matter.)

A second consideration arises from the implications of an expansive picture of responsible agency. Fischer's view seems to allow that agents can be morally responsible in universes in which there are no moral considerations whatsoever. So, universes in which there are no genuinely moral considerations—consider a world in which an error-theory of morality is correct—an agent might satisfy Fischer-style requirements of reasons responsiveness, and thus be morally responsible for any number of acts—*even though morality is a sham*. That strikes me as clear drawback of a Fischer-style view. In contrast, on my view one might possess the capacities for responsible agency in such a world. However, no one would be responsible for anything precisely because there are no moral considerations in play that make such agents blameworthy for their actions.

I grant that the power of this thought experiment turns on any number of contestable assumptions, so it is not decisive. Moreover, one might object that my account falls victim to an analogous difficulty. It seems that my account also allows that there could be responsible agents in a universe where there are no moral considerations. After all, even in that universe agents might have the unexercised *capacity* to recognize and respond to moral considerations—it is just that there are none.

I'm not sold on this being a problem for my account. Recall that *responsible agent* is a technical term for a special form of agency. I've chosen the present label only because it helped identify why that form of agency was important. But the label itself does not entail anything about there being actions for which we are morally responsible. That is, it does not commit us to describing acts flowing from that agency as acts for which the agent is morally responsible. In contrast, it appears that Fischer's view requires us to say as much. So, I do not think an analogous problem arises for my account.

Part of what may fund the temptation to permit talk of agents being morally responsible for non-moral outcomes is that in ordinary discourse the judgment that someone "is responsible" is an ambiguous one. The ambiguity corresponds to the difference between a judgment that someone is a morally responsible agent—a candidate for praise and blame judgments—and the "all-in" judgments that someone is morally responsible for some outcome (a judgment that presumes that someone is a responsible agent and that they have done something praiseworthy or blameworthy).

The theory I have offered has no difficulty accounting for this ambiguity in ordinary language. It does so by providing a distinction between responsible agency and being responsible for some bit of behavior. So, one can be a responsible agent at some time—alive to relevant moral considerations— without it following that one is blameworthy for some act. And, in cases where there are no moral considerations in play, where the considered act is devoid of moral significance, the issue of being morally responsible for some behavior is simply not live.

4. So, are we really responsible?

Earlier, I noted that one persistent source of dissatisfaction with P. F. Strawson's account of responsibility has been that it did not have much of an answer to the skeptic who wondered whether we are *really* responsible. What Strawson gives us, critics objected, is an account of why we cannot help holding each other responsible. Even if we cannot help doing so, or even if there is merely very good reason to hold one another responsible, this would still fail to show that we are ever *actually* morally responsible.

It is not hard to imagine that one might raise a similar charge against my account. Even if persuaded that I've given a plausible enough defense of why we have reason to participate in and perpetuate the responsibility system, a critic might object I have simply changed the subject, for we can ask again: even if there is good reason for us to engage in the practices, *are we really responsible?*

I think the most plausible answer here is yes, for reasons I have endeavored to motivate throughout this book, although I won't pretend that the revisionist pill is easy swallow. The most I can hope to offer here is some recapitulation of the claims I take to be most telling on this matter.

First, there is a (to my mind, plausible) view on which responsibility just is the kind of thing, whatever it is, that licenses praise and blame and makes sense of the bulk of our ordinary practices, inferences, and the like surrounding responsibility. The account I have offered explains how praise and blame are licensed, and how the web of statuses, judgments, and practices surrounding differential moral praise and blame are organized and how they can be deserved.

Given that my account makes sense of our practices, largely as we find them, and given that it explains how we are properly licensed in differential praising and blaming, I don't see why we ought to call it anything other than an account of moral responsibility. Put differently, the plausibility of the account gives us reason for concluding that we are indeed responsible, even if our being responsible is somewhat differently constituted than we might have thought (at least, according to the diagnostic account I offered in Part I). For this reason, my account is plausibly a version of connotational revisionism.

Second, even if you reject the conceptual or semantic picture given above (and thus we remain agnostic or doubtful that the account we have in hand shows that we are *really* morally responsible) the account will nevertheless have shown something important. What it shows is that there is a coherent package of morally significant statuses, judgments, and practices that licenses a wide range of behaviors and inferences characteristic of responsibility.

So, perhaps it is only responsibility* that exists, and not responsibility. If so, then so much the worse for responsibility. If my account works, the non-existence of responsibility entails virtually no significant deviation from the practices, attitudes, and judgment-licensing statuses that were thought to be at stake in light of the threat of responsibility nihilism. Of course, I'm also inclined to think that if my account does secure the integrity of such practices, and there is nevertheless reason to reject the idea that it is an account of responsibility, then it is not unreasonable to advocate for denotational revision, re-anchoring responsibility talk in the responsibility* features of the world.

Suppose, though, that we accept that we are at best sometimes morally responsible* and never morally responsible, full stop. The responsibility nihilist could claim a kind of victory, however pyrrhic. If all that responsibility nihilism comes to is the claim that we cannot use certain words, but nothing else about our practices must go, then that's good enough for me.

There is a different way one might get at the worry that I have not yet provided a theory of moral responsibility. A critic might grant that I have provided a kind of reply to the skeptic, but that I have nevertheless mischaracterized the normative heart of moral responsibility, and thus, I have failed to provide an account of the nature of moral responsibility and its conditions.

I imagine that this sort of criticism will mainly appeal to those who have importantly different views about the work of the concept of responsibility, or are inclined to ground the responsibility system in a different story of its justification. Although I have not and will not attempt to argue against all potential and actual alternative accounts of moral responsibility, perhaps I can forestall some of this concern.

Let's start with an ecumenical idea I advanced earlier (in chapter 6), regarding the justification of the responsibility-characteristic practices. What I claimed about my particular justification of the responsibility-characteristic practices was that it was not intended to be normatively exclusive. That is, I explicitly allowed that there might be other justificatory accounts available to us that would permit us to explain why we are licensed in praising and blaming, and how such licenses connect to the various statuses, judgments, and inferences that are characteristic of moral responsibility as we tend to think of it. The thought there was that my particular proposal was one among many potential accounts, but that it was especially promising given its relatively minimal commitments to substantive views about normative ethics and the metaphysics of agency. The ensuing account was to be judged in terms of its fruitfulness and the various methodological injunctions I have outlined.

Although these thoughts were mustered largely in the context of reflections about the justification of responsibility-characteristic practices, I take it that many of the same basic lessons apply to disagreements about the work of the concept or the convictions about the essential nature of moral responsibility. That is, it might be that alternative accounts overlap or complement the present account in some illuminating way. If so, then alternative accounts or apparent disagreements at the level of the characterization of the work of the concept might be reconsidered as complements or emendations, rather than as something that necessarily competes with my account.

In particular, I am happy to allow that alternative accounts of the blaming norms might complement or supersede the quality of will account I have offered. I have already noted that various aspects of the account are explicitly modular, so that one can accept any number of elements in this account without accepting other aspects of the account. One can embrace revisionism, for example, without accepting my particular prescriptive account. Similarly, one can accept the justificatory account without accepting the revisionist element or the quality of will element or the "priority of reasons" element or the circumstantialist conception of agential capacities, and so on. Naturally, I prefer the package as it stands, but I see no reason to think that the central elements rise and fall together.

To be sure, when alternative accounts with comparable credentials do conflict, we'll have to carefully adjudicate the matter. However, it does not follow from the thought that one might think there is an alternative way of justifying our responsibility-characteristic practices that the present account has not taught us something about the nature of responsibility. So, I am happy to be conciliatory, especially if it nets us a better account.

As open as I am to ecumenical overtures, I do not wish to suggest that there is no challenge to formulating a viable competitor prescriptive account. If I am right about the general diagnostic account—that we have diverse intuitions about free will and moral responsibility, and that conventional (i.e., non-revisionist) theorists have been largely deaf to concerns that are not their own, that threads of ordinary convictions give rise to a threat of responsibility skepticism, and that many accounts (both conventionally compatibilist and incompatibilist) have failed to take seriously what we know about how human agency operates in the world—then any alternative prescriptive account that would have us jettison some or all of the present account will need to be able to do at least as well on these diverse matters.

Moreover, it is not as though the present account altogether lacks fruits of its own. It provides a defense of the bulk of responsibility-characteristic attitudes and practices in the face of skeptical concerns. Moreover, it does so in a naturalistically plausible and normatively adequate way that illuminates a variety of long-standing puzzles in the literature. The account also gives us a new way of understanding the complex interaction of paths to exculpation. Importantly, it provides us with some sense of a new class of underappreciated but important concerns about our ability to structure our capacity-constituting ecology, and so on. These are non-trivial virtues. To the extent that they are earned, they provide reasons for thinking that the present prescriptive account's particular cocktail of conceptual innovations and methodological elaborations have gotten right the normative core of moral responsibility. So, concessions to a more ecumenical revisionism will have to be earned.

★★★

It is time to conclude.

A key part of the modern philosophical imagination about free will and moral responsibility is the idea that the integrity of our responsibility-characteristic practices and attitudes depends on the vindication of our self-conception, on which we are free and morally responsible agents. The debate between conventional compatibilists and incompatibilists has too often started and ended with the characterization of that self-conception. The difficulty with trying to shoehorn our best philosophical theories into the constraints of our presumably contingent and culturally inherited intuitions is well illustrated by the strange combination of brilliant innovation and sterile familiarity in the philosophical literature on these issues. Too often our intuitions clash with the normative aims of our theories.

The account I have offered advocates changes to our self-conception. In particular, it calls for recognition that we are unlikely to be agents with libertarian powers, that this is a kind of loss, but that we can nevertheless justify much of what we were concerned to account for in the first place. We can be open to the idea that ordinary thinking about responsibility may well be historical in the way some insist, that it may involve libertarian-style alternative possibilities, that it require some notion of ultimacy, or even basic desert. In conceding these claims, we can still insist that an adequate theory will depart from the folk concept in ways counterintuitive but principled. Indeed, counterintuitiveness is a predictable consequence of the approach. That is, we will find the theory counterintuitive in just those instances where the theory revises away from the elements of our practices, attitudes, and beliefs that are either unjustifiable or naturalistically implausible. Of course, the point and the promise of a revisionist approach is that it captures what matters, and no more. That should be enough.

Appendix: Activity and Origination

1. Activity, origination, and freedom

The function of this Appendix is to consider a collection of issues that arise from considering ways in which free will and responsible agency might be thought to rely upon, or be interestingly integrated with a causal theory of action more generally. I start with the idea that sometimes free will is characterized as an active power.

On my account, free will can be had by possession of a capacity. One might object that this is entirely too passive to be an adequate account of free will. After all, the critic might say, we readily recognize free will as an *active* power, the sort of thing characteristic of activity and origination.

A commitment to free will as an active thing seems to be operative in the following passage by Peter van Inwagen:

The concept of a causal power or capacity would seem to be the concept of an invariable disposition to react to certain determinate changes in the environment in certain determinate ways, whereas the concept of an agent's power to act would seem not to be the concept of a power that is dispositional or reactive, but rather the concept of a power to *originate* changes in the environment.[1]

One way to think about these remarks is as an expression of the sourcehood impulse I noted earlier. Perhaps that's what van Inwagen is giving expression to in this passage. I take it that the core issue, though, is that we need some distinction between when an agent originates changes and when the agent is subject to or passive with respect to such a change. We can think of this as a concept of origination or activity.

To be sure, on some views, sourcehood and origination may come to the same thing. They need not. One might think that sourcehood can only be satisfied by an agent causal picture, for example, but still hold that there is a different notion of activity and origination that is compatible with forms of agency that do not invoke irreducible agent causation. I will bracket questions about the more demanding conception of sourcehood, and instead focus on the issues of whether, given the

---

[1] Van Inwagen, *An Essay on Free Will*, p. 11.

present account, we can account for the ordinary idea of there being a difference between agency that actively originates behavior as opposed to being passive with respect to it. (Recall: however we think about sourcehood, if it is to have any claim on our prescriptive theorizing, it cannot commit us to an essentially impossible power.)

It is reasonable to think that, *at least paradigmatically,* free will involves a power of originating activity. This does not entail that there are no cases of free will that lack the characteristic structure, however. It simply means that whatever we say about free will, if it is to correspond to this aspect of our ordinary convictions, it will need to explain how activity can be ordinarily present in instances of free will.

Next, note that the present account is not *just* appealing to the presence of a disposition. There are plausibly dispositions involved in considerations-responsiveness, to be sure. But, at least in a case of original responsibility, the burden of accounting for the active element does not rest internal to a theory of free will so much as a broader theory of agency.

So, my proposal is that we grant the originating/non-originating distinction, allow that many paradigmatic instances of free will-exercising agency will be originating, but locate the source of this distinction in the operations of self-governed agency. As I noted in chapter 7, such agency could include higher-ordered desires, identity-fixing policies that govern practical reasoning, and so on.[2] On this picture, the idea is that we account for the originating activity of agents, something above and beyond the trigger of dispositional properties, by appealing to various features of agents that are not particular to free will and moral responsibility but that arise more generally in sophisticated forms of self-directed agency.

Here is how an independently generated account of self-governance can address such questions in the context of free will. Start with Bratman's idea that his planning theory of intention constitutes "a modest theory of the will." The idea is that we can identify an agent's will with his or her intentions, and we can understand the various rational constraints on willing in terms of the rational constraints on intending. In light of such an account, one might think it would be an elegant extension of both that account and the present revisionist, prescriptive

---

[2] Accounts of what I am here characterizing as "self-governed agency" can be found in: John Bishop, *Natural Agency: An Essay on the Causal Theory of Action* (New York: Cambridge University Press, 1990); Bratman, *Structures of Agency: Essays*; Harry G. Frankfurt, *Necessity, Volition, and Love* (New York: Cambridge University Press, 1999); J. David Velleman, *Practical Reflection* (Princeton, NJ: Princeton University Press, 1989). Note that such accounts are not always centrally concerned with the phenomenology of activity, although I take it that they are intended to be compatible with such phenomenology. Rather, what is central is the thought that a plausible account of, roughly, the metaphysics of agency will have the resources for drawing a distinction between the active and the passive, that which originates from the agent and that which originates without, and so on.

account of responsibility if there were a way to bridge the notion of the will-as-an-agent's-intentions and free will-as-moral-considerations-responsiveness.

I think there is a way to do just that. It requires a bit of linguistic regimentation, but this is easy enough to provide. I have already said that one has free will when one has the capacities to recognize and respond to moral considerations in the appropriate ways. This is a picture on which one's *possessing* free will occurs only under conditions in which there are moral considerations in play. We can say that one retains that *capacity for free will* even in circumstances where no such considerations are active. This is just to say that one has a capacity for having the distinctive responsibility-relevant capacities.

Perhaps this sounds strange to you. It should not. In ordinary discourse we regularly acknowledge the capacity to have other capacities. I am capable of being proficient at sewing freehand, although I am not currently proficient in that way. You are capable of becoming able to distill bourbon, even though (I imagine) you currently lack that capacity. Our general capacity to acquire more particular capacities is expansive.

At least in ordinary language, there are relatively loose constraints on whether and when we treat the capacity to develop a capacity as constituting the possession of the latter capacity. Indeed, I am suspicious about there being more than conventional or pragmatic considerations at work here. I find it hard to see how there could be a sharp metaphysical distinction about whether, for example, I am able to buy a luxury sedan in the general "now," if it is the case that in order to buy a luxury sedan I would first need to secure a loan from the bank. If we are confident that I could secure that loan, it doesn't seem odd to me to insist that I can now buy a luxury sedan.

Of course, we could sharpen up matters with a bit of time-indexing. So: I can't *now* buy that luxury sedan, but I can now get the loan so that post-loan, in the car dealership, I will be able to buy the car. Still, it doesn't seem to get rid of the basic problem. After all, when does it become true that I can buy the car—when I walk into the dealership? When I first broach the subject with a salesperson? When I am presented with the paperwork? When I've had an opportunity to put the pen to paper? When my final signature on the documents is nearly complete?

We could try to finesse the metaphysics in various ways. I suspect we are better off thinking about matters differently. Instead, I prefer to think that the propriety of whether and how we narrow or expand the time-indexing for capacity-talk is primarily a function of our practical interests and our local conventions. That is, the interesting truths about agent-involving capacities and abilities are less a matter of carving the mind-independent world at its joints than it is of carving our practical interests at their joints. But you don't have to agree with me about all of this (except, of course, in the aforementioned, normatively structured case of the responsibility-relevant capacities!). The point here is that it is not especially unusual to talk about higher-order capacities.

Now consider the following picture of what it is to have *a capacity for one's will to be free*. We characterize this capacity in terms of the twin capacities to recognize and appropriately respond to relevant moral considerations in the given context. This capacity must be taken to include the forming of intentions to act, in its "appropriately respond" condition. One's *willing* is free—in the sense of manifesting a responsibility-centric conception of free will—when one's intentions are produced via those considerations-responsive capacities. One *acts* from free will when one's actions proceed from a will that is free in the sense just specified.

On this picture, we can further distinguish between the possession and exercise of free will. In saying that one possesses a free will, what is properly expressed is the thought that one has the occurrent capacity to recognize and respond to moral considerations. As I have already noted, this is a capacity that might, in a given situation, go unexercised. If I am sitting in my chair, dozing off, but not quite asleep, I plausibly retain a suitably robust ability to recognize and respond to a range of moral considerations in light of whatever morally salient activities are occurring in the room.

So, for example, I may be alive to the fact that one of my daughters is ravaging the puzzle that was recently assembled by her sister. In just sitting there, I am not obviously exercising my capacity to self-governance in light of various concerns about the ruthless destruction of the puzzle's arrangement by the transgressing sister. I am mostly passive to the world. Still, I retain my free will.

However, I might exercise those capacities that constitute free will. In exercising the relevant capacities and producing an intention (or intentions) that operate through or function at least partly through those responsibility-relevant capacities, I can be said to *exercise* my free will.

In chapter 3, I noted that one defeasible aspiration for an account of free will is that it capture the idea that our freedom is not mere arbitrariness, nor something that bypasses agency, but that is instead a kind of freedom where we are contributors, contributors whose input in the causal process reflects agent-level control.

We might again borrow resources from contemporary philosophy of action to give us a way to satisfy that desideratum. Consider an important challenge for contemporary accounts of agency, especially those that aim to roughly reduce agency to the functioning of various mental states. The challenge is this: why do some mental states or their arrangements, and not others, count as having "agential authority"? After all some of my mental states can be said to "speak for me" but others we regard as wayward impulses, desires we dismiss as contrary to our values, or thoughts we regard as outlaw or from which we are alienated. In trying to articulate a privileged set of structures or elements in our psychic economy, these accounts can be understood as articulating various possible structures of interest to us, but among them is the thought that some or perhaps many of these structures can count as *constituting* the agent's standpoint.

Return to the Bratmanian model. Simplifying a bit, we can say that what gives particular plan-like structures the authority to "speak for the agent" is their role in constituting the agent's identity over time.[3] In turn, these structures filter various plans of action. They support the recognition and implementation of some considerations while suppressing the recognition and implementation of others. Accordingly, self-governing policies (standing plans about what is to be given how much weight in one's deliberation) can structure what reasons there are for an agent. If there are external reasons, such policies filter what reasons the agent recognizes and/or embraces as his or her own. The involved policies and plan-like structures do this by, among other things, ruling out some considerations and treating others as reasons-giving in practical deliberation.

In such a picture, where considerations-sensitive structures are coupled with a rich account of the operations of sophisticated self-directed agency, we have a natural way to account for the thought that freedom (of the responsibility-relevant sort) is indeed partly a function *of the agent*. What difference-making our agency provides, even embedded in the ebb and flow of psychological phenomena, is to be found in the operations of those privileged features of the agent that constitute the agent's own standpoint. It will not provide a complete stopping point for the causal nexus, some point that does not extend past the agent. I've already rejected that demand for a variety of reasons (see chapter 3). What a Bratman-like picture does provide, however, is a principled reason for attributing at least some actions to the agent in a non-arbitrary way.

Where free will and origination come together, then, are in those cases where policies interact with, and indeed structure, our capacities for recognizing moral considerations and acting upon them. When those capacity-structuring policies stand in the right relationship to the agent's identity and other aspects of the agent's psychic economy, the actions that flow from intentions thus formed are both free (in the responsibility-relevant sense) and originating in the agent in a non-arbitrary sense. The grounds for the *freedom* claim derives from the role those capacities play in, among other things, supporting and licensing a system of moralized praising and blaming. The grounds for the *origination* claim derive

---

[3] See Bratman, *Structures of Agency: Essays.*

from the role those privileged elements of the psyche play in constituting the agent's identity and standpoint.

This picture gives us resources to make sense of several familiar ideas. For example, we have the resources to explain how, in some sense, we (at least sometimes) *give ourselves* a kind of freedom with agent-level control. We give that freedom to ourselves, by adopting policies that support the recognition of moral considerations and action that derives from or reflects the recognition of those considerations. Such policies can contribute to making us agents of a particular kind—responsible agents, i.e., moral considerations-responsive agents. *We* are the ones giving it to ourselves inasmuch as the doing so is grounded in identity- and standpoint-constituting features.[4]

It is in virtue of being responsible agents (agents capable of recognizing and responding to moral considerations, and capable of embedding such concern in a privileged network of identity-constituing plans and policies) that larger social networks of practices and judgments interlock with the agent-level control-constituting aspects of responsibility. That is, (partly) in virtue of instituting policies of appropriately responding to moral considerations we come to be moral considerations-responsive agents. Structure of agency and structures of norm-governed social practices are mutually supporting.

2. Willpower

Recently, Richard Holton has drawn on work in experimental psychology to argue that a plausible picture of agency will need to include the notion of will-power.[5] As he understands it, willpower is a faculty, a power distinct from various mental states such as desires, beliefs, and intentions. It can be strengthened through exercise, and its strength plays an important role in successful self-regulation. Its principal significance for Holton is that it contributes to efficacy of resolutions, or intentions to X that are accompanied by the intention not to be deflected from doing X.

These ideas can give some texture to the present account. Someone might act of their own free will—intending to X, and choosing so on the basis of the operation of responsibility-relevant capacities. The stability of the agent's intention to X—his or her strength of will, in Holton's terms—depends on a number of things,

---

[4] It is also something we give to ourselves in another sense. Our control involves capacities we indirectly foster and develop in light of our participation in and perpetuation of the responsibility system.

[5] Richard Holton, *Willing, Wanting, Waiting* (Oxford: Clarendon Press, 2009): 125–35.

including whether the action is habitual and whether it is implemented and sustained in the context of temptations to not X. In these latter cases, an agent's willpower will plausibly have some role to play in whether the agent can carry through on his or her will to X.

This suggests that willpower ordinarily has a special significance for freely willed action. An agent might form an intention to X in a moral considerations-responsive fashion. However, if that agent is subject to constant temptation, or finds him- or herself deficient in willpower, that agent is less likely to retain the capacity for self-governance in light of moral considerations. Of course, where that threshold is set may vary across contexts and classes of considerations. And, the presence of the capacity does not guarantee its exercise. However, other things equal, greater willpower provides greater capacity for self-governance precisely by amplifying the capacity to sustain those intentions formed in response to the content of moral considerations.

One upshot of this picture is that there may be irresolute agents who nevertheless retain freedom of the will across vacillations of resolutions. Consider an agent who is terrible about resisting temptation, but only in circumstances where there are moral considerations that favor alternate but distinct courses of action. Perhaps some cases of vacillation between competing courses of actions favoring incommensurable moral goods are like this. If so, the agent may act from free will in one way, and then act from free will in the contrary instance of intending.

Recall the example from Sartre of a son that is deciding between caring for his sick mother and joining the Resistance. This son might act from free will in first deciding to join the Resistance and acting accordingly (for example, packing up, saying his goodbyes, apologizing to his mother, and so on). However, after walking out the front door, should the son decide (let us suppose) to overturn the involved resolution (recall: both the intention to join the Resistance and the intention to not reconsider that intention), this new course of action could be freely willed. All that is required is that the new will be formed in a fashion responsive to the relevant moral considerations in that context, and that the agent has the relevant capacity to self-govern in light of that intention. Is this possible?

I think so. What is crucial is that the agent be sufficiently capable of self-governance in light of either course of action, without that standard of self-governance being so high as to rule out failures of self-governance. We've already seen that the self-governance condition plausibly allows that one may be capable of self-governance in light of a consideration without one actually exercising that capacity. All that the present case requires is that the agent is capable of self-guidance on either option. And, at least prima facie, I don't see any reason to think this cannot happen, even if in fact the agent vacillates back and forth.

The example may be made more plausible if we assume that the relevant psychological trigger for revising the resolution is relatively specific. Suppose the son will not revise the resolution to join the Resistance so long as when he walks out the door, his mother does not begin to wail. Quiet sobbing won't do the trick—it must be full-blown wailing. And, suppose too that were the son to resolve to stay with mom, the only condition under which he would revisit that temptation is if in the first ten minutes of doing so he hears gunfire.[6] In such a case it seems to me that both as a matter of our current intuitions and the regimentation provided by the present account, we can conclude that the agent possesses the capacity for self-governance in either direction, regardless of whether he happens to be in a world where the relevant triggers are present or not.

So, I think we should allow that it is possible for an agent to vacillate between distinct wills and to be free and responsible in so acting under each then-controlling intention.

In allowing for this possibility, I do not think we need to take a stand on the difficult issue of the conditions under which it is *rational* to revise an intention. For present purposes, it is enough to allow that one might form a future-directed intention, and form it in a moral considerations-responsive way. Such an intention would constitute a free will, so long as it was action guiding. Were the agent to abandon that intention and form a new intention, the new intention would also be free, so long as it was produced in the right way, and appropriately governed action. So, an agent might irrationally abandon a will to X that is free, but settle on a new will to X that is free, and that doing so might itself be free. That production of a replacement intention is responsive to moral considerations does not guarantee that revision of the original intention was not irrational, or even, that the new will itself is not irrational with respect to non-moral considerations.

In sum, whether willpower-dependent deficits of self-governance render an agent non-responsible depends on the effect of the deficit on the agent and the precise standard for self-governance for agents in that type of circumstance. Nevertheless, the basic picture here is one on which the various properties can, at least in principle, operate independently of one another. So, an agent might will freely but might also have a relatively low-powered will. This might occur when an agent's moral-considerations-responsively formed will governs, and succeeds in doing so

---

[6] If you like, you can even imagine that nothing about the bare fact of the agent reconsidering in those circumstances guarantees that the reconsideration will result in the alternate resolution. This can be imagined to occur in any of a variety of ways. We could suppose that the process is indeterministic in the agent, but we need not. It might be that the timing of the triggering event matters for the outcome of reconsideration, and that might be a fully deterministic matter. Here, my account's moderately coarse-grained way of individuating circumstances permits us to treat such variation as variation in the same set of circumstances, even though a finer-grained way of individuating circumstances would preclude it.

despite low willpower because of the absence of relevant temptations. In other cases, an agent might lack free will in some context (e.g., in non-moral circumstances, or in cases of coercion) but be possessed of considerable reserves of willpower (but, perhaps, willpower insufficient to resist the coercion). Alternately, an agent might have both considerable willpower and have free will, but simply not will (as in the case of indecision about what to do). This diversity of arrangements between the will, free will, and willpower seems consonant with the complexity of agency as we find it and experience it in the world.

These thoughts point to some reasons why *efforts of will*, or exercises of willpower, have a special significance for responsibility. First, the exercise of willpower can make self-governance effective when it would not otherwise be. Second, even when the exercise of willpower is not effective, if willpower can be strengthened through exercise, whether it was exercised or not is significant for the development of moral considerations-responsive agency. In light of this, judgments of blameworthiness (recall: assessments of quality of will) have reason to be sensitive to both aspects of willpower's significance. Mitigation follows from earnest but failing efforts to bring willpower to bear, whereas failures to bring willpower to bear usually intensify blame. The systemic effects of judgments and practices that are responsive to these willpower-assessing norms plausibly contribute to the ends of the responsibility system.

3. Activity and passivity

Let us return to the issue that motivated these reflections: origination and activity in the exercise of free will. As I noted at the outset, the present approach deflects questions of origination and action-initiation about free will to accounts of self-directed agency and their pictures of action attribution and action initiation. In this section, I aim to pull together several of the threads developed in the preceding discussion.

The present prescriptive, responsibility-centric conception of free will cross-cuts the active/passive distinction. Responsiveness to moral considerations might sometimes work through an active self and other times not. An agent might be active in making a decision—and that decision might reflect a suitable ability to recognize and respond to reasons—or she might not.[7] In a given instance, then, action

---

[7] Richard Holton has argued that choice is an act that can occur in the absence of a judgment about the quality of the options. See his Richard Holton, "The Act of Choice," *Philosopher's Imprint* 6, no. 3 (2006): 1–15.

flowing from moral considerations-sensitive capacities might not operate through whatever features of agency prove to be origination-producing.

I have already implicitly pointed to one way in which conditions of origination separate from free will: origination is to be given by an independent account of agency whereas free will is given by the considerations-responsive mechanisms identified by this account. Free will satisfies conditions of origination only when both conditions are simultaneously satisfied. There is some reason to think that this will happen in mature forms of agency whenever agents settle on policies to treat particular moral considerations as action-determining.

Let's return to the question of activity, however. In the case where an agent is active with respect to some choice, perhaps launching some effort of will to consider what considerations are alive in the circumstances of practical reasoning (or perhaps struggling to bring one's intentions in line with the relevant considerations), we have reason to hope that the relevant capacities to recognize and respond to moral considerations are "alive" or present in the agent. But it is not a matter of necessity that such capacities are live.

For example, one's active, conscious deliberations might be in the grip of an ideology or self-conception that filters reasons worse than they would have been if one's mechanisms for judgment-making were never engaged. In other cases, one might (perhaps through habituation or native endowment) recognize and respond to moral considerations in ways that seem to bypass any engagement of active, conscious agency. So, I think it is not only possible but also sometimes desirable to think of the control-constituting capacities of responsibility as not always involving the activity of conscious deliberative agency.

We might then wonder whether there is any role whatsoever for the active exercise of specifically conscious agency. The role of consciousness in general is a notoriously difficult thing to pin down, but at least here there is a plausible enough role for it, supposing conscious agency is causally efficacious. Suppose that we accept that some of our reasons-detecting processes are conscious and others are not, and that some move from conscious to unconscious (or in the opposite direction) through sufficient attention or practice. The outputs of these varied mechanisms will sometimes converge, and other times conflict. Conscious activity might have some role to play as manager or arbiter of these conflicts, and as a monitoring system for when psychic conflict is pending or occurring.

That's the general picture. However, let's start with the thought that much of the time it is obvious what the agent should do, and what counts as a satisfactory way of doing it. Amongst adults it may frequently be the case that conscious deliberation only injects itself into the psychological tide when there is a special reason to do so. Such economy of intervention reflects different features of conscious mental processes. Conscious deliberation is slow and demanding of neurochemical resources. Like all mechanisms, it is capable of error. Even so, to the extent to which it effectively resolves conflicts and sets in motion constraints on deliberation and action through planning and related mechanisms of psychological disciplining, it has an important role to play.

Plausible as it may be, this picture has been attacked by skeptics about the causal efficacy of conscious exercises of will-setting. *Willusionists*—Eddy Nahmias' helpful term for those who reject that conscious, deliberative willing is in any way effective in the causal production of action—deny that our conscious, deliberative self can play any such active role.[8] I think there are compelling reasons to reject willusionism on both conceptual and empirical grounds, so I am not much concerned.[9]

Even if we allow that willusionism is an open possibility, it seems to be an unduly narrow conception of the role of conscious, active agency that it *only* adjudicate between occurrent or pending psychic conflicts. Minimally, our conscious ability to form plan-like intentions functions as a way of extending our conscious, reasoning agency into the future. It does so by committing ourselves to one course of action rather than another in the chronological downstream.[10]

I am agnostic about what it would mean if it could somehow be shown that consciousness has no role to play in the setting of plans. Here, however, I will suppose that consciousness is implicated in at least the settling on courses of action, the forming of policies, the filtering of considerations, and in tapping the resources of willpower. If that is right, then we have a plausible role for conscious, active agency.

First, agential activity grounded in conscious monitoring of one's actions and reasons provides a degree of control in light of considerations one endorses, even if those considerations do not have a strong grip on one's non-conscious dispositions. After all, left to non-conscious processes, I might not self-govern in light of otherwise motivationally weak commitments. So consciousness may provide re-inforcement by explicitly settling courses of action and by triggering exertions of resolution-armoring willpower. Second, active exercise of conscious willing can resolve conflicts in ways that track commitments that I espouse, even when such commitments wouldn't govern if I were not attending to them.

So, if we accept that free will can operate in conditions where agents are both active and passive, we can still leave room for the thought that there may be special work for conscious mental life. Our conscious selves may sometimes turn the

---

[8] The best-known proponent of this view is Wegner, *The Illusion of Conscious Will.*

[9] Alfred R. Mele, *Effective Intentions: The Power of the Conscious Will* (New York: Oxford University Press, 2009).

[10] This is a point Mele also emphasizes in *Effective Intentions: The Power of the Conscious Will.*

psychic tide, by consciously rejecting what we would unreflectively do, if left to our own devices. And such tide-turning is plausibly a function of the faculty of willpower. However, conscious deliberation also has forward-looking virtues, setting up plans or weighing values that structure downstream operation. So, we can hold that the operation of free will may cross-cut the activity/passivity distinction in agency, but in doing so it does not entail that there is no benefit to be had from the engagement of agency in its active, conscious, deliberative mode.

In sum, one might exercise one's free will in a way that provides for a variety of origination; however, one's blameworthiness may sometimes fail to track that sense of origination. And, one might exercise free will and be either active with respect to that exercise (when one settles on a course of action) or passive to it (when, in acting, one merely continues to adhere to a policy of, say, disregarding avaricious impulses). What intuitions there are that free will requires origination and active, conscious agency are only partly preserved on the present prescriptive account. Still, there is some place for these thoughts, for origination and activity will frequently be important elements in the constitution of self-governance, and thus, in the constitution of free will. So, origination and activity are, in the ordinary course of things, plausibly important for and frequently compresent with free will. For all that, they are not essential to it.

Bibliography

Adams, Robert Merrihew. "Motive Utilitarianism." *Journal of Philosophy* 73 (1976): 467–81.

Appiah, Kwame Anthony. *Cosmopolitanism: Ethics in a World of Strangers.* New York: W. W. Norton, 2007.

Arneson, Richard J. "The Smart Theory of Moral Responsibility and Desert." In *Desert and Justice,* edited by Serena Olsaretti, 233–58. Oxford: Oxford University Press, 2003.

Aronson, Joshua, Lustina, Michael J., Good, Catherine, Keough, Kelli, Steele, Claude M., and Brown, Joseph. "When White Men Can't Do Math: Necessary and Sufficient Factors in Stereotype Threat." *Journal of Experimental Social Psychology* 35 (1999): 29–46.

Arpaly, Nomy. *Unprincipled Virtue: An Inquiry into Moral Agency.* New York: Oxford University Press, 2003.

Bargh, John A. "Free Will is Un-Natural." In *Are We Free? Psychology and Free Will,* edited by John Baer, James C. Kaufman, and Roy F. Baumeister, 128–54. New York: Oxford University Press, 2008.

Bennett, Christopher. "The Varieties of Retributive Experience." *Philosophical Quarterly* 52, no. 207 (2002): 145–63.

Bennett, Jonathan. "Accountability." In *Philosophical Subjects: Essays Presented to P. F. Strawson,* edited by Zak Van Straaten, 14–47. Oxford: Clarendon Press, 1980.

Bishop, John. *Natural Agency: An Essay on the Causal Theory of Action.* New York: Cambridge University Press, 1990.

Bobzien, Susanne. "The Inadvertent Conception and Late Birth of the Free-Will Problem." *Phronesis* 43 (1988): 132–75.

Borges, Jorge Luis. *Collected Fictions.* New York: Penguin, 1998.

Brandt, Richard B. *A Theory of the Good and the Right.* Oxford: Clarendon Press, 1979.

Bratman, Michael E. "Identification, Decision, and Treating as a Reason." *Philosophical Topics* 24, no. 2 (1996): 1–18.

Bratman, Michael E. "Identification, Decision, and Treating as a Reason." In *Faces of Intention: Selected Essays on Intention and Agency,* 185–206. Cambridge: Cambridge University Press, 1999.

Bratman, Michael. "Fischer and Ravizza on Moral Responsibility and History." *Philosophy and Phenomenological Research* 61, no. 2 (2000): 453–58.

Bratman, Michael E. "Autonomy and Hierarchy." *Social Philosophy and Policy* 20, no. 2 (2003): 156–76.

Bratman, Michael E. *Structures of Agency: Essays.* New York: Oxford University Press, 2007.

Bratman, Michael. "Agency, Time, and Sociality." *Proceedings and Addresses of the American Philosophical Association* 84, no. 2 (2010): 7–26.

Campbell, C. A. "Is 'Free Will' a Pseudo-Problem?" *Mind* 60, no. 240 (1951): 441–65.

Carlsmith, Kevin M., Darley, John, and Robinson, Paul H. "Why Do We Punish? Deterrence and Just Deserts as Motives for Punishment." *Journal of Personality and Social Psychology* 83, no. 2 (2002): 284–99.

Catechism of the Catholic Church (2nd edn.) New York: Doubleday, 1997.

Clarke, Randolph. "Toward a Credible Agent-Causal Account of Free Will." *Nous* 27 (1993): 191–203.

Clarke, Randolph. 2009. Incompatibilist (Nondeterministic) Theories of Free Will <http://plato.stanford.edu/entries/incompatibilism-theories>, accessed July 19, 2010.

Clarke, Randolph. "Dispositions, Abilities to Act, and Free Will: The New Dispositionalism." *Mind* 118, no. 470 (2009): 323–51.

Collins, Randall. *Sociology of Philosophies.* Cambridge, MA: Belknap, 1998.

Copp, David. *Morality, Normativity, and Society.* New York: Oxford University Press, 1995.

Daniels, Norman. 2011. "Reflective Equilibrium." *Stanford Encyclopedia of Philosophy* (Spring edn.) <http://plato.stanford.edu/archives/spr2011/entries/reflective-equilibrium/>, accessed January 23, 2012.

Daw, Russell and Alter, Torin. "Free Acts and Robot Cats." *Philosophical Studies* 102, no. 3 (2001): 345–57.

de Beauvoir, Simone. *The Second Sex.* Translated by Constance Borde and Sheila Malovany-Chevallier. New York: Alfred A. Knopf, 2010.

Dennett, Daniel. *Elbow Room.* Cambridge, MA: MIT Press, 1984.

Dennett, Daniel. *Freedom Evolves.* New York: Viking, 2003.

DePaul, Michael R. "Why Bother With Reflective Equilibrium?" In *Rethinking Intuition: The Psychology of Intuition and Its Role in Philosophical Inquiry*, edited by Michael R. DePaul and William Ramsey, 293–309. Lanham, MD: Rowman & Littlefield, 1998.

DePaul, Michael R. and Ramsey, William, eds, *Rethinking Intuition: The Psychology of Intuition and Its Role in Philosophical Inquiry.* Lanham, MD: Rowman & Littlefield, 1998.

Doris, John. *Lack of Character: Personality and Moral Behavior.* New York: Cambridge University Press, 2002.

Doris, John. *Talking to Ourselves: Reflection, Skepticism, and Agency*. New York: Oxford University Press, forthcoming.

Doris, John, Knobe, Joshua, and Woolfolk, Robert L. "Variantism About Moral Responsibility." *Philosophical Perspectives* 21, no. 1 (2007): 183–21.

Doris, John and Murphy, Dominic. "From My Lai to Abu Ghraib: The Moral Psychology of Atrocity." *Midwest Studies in Philosophy* 31 (2007): 25–55.

Doris, John and Stich, Stephen. "As a Matter of Fact: Empirical Perspectives on Ethics." In *The Oxford Handbook of Contemporary Philosophy*, edited by Frank Jackson and Michael Smith, 114–52. Oxford: Oxford University Press, 2005.

Double, Richard. *The Non-Reality of Free Will*. New York: Oxford University Press, 1991.

Double, Richard. *Metaphilosophy and Free Will*. New York: Oxford University Press, 1996.

Dweck, Carol S. and Molden, Daniel C. "Self-Theories: The Construction of Free Will." In *Are We Free? Psychology and Free Will*, edited by John Baer, James C. Kaufman, and Roy F. Baumeister, 44–64. New York: Oxford University Press, 2008.

Dworkin, Gerald. "Review of *Elbow Room*." *Ethics* 96, no. 2 (1986): 423–25.

Dworkin, Gerald. *The Theory and Practice of Autonomy*. New York: Cambridge University Press, 1988.

Ekstrom, Laura Waddell. *Free Will: A Philosophical Study*. Boulder, CO: Westview Press, 2000.

Ekstrom, Laura. "Free Will, Chance, and Mystery." *Philosophical Studies* 113, no. 2 (2003): 153–80.

Feltz, Adam, Cokely, Edward T., and Nadelhoffer, Thomas. "Natural Compatibilism Versus Natural Incompatibilism: Back to the Drawing Board." *Mind and Language* 24, no. 1 (2009): 1–23.

Fischer, John Martin. "Recent Work on Moral Responsibility." *Ethics* 110, no. 1 (1999): 93–139.

Fischer, John Martin. "Chicken Soup for the Semi-Compatibilist Soul: Reply to Haji and Kane." *Journal of Ethics* 4, no. 4 (2000): 404–7.

Fischer, John Martin. "Précis of *Responsibility and Control: A Theory of Moral Responsibility*," *Philosophy and Phenomenological Research* 61, no. 2 (2000): 441–6.

Fischer, John Martin. "Replies." *Philosophy and Phenomenological Research* 61, no. 2 (2000): 467–80.

Fischer, John Martin. *My Way: Essays on Moral Responsibility*. New York: Oxford University Press, 2006.

Fischer, John Martin and Ravizza, Mark. "Responsibility and History." In *Midwest Studies in Philosophy*, edited by Peter A. French, Theodore E. Uehling, and

Howard K. Wettstein, 430–51. Notre Dame: Notre Dame University Press, 1994.

Fischer, John Martin and Ravizza, Mark. *Responsibility and Control: A Theory of Moral Responsibility.* New York: Cambridge University Press, 1998.

Fischer, John Martin and Tognazinni, Neal. "The Truth About Tracing." *Nous* 43, no. 3 (2009): 531–56.

Fischer, John Martin and Tognazinni, Neal. "The Physiognomy of Responsibility." *Philosophy and Phenomenological Research* 82, no. 2 (2011): 381–417.

Fischer, John Martin, Kane, Robert, Pereboom, Derk, and Vargas, Manuel. *Four Views on Free Will.* Malden, MA: Blackwell, 2007.

Frankfurt, Harry. "Freedom of the Will and the Concept of a Person." *Journal of Philosophy* 68, no. 1 (1971): 5–20.

Frankfurt, Harry G. *The Importance of What We Care About: Philosophical Essays.* Cambridge: Cambridge University Press, 1988.

Frankfurt, Harry G. *Necessity, Volition, and Love.* New York: Cambridge University Press, 1999.

Franklin, Chris. "The Problem of Enhanced Control." *Australasian Journal of Philosophy* 89, no. 4 (2011): 687–706.

Freud, Sigmund. *Civilization and Its Discontents.* New York: Norton, 1989.

Gatchel, Robert J., Peng, Yuan Bo, Peters, Madelon L., Fuchs, Perry N., and Turk, Dennis C. "The Biopsychosocial Approach to Chronic Pain: Scientific Advances and Future Directions." *Psychological Bulletin* 133, no. 4 (2007): 581–624.

Ginet, Carl. "Might We Have No Choice?" In *Freedom and Determinism*, edited by Keith Lehrer, 87–104. New York: Random House, 1966.

Ginet, Carl. *On Action.* Cambridge: Cambridge University Press, 1990.

Ginet, Carl. "In Defense of the Principle of Alternative Possibilities." *Philosophical Perspectives* 10 (1996): 403–17.

Ginet, Carl. "The Epistemic Requirements for Moral Responsibility." In *Philosophical Perspectives 14: Action and Freedom, 2000*, edited by James Tomberlin, 267–77. Malden, MA: Blackwell, 2000.

Hacking, Ian. *Rewriting the Soul: Multiple Personality and the Sciences of Memory.* Princeton, NJ: Princeton University Press, 1995.

Haslanger, Sally. "Changing the Ideology and Culture of Philosophy: Not By Reason (Alone)." *Hypatia* 23, no. 2 (2008): 210–23.

Heller, Mark. "The Mad Scientist Meets the Robot Cats: Compatibilism, Kinds, and Counterexamples." *Philosophy and Phenomenological Research* 56 (1996): 333–7.

Henrich, Joseph, Heine, Steven J., and Norenzayan, Ara. "The Weirdest People in the World?" *Behavioral and Brain Sciences* 32, nos 2–3 (2010): 1–23.

Holton, Richard. "The Act of Choice." *Philosopher's Imprint* 6, no. 3 (2006): 1–15.

Holton, Richard. "Determinism, Self-Efficacy, and the Phenomenology of Free Will." *Inquiry* 52 (2009): 412–28.

Holton, Richard. *Willing, Wanting, Waiting*. Oxford: Clarendon Press, 2009.

Honderich, Ted. *A Theory of Determinism*. New York: Oxford University Press, 1988.

Honderich, Ted. "After Compatibilism and Incompatibilism." In *Freedom and Determinism*, edited by Joseph Keim Campbell, Michael O'Rourke, and David Shier, 305–22. Cambridge MA: MIT Press, 2004.

Hooker, Brad. *Ideal Code, Real World: A Rule-Consequentialist Theory of Morality*. New York: Oxford University Press, 2000.

Hume, David. *A Treatise of Human Nature*. Translated by L. A. Selby-Bigge, and P. H. Nidditch (2nd edn.) New York: Oxford University Press, 1978.

Hurley, S. L. *Justice, Luck, and Knowledge*. Cambridge, MA: Harvard University Press, 2003.

Hurley, Susan. "Is Responsibility Essentially Impossible?" *Philosophical Studies* 99 (2000): 229–68.

Huxley, Aldous. *Brave New World*. New York: Perennial, 1942.

Jackson, Frank and Pettit, Philip. "Moral Functionalism and Moral Motivation." *Philosophical Quarterly* 45, no. 178 (1995): 20–40.

Jones, Karen. "Emotion, Weakness of Will, and the Normative Conception of Agency." *Supplement to Philosophy* 52 (2003): 181–200.

Kane, Robert. *Free Will and Values*. Albany: SUNY Press, 1985.

Kane, Robert. *The Significance of Free Will*. Oxford: Oxford University Press, 1996.

Kane, Robert. "Non-Constraining Control and the Threat of Social Conditioning." *Journal of Ethics* 4, no. 4 (2000): 357–60.

Kane, Robert. *A Contemporary Introduction to Free Will*. New York: Oxford University Press, 2005.

Kane, Robert. "Review of *Libertarian Accounts of Free Will*." *Mind* 115 (2006): 136–42.

Kennett, Jeanette. "Autism, Empathy and Moral Agency." *Philosophical Quarterly* 52, no. 208 (2002): 340–57.

Kiehl, Kent A. and Buckholtz, Joshua W. "Inside the Mind of a Psychopath." *Scientific American Mind* (Sept./Oct. 2010): 22–9.

King, Matt. "The Structure of Responsibility." Ph.D. Dissertation, University of Maryland, 2008.

Knobe, Joshua and Leiter, Brian. "The Case for Nietzschean Moral Psychology." In *Nietzsche and Morality*, edited by Brian Leiter and Neil Sinhababu, 83–109. New York: Oxford University Press, 2007.

Levy, Neil. "Review of *Four Views on Free Will*." *Metapsychology Online Reviews* 11.40 (2007) <http://metapsychology.mentalhelp.net/poc/view_doc.php?type=book&id=3851&cn=394>.

Levy, Neil. *Hard Luck: How Luck Undermines Freedom.* New York: Oxford University Press, 2011.

Lewis, David. "How to Define Theoretical Terms." In *Philosophical Papers*, 78–95. New York: Oxford University Press, 1983.

Lowry, Malcolm. *Under the Volcano.* New York: Harper Perennial, 2007.

McGeer, Victoria. "Varieties of Moral Agency: Lessons From Autism (and Psychopathy)." In *Moral Psychology, Volume 3: The Neuroscience of Morality: Emotions, Brain Disorders, and Development*, edited by Walter Sinnott-Armstrong, 227–58. Cambridge, MA: MIT Press, 2008.

McGinn, Colin. *Problems in Philosophy: The Limits of Inquiry.* Cambridge, MA: Blackwell, 1993.

Machery, E., Mallon, R., Nichols, Shaun, and Stich, Stephen. "Semantics, Cross-Cultural Style." *Cognition* 92 (2004): B1–B12.

McKenna, Michael. "Source Incompatibilism, Ultimacy, and the Transfer of Non-Responsibility." *American Philosophical Quarterly* 38, no. 1 (2001): 37–51.

McKenna, Michael. "Robustness, Control, and the Demand for Morally Significant Alternatives." In *Moral Responsibility and Alternative Possibilities*, edited by David Widerker and Michael McKenna, 201–17. Burlington, VT: Ashgate, 2003.

McKenna, Michael. "Compatibilism and Desert: Critical Comments on Four Views on Free Will." *Philosophical Studies* 144 (2009): 3–13.

McLeod, Owen. "Desert." In *The Stanford Encyclopedia of Philosophy* (Spring 2009 edn.), edited by Edward Zalta <https://leibniz.stanford.edu/friends/members/view/desert/>.

Mallon, Ron. "A Field Guide to Social Construction." *Philosophy Compass* 2, no. 1 (2007): 93–108.

Mallon, Ron. "Making Up Your Mind and Explaining Yourself." Unpublished manuscript: In progress.

Mason, Elinor. "Recent Work on Moral Responsibility." *Philosophical Books* 46, no. 4 (2005): 343–53.

Mele, Alfred. *Autonomous Agents: From Self-Control to Autonomy.* New York: Oxford University Press, 1995.

Mele, Alfred. *Free Will and Luck.* New York: Oxford University Press, 2006.

Mele, Alfred R. *Effective Intentions: The Power of the Conscious Will.* New York: Oxford University Press, 2009.

Mele, Alfred. "Moral Responsibility and History Revisited." *Ethical Theory and Moral Practice* 12, no. 5 (2009): 463–75.

Merritt, Maria, Doris, John, and Harman, Gilbert. "Character." In *The Moral Psychology Handbook*, edited by John Doris, 355–401. New York: Oxford University Press, 2010.

Miller, DeMond, Gill, D. A., and Picou, J. Steven. "Assigning Blame: The Interpretation of Social Narratives and Environmental Disasters." *Southeastern Sociological Review* 1 (2000): 13–31.

Moll, Jorge, Zahn, Roland, de Olliveira-Souza, R., Krueger, Frank, and Grafman, Jordan. "The Neural Basis of Human Moral Cognition." *Nature Reviews Neuroscience* 6 (2005): 799–809.

Montague, P. Read. "Free Will." *Current Biology* 18, no. 14 (2008): R584–R585.

Montero, Barbara. "Post-Physicalism." *Journal of Consciousness Studies* 8, no. 2 (2001): 61–80.

Nahmias, Eddy. "Folk Fears About Freedom and Responsibility: Determinism and Reductionism." *Journal of Culture and Cognition* 6, nos 1–2 (2006): 215–38.

Nahmias, Eddy. "Autonomous Agency and Social Psychology." In *Cartographies of the Mind: Philosophy and Psychology in Intersection*, edited by Massimo Marraffa, Mario De Caro, and Francesco Ferretti, 169–85. Berlin: Springer, 2007.

Nahmias, Eddy. "Intuitions About Free Will, Determinism, and Bypassing." In *The Oxford Handbook of Free Will* (2nd edn.), edited by Robert Kane, 55–576. New York: Oxford University Press, 2011.

Nahmias, Eddy, Morris, Stephen, Nadelhoffer, Thomas, and Turner, Jason. "Is Incompatibilism Intuitive?" *Philosophy and Phenomenological Research* 73, no. 1 (2006): 28–53.

Nahmias, Eddy, Coates, D. Justin, and Kvaran, Trevor. "Free Will, Moral Responsibility, and Mechanism: Experiments on Folk Intuitions." *Midwest Studies in Philosophy* XXXI (2007): 214–41.

Nelkin, Dana. "Freedom, Responsibility, and the Challenge of Situationism." *Midwest Studies in Philosophy* 29, no. 1 (2005): 181–206.

Nelkin, Dana. "Do We Have a Coherent Set of Intuitions About Moral Responsibility?" *Midwest Studies in Philosophy* 31 (2007): 243–59.

Nelkin, Dana. "Responsibility and Rational Abilities: Defending an Asymmetrical View." *Pacific Philosophical Quarterly* 89 (2008): 497–515.

Newman, Philip L. "'Wild Man' Behavior in a New Guinea Highlands Community." *American Anthropologist* 66, no. 1 (1964): 1–19.

Nichols, Shaun. *Sentimental Rules: On the Natural Foundations of Moral Judgment.* Oxford: Oxford University Press, 2004.

Nichols, Shaun. "Folk Intuitions on Free Will." *Journal of Cognition and Culture* 6, nos 1 & 2 (2006): 57–86.

Nichols, Shaun. "After Incompatibilism: A Naturalistic Defense of the Reactive Attitudes." *Philosophical Perspectives* 21 (2007): 405–28.

Nichols, Shaun. "Why Do We Believe in Free Will?" Unpublished manuscript (forthcoming).

Nichols, Shaun and Knobe, Joshua. "Moral Responsibility and Determinism: The Cognitive Science of Folk Intuitions." *Nous* 41, no. 4 (2007): 663–85.

Nichols, Shaun and Knobe, Joshua. "Free Will and the Bounds of the Self." In *The Oxford Handbook of Free Will* (2nd edn.), edited by Robert Kane, 530–54. New York: Oxford University Press, 2011.

Nietzsche, Friedrich Wilhelm. *On the Genealogy of Morality*. Translated by Maudemarie Clark and Alan Swenson. Indianapolis, IN: Hackett Publishing, 1996.

Nisbett, Richard E. *The Geography of Thought: How Asians and Westerners Think Differently—And Why*. New York: Free Press, 2003.

Nozick, Robert. *Philosophical Explanations*. Oxford: Clarendon Press, 1981.

O'Connor, Timothy. *Persons and Causes*. New York: Oxford University Press, 2000.

Olsaretti, Serena. "Introduction: Debating Desert and Justice." In *Desert and Justice*, 1–24. Oxford: Oxford University Press, 2003.

Ortega y Gasset, José. *Meditations on Quixote* (1st American edn.) New York: Norton, 1961.

Pereboom, Derk. *Living Without Free Will*. Cambridge: Cambridge University Press, 2001.

Pereboom, Derk. "Defending Hard Incompatibilism." *Midwest Studies in Philosophy* 29, no. 1 (2005): 228–47.

Pereboom, Derk. "Kant on Transcendental Freedom." *Philosophy and Phenomenological Research* 73, no. 3 (2006): 537–67.

Pereboom, Derk. "Hard Incompatibilism and Its Rivals." *Philosophical Studies* 144 (2009): 21–33.

Perry, John. "Wretched Subterfuge: A Defense of the Compatibilism of Freedom and Natural Causation." *Proceedings and Addresses of the American Philosophical Association* 84, no. 2 (2010): 93–113.

Picou, J. Steven. "When the Solution Becomes the Problem: The Impacts of Adversarial Litigation on Survivors of the *Exxon Valdez* Oil Spill." *University of St. Thomas Law Journal* 7, no. 1 (2009): 68–88.

Pockett, Susan. "The Concept of Free Will: Philosophy Neuroscience, and the Law." *Behavioral Sciences and the Law* 25 (2007): 281–93.

Rose, Julie. 2010. "Weathering Emotional Storms Over Gulf Oil Spill." <http://www.npr.org/templates/story/story.php?storyId=128334355>, accessed July 19, 2010.

Roskies, Adina. "Neuroscientific Challenges to Free Will and Responsibility." *Trends in Cognitive Science* 10, no. 9 (2006): 419–23.

Roskies, Adina. "How Does Neuroscience Affect Our Conception of Volition?" *Annual Review of Neuroscience* 33 (2010): 109–30.

Roskies, Adina and Nichols, Shaun. "Bringing Responsibility Down to Earth." *Journal of Philosophy* 105, no. 7 (2008): 371–88.

Sacks, Oliver W. *The Man Who Mistook His Wife for a Hat and Other Clinical Tales.* New York: Summit Books, 1985.

Sarkissian, Hagop, Chatterjee, Amita, De Brigard, Felipe, Knobe, Joshua, Nichols, Shaun, and Sirker, Smita. "Is Belief in Free Will a Cultural Universal?" *Mind and Language* 25, no. 3 (2010): 346–58.

Scanlon, T. M. "The Significance of Choice." In *The Tanner Lectures on Human Values*, edited by Sterling M. McMurrin, 150–216. Cambridge: Cambridge University Press, 1988.

Scanlon, T. M. *What We Owe to Each Other.* Cambridge, MA: Belknap Press of Harvard University Press, 1998.

Scanlon, Thomas. *Moral Dimensions: Permissibility, Meaning, Blame.* Cambridge, MA: Belknap Press of Harvard University Press, 2008.

Scheffler, Samuel. "Responsibility, Reactive Attitudes, and Liberalism in Philosophy and Politics." *Philosophy & Public Affairs* 21, no. 4 (1992): 299–324.

Schlick, Moritz. *The Problems of Ethics.* Translated by D. Rynin. New York: Prentice Hall, 1939.

Schmidtz, David. "How to Deserve." *Political Theory* 30, no. 6 (2002): 774–99.

Schroeder, Timothy. "Moral Responsibility and Tourette Syndrome." *Philosophy and Phenomenological Research* 71, no. 1 (2005): 106–23.

Sher, George. *Who Knew? Responsibility Without Awareness.* New York: Oxford University Press, 2009.

Sidgwick, Henry. *The Methods of Ethics* (7th edn.) Indianapolis, IN: Hackett, 1981.

Skinner, B. F. *Walden Two.* New York: Macmillan, 1948.

Slote, Michael. "Ethics Without Free Will." *Social Theory and Practice* 16, no. 3 (1990): 369–83.

Smart, J. J. C. "Free Will, Praise, and Blame." *Mind* 70 (1961): 291–306.

Smilansky, Saul. *Free Will and Illusion.* New York: Clarendon Press, 2000.

Smith, Angela. "Responsibility for Attitudes: Activity and Passivity in Mental Life." *Ethics* 115 (2005): 236–71.

Smith, Angela. "Control, Responsibility, and Moral Assessment." *Philosophical Studies* 138 (2008): 367–92.

Sommers, Tamler. *Relative Justice.* Princeton, NJ: Princeton University Press, 2011.

Sorabji, Richard. "The Concept of the Will From Plato to Maximus the Confessor." In *The Will*, edited by Thomas Pink and Martin Stone, 6–28. London: Routledge, 2003.

Speak, Daniel. "Towards an Axiological Defense of Libertarianism." *Philosophical Topics* 32, nos 1 & 2 (2004): 353–69.

Speak, Daniel. "The Consequence Argument Revisited." In *The Oxford Handbook of Free Will* (2nd edn.), edited by Robert Kane, 115–30. New York: Oxford University Press, 2011.

Sripada, Chandra and Stich, Stephen. "A Framework for the Psychology of Norms." In *The Innate Mind: Volume 2: Culture and Cognition*, edited by Peter Carruthers, Stephen Laurence, and Stephen Stich, 280–301. New York: Oxford University Press, 2006.

Steele, Claude M. "A Threat in the Air: How Stereotypes Shape Intellectual Identity and Performance." *American Psychologist* 52, no. 6 (1997): 613–29.

Steele, Claude M., Spencer, Steven J., and Aronson, Joshua. "Contending With Group Image: The Psychology of Stereotype and Social Identity Threat." *Advances in Experimental Social Psychology* 34 (2002): 379–440.

Stern, Lawrence. "Freedom, Blame, and the Moral Community." *Journal of Philosophy* 71, no. 3 (1974): 72–84.

Strawson, Galen. "The Impossibility of Moral Responsibility." *Philosophical Studies* 75 (1994): 5–24.

Strawson, P. F. "Freedom and Resentment." *Proceedings of the British Academy* XLVIII (1962): 1–25.

Taylor, James Stacey, ed., *Personal Autonomy: New Essays on Personal Autonomy and Its Role in Contemporary Moral Philosophy*. New York: Cambridge University Press, 2005.

Thaler, Richard H. and Sunstein, Cass R. *Nudge: Improving Decisions About Health, Wealth, and Happiness*. New York: Penguin, 2009.

Timpe, Kevin. *Free Will: Sourcehood and Its Alternatives*. New York: Continuum, 2008.

van Inwagen, Peter. *An Essay on Free Will*. New York: Oxford University Press, 1983.

van Inwagen, Peter. "When is the Will Free?" In *Philosophical Perspectives, 3, Philosophy of Mind and Action Theory, 1989*, edited by James E. Tomberlin, 399–422. Atascadero, CA: Ridgeview, 1989.

van Inwagen, Peter. "Review of Problems in Philosophy." *Philosophical Review* 105, no. 2 (1996): 253–56.

van Inwagen, Peter. "Free Will Remains a Mystery." In *Philosophical Perspectives (14: Action and Freedom, 2000)*, edited by James Tomberlin, 1–20. Boston: Blackwell, 2000.

van Inwagen, Peter. *Metaphysics* (3rd edn.) Boulder, CO: Westview Press, 2008.

van Roojen, Mark. 2009. "Moral Cognitivism vs. Non-Cognitivism." <http://plato.stanford.edu/archives/fall2009/entries/moral-cognitivism/>, accessed July 19, 2010.

Vargas, Manuel. "Responsibility and the Aims of Theory: Strawson and Revisionism." *Pacific Philosophical Quarterly* 85, no. 2 (2004): 218–41.

Vargas, Manuel. "Compatibilism Evolves? On Some Varieties of Dennett Worth Wanting." *Metaphilosophy* 36, no. 4 (2005): 460–75.

Vargas, Manuel. "The Revisionist's Guide to Responsibility." *Philosophical Studies* 125, no. 3 (2005): 399–429.

Vargas, Manuel. "The Trouble With Tracing." *Midwest Studies in Philosophy* 29, no. 1 (2005): 269–91.

Vargas, Manuel. "On the Importance of History for Responsible Agency." *Philosophical Studies* 127, no. 3 (2006): 351–82.

Vargas, Manuel. "Revisionism About Free Will: A Statement & Defense." *Philosophical Studies* 144, no.1 (2009): 45–62.

Vargas, Manuel. "Revisionist Accounts of Free Will: Origins, Varieties, and Challenges." In *The Oxford Handbook of Free Will* (2nd edn.), edited by Robert Kane, 457–84. New York: Oxford University Press, 2011.

Vargas, Manuel. "The Revisionist Turn: Reflection on the Recent History of Work on Free Will." In *New Waves in the Philosophy of Action*, edited by Jesus Aguilar, Andrei Buckareff, and Keith Frankish, 143–72. New York: Palgrave Macmillan, 2011.

Vargas, Manuel. "Situationism and Moral Responsibility: Free Will in Fragments." In *Decomposing the Will*, edited by Till Vierkant, Julian Kiverstein, and Andy Clark. New York: Oxford University Press, forthcoming.

Vargas, Manuel. "Why the Luck Problem Isn't." *Philosophical Issues: A Supplement to Nous* 22 (forthcoming).

Velleman, J. David. *Practical Reflection*. Princeton, NJ: Princeton University Press, 1989.

Velleman, David. "What Happens When Someone Acts?" In *The Possibility of Practical Reason*, 123–43. Oxford: Clarendon Press, 2000.

Walker, Lawrence J., Frimer, Jeremy A., and Dunlop, William L. "Paradigm Assumptions About Moral Behavior: An Empirical Battle Royal." In *The Social Psychology of Morality: Exploring the Causes of Good and Evil*, edited by M. Mikulincer and P. R. Shaver, 275–92. Washington, DC: The American Psychological Association, 2011.

Wallace, R. Jay. *Responsibility and the Moral Sentiments*. Cambridge, MA: Harvard University Press, 1994.

Wallace, R. Jay. "Dispassionate Opprobrium: On Blame and the Reactive Sentiments." In *Reasons and Recognition: Essays on the Philosophy of T. M. Scanlon*, edited by R. Jay Wallace, Rahul Kumar, and Samuel Freeman, 348–72. New York: Oxford University Press, 2011.

Watson, Gary. "Free Agency." *Journal of Philosophy* 72, no. 8 (1975): 205–20.

Watson, Gary. "Skepticism About Weakness of Will." *Philosophical Review* 86 (1977): 316–39.

Watson, Gary. "Review of *Elbow Room.*" *Journal of Philosophy* 83, no. 9 (1986): 517–22.

Watson, Gary. "Responsibility and the Limits of Evil." In *Responsibility, Character, and the Emotions,* edited by Ferdinand David Schoeman, 256–86. New York: Cambridge University Press, 1987.

Watson, Gary. "Two Faces of Responsibility." *Philosophical Topics* 24 (1996): 227–48.

Wegner, Daniel M. *The Illusion of Conscious Will.* Cambridge, MA: MIT Press, 2002.

Weinberg, Jonathan M., Nichols, Shaun, and Stich, Stephen P. "Normativity and Epistemic Intuition." *Philosophical Topics* 29 (2001): 429–60.

Widerker, David. "Libertarianism and Frankfurt's Attack on the Principle of Alternative Possibilities." *Philosophical Review* 104 (1995): 247–61.

Widerker, David and McKenna, Michael, eds, *Moral Responsibility and Alternative Possibilities: Essays on the Importance of Alternative Possibilities.* Burlington, VT: Ashgate, 2003.

Wolf, Susan. "The Importance of Free Will." *Mind* 90 (1981): 386–405.

Wolf, Susan. *Freedom Within Reason.* New York: Oxford University Press, 1990.

Wolf, Susan. "Sanity and the Metaphysics of Responsibility." In *Free Will,* edited by Gary Watson, 372–87. New York: Oxford University Press, 2003.

Woolfolk, Robert L., Doris, John, and Darley, John. "Identification, Situational Constraint, and Social Cognition: Studies in the Attribution of Moral Responsibility." *Cognition* 100 (2006): 283–401.

Zimmerman, David. "Reasons-Responsiveness and Ownership-of-Agency." *Journal of Ethics* 6 (2002): 199–234.

Index

Ingram Content Group Australia Pty Ltd
Printed in Australia
AUHW011852140423
377011AU00006B/69